BRITISH REGIMENTS
1914-1918

by
Brigadier E. A. James, O.B.E., T.D.
(late Royal Signals, T.A.)

Previously published as two Volumes:
　　British Cavalry and Yeomanry Regiments in the Great War
　　　　First published　July, 1969
　　　　2nd Edition　　　April, 1975
　　　　3rd Edition　　　August, 1976

　　British Infantry Regiments in the Great War
　　　　First Published　July, 1974
　　　　2nd Edition　　　July, 1975
　　　　3rd Edition　　　January, 1976

This joint Edition contains the two Volumes under one cover
　　　　First impression, 1978
　　　　4th Edition　　　September, 1993
　　　　5th Edition　　　April, 1998

Published by:
Naval & Military Press Ltd, PO Box 61, Dallington, Heathfield, East Sussex TN21 9ZS

Foreword

In 1929 the Record of the Cavalry, Yeomanry, and Infantry Regiments of the British Army in the Great War, 1914-18 was published in a very limited edition. The Author, Edward Antrobus James, who was born in 1899, had joined the Royal Warwickshire Regiment on leaving King Edward's School, Birmingham, and shortly afterwards transferred to the Signals Service Training Centre at Haynes Park, where he gained a commission in the Royal Engineers Signal Service, and began his long association with Signals, which was to extend beyond the end of the Second World War.

The Record was the result of his deep interest in the history of the units, which served during the First World War, and his work assisting the historian in the production of the monumental official history, *Military Operations in the Great War*.

Prior to the appearance of the Record came another valuable contribution in the *Record of the Battles and Engagements of the British Armies in France and Flanders, 1914-17*, published in 1924.

These two volumes became possibly two of the most used works in the Library of the Imperial War Museum. Captain James, as he then was, had first made use of the Library in 1919, and continued to be one of the regular readers until shortly before his death in 1976. He became the acknowledged expert on the disposition of units on the various fronts and at home, and as such, was frequently consulted.

In France he joined the 33rd Divisional Signal Company, and was gassed. He later commanded a Cable Section of 2 Corps Signal Company. After demobilization in 1919, he entered the family firm of wine and spirit merchants in Birmingham, but all his spare time was devoted to the Signal Service of the Territorial Army.

In 1921, he was commissioned into the 48th Divisional Signals, and over the next fifteen years, held the commands of various sections and companies until he became Second in Command. He was given command of the 61st Divisional Signals in 1939, and took the unit to Northern Ireland the next year.

He became District Signals Officer, Southern Command in 1942, later being appointed Chief Signals Officer 2 Corps. After a brief period as Commandant of the 3rd Signal Training School at Huddersfield in 1944, he went to 21st Army Group as Chief Signals Officer of the Lines of Communication, having responsibility from Bayeux to the Dutch border with Belgium.

By 1946 he had returned to his family business, but remained a dedicated member of the Territorial Army, becoming Hon. Colonel of the 48th (South Midland) Signal Regiment from 1950 to 1957, he was also a member of the Territorial and Auxiliary Forces Association.

All through his career with the Territorial Army, he had shown interest in all the military activities offered, taking part in manoeuvres, and of course the parades, and exercises, which were held both before and after the Second World War all over the U.K.

As if this was not enough, he was also in the forefront of local affairs, and in 1945 was appointed a Deputy Lieutenant for Warwickshire. In 1951 he became a Justice of the Peace, and from 1961 to 1969, was Chairman of the Royal Sutton Coldfield Bench.

Never losing his interest in his hobby of investigating the records of the units of the British Army, he retired from business, and gave more and more of his time to revising and rewriting his Record, and in 1969, he published the Revised edition of the *Historical Records of British Cavalry and Yeomanry Regiments in the Great War, 1914-18* in a much enlarged form to the original.

In 1975 came the Infantry Regiments, he also wrote articles on Signal Communication, and was a member of the Military Historical Society.

For his services in 1944-45, he was appointed O.B.E., and a Knight of the Netherlands Order of Orange Nassau.

He married Lilian Patricia Edwards, M.B., B.S., in 1932, and they had two daughters. He died suddenly at his home in Sutton Coldfield on 2nd October, 1976.

This volume of ready reference to all the Regiments of the British Army in 1914-18, contains the vital information he had gathered during years of research in the official records at the Public Record Office, the War Office, the Imperial War Museum and other sources. Set out in such concise manner, this volume forms a fitting memorial to him.

Rose E.B. Coombs
East Grinstead
May 1978

BRITISH REGIMENTS
1914 – 1918

Brigadier E. A. James, O.B.E., T.D.
(1899-1976)

Contents

Publisher's Notes
Foreword

PART I

Introduction to Part I
Household Cavalry
Cavalry of the Line
Reserve Cavalry Regiments
Special Reserve Cavalry Regiments
Yeomanry Regiments (in alphabetical order)

Appendix I
   Analysis of the service of Cavalry Regiments

Appendix II
   Analysis of the service and employment of Yeomanry Regiments

Appendix III
   Outline Histories of Yeomanry Formations

PART II

Introduction to Part II

FOOT GUARDS

Grenadier Guards
Coldstream Guards
Scots Guards
Irish Guards
Welsh Guards
Guards Machine Gun Regiment

INFANTRY REGIMENTS

The Royal Scots (Lothian Regiment)
The Queen's (Royal West Surrey Regiment)
The Buffs (East Kent Regiment)
The King's Own (Royal Lancaster Regiment)
The Northumberland Fusiliers
The Royal Warwickshire Regiment
The Royal Fusiliers (City of London Regiment)
The King's (Liverpool Regiment)
The Norfolk Regiment
The Lincolnshire Regiment
The Devonshire Regiment
The Suffolk Regiment
Prince Albert's (Somerset Light Infantry)
The Prince of Wales's Own (West Yorkshire Regiment)
The East Yorkshire Regiment
The Bedfordshire Regiment
The Leicestershire Regiment
The Royal Irish Regiment
Alexandra, Princess of Wales's Own (Yorkshire Regiment)
The Lancashire Fusiliers
The Royal Scots Fusiliers
The Cheshire Regiment
The Royal Welsh Fusiliers
The South Wales Borderers
The King's Own Scottish Borderers
The Cameronians (Scottish Rifles)
The Royal Inniskilling Fusiliers
The Gloucestershire Regiment
The Worcestershire Regiment
The East Lancashire Regiment
The East Surrey Regiment
The Duke of Cornwall's Light Infantry
The Duke of Wellington's (West Riding Regiment)
The Border Regiment
The Royal Sussex Regiment
The Hampshire Regiment
The South Staffordshire Regiment
The Dorsetshire Regiment
The Prince of Wales's Volunteers (South Lancashire Regiment)
The Welsh Regiment
The Black Watch (Royal Highlanders)
The Oxfordshire and Buckinghamshire Light Infantry
The Essex Regiment
The Sherwood Foresters (Nottinghamshire and Derbyshire Regiment)
The Loyal North Lancashire Regiment
The Northamptonshire Regiment
Princess Charlotte of Wales's (Royal Berkshire Regiment)
The Queen's Own (Royal West Kent Regiment)
The King's Own (Yorkshire Light Infantry)
The King's (Shropshire Light Infantry)
The Duke of Cambridge's Own (Middlesex Regiment)
The King's Royal Rifle Corps
The Duke of Edinburgh's (Wiltshire Regiment)
The Manchester Regiment
The Prince of Wales's (North Staffordshire Regiment)
The York and Lancaster Regiment
The Durham Light Infantry
The Highland Light Infantry
Seaforth Highlanders (Ross-shire Buffs, The Duke of Albany's)
The Gordon Highlanders
The Queen's Own Cameron Highlanders
The Royal Irish Rifles
Princess Victoria's (Royal Irish Fusiliers)
The Connaught Rangers
Princess Louise's (Argyll and Sutherland Highlanders)
The Prince of Wales's Leinster Regiment (Royal Canadians)
The Royal Munster Fusiliers
The Royal Dublin Fusiliers
The Rifle Brigade (The Prince Consort's Own)

INFANTRY TERRITORIAL FORCE

Honourable Artillery Company Infantry
The Monmouthshire Regiment
The Cambridgeshire Regiment
The London Regiment
Inns of Court Officers Training Corps
The Hertfordshire Regiment
The Herefordshire Regiment
The Northern Cyclist Battalion
The Highland Cyclist Battalion
The Kent Cyclist Battalion
The Huntingdonshire Cyclist Battalion

CHANNEL ISLANDS MILITIA

The Royal Militia of the Island of Jersey
Royal Guernsey

Officer Cadet Battalions
The Household Battalion
Wartime Camps in the United Kingdom

Sources

Appendix I
　Regiments and their Battalions
Appendix II
　The New Army Battalions
Appendix III
　The Training Reserve

Appendix IV
　Third Line and Provisional Territorial Battalions
Appendix V
　List of British Divisions (Infantry) which served in the Great War, 1914–198
Appendix VI
　Titles of Infantry Regiments in 1914 and 1974
Appendix VII
　Battle Honours, Victoria Crosses & Casualties

Index

Part 1

BRITISH CAVALRY AND YEOMANRY REGIMENTS IN THE GREAT WAR 1914-1918

Introduction to Part 1

This work is based on a previous one completed in 1929. The original version was a Record of the Cavalry, Yeomanry, and Infantry Regiments of the British Army in the Great War, 1914-18. The present one deals only with the Cavalry and Yeomanry Regiments but in much more detail: the eleven pages of 1929 have increased to sixty-nine. This expansion is partly due to the fact that there is now more information available and partly because the Reserve Cavalry Regiments and the 2nd and 3rd Line Yeomanry are now included, to make a total of 227 regiments.

The account of each pre-war unit starts with its station and brigade on 4th August 1914: others start with the date of formation. The dates of moves overseas are given with changes in allotment to formation also subsequent moves to other theatres of war. Campaign Battle Honours are shown under the titles of the regiments as they indicate roughly where they served. Moves in the United Kingdom have been given in more detail as this information is not easily available elsewhere. Few units at home kept war diaries and there were none after April 1916.

It may be useful to explain the method of expansion of the Territorial Force—the Yeomanry was its mounted arm—in 1914 and 1915. Soon after the outbreak of war each unit formed a reserve one to provide it with reinforcements. In November 1914 it was decided that when a T.F. unit went overseas its reserve would take its place and another reserve one formed, which was named the 2nd Reserve. In March 1915 all Territorial units were ordered to form a third reserve unit. The first and second line would be operational while the third would supply drafts for the other two. At this time the fractional designations, 1/1st, 2/1st and 3/1st, came into use.

Although the hundred and fourteen 2nd and 3rd Line Yeomanry units nearly all remained at home during the war, it must be remembered that they were constantly called on to provide drafts for overseas reinforcements and that, in act, all fit officers and men were eventually posted abroad.

For example, in 1916 the 2/1st Worcestershire Yeomanry sent 100 men to the county regiment and the 2/1st Oxfordshire Hussars, 200 to the 6th Oxford & Bucks L.I. in France. Again, in 1918 the 2/1st Montgomeryshire Yeomanry and the 2/1st South Nottinghamshire Hussars both posted all available fit men to the infantry. There are a number of references in various regimental histories to the good quality of the drafts from the Yeomanry.

This record has been compiled from information collected over a wide range: the sources are given on page 121. The most useful source for the Reserve Cavalry Regiments and 2nd and 3rd Line Yeomanry between 1916 and 1918 was the series of books issued by G.H.Q., Home Forces from time to time under the title Commanders, or, Officers in Command, Home Forces. They contain valuable lists of units and their locations but, unfortunately, no similar source has been found for 1914 and 1915.

I have also used my notes made during many years of research on the War Diaries while they were with the Historical Section, Committee of Imperial Defence, with War Office Records at Droitwich and Hayes and with the Public Record Office at Ashridge and, finally, at Chancery Lane. I have always had the most willing assistance from the staff of the various establishments storing the diaries.

I am most grateful to Miss R. E. B. Coombs, the Librarian of the Imperial War Museum and to Mr. D. W. King, Chief Librarian, Ministry of Defence Library (Central and Army) who allowed me to use their fine libraries—rich storehouses of military history.

Nearly all the details given have documentary support but, in a few cases, they are the result of deduction, particularly in the case of home service units. Where there was any doubt the qualifying words 'about', 'by', 'in the early part of', 'apparently' and so on have been used.

E.A.J.

Sutton Coldfield,
August 1976.

British Cavalry and Yeomanry Regiments in the Great War 1914-1918

HOUSEHOLD CAVALRY

1st LIFE GUARDS
'France and Flanders, 1914–18'
4.8.14 Hyde Park. On mobilization one squadron to Household Cavalry Composite Regiment (see below). 1.9.14 to 7th Cav. Bde. 3rd Cav. Div. at Ludgershall. 7.10.14 landed at Zeebrugge. 10.3.18 left 3rd Cav. Div. and formed No. 1 (1st Life Guards) Bn. Guards M.G. Regt. April/May 1918 trained at Etaples. 24.5.18 to First Army as Army Troops. No further change.

2nd LIFE GUARDS
'France and Flanders, 1914–18'
4.8.14 Regent's Park. On mobilization one squadron to Household Cavalry Composite Regiment (see below). 1.9.14 to 7th Cav. Bde. 3rd Cav. Div. at Ludgershall. 7.10.14 landed at Zeebrugge. 10.3.18 left 3rd Cav. Div. and formed No. 2 (2nd Life Guards) Bn. Guards M.G. Regt. April/May 1918 trained at Etaples. 23.5.18 to First Army as Army Troops. No further change.

ROYAL HORSE GUARDS
'France and Flanders, 1914–18'
4.8.14 Windsor. On mobilization one squadron to Household Cavalry Composite Regiment (see below). 1.9.14 to 7th Cav. Bde. 3rd Cav. Div. at Ludgershall. 7.10.14 landed at Zeebrugge. 21.11.14 to 8th Cav. Bde. 3rd Cav. Div. 7.11.17 returned to 7th Cav. Bde. 3rd Cav. Div. 10.3.18 left 3rd Cav. Div. and formed No. 3 (Royal Horse Guards) Bn. Guards M.G. Regt. April/May 1918 trained at Etaples. 22.5.18 to First Army as Army Troops. No further change.

HOUSEHOLD CAVALRY COMPOSITE REGIMENT
August 1914 formed on mobilization with one squadron from each of the Household Cavalry Regts. in 4th Cav. Bde. The Cav. Div. 16.8.14 to France. 16.9.14 The Cav. Div. became 1st Cav. Div. 11.11.14 Composite Regt. broken up and the three squadrons returned to their regiments.

HOUSEHOLD BATTALION
Formed at Knightsbridge Barracks on 1.9.16 as an infantry battalion with personnel from the Household Cavalry Reserve Regiments. 9.11.16 to France. 17.11.16 to 10th Bde. 4th Div. 10.2.18 disbanded in France sending drafts to Household Cavalry and Foot Guards.

GUARDS DIVISIONAL CAVALRY SQUADRON
Formed about July 1915 by the 1st Life Guards Reserve Regiment. 4.8.15 to France joining the Guards Div. in the Lumbres area. 19.6.16 broken up at Rouen and personnel to 1st Life Guards.

520th (SIEGE) BATTERY R.G.A.
Formed with Household Cavalry personnel and served in France in 1918 with six inch guns.

CAVALRY OF THE LINE

1st (KING'S) DRAGOON GUARDS
'France and Flanders, 1914–17'
4.8.14 Lucknow: Lucknow Cav. Bde. 16.10.14 sailed from Bombay. 7.11.14 landed at Marseilles in Lucknow Cav. Bde. 1st Indian Cav. Div. 26.11.16 1st Indian Cav. Div. became 4th Cav. Div. 7.10.17 left 4th Cav. Div. and returned to India where it remained.

2nd DRAGOON GUARDS (QUEEN'S BAYS)
'France and Flanders, 1914–18'
4.8.14 Aldershot: 1st Cav. Bde. Aug. 1914 to France in 1st Cav. Bde. The Cav. Div. 16.9.14 The Cav. Div. became 1st Cav. Div. No further change.

3rd (PRINCE OF WALES'S) DRAGOON GUARDS
'France and Flanders, 1914–18'
4.8.14 Cairo. 29.9.14 sailed from Alexandria. 18.10.14 landed at Liverpool. 31.10.14 to France. 4.11.14 to 6th Cav. Bde. 3rd Cav. Div. No change.

4th (ROYAL IRISH) DRAGOON GUARDS
'France and Flanders, 1914–18'
4.8.14 Tidworth: 2nd Cav. Bde. Aug. 1914 to France in 2nd Cav. Bde. The Cav. Div. 16.9.14 The Cav. Div. became 1st Cav. Div. No further change.

5th (PRINCESS CHARLOTTE OF WALES'S) DRAGOON GUARDS
'France and Flanders, 1914–18'
4.8.14 Aldershot: 1st Cav. Bde. 16.8.14 to France in 1st Cav. Bde. The Cav. Div. 16.9.14 The Cav. Div. became 1st Cav. Div. No further change.

6th DRAGOON GUARDS (CARABINIERS)
'France and Flanders, 1914–18'
4.8.14 Canterbury: 4th Cav. Bde. August, 1914 to France in 4th Cav. Bde. The Cav. Div. 16.9.14 The Cav. Div. became 1st Cav. Div. 14.10.14 4th Cav. Bde. to 2nd Cav. Div. No further change.

7th (PRINCESS ROYAL'S) DRAGOON GUARDS
'France and Flanders, 1914–18'
4.8.14 Secunderabad: Secunderabad Cav. Bde. 10.9.14 sailed from Bombay. 13.10.14 landed at Marseilles in Secunderabad Cav. Bde. which was attached to Indian Corps. 23.12.14 Secunderabad Cav. Bde. to 2nd Indian Cav. Div. 26.11.16 2nd Indian Cav. Div. became 5th Cav. Div. Feb. 1918 5th Cav. Div. broken up. 10.3.18 to 7th Cav. Bde. 3rd Cav. Div. No further change.

1st (ROYAL) DRAGOONS
'France and Flanders, 1914–18'
4.8.14 Potchefstroom. 27.8.14 sailed from Cape Town. 19.9.14 arrived in England and to 6th Cav. Bde. 3rd Cav. Div. at Ludgershall. 8.10.14 landed at Ostend. No change.

2nd DRAGOONS (ROYAL SCOTS GREYS)
'France and Flanders, 1914–18'
4.8.14 York: 5th Cav. Bde. Aug., 1914 to France in 5th Cav. Bde. which was independent. 6.9.14 5th Cav. Bde. to Gough's Command. 13.9.14 Gough's Command became 2nd Cav. Div. No further change.

3rd (KING'S OWN) HUSSARS
'France and Flanders, 1914–18'
4.8.14 Shorncliffe: 4th Cav. Bde. 17.8.14 landed at Rouen in 4th Cav. Bde. The Cav. Div. 16.9.14 The Cav. Div.

became 1st Cav. Div. 14.10.14 4th Cav. Bde. to 2nd Cav. Div. No further change.

4TH (QUEEN'S OWN) HUSSARS
'France and Flanders, 1914–18'

4.8.14 Curragh: 3rd Cav. Bde. Aug., 1914 to France in 3rd Cav. Bde. The Cav. Div. 6.9.14 3rd Cav. Bde. to Gough's Command. 13.9.14 Gough's Command became 2nd Cav. Div. No further change.

5TH (ROYAL IRISH) LANCERS
'France and Flanders, 1914–18'

4.8.14 Dublin: 3rd Cav. Bde. Aug., 1914 to France in 3rd Cav. Bde. The Cav. Div. 6.9.14 3rd Cav. Bde. to Gough's Command. 13.9.14 Gough's Command became 2nd Cav. Div. No further change.

6TH (INNISKILLING) DRAGOONS
'France and Flanders, 1914–18'

4.8.14 Muttra. 9.11.14 to Mhow Cav. Bde. 19.11.14 sailed from Bombay. 14.12.14 landed at Marseilles in Mhow Cav. Bde. 2nd Indian Cav. Div. Sept. 1915 Mhow Cav. Bde. to 1st Indian Cav. Div. 26.11.16 1st Indian Cav. Div. became 4th Cav. Div. Feb. 1918 4th Cav. Div. broken up. 10.3.18 to 7th Cav. Bde. 3rd Cav. Div. No further change.

A Service Squadron was formed at Enniskillen in Nov. 1914 as Div. Cav. for the 36th (Ulster) Div. July 1915 to England (Seaford and Bordon). 6.10.15 landed in France. 21.6.16 to X Corps Cavalry Regt. Summer 1917 X Corps Cavalry Regt. broken up and squadron was dismounted and personnel posted to 9th Royal Irish Fusiliers in 108th Bde. 36th Div.

7TH (QUEEN'S OWN) HUSSARS
'Mesopotamia, 1917–18'

4.8.14 Bangalore. Dec. 1917 landed in Mesopotamia: to 11th Indian Cav. Bde. Cav. Div. April 1918 Cav. Div. broken up and 11th Cav. Bde. became independent.

8TH (KING'S ROYAL IRISH) HUSSARS
'France and Flanders, 1914–18'

4.8.14 Ambala: Ambala Cav. Bde. 16.10.14 sailed from Bombay. 10.11.14 landed at Marseilles in Ambala Cav. Bde. 1st Indian Cav. Div. 15.9.15 Ambala Cav. Bde. to 2nd Indian Cav. Div. 26.11.16 2nd Indian Cav. Div. became 5th Cav. Div. Feb. 1918 5th Cav. Div. broken up. 10.9.18 to 9th Cav. Bde. 1st Cav. Div. No further change.

9TH (QUEEN'S ROYAL) LANCERS
'France and Flanders, 1914–18'

4.8.14 Tidworth: 2nd Cav. Bde. Aug., 1914 to France in 2nd Cav. Bde. The Cav. Div. 16.9.14 The Cav. Div. became 1st Cav. Div. No further change.

10TH (PRINCE OF WALES'S OWN ROYAL) HUSSARS
'France and Flanders, 1914–18'

4.8.14 Potchefstroom. Aug. 1914 sailed from Cape Town. 22.9.14 joined 6th Cav. Bde. 3rd Cav. Div. at Ludgershall. 8.10.14 landed at Ostend. 20.11.14 to 8th Cav. Bde. 3rd Cav. Div. 12.3.18 to 6th Cav. Bde. 3rd Cav. Div. No further change.

11TH (PRINCE ALBERT'S OWN) HUSSARS
'France and Flanders, 1914–18'

4.8.14 Aldershot: 1st Cav. Bde. Aug. 1914 to France in 1st Cav. Bde. The Cav. Div. 16.9.14 The Cav. Div. became 1st Cav. Div. No further change.

12TH (PRINCE OF WALES'S ROYAL) LANCERS
'France and Flanders, 1914–18'

4.8.14 Norwich: 5th Cav. Bde. Aug. 1914 to France in 5th Cav. Bde. which was independent. 6.9.14 5th Cav. Bde. to Gough's Command. 16.9.14 Gough's Command became 2nd Cav. Div. No further change.

13TH HUSSARS
'France and Flanders, 1914—16'
'Mesopotamia, 1916–18'

4.8.14 Meerut: Meerut Cav. Bde. 19.11.14 sailed from Bombay. Dec. 1914 landed at Marseilles in Meerut Cav. Bde. 2nd Indian Cav. Div. July 1916 Meerut Cav. Bde. left 2nd Indian Cav. Div. for Mesopotamia. Aug. 1916 landed at Basra: now in 7th Indian Cav. Bde. Dec. 1916 7th Indian Cav. Bde. to Cav. Div. April 1918 Cav. Div. broken up and 7th Indian Cav. Bde. became independent.

14TH (KING'S) HUSSARS
'Mesopotamia, 1915–18'
'Persia, 1918'

4.8.14 Mhow. Nov. 1915 landed in Mesopotamia in 6th Indian Cav. Bde. Dec. 1915 6th Indian Cav. Bde. to Cav. Div. April 1918 Cav. Div. broken up and 6th Indian Cav. Bde. became independent. May 1918 left 6th Indian Cav. Bde. and went to Persia.

15TH (THE KING'S) HUSSARS
'France and Flanders, 1914–18'

4.8.14 Longmoor. On mobilization the regiment was split up as divisional cavalry. 18.8.14 landed at Rouen and joined divisions. 'A' Squadron to 3rd Div. 'B' Squadron to 2nd Div. 'C' Squadron to 1st Div. April 1915 squadrons withdrawn from divisions and the regiment concentrated. 14.4.15 to 9th Cav. Bde. 1st Cav. Div. No further change.

16TH (THE QUEEN'S) LANCERS
'France and Flanders, 1914–18'

4.8.14 Curragh: 3rd Cav. Bde. Aug. 1914 to France in 3rd Cav. Bde. The Cav. Div. 6.9.14 3rd Cav. Bde. to Gough's Command. 16.9.14 Gough's Command became 2nd Cav. Div. No further change.

17TH (DUKE OF CAMBRIDGE'S OWN) LANCERS
'France and Flanders, 1914–18'

4.8.14 Sialkot: Sialkot Cav. Bde. 16.10.14 sailed from Bombay. 7.11.14 landed at Marseilles in Sialkot Cav. Bde. 1st Indian Cav. Div. 26.11.16 1st Indian Cav. Div. became 4th Cav. Div. Feb. 1918 4th Cav. Div. broken up 10.3.18 to 7th Cav. Bde. 3rd Cav. Div. No further change.

18TH (QUEEN MARY'S OWN) HUSSARS
'France and Flanders, 1914–18'

4.8.14 Tidworth: 2nd Cav. Bde. Aug. 1914 to France in 2nd Cav. Bde. The Cav. Div. 16.9.14 The Cav. Div. became 1st Cav. Div. No further change.

19TH (QUEEN ALEXANDRA'S OWN ROYAL) HUSSARS
'France and Flanders, 1914–18'

4.8.14 Hounslow: On mobilization the regiment was split up as divisional cavalry. Aug. 1914 'A' and 'B' Squadrons to France with 5th and 4th Divs. Sept. 1914 'C' Squadron to France with 6th Div. April 1915 Squadrons withdrawn from divisions and the regiment concentrated. 14.4.15 to 9th Cav. Bde. 1st Cav. Div. No further change.

20TH HUSSARS
'France and Flanders, 1914–18'

4.8.14 Colchester: 5th Cav. Bde. Aug. 1914 to France in 5th Cav. Bde. which was independent. 6.9.14 5th Cav. Bde. to Gough's Command. 16.9.14 Gough's Command became 2nd Cav. Div. No further change.

21ST (EMPRESS OF INDIA'S) LANCERS
'N.W. Frontier, India, 1915, '16'

4.8.14 Rawal Pindi. Remained in India throughout the war. A service squadron formed part of the XIV Corps Cavalry Regiment in France, from June 1916 to August 1917.

RESERVE CAVALRY REGIMENTS

On mobilization in August 1914 seventeen reserve cavalry regiments were formed. Three for the Household Cavalry, which remained unchanged until the end of the war, and fourteen for the Cavalry of the Line which was one for each pair of regiments.

In June 1915 instructions were issued for the affiliation of 3rd Line Yeomanry units to Reserve Cavalry Regiments. The Yeomanry in a command were allotted to one Reserve Regiment or group of Regiments e.g. the 10 Yeomanry units in Western Command went to Reserve Regiments in Ireland and the 13 in Southern Command to the Reserve Regiments at Tidworth. All men who had completed elementary training were to join the reserve regiments. If there were over one hundred they would be formed into a squadron, if less, they would be attached to squadrons of the reserve regiment. Regiments carried out these instructions in varying ways: some sent a squadron or less to the reserve regiment and continued to train as a cavalry regiment, others moved almost complete to the affiliated reserve cavalry regiment leaving only a small detachment at the 3rd Line depot.

By April 1916 eleven of the reserve cavalry regiments had been grouped in three brigades at Aldershot, Tidworth and the Curragh: the remaining three regiments were independent.

In April 1916 the 3rd Line depots of the 23 Yeomanry Regiments whose 1st Line units were serving as infantry in Egypt were withdrawn from Reserve Cavalry Regiments and attached to 3rd Line Groups of T.F. Divisions for training as infantry. At the same time there were a number of changes in the affiliations to Reserve Cavalry Regiments of the 3rd Line depots of the 34 Yeomanry Regiments serving abroad as mounted units.

Early in 1917 there was a major reorganization of the Cavalry Reserves when the fourteen Reserve Regiments and the Reserve Squadrons of mounted Yeomanry Regiments were amalgamated to form six Reserve Regiments. The 3rd Line units of mounted Yeomanry were abolished and these regiments were reinforced from the Reserve Cavalry Regiments.

In the autumn of 1917 five 1st Line Yeomanry Regiments, which had been serving in France as Corps Cavalry Regiments, were dismounted and absorbed in service battalions of Infantry Regiments. They ceased to be affiliated to Reserve Cavalry Regiments and were reinforced from Reserve Infantry Battalions.

By 1918 the 1st and 2nd Reserve Cavalry Brigades were abolished and the regiments were unbrigaded but the 3rd Reserve Cavalry Brigade at the Curragh remained until the end of the war.

HOUSEHOLD CAVALRY

1st Life Guards Reserve Regiment
Formed on mobilization in Aug. 1914 and stationed at Hyde Park throughout the war.

2nd Life Guards Reserve Regiment
Formed on mobilization in Aug. 1914 and stationed at Windsor throughout the war.

Royal Horse Guards Reserve Regiment
Formed on mobilization in Aug. 1914 and stationed at Regents Park throughout the war.

Reserve Household Battalion
Formed about Sept. 1916 to supply reinforcements for the Household Battalion in France. Stationed at Windsor until disbandment early in 1918.

CAVALRY OF THE LINE

1ST RESERVE CAVALRY REGIMENT

Formed on mobilization in Aug. 1914 at Aldershot affiliated to 1st and 5th Dragoon Guards. In the summer of 1915 some 3rd Line Yeomanry regiments from Scottish Command were affiliated. By April 1916 the Regiment was in the 1st Reserve Cav. Bde. and the affiliated Yeomanry were the Glasgow Yeomanry and the Sherwood Rangers (Nottinghamshire). Early in 1917 the 1st Reserve Cavalry Regiment was absorbed in the 4th Reserve Regiment, also at Aldershot.

A new 1st Reserve Regiment was formed at the Curragh early in 1917 mainly from the 6th, 7th and 8th Regiments. It was in the 3rd Reserve Cav. Bde. The affiliated regiments were the 5th, 9th, 12th, 16th, 17th and 21st Lancers with the Bedford, Lincoln, City of London, Surrey and East Riding Yeomanry.

The Regiment remained at the Curragh in the 3rd Reserve Cav. Bde. until the end of the war.

2ND RESERVE CAVALRY REGIMENT

Formed on mobilization in Aug. 1914 at Aldershot affiliated to 2nd Dragoon Guards and 6th Dragoons. In the summer of 1915 some 3rd Line Yeomanry from Scottish Command were affiliated. By April 1916 the regiment was in 1st Reserve Cav. Bde. and the affiliated Yeomanry were Essex Yeomanry and the Lothians & Border Horse. Early in 1917 the regiment was absorbed in the new 4th Reserve Cavalry Regiment at Aldershot.

A new 2nd Reserve Regiment was formed at the Curragh early in 1917 mainly from the 9th and 10th Reserve Regiments; in 3rd Reserve Cav. Bde. The affiliated regiments were 3rd, 4th, 7th and 8th Hussars and the Dorset Yeomanry, Lancashire Hussars, 1st and 3rd County of London Yeomanry, South Notts. Hussars with the Oxfordshire and Westmorland & Cumberland Yeomanry.

The Regiment remained at the Curragh until the end of the war. In 1918 the Lancashire Hussars and Westmorland & Cumberland Yeomanry left for reserve infantry battalions as the 1st Line regiments had been dismounted and absorbed in infantry regiments.

3RD RESERVE CAVALRY REGIMENT

Formed on mobilization in Aug. 1914 at Canterbury affiliated to 3rd and 6th Dragoon Guards. In the summer of 1915 the 3rd Line units of Northamptonshire, Surrey and Sussex Yeomanry were affiliated. By April 1916 only the first two Yeomanry remained and the regiment was at Canterbury until early in 1917 when it was absorbed in the new 6th Reserve Regiment at Tidworth.

A new 3rd Reserve Regiment was formed at Aldershot early in 1917 mainly from the 12th and 14th Reserve Cavalry Regiments; in 1st Reserve Cavalry Bde. The affiliated regiments were the 11th, 13th, 15th and 19th Hussars and the Buckinghamshire, Leicester, Stafford and Wiltshire Yeomanry with the Sherwood Rangers. Remained at Aldershot but no longer brigaded in 1918 and the Wiltshire Yeomanry left for a reserve infantry battalion as the 1st Line Regiment had been dismounted and absorbed in the Wiltshire Regiment.

4TH RESERVE CAVALRY REGIMENT

Formed on mobilization in Aug. 1914 at Tidworth affiliated to 4th and 7th Dragoon Guards. In the summer of 1915 some 3rd Line Yeomanry from Southern Command were affiliated. By April 1916 the regiment was in 2nd Reserve Cav. Bde. and the affiliated 3rd Line Yeomanry were the Warwickshire, Gloucestershire and Worcestershire. Early in 1917 the 4th Reserve Cavalry Regiment was absorbed in the new 6th Reserve Cavalry Regiment at Tidworth.

A new 4th Reserve Regiment was formed at Aldershot early in 1917.[1] The cavalry regiments affiliated were the 1st, 2nd and 5th Dragoon Guards and the 6th Dragoons. The Yeomanry affiliated were the Derbyshire, Essex, Glasgow, Hampshire, 2nd County of London and the Lothians & Border Horse. There were no further changes except that the regiment ceased to be brigaded in 1918 and the Hampshire Yeomanry left for an infantry reserve battalion as the 1st Line Regiment was dismounted and absorbed in the Hampshire Regiment.

5TH RESERVE CAVALRY REGIMENT

Formed on mobilization in Aug. 1914 at York affiliated to 1st and 2nd Dragoons. In the summer of 1915 the 3rd Line units of four yeomanry regiments were affiliated: Northumberland Hussars, Yorkshire Dragoons, Yorkshire Hussars and the East Riding Yeomanry. There were no changes until early in 1917 when the regiment was absorbed in the new 6th Reserve Regiment at Tidworth.

A new 5th Reserve Regiment was formed early in 1917 at Tidworth from the 11th and 13th Regiments, affiliated to the 10th, 14th, 18th and 20th Hussars and the Gloucestershire Yeomanry, Northumberland Hussars, Warwickshire and Worcester Yeomanry and the Yorkshire Hussars. Early in 1918 the Regiment ceased to be brigaded and the Yorkshire Hussars left when the 1st Line unit was dismounted and absorbed in the West Yorkshire Regiment.

6TH RESERVE CAVALRY REGIMENT

Formed on mobilization in Aug. 1914 at Dublin affiliated to the 5th and 12th Lancers. In the summer of 1915 some 3rd Line Yeomanry regiments from Western Command were affiliated. By April 1916 the regiment was in the 3rd Reserve Cav. Bde. and the affiliated Yeomanry were the City of London and the 1st County of London. Early in 1917 the Regiment was absorbed in the new 1st Reserve Regiment at the Curragh.

Early in 1917 a new 6th Reserve Regiment was formed at Tidworth mainly from the 3rd, 4th and 5th Reserve Regiments. It was affiliated to the 3rd, 4th, 6th and 7th Dragoon Guards and the 1st and 2nd Dragoons and the Yeomanry were the Berkshire, Hertford, Duke of Lancasters, Northampton, North Somerset and the Yorkshire Dragoons. The Regiment remained at Tidworth and was in the 2nd Reserve Cav. Bde. until 1918, when the brigade ceased to exist.

[1] Mainly from the 1st and 2nd Reserve Regiments.

7TH RESERVE CAVALRY REGIMENT

Formed on mobilization in Aug. 1914 at Tidworth affiliated to the 9th and 21st Lancers. In the summer of 1915 some 3rd Line Yeomanry from regiments in Southern Command were affiliated. By April 1916 the Regiment was in the 2nd Reserve Cav. Bde. and the affiliated Yeomanry were the Buckingham and Berkshire. Early in 1917 the Regiment was absorbed in the new 1st Reserve Regiment at the Curragh.

8TH RESERVE CAVALRY REGIMENT

Formed on mobilization in Aug. 1914 at the Curragh affiliated to the 16th and 17th Lancers. In the summer of 1915 some 3rd Line Yeomanry from regiments in Western Command were affiliated. By April 1916 the Regiment was in the 3rd Reserve Cav. Bde. and the affiliated Yeomanry were the Dorset and Oxford. Early in 1917 the Regiment was absorbed in the new 1st Reserve Regiment, also at the Curragh.

9TH RESERVE CAVALRY REGIMENT

Formed on mobilization in Aug. 1914 at Shorncliffe affiliated to the 3rd and 7th Hussars. In the summer of 1915 some 3rd Line Yeomanry from regiments in Eastern Command were affiliated and later in 1915 the Regiment moved to Newbridge in Ireland. In April 1916 it was in the 3rd Reserve Cav. Bde. and the affiliated Yeomanry were the 2nd and 3rd County of London. Early in 1917 the Regiment was absorbed in the new 2nd Reserve Regiment at the Curragh.

10TH RESERVE CAVALRY REGIMENT

Formed on mobilization in Aug. 1914 at the Curragh affliated to the 4th and 8th Hussars. In the summer of 1915 some 3rd Line Yeomanry from regiments in Western Command were affiliated. In April 1916 the Regiment was in the 3rd Reserve Cav. Bde. and the affliated Yeomanry were the Duke of Lancaster's, the Lancashire Hussars and the Westmorland and Cumberland. Early in 1917 the Regiment was absorbed in the new 2nd Reserve Regiment at the Curragh.

11TH RESERVE CAVALRY REGIMENT

Formed on mobilization in Aug. 1914 at Tidworth affiliated to the 10th and 18th Hussars. In the summer of 1915 some 3rd Line Yeomanry from regiments in Southern Command were affiliated. In April 1916 the Regiment was in the 2nd Reserve Cav. Bde. and the affiliated Yeomanry were the Hampshire, North Somerset and Wiltshire. Early in 1917 the Regiment was absorbed in the new 5th Reserve Regiment at Tidworth.

12TH RESERVE CAVALRY REGIMENT

Formed on mobilization in Aug. 1914 at Aldershot affiliated to the 11th and 13th Hussars. In the summer of 1915 some 3rd Line Yeomanry from regiments in Northern Command were affiliated. In April 1916 the Regiment was in the 1st Reserve Cavalry Brigade and the affiliated Yeomanry were the Leicester, Lincolnshire and Staffordshire. Early in 1917 the Regiment was absorbed in the new 3rd Reserve Regiment at Aldershot.

13TH RESERVE CAVALRY REGIMENT

Formed on mobilization in Aug. 1914 at Colchester affiliated to the 14th and 20th Hussars. In the summer of 1915 the 3rd Line units of the Bedfordshire and Hertfordshire Yeomanry were affiliated. Early in 1916 the Regiment moved to Maresfield, Sussex. Early in 1917 the Regiment was absorbed in the new 5th Reserve Regiment at Tidworth.

14TH RESERVE CAVALRY REGIMENT

Formed on mobilization in Aug. 1914 at Longmoor, near Liss, Hampshire affiliated to 15th and 19th Hussars. In the summer of 1915 some 3rd Line Yeomanry from regiments in Northern Command were affiliated. In April 1916 the Regiment was in the 1st Reserve Cav. Bde. and the affiliated Yeomanry were the Derbyshire and the South Nottinghamshire Hussars. In the autumn of 1916 the Regiment moved to Ireland, joining the 3rd Reserve Cav. Bde. Early in 1917 it was absorbed in the new 3rd Reserve Regiment at Aldershot.

SPECIAL RESERVE

NORTH IRISH HORSE
'France and Flanders, 1914–18'

4.8.14 Belfast: attached to 3rd Cav. Bde. On mobilization the regiment was split up and the squadrons were employed mainly as divisional cavalry until 1916. After this as corps cavalry and, finally in 1918, as corps cyclists and infantry. Three new squadrons were formed.

'A' Squadron landed at Havre on 19.8.14 as G.H.Q. Troops. 4.1.16 to 55th Div. as Div. Cav. 10.5.16 to VII Corps Cav. Regt.

'B' Squadron was attached to 59th Div. in Hertfordshire from Aug. 1915 to April 1916. In May 1916 'F' Squadron in France became 'B' Squadron.

'C' Squadron landed in France on 22.8.14 as G.H.Q. Troops. 14.4.15 to 3rd Div. as Div. Cav. 11.5.16 to X Corps Cav. Regt.

'D' Squadron. In 1915 joined 51st Div. at Bedford as Div. Cav. 2.5.15 landed at Havre. 10.5.16 to VII Corps Cav. Regt.

'E' Squadron. In 1915 joined 34th Div. on Salisbury Plain as Div. Cav. 1.1.16 landed at Havre. 10.5.16 to VII Corps Cav. Regt.

'F' (later 'B') Squadron. In 1915 joined 33rd Div. on Salisbury Plain as Div. Cav. 18.11.15 landed at Havre. On 19.4.16 left 33rd Div. and after short attachments to 1st Cav. 49th and 32nd Divs. joined X Corps Cav. Regt. on 21.6.16. Became 'B' Squadron on 25.5.16.

On 10.5.16 'A', 'D' and 'E' Squadrons formed what was known as the 1st North Irish Horse and served as VII Corps Cav. Regt. On 16.7.17 it became XIX Corps Cav. Regt. and transferred to V Corps on 7.9.17. Early in March the regiment was dismounted and converted to cyclists and was V Corps Cyclist Bn. until the end of the war.

On 21.6.16 'B' and 'C' Squadrons with the service sqdn. of the 6th (Inniskilling) Dragoons (from 36th Div.) formed the 2nd North Irish Horse at Toutencourt as X Corps Cav. Regt. In August 1917 the X Corps Cav. Regt. was broken up and the squadrons went to a base depot for infantry training. On 25.9.17 the 9th Bn. Royal Irish Fusiliers absorbed 304 men of the two North Irish Horse squadrons adding (North Irish Horse) to its title. The unit was in 108th Bde. 36th Div.

A reserve regiment was formed and remained in Ireland all the war, for most of the time at Antrim.

SOUTH IRISH HORSE
'France and Flanders, 1915–18'

4.8.14 Dublin: attached to 3rd Cav. Bde. On mobilization the regiment was split up and the squadrons were employed mainly as divisional cavalry until 1916. After this as corps cavalry and after September 1917 as infantry. Three new squadrons were formed.

'A' Squadron joined 21st Div. at Aldershot in 1915 as divisional cavalry. 12.9.15 landed at Havre. 11.5.16 to XV Corps Cav. Regt. Nov. 1916 to IX Corps Cav. Regt. 16.1.17 to XVIII Corps Cav. Regt.

'B' (later 'S') Squadron went to France on 17.8.14 as G.H.Q. Troops. 4.5.15 to 2nd Div. as Div. Cav. 15.5.16 to I Corps Cav. Regt. and became 'S' Sqdn.

'C' Squadron joined 16th Div. at Aldershot in 1915 as Div. Cav. 16.12.15 to France 17.5.16 to I Corps Cav. Regt.

'E' Squadron landed at Havre and joined 39th Div. as Div. Cav. on 17.3.16. 17.5.16 to I Corps Cav. Regt.

'F' Squadron landed in France from Ireland on 18.5.17 and on 27.5.17 replaced 'B' Sqdn. 1/1st Herts. Yeo. in XVIII Corps Cav. Regt.

'S' (later 'B') Squadron joined 32nd Div. on Salisbury Plain in 1915 as Div. Cav. 25.11.15 landed at Havre. 14.5.16 to XV Corps Cav. Regt. and became 'B' Sqdn. 21.11.16 to IX Corps Cav. Regt. Jan. 1917 to XVIII Corps Cav. Regt.

On 17.5.16 'C', 'E' and 'S' Squadrons formed I Corps Cav. Regt. and were known as the 1st South Irish Horse. It left I Corps in Aug. 1917, was dismounted and went to Etaples. At the end of Aug. it amalgamated with the 2nd South Irish Horse and on 1.9.17 formed the 7th (South Irish Horse) Bn. Royal Irish Regt. 14.10.17 to 49th Bde. 16th Div. 18.4.18 reduced to cadre. End of June reformed and on 4.7.18 to 21st Bde. 30th Div. until the end of the war.

On 11 & 14.5.16 'A' and 'S' Squadrons went to XV Corps as Corps Cavalry when 'S' Squadron became 'B'. On 21.5.16 RHQ and 'D' Squadron Wiltshire Yeomanry joined XV Corps Cav. Regt. Nov. 1916 the two South Irish Horse Squadrons joined 'C' Squadron Hampshire Yeomanry in IX Corps Cav. Regt. Jan. 1917 'A' and 'B' Squadrons with 'B' Squadron 1/1st Herts. Yeomanry formed XVIII Corps Cav. Regt. May 1917 'F' Squadron from Ireland joined in place of 'B' Herts. Yeo. In Aug. 1917 2nd South Irish Horse were dismounted and went to Etaples. Joined 1st S.I.H. and formed 7th (S.I.H.) Bn. Royal Irish Regt. (see above).

A reserve regiment was formed and remained in Ireland for the war, most of the time stationed at Cahir, in Tipperary.

KING EDWARD'S HORSE
(The King's Overseas Dominions Regiment)
'France and Flanders, 1915–17, 1918'
'Italy, 1917–18'

1st King Edward's Horse

4.8.14 Chelsea: attached to 4th Cav. Bde. for training. On mobilization to Watford. Mar. 1915 to Bishops Stortford. April 1915 regiment split up and squadrons employed as divisional cavalry until June 1916 and after this as a corps cavalry regiment.

RHQ and 'C' Squadron landed at Havre 22.4.15 and went to 47th Div. 1.6.16 Corps Cav. Regt.

'A' Squadron to 12th Div. at Aldershot on 23.5.15. Landed at Havre 2.6.15. 1.6.16 to IV Corps Cav. Regt.

'B' Squadron landed at Havre 22.4.15 and joined 48th Div. 1.6.16 to IV Corps Cav. Regt.

The regiment concentrated at Valhuon as IV Corps Cav. Regt. on 1.6.16. On 17.7.17 to XVIII Corps and in Nov. 1917 returned on IV Corps. 15.12.17 to Italy joining XI Corps. Mar. 1918 returned to France with XI Corps. In May 1918 the regiment was divided among the corps of First Army: 'A' Squadron to XI Corps, 'B' Squadron to I Corps and 'C' Squadron to XIII Corps (Oct. to III Corps).

A reserve squadron was formed at Chelsea in Aug. 1914 and went to Bishops Stortford in May 1915. In July 1915 the squadron crossed to Ireland and was attached to 8th Reserve Cavalry Regiment at the Curragh. April 1916 to

Longford. Feb. 1917 to Dublin and expanded to a reserve regiment. Remained in Dublin.

2nd King Edward's Horse
Formed in London on 10.8.14. Dec. 1914 replaced Essex Yeo. in Eastern Mtd. Bde. 1st Mtd. Div. in Essex. 1.2.15 to Canadian Cav. Bde. at Maresfield. 4.5.15 Canadian Cav. Bde. to France, dismounted, as Seely's Detachment and attached to 1st Canadian Div. until Sept. and then became Canadian Cav. Bde. again. 27.1.16 regiment mounted again and formed as a two squadron cavalry regiment with G.H.Q. Troops. R.H.Q. and 'A' Squadron remained with G.H.Q. Troops and 'B' Squadron went to 56th Div. as divisional cavalry on 23.3.16 until 30.5.16.

In June 1916 the regiment was joined by a service squadron of 21st Lancers from England and formed XIV Corps Cavalry Regiment. This unit was broken up in Aug. 1917, 2nd King Edward's Horse left France for Wareham on 5 Aug. and was absorbed by the Tank Corps. The squadron 21st Lancers went to No. 5 Base Depot on 29th Aug. and broken up.

A reserve squadron was formed which crossed to Ireland in July 1915. Later it expanded to a regiment and was stationed at Kilkenny in 1917 and 1918.

YEOMANRY

AYRSHIRE YEOMANRY
(Earl of Carrick's Own)
'Gallipoli, 1915'
'Egypt, 1916-17'
'Palestine, 1917-18'
'France and Flanders, 1918'

1/1st Ayrshire Yeomanry.
4.8.14 Ayr: Lowland Mtd. Bde. In Scotland until Sept. 1915 then sailed for Gallipoli, dismounted. 11.10.15 landed at Helles and brigade attached to 52nd Div. Jan. 1916 to Mudros. Feb. 1916 Egypt and brigade to 1st Dismounted Bde. 16.10.16 1st Dismounted Bde. broken up and regiment to 2nd Dismounted Bde. Jan. 1917 with Lanarkshire Yeomanry formed 12th (Ayr & Lanark Yeomanry) Bn. Royal Scots Fusiliers in 229th Bde. 74th Div. May 1918 to France. 21.6.18 to 94th Bde. 31st Div.

2/1st Ayrshire Yeomanry.
Formed Sept. 1914 and remained in Scotland in 2/1st Lowland Mtd. Bde. Mar. 1916 stationed at Dunbar when brigade became 20th Mtd. Bde. July 1916 converted to a cyclist unit in 13th Cyclist Bde. Nov. 1916 brigade became 9th Cyclist Bde. Regiment remained at Dunbar until about May 1918 when it moved to Ireland in 9th Cyclist Bde. Stationed at Omagh until the end of the war.

3/1st Ayrshire Yeomanry.
Formed in 1915 and in the summer was affiliated to a reserve cavalry regiment at Aldershot. June 1916 left reserve regiment and went to Perth. Early in 1917 the unit was disbanded the personnel going to the 2nd Line unit and the 4th (Reserve) Bn. Royal Scots Fusiliers at Catterick.

BEDFORDSHIRE YEOMANRY
'France and Flanders, 1915-18'

1/1st Bedfordshire Yeomanry.
4.8.14 Bedford: attached to Eastern Mtd. Bde. Stationed at Hatfield Peverel and Stansted until June 1915 then to France. 12.6.15 to 9th Cav. Bde. 1st Cav. Div. 10.3.18 withdrawn from 1st Cav. Div. to become a cyclist unit, then to form a machine gun battalion with the Essex Yeomanry, but after German offensive mounted again and sent to 1st Cav. Div. April 1918 regiment split up sending one squadron to each regiment of 9th Cav. Bde. (8th, 15th, and 19th Hussars). No further change.

2/1st Bedfordshire Yeomanry.
Formed Sept. 1914. Oct. 1915 to Feb. 1916 with 61st Div. in Chelmsford area. June 1916 in 16th Mtd. Bde. 4th Mtd. Div. in Essex. Later in 1916 the regiment was split up as divisional cavalry: 'A' Squadron to 57th Div. at Aldershot, 'B' Squadron to 66th Div. at Colchester and 'C' Squadron to 68th Div. at Turvey. By Mar. 1917 the regiment had concentrated at Ware attached to the 1st Mtd. Div. 'C' Squadron was attached to 71st Div. at Colchester. By July 1917 the regiment had been absorbed in the 1st Reserve Cavalry Regiment at the Curragh.

3/1st Bedfordshire Yeomanry.
Formed in 1915 and in June affiliated to 13th Reserve Cavalry Regiment at Colchester. Jan. 1917 absorbed in 1st Reserve Cavalry Regiment at the Curragh.

BERKSHIRE YEOMANRY
(Hungerford)
'Gallipoli, 1915'
'Egypt, 1915-17'
'Palestine, 1917-18'
'France and Flanders, 1918'

1/1st Berkshire Yeomanry.
4.8.14 Reading: 2nd South Midland Mtd. Bde. Aug. 1914 brigade to Mtd. Div. 2.9.14 brigade to 2nd Mtd. Div. at Churn. Nov. 1914 to Fakenham area. April 1915 to Egypt. Aug. 1915 to Gallipoli, dismounted. Dec. 1915 returned to Egypt. Jan. 1916 2nd Mtd. Div. broken up and brigades became independent. 2nd S.M. Bde. became 6th Mtd. Bde. Feb. 1917 6th Mtd. Bde. to Imperial Mtd. Div. June 1917 Bde. to Yeomanry Mtd. Div. 4.4.18 regiment left brigade and with Buckinghamshire Yeo. formed C Bn. Machine Gun Corps. 21.6.18 landed at Taranto and on to France. Mid Aug. numbered 101st Bn. M.G.C. At end of war was with Second Army.

2/1st Berkshire Yeomanry.
Formed Sept. 1914. Mar. 1915 in 2/2nd South Midland Mtd. Bde. from Reading. Now in 2/2nd Mtd. Div. in Kings Lynn area. Mar. 1916 now in 11th Mtd. Bde. 3rd Mtd. Div. July 1916 became a cyclist unit in 8th Cyclist Bde. 2nd Cyclist Div. in Maidstone area. Sept. 1916 to Ipswich area. Nov. 1916 2nd Cyclist Div. broken up and the unit amalgamated with 2/1st Hampshire Yeo. to form 11th (Hampshire & Berkshire) Yeomanry Cyclist Regt. in the 4th Cyclist Bde. in Essex. Mar. 1917 composite regiment discontinued and resumed identity. By July at Wivenhoe. About Jan. 1918 to Ireland in 4th Cyclist Bde. Stationed at Dublin and Dundalk.

3/1st Berkshire Yeomanry.
Formed in 1915 and in the summer affiliated to the 7th Reserve Cavalry Regiment at Tidworth. Early in 1917 absorbed in 6th Reserve Cavalry Regiment at Tidworth.

BUCKINGHAMSHIRE YEOMANRY
(Royal Bucks. Hussars)
'Gallipoli, 1915'
'Egypt, 1915-17'
'Palestine, 1917-18'
'France and Flanders, 1918'

1/1st Buckinghamshire Yeomanry.
4.8.14 Buckingham: 2nd South Midland Mtd. Bde. Subsequent record same as 1/1st Berkshire Yeomanry.

2/1st Buckinghamshire Yeomanry.

Formed Sept. 1914. Mar. 1915 from Buckingham to Kings Lynn area in 2/2nd South Midland Mtd. Bde. of 2/2nd Mtd. Div. Mar. 1916 Brigade became 11th Mtd. Bde. of 3rd Mtd. Div. July 1916 now in 1st Mtd. Bde. of 1st Mtd. Div. at Brentwood. Mar. 1917 at Much Hadham and in April back to Brentwood. Aug. 1917 became a cyclist unit in 11th Cyclist Bde. of the Cyclist Div. and was stationed at Canterbury in 1918 until the end of the war.

3/1st Buckinghamshire Yeomanry.
Formed in 1915 and in the summer affiliated to the 7th Reserve Cavalry Regiment at Tidworth. Early in 1917 absorbed in 3rd Reserve Cavalry Regiment at Aldershot.

CHESHIRE YEOMANRY
(Earl of Chester's)
'Egypt, 1916–17'
'Palestine, 1917–18'
'France and Flanders, 1918'

1/1st Cheshire Yeomanry.
4.8.14 Chester: Welsh Border Mtd. Bde. Sept. 1914 with brigade to Beccles and Bungay area in 1st Mtd. Div. Nov. 1915 dismounted. Mar. 1916 to Egypt and on 20 Mar., with South Wales Mtd. Bde., formed 4th Dismounted Bde. 2.3.17 with 1/1st Shropshire Yeomanry formed 10th (Shropshire & Cheshire Yeo.) Bn. K.S.L.I. in 231st Bde. 74th Div. May 1918 to France with 74th Div. where it remained.

2/1st Cheshire Yeomanry.
Formed Sept. 1914. 1915 in Northumberland with 2/1st Welsh Border Mtd. Bde. In Mar. 1916 brigade became 17th Mtd. Bde. and was for a short time in 1st Mtd. Div. in East Anglia and then to Morpeth. July 1916 became cyclist unit in 10th Cyclist Bde. Nov. 1916 brigade became Cyclist Bde. Mar. 1917 still at Morpeth and in July at Acklington. Early in 1918 from Acklington, in 6th Cyclist Bde., to Ireland and stationed at the Curragh until the end of the war.

3/1st Cheshire Yeomanry.
Formed in 1915 and in the summer affiliated to a reserve cavalry regiment at the Curragh. In the summer of 1916 attached to 3rd Line Groups of West Lancs. Div. Early in 1917 the unit was disbanded. The personnel going to the 2nd Line unit and the 4th (Reserve) Bn. Cheshire Regt. at Oswestry.

DENBIGHSHIRE YEOMANRY
'Egypt, 1916–17'
'Palestine, 1917–18'
'France and Flanders, 1918'

1/1st Denbighshire Yeomanry.
4.8.14 Wrexham: Welsh Border Mtd. Bde. Sept. 1914 with brigade to north-east Suffolk in 1st Mtd. Div. Nov. 1915 dismounted. Mar. 1916 to Egypt and on 20 Mar. the Welsh Border Mtd. Bde. with South Wales Mtd. Bde. formed the 4th Dismounted Bde. Feb. 1917 formed 24th (Denbighshire Yeo.) Bn. Royal Welsh Fusiliers in 231st Bde. 74th Div. May 1918 to France with 74th Div. 21.6.18 to 94th Bde. 31st Div.

2/1st Denbighshire Yeomanry.
Formed Sept. 1914. Jan. 1915 2/1st Welsh Border Mtd. Bde. in Newcastle area until Nov. 1915 then Yorkshire. In Mar. 1916 brigade became 17th Mtd. Bde. and was in 1st Mtd. Div. in East Anglia for a short time and then to Morpeth area. July 1916 became a cyclist unit in 10th Cyclist Bde. Nov. 1916 to 1st Cyclist Bde. at Beccles and with 2/1st Montgomery Yeomanry formed 3rd (Montgomery & Denbigh Yeo.) Cyclist Bn. at Beccles in 1st Cyclist Bde. Mar. 1917 resumed identity. July at Worlingham (Beccles). Jan. and April 1918 at Aldeburgh but afterwards at Worlingham in 1st Cyclist Bde. until the end of the war.

3/1st Denbighshire Yeomanry.
Formed in 1915 and in the summer affiliated to a reserve cavalry regiment at the Curragh. Summer 1916 dismounted and attached to 3rd Line Groups of West Lancs. Div. Early in 1917 the unit was disbanded the personnel going to the 2nd Line unit and the 4th (Reserve) Bn. Royal Welsh Fusiliers at Oswestry.

DERBYSHIRE YEOMANRY
'Gallipoli, 1915'
'Egypt, 1915–16'
'Macedonia, 1916–18'

1/1st Derbyshire Yeomanry.
4.8.14 Derby: Notts. and Derby Mtd. Bde. Sept. 1914 Brigade to 2nd Mtd. Div. at South Stoke, Berkshire. Nov. 1914 with division to Norfolk coast. April 1915 to Egypt. Aug. 1915 to Gallipoli, dismounted. Dec. 1915 returned to Egypt. Jan. 1916 Notts. and Derby Mtd. Bde. left 2nd Mtd. Div. and in Feb. 1916 went to Salonika as 7th Mtd. Bde. June 1917 7th Mtd. Bde. returned to Egypt but 1/1st Derbyshire Yeomanry remained in Macedonia till the end of the war, most of the time as G.H.Q. Troops of British Salonika Army.

2/1st Derbyshire Yeomanry.
Formed Sept. 1914. Feb. 1915 at Chatsworth in 2/1st Notts. and Derby Mtd. Bde. Mar. 1915 brigade to 2/2nd Mtd. Div. in Kings Lynn area. Mar. 1916 brigade became 9th Mtd. Bde. and 2/2nd Mtd. Div. became 3rd Mtd. Div. July 1916 3rd Mtd. Div. became 1st Mtd. Div., 9th Mtd. Bde. became 9th Cyclist Bde. and the regiment became a cyclist unit: now in Canterbury area. Nov. 1916 brigade became 5th Cyclist Bde. at Bridge near Canterbury. Sept. 1917 5th Cyclist Bde. became independent brigade. Nov. 1917 brigade to The Cyclist Div. and the regiment remained in this formation at Ash, near Canterbury until the end of the war.

3/1st Derbyshire Yeomanry.
Formed 1915 and in the summer affiliated to a reserve cavalry regiment at Aldershot. April 1916 affiliated to 14th Reserve Cavalry Regiment at Aldershot and in autumn with regiment to Ireland. Early in 1917 absorbed by 4th Reserve Cavalry Regiment at Aldershot.

ROYAL 1st DEVON YEOMANRY
'Gallipoli, 1915'
'Egypt, 1916–17'
'Palestine, 1917–18'
'France and Flanders, 1918'

1/1st Royal 1st Devon Yeomanry.
4.8.14 Exeter: 2nd South Western Mtd. Bde. Aug. 1914 with brigade to Colchester area. Sept. 1915 dismounted and sailed from Liverpool on 24.9.15. 9.10.15 landed at Gallipoli. 30.12.15 landed at Alexandria. Feb. 1916 2nd South Western Mtd. Bde. absorbed in 2nd Dismounted Bde. 4.1.17 with 1/1st North Devon Yeomanry formed 16th (Royal 1st Devon and Royal North Devon Yeomanry) Bn. Devonshire Regt. in 229th Bde. 74th Div. 7.5.18 landed at Marseilles and remained in France with the 74th Div. until the end of the war.

2/1st Royal 1st Devon Yeomanry.
Formed Sept. 1914 and stationed at Teignmouth. May 1915 in 2/2nd South Western Mtd. Bde. to Woodbury. Sept. 1915 to Colchester area taking over horses from the

1st Line regiment. April 1916 with brigade to Norfolk joining 1st Mtd. Div. July 1916 to 2nd Mtd. Bde. of new 1st Mtd. Div. and stationed at Thornton Park near Brentwood. Nov. 1916 became a cyclist unit, returning to Norfolk and with North Devon Yeomanry forming 4th (Royal 1st Devon and North Devon) Yeomanry Cyclist Regiment in 2nd Cyclist Bde. Mar. 1917 resumed identity, now at Holt, Norfolk. Remained in Holt and area until May 1918 and then went to Ireland with the 2nd Cyclist Bde. The unit was stationed at the Curragh and Mullingar.

3/1st Royal 1st Devon Yeomanry.
Formed at Exeter in 1915. In the summer affiliated to a reserve cavalry regiment at Tidworth. Summer 1916 dismounted and attached to 3rd Line Groups of Wessex Division, probably in Winchester area. Early in 1917 disbanded, personnel going to the 2nd Line regiment and the 4th (Reserve) Bn. Devonshire Regiment at Bournemouth.

ROYAL NORTH DEVON YEOMANRY
'Gallipoli, 1915'
'Egypt, 1916–17'
'Palestine, 1917–18'
'France and Flanders, 1918'

1/1st Royal North Devon Yeomanry.
4.8.14 Barnstaple: 2nd South Western Mtd. Bde. Subsequent record the same as 1/1st Royal 1st Devon Yeomanry.

2/1st Royal North Devon Yeomanry.
Formed at Barnstaple in Sept. 1914. May 1915 in 2/2nd South Western Mtd. Bde. to Woodbury. Sept. 1915 to Colchester area taking over horses from the 1st Line unit. April 1916 with brigade to Norfolk joining 1st Mtd. Div. July 1916 became a cyclist unit in 2nd Cyclist Bde. of 1st Cyclist Div. in Yoxford area. Nov. 1916 1st Cyclist Div. broken up and regiment with 2/1st Royal 1st Devon (from 1st Mtd. Div.) formed 4th (Royal 1st Devon and North Devon) Yeomanry Cyclist Regt. in 2nd Cyclist Bde. in Norfolk. Mar. 1917 resumed identity still in 2nd Cyclist Bde. and stationed at Melton Constable. Later in 1917 to East Dereham until May 1918 then to Ireland with 2nd Cyclist Bde. and stationed at Longford until the end of the war.

3/1st Royal North Devon Yeomanry.
Formed at Barnstaple in 1915. Subsequent record same as 3/1st Royal 1st Devon Yeomanry.

DORSET YEOMANRY
(Queen's Own)
'Gallipoli, 1915'
'Egypt, 1915–17'
'Palestine, 1917–18'

1/1st Dorset Yeomanry.
4.8.14 Sherborne: attached 1st South Western Mtd. Bde. Sept. 1914 to 2nd South Midland Mtd. Bde. (replacing Oxford Yeomanry) in Churn area, in 2nd Mtd. Div. Nov. 1914 to Fakenham area. April 1915 to Egypt with 2nd Mtd. Div. Aug. 1915 to Gallipoli, dismounted. Dec. 1915 returned to Egypt. Jan. 1916 2nd Mtd. Div. broken up and brigade became 6th Mtd. Bde. and independent. Feb. 1917 brigade to Imperial Mtd. Div. June 1917 to Yeomanry Mtd. Div. July 1918 formation names now 10th Cav. Bde. 4th Cav. Div. and remained with them in Palestine until the end of the war.

2/1st Dorset Yeomanry.
Sept. 1914 formed at Sherborne. In May 1915 at Chippenham in 2/1st South Western Mtd. Bde. Sept. 1915 to Maresfield. Oct. 1915 to Lewes in 1/1st South Western Mtd. Bde. replacing 1/1st Wiltshire Yeomanry. Brigade became 2/1st Southern Mtd. Bde. then 16th Mtd. Bde. in Mar. when it joined 4th Mtd. Div. Now at Manningtree. July 1916 became cyclist unit in 7th Cyclist Bde. of 2nd Cyclist Div., now at Woodbridge. Nov. 1916 2nd Cyclist Div. broken up. Regiment to Maidstone taking over horses from 2/1st West Kent Yeomanry and replacing them in 3rd Mtd. Bde. 1st Mtd. Div. Mar. 1917 at Sevenoaks. Sept. 1917 became a cyclist unit again, now in 13th Cyclist Bde. of The Cyclist Div. still at Sevenoaks. Dec. 1917 13th Cyclist Bde. broken up and early in 1918 the Regiment went to Ireland joining the 6th Cyclist Bde. at the Curragh till the end of the war.

3/1st Dorset Yeomanry.
Formed 1915 and in the summer affiliated to a reserve cavalry regiment at Tidworth. July 1916 affiliated to 8th Reserve Cavalry Regiment at the Curragh. Early in 1917 absorbed by the 2nd Reserve Cavalry Regiment at the Curragh.

ESSEX YEOMANRY
'France and Flanders, 1914–18'

1/1st Essex Yeomanry.
4.8.14 Colchester: Eastern Mtd. Bde. Aug. 1914 with brigade to 1st Mtd. Div. in Ipswich area then at the end of Aug. to Woodbridge area. Nov. 1914 left brigade and landed at Havre on 1.12.14. 12.12.14 to 8th Cav. Bde. 3rd Cav. Div. near Hazebrouck. Mar. 1918 withdrawn from 3rd Cav. Div. for conversion to a cyclist unit. 12.3.18 decision to form a machine gun battalion from Bedford and Essex Yeomanry. 28.3.18 regiment mounted again and sent to 1st Cav. Div. 4.4.18 regiment split up sending one squadron to each regiment of 1st Cav. Bde. (2 D.G., 5 D.G. and 11 Hussars) in 1st Cav. Div. No further change.

2/1st Essex Yeomanry.
Formed Sept. 1914 at Colchester. Oct. 1914 Wickham Market. Jan. 1915 in 2/1st Eastern Mtd. Bde. at Huntingdon. June 1915 to Mar. 1916 at Hounslow: then, now 13th Mtd. Bde., joined the new 4th Mtd. Div. with unit at Great Bentley, Essex. July 1916 to 3rd Mtd. Bde. of new 1st Mtd. Div. and stationed at Leybourne Park, Kent. Mar. 1917 at Brasted, near Sevenoaks. Sept. 1917 1st Mtd. Div. became The Cyclist Div. and regiment became a cyclist unit in 13th Cyclist Bde. at Sevenoaks. Dec. 1917 13th Cyclist Bde. broken up and in Jan. 1918 to Ireland joining 6th Cyclist Bde. Stationed at the Curragh.

3/1st Essex Yeomanry.
Formed in 1915 and in the summer affiliated to a reserve cavalry regiment in Eastern Command and in April 1916 affiliated to 2nd Reserve Cavalry Regiment at Aldershot. Early in 1917 absorbed in 4th Reserve Cavalry Regiment at Aldershot.

FIFE AND FORFAR YEOMANRY
'Gallipoli, 1915'
'Egypt, 1915–17'
'Palestine, 1917–18'
'France and Flanders, 1918'

1/1st Fife and Forfar Yeomanry.
4.8.14 Kirkaldy: Highland Mtd. Bde. 12.8.14 with brigade to Blairgowrie then to Huntingdon area with regiment at St. Ives. Nov. 1914 brigade to Lincolnshire with regiment at Skegness. April 1915 to north Norfolk at Fakenham. Aug. 1915 dismounted and horses to 2nd Line unit and remount depot. 8.9.15 sailed from Devonport.

18.9.15 Alexandria. 26.9.15 landed at Gallipoli. Dec. 1915 to Egypt. Feb. 1916 Highland Mtd. Bde. in 2nd Dismtd. Bde. 21.12.16 formed 14th (Fife and Forfar Yeo.) Bn. The Black Watch in 229th Bde. 74th Div. 7.5.18 landed at Marseilles and remained in France in 74th Div. until the end of the war.

2/1st Fife and Forfar Yeomanry.
Formed Sept. 1914. Jan. 1915 in 2/1st Highland Mtd. Bde. April 1916 brigade, now 1st Mtd. Bde., to 1st Mtd. Div. in Norfolk. July 1916 1st Mtd. Div. became 1st Cyclist Div. and regiment went, mounted, to 2nd Mtd. Bde. in new 1st Mtd. Div. and stationed in Brentwood area. Nov. 1916 became a cyclist unit and joined 6th Cyclist Bde. in Northumberland at Ashington. By July 1917 at Acklington. Remained here until early in 1918 and then to Ireland with 6th Cyclist Bde. and stationed at the Curragh until the end of the war.

3/1st Fife and Forfar Yeomanry.
Formed 1915 and in the summer affiliated to a reserve cavalry regiment at Aldershot. June 1916 to Perth. Early in 1917 disbanded and personnel absorbed in the 2nd Line unit and the 4th (Reserve) Bn. The Black Watch at Ripon.

GLAMORGAN YEOMANRY
'Egypt, 1916–17'
'Palestine, 1917–18'
'France and Flanders, 1918'

1/1st Glamorgan Yeomanry.
4.8.14 Bridgend: South Wales Mtd. Bde. 12.8.14 with brigade at Hereford. End of Aug. to Thetford area, joining 1st Mtd. Div., and then to Aylsham. Oct. 1915 to Cromer area. Nov. 1915 dismounted. Mar. 1916 to Egypt and on 20.3.16 the South Wales Mtd. Bde. was absorbed in 4th Dismounted Bde. 2.2.17 with 1/1st Pembroke Yeomanry formed 24th (Pembroke & Glamorgan Yeo.) Bn. Welsh Regt. in 231st Bde. 74th Div. May 1918 to France and remained here until the end of the war in the 74th Div.

2/1st Glamorgan Yeomanry.
Formed 1914. Jan. 1915 in 2/1st South Wales Mtd. Bde. July 1915 Dorchester area. Sept. 1915 with brigade to east Suffolk joining 1st Mtd. Div. Mar. 1916 brigade became 4th Mtd. Bde. July 1916 1st Mtd. Div. became 1st Cyclist Div. and unit became a cyclist unit in 2nd Cyclist Bde. of the division at Yoxford. Nov. 1916 division broken up and unit with 2/1st Pembroke Yeomanry formed 2nd (Pembroke & Glamorgan Yeo.) Cyclist Bn. in 1st Cyclist Bde. Mar. 1917 resumed identity, now at Leiston. By July 1917 at Benacre. By the end of 1917 at Worlingham, near Beccles, where it remained, in 1st Cyclist Bde., until the end of the war.

3/1st Glamorgan Yeomanry.
Formed in 1915 and in summer attached to a reserve cavalry regiment at the Curragh. Summer 1916 dismounted and attached to 3rd Line Groups of Welsh Div. Early in 1917 the unit was disbanded the personnel going to the 2nd Line unit and the 4th (Reserve) Bn. Welsh Regt. at Milford Haven.

QUEEN'S OWN ROYAL GLASGOW YEOMANRY
'France and Flanders, 1915–18'

1/1st Glasgow Yeomanry.
4.8.14 Glasgow: attached to Lowland Mtd. Bde. Aug. 1914 with brigade to Cupar, Fife on coast defence. May 1915 left brigade and split up.

RHQ and 'C' Squadron went to Egypt, arriving at Port Said 22.6.15. Oct. 1915 joined 52nd Div. at Gallipoli and in Jan. 1916 returned to Egypt with 52nd Div. In May 1916 RHQ went to France and joined V Corps Cavalry Regiment. 'C' Sqdn. remained with 52nd Div. until 21.8.17 when it joined XXI Corps Cav. Regt. In May 1918 to Palestine L. of C. until the end of the war.

'A' Squadron to 11th Div. at Aldershot on 2.6.15 and on 30.6.15 to 24th Div. at Aldershot. 1.9.15 landed at Havre. Attached to 2nd Cav. Div. 30.4.16 to 14.5.16 and joined V Corps Cav. Regt. on 21.45.16.

'B' Squadron landed at Havre on 13.5.15 and joined 9th Div. at St. Omer. 10.5.16 to V Corps Cav. Regt.

The V Corps Cavalry Regiment was formed in France in May 1916 with RHQ, 'A' and 'B' Squadrons Glasgow Yeomanry and 'B' Squadrons Lothians and Border Horse. In July 1917 the regiment was dismounted and the horses sent to Egypt. The squadrons went to No. 21 Infantry Base Depot at Etaples for infantry training on 23.8.17. The Glasgow Yeomanry (4 O. & 146 OR) on 23.9.17 joined 18th H.L.I. in 106th Bde. 35th Div. at Aizecourt le Bas. They were absorbed in the battalion which became 18th (R. Glasgow Yeo.) Bn. H.L.I. and remained in France until the end of the war.

2/1st Glasgow Yeomanry.
Formed in Glasgow in 1914 and remained here till May 1915 and then to Hawick. In Mar. 1916 RHQ with 'A' and 'B' Squadrons joined 65th Div. in Essex and were later reduced to one squadron. In Jan. 1917 with 65th Div. to Ireland and in Feb. 1918 absorbed by 1st Res. Cav. Regt. at the Curragh. 'C' Squadron went to the 64th Div. in Norfolk in 1916 and was disbanded in 1917.

3/1st Glasgow Yeomanry.
Formed 1915 and in summer affiliated to a reserve cavalry regiment at Aldershot. June 1916 affiliated to 1st Res. Cav. Regt. at Aldershot. Early 1917 absorbed by 4th Res. Cav. Regt. at Aldershot. It is probable that some of the men went to the 5th (Reserve) Bn. H.L.I. at Catterick.

NOTE. The title of this regiment in 1914 was LANARKSHIRE YEOMANRY (QUEEN'S OWN ROYAL GLASGOW AND LOWER WARD OF LANARKSHIRE). The designation QUEEN'S OWN ROYAL GLASGOW YEOMANRY was approved in Army Order 91 of Mar., 1960.

GLOUCESTERSHIRE YEOMANRY
(Royal Gloucestershire Hussars)
'Gallipoli, 1915'
'Egypt, 1915–17'
'Palestine, 1917–18'

1/1st Gloucestershire Yeomanry.
4.8.14 Gloucester: 1st South Midland Mtd. Bde. With brigade to Bury St. Edmunds area in 1st Mtd. Div. End Aug. with brigade to Newbury to 2nd Mtd. Div. Nov. 1914 to Kings Lynn area. April 1915 to Egypt, landing at Alexandria on 24th April. Aug. 1915 to Gallipoli with 2nd Mtd. Div., dismounted. Dec. 1915 returned to Egypt. Jan. 1916 2nd Mtd. Div. broken up and brigade became 5th Mtd. Bde. which was independent. Feb. 1917 Brigade to Imperial Mtd. Bde. June 1917 Division became Australian Mtd. Div. Aug. 1918 5th Mtd. Bde. became 13th Cav. Bde. in 5th Cav. Div. where it remained until the end of the war.

2/1st Gloucestershire Yeomanry.
Sept. 1914 formed at Gloucester. April 1915 joined 2/1st South Midland Mtd. Bde. at Cirencester. June 1915 with brigade to north Norfolk joining 2/2nd Mtd. Div. Mar.

1916 brigade became 10th Mtd. Bde. Summer 1916 became a cyclist unit and moved to 8th Cyclist Bde. 2nd Cyclist Div. at first in Kent and then to Ipswich. Nov. 1916 2nd Cyclist Div. broken up. With Worcestershire Yeo. formed 12th (Gloucester & Worcester Yeomanry) Cyclist Regt. at Ipswich in 4th Cyclist Bde. Mar. 1917 resumed identity probably at Ipswich. July 1917 at Wivenhoe. Jan. 1918 Clacton. By April 1918 in Ireland still in the Cyclist Bde. and stationed in Dublin until the end of the war.

3/1st Gloucestershire Yeomanry.
Formed 1915 and in summer affiliated to a reserve cavalry regiment at Tidworth. April 1916 affiliated to 4th. Reserve Cavalry Regiment at Tidworth. Early in 1917 absorbed by 5th Reserve Cavalry Regiment at Tidworth.

HAMPSHIRE YEOMANRY
(Carabiniers)
'France and Flanders, 1916–17, 1918'
'Italy, 1917–18'

1/1st Hampshire Yeomanry.
4.8.14 Winchester: 1st South Western Mtd. Bde. Aug. 1914 Portsmouth Defences. Oct. 1914 with brigade in Forest Row area. Oct. 1915 Eastbourne. Mar. 1916 regiment split up became divisional cavalry.
'A' Squadron to 58th Div. at Ipswich 21.3.16. July 1916 with division to Sutton Veny area. 20.1.17 landed at Havre and on 25 Jan. 1917 rejoined the regiment in IX Corps Cav. Regt. at Bailleul.
'B' Squadron and RHQ to 60th Div. at Warminster on 26.4.16. Landed at Havre 25.6.16. 28.6.16 RHQ joined IX Corps Cav. Regt. ('A' and 'B' Sqdns. Wiltshire Yeo. and 'C' Sqdn. Hampshire Yeo.) at Bailleul and 'B' Sqdn. attached to XVII Corps Cav. Regt. 8 July to 4 Sept. 5.9.16 to Cav. Corps Troops. 19.1.17 rejoined regiment in IX Corps Cav. Regt.
'C' Squadron to 61st Div. at Ludegershall on 18.3.16. 25.5.16 landed at Havre. 31 May to 16 June attached 1st Cav. Div. 17.6.16 joined IX Corps Cav. Regt.
The IX Corps Cavalry Regiment was formed at Bailleul at the end of June 1916 consisting of RHQ and 'C' Squadron 1/1st Hampshire Yeomanry and 'A' and 'B' Squadrons 1/1st Wiltshire Yeomanry. The latter left in Nov. and in Jan. 1917 the other two Hampshire squadrons joined so the regiment was complete. 25.7.17 left IX Corps. 25.8.17 now dismounted and to No. 3 Infantry Base Depot at Rouen for training. 27.9.17 joined 15th Bn. Hampshire Regt. at Caestre in 122 Bde. 41st Div. which became 15th (Hampshire Yeomanry) Bn. Hampshire Regt. 12.11.17 to Italy with 41st Div. Early Mar. returned to France and remained there until the end of the war in 41st Div.

2/1st Hampshire Yeomanry.
Oct. 1914 formed at Winchester and in May 1915 to Calne in 2/1st South Western Mtd. Bde. Sept. 1915 Canterbury. Oct. 1915 to Maresfield. Mar. 1916 to Tiptree: Bde. now 15th Mtd. and joined 4th Mtd. Div. July 1916 became a cyclist unit in 6th Cyclist Bde. 2nd Cyclist Div. Aug. to Preston, near Canterbury. Nov. 1916 to Ipswich and with 2/1st Berkshire Yeo. formed 11th (Hampshire and Berkshire) Yeomanry Cyclist Regt. in 4th Cyclist Bde. Feb. 1917 to Coltishall and to 5th (Hampshire and West Somerset) Yeomanry Cyclist Regt. in 2nd Cyclist Bde. Mar. 1917 resumed identity. Oct. 1917 to Reepham, Norfolk. 16.5.18 landed at Dublin and was stationed at Maryborough, with companies at Tullamore and Birr, still in 2nd Cyclist Bde., until the end of the war.

3/1st Hampshire Yeomantry.
Formed in 1915. In the summer affiliated to 11th Res. Cav. Regt. at Tidworth. Early 1917 absorbed in 4th Res. Cav. Regt. at Aldershot. By 1918 had left 4th Reserve Cav. Regt., when 1st Line unit became infantry, and joined 4th (Reserve) Bn. Hampshire Regt. at Larkhill.

HERTS YEOMANRY
'Gallipoli, 1915'
'Egypt, 1915–16'
'Palestine, 1918'

1/1st Herts Yeomanry.
4.8.14 Hertford: attached Eastern Mtd. Bde. 10.9.14 sailed for Egypt. 19.1.15 with 2nd County of London Yeomanry formed Yeomanry Mtd. Bde. in Egypt. Aug. 1915 to Gallipoli joining 2nd Mtd. Div. as 5th Mtd. Bde. Dec. 1915 returned to Egypt and left 2nd Mtd. Div. for Western Frontier. Mar. 1916 regiment split up to serve as divisional cavalry.
RHQ and 'A' Squadron joined 54th Div. at Mena 20.3.16. Sept. 1916 RHQ broken up. 26.8.17. to XXI Corps Cav. Regt. in Palestine.
'B' Squadron to 11th Div. 11.3.16 and landed in France with division on 4.7.16. 12.7.16 attached to VI Corps Cav. Regt. (1/1st Northants Yeo.). Early 1917 to XVIII Corps Cav. Regt. 27.5.17 to G.H.Q. Troops. 6.7.17 arrived back in Egypt and became Depot Squadron at Zeitoun. 9.5.18 joined 'A' Squadron in XXI Corps Cav. Regt. in Palestine.
'D' Squadron to Mesopotamia Mar. 1916 and to L of C 8.7.16 to 13th Div. Dec. 1916 to III (Tigris) Corps Cav. Regt. 6.8.17 to 15th Indian Div. May 1918 to North Persia Force L of C.

2/1st Herts Yeomanry.
Formed at Hertford 1.9.14. Aug. 1915 to 69th Div. in Thetford–Newmarket area, at Huntingdon. 28.4.16 to 16th (2/1st Southern) Mtd. Bde. 4th Mtd. Div. in Manningtree area. July 1916 to 3rd Mtd. Bde. of new 1st Mtd. Div. in Maidstone area. Oct. 1916 West Malling area. Mar. 1917 Sevenoaks area. Regiment became a cyclist unit in Sept. 1917 in 13th Cyclist Bde. of the Cyclist Div. 26.10.17 to 214th Bde. 71st Div. This brigade was a special formation for possible service in Murmansk. Now at Colchester. 12.2.18 with brigade to 67th Div. still at Colchester. In Mar. 1918 all fit men in 214th Bde. were used as drafts for France and the Murmansk operation was cancelled. The unit appears to have left the 67th Div. by Sept. but probably remained in East Anglia until the end of the war.

3/1st Herts Yeomanry.
Formed at Hertford Dec. 1914. Mar. 1915 affiliated to 13th Reserve Cav. Regt. at Colchester. 1916 at Maresfield. Feb. 1917 absorbed in 6th Reserve Cav. Regt. at Tidworth.

ROYAL EAST KENT YEOMANRY
(The Duke of Connaught's Own)
(Mounted Rifles)
'Gallipoli, 1915'
'Egypt, 1916–17'
'Palestine, 1917–18'
'France and Flanders, 1918'

1/1st Royal East Kent Yeomanry.
4.8.14 Canterbury: South Eastern Mtd. Bde. Aug. 1914 with brigade to Canterbury area till Sept. 1915. Dismounted and sailed from Liverpool on 24.9.15 in s.s. 'Olympic' 8.10.15 landed on Gallipoli and attd. to 42nd

Div. Jan. 1916 to Mudros. Feb. 1916 to Egypt and S.E. Mtd. Bde. was absorbed in 3rd Dismounted Bde. 1.2.17 with 1/1st West Kent Yeo. formed 10th (Royal E. Kent and W. Kent Yeo.) Bn. The Buffs in 230th Bde. 74th Div. 7.5.18 landed at Marseilles and remained in France until the end of the war in 74th Div.

2/1st Royal East Kent Yeomanry.
Formed in 1914. 1915 in 2/1st South Eastern Mtd. Bde. Sept. 1915 in Canterbury area. Mar. 1916 Brigade became 14th Mtd. Bde. and joined 4th Mtd. Div., still in Canterbury area. July 1916 became a cyclist unit in 7th Cyclist Bde. 2nd Cyclist Div. in Manningtree area. Nov. 1916 division broken up: with W. Kent Yeo. unit formed 9th (East Kent and West Kent) Yeomanry Cyclist Regiment in 3rd Cyclist Bde. in Ipswich area. Mar. 1917 resumed identity, in Woodbridge, still in 3rd Cyclist Bde. April 1918 to Ireland with brigade and was in Co. Mayo until the end of the war.

3/1st Royal East Kent Yeomanry.
Formed in 1915 and in the summer was affiliated to a Reserve Cav. Regt. in Eastern Command. Summer 1916 attached to Third Line Groups, Home Counties Div. at Crowborough. Early 1917 disbanded, personnel to 2nd Line unit and 4th (Reserve) Bn. The Buffs at Crowborough.

WEST KENT YEOMANRY
(Queen's Own)
'Gallipoli, 1915'
'Egypt, 1916–17'
'Palestine, 1917–18'
'France and Flanders, 1918'

1/1st West Kent Yeomanry.
4.8.14 Maidstone: South Eastern Mtd. Bde. Subsequent record the same as 1/1st Royal East Kent Yeomanry.

2/1st West Kent Yeomanry.
Aug. 1914 formed at Maidstone. Jan. 1915 Hounslow Barracks April 1915 to Maresfield and took over horses from Royal Canadian Dragoons and Lord Strathcona's Horse, who were going to France dismounted. Oct. 1915 Westbere, near Canterbury, in 2/1st South Eastern Mtd. Bde. Mar. 1916 brigade became 14th Mtd. Bde. and joined 4th Mtd. Div. July 1916 to 3rd Mtd. Bde. 1st Mtd. Div. near Maidstone. Oct. 1916 handed over horses to 2/1st Dorset Yeo. and became a cyclist unit. With 2/1st East Kent Yeo. formed 9th (East Kent and West Kent) Yeomanry Cyclist Regiment in 3rd Cyclist Bde. in Ipswich area. Mar. 1917 resumed identity at Woodbridge in 3rd Cyclist Bde. Remained there until April 1918 and then to Ireland still in 3rd Cyclist Bde. Stationed at Dublin and then Claremorris till the end of the war.

3/1st West Kent Yeomanry.
Formed end of 1914 at Canterbury. June 1915 affiliated to 3rd Reserve Cav. Regt. at Canterbury. Summer 1916 attached to Third Line Groups, Home Counties Div. at Crowborough. Nov. 1916 Tunbridge Wells. Feb. 1917 disbanded. Personnel to 2nd Line unit and 4th (Reserve) Bn. Royal West Kent Regt. at Crowborough.

LANARKSHIRE YEOMANRY
'Gallipoli, 1915'
'Egypt, 1916–17'
'Palestine, 1917–18'
'France and Flanders, 1918'

1/1st Lanarkshire Yeomanry.
4.8.14 Lanark: Lowland Mtd. Bde. Aug. 1914 to Cupar. Sept. 1915 dismounted and sailed for Gallipoli. 11.10.15 landed at Helles and brigade attached to 52nd Div. Jan. 1916 Mudros. 7 Feb. 1916 Egypt and brigade to 1st Dismtd. Bde. 16.10.16 1st Dismtd. Bde. broken up and regiment to 2nd Dismtd. Bde. 4.1.17 with Ayrshire Yeo. formed 12th (Ayr and Lanark Yeomanry) Bn. Royal Scots Fusiliers in 229th Bde. 74th Div. May 1918 landed in France. 21.6.18 Battalion to 94th Bde. 31st Div. until the end of the war.

2/1st Lanarkshire Yeomanry.
Formed 1914. Remained in Scotland with 2/1st Lowland Mtd. Bde. Mar. 1916 brigade became 20th Mtd. Bde. at Dunbar. July 1916 became a cyclist unit in 13th Cyclist Bde. Nov. 1916 brigade became 9th Cyclist Bde. Regiment remained at Dunbar until about May 1918 and then to Ireland with 9th Cyclist Bde. Stationed at Londonderry until the end of the war.

3/1st Lanarkshire Yeomanry.
Formed in 1915. Summer 1915 affiliated to a reserve cavalry regiment at Aldershot. June 1916 left reserve regiment and went to Perth. Early 1917 disbanded: personnel to 2nd Line unit and the 5th (Reserve) Bn. Scottish Rifles at Leven.

LANCASHIRE HUSSARS YEOMANRY
'France and Flanders, 1916–18'

1/1st Lancashire Hussars.
4.8.14 Liverpool: attached to Welsh Border Mtd. Bde. Aug. 1914 to West Lancs. Div. and with division to Kent. April 1915 with remaining units of division to 2/West Lancs. Div. still in Kent. Oct. 1915 unit split up as divisional cavalry.

RHQ and 'B' Squadron on 27.11.15 to 31st Div. on Salisbury Plain. Dec. 1915 to Egypt with division. Mar. 1916 to France. 27 April to 10 May attd. to 2nd Indian Cav. Div. 11.5.16 to VIII Corps Cav. Regt.

'C' Squadron on 14.11.15 to 35th Div. on Salisbury Plain. 1.2.16 landed at Havre. 10.5.16 to VIII Corps Cav. Regt.

'D' Squadron on 29.10.15 to 30th Div. on Salisbury Plain. 10.11.15 landed at Havre. 13 to 26 April attd. to 2nd Indian Cav. Div. 11.5.16 to VIII Corps Cav. Regt.

In May 1916 the VIII Corps Cav. Regt. was formed by the regiment. About July 1917 dismounted and went to Base Depot for infantry training. 24.9.17 with a strength of 16 officers and 290 other ranks absorbed by 18th Bn. The King's Regt. in 21st Bde. 30th Div. Became 18th (Lancashire Hussars Yeo.) Bn. The King's Regt. 11.2.18 to 89th Bde. 30th Div. 14.5.18 reduced to training cadre and on 19.6.18 to 66th Div. 13.8.18 reconstituted and on 19.9.18 to 199th Bde. 66th Div. where it remained.

2/1st Lancashire Hussars.
Formed in 1914. In 1915 in newly formed Western Mtd. Bde. By Mar. 1916 at Cupar, Fife and brigade became 21st Mtd. Bde. July 1916 became a cyclist unit in 14th Cyclist Bde. Oct. 1916 became 10th Cyclist Bde. and at Cupar. Brigade remained at Cupar until the end of 1917 but the unit was at St. Andrews from July. About Jan. the 10th Cyclist Bde. moved to Lincolnshire and the unit was at Skegness. May 1918 to Ireland with brigade and stationed at Bandon and Buttevant until the end of the war.

3/1st Lancashire Hussars.
Formed 1915 and in summer affiliated to a reserve cav. regt. at the Curragh. Summer 1916 affiliated to 10th

Reserve Cav. Regt. at the Curragh. Early 1917 absorbed by 2nd Reserve Cav. Regt. at the Curragh. By 1918 had left 2nd Reserve Cav. Regt., when 1st Line unit became infantry, and joined 5th (Reserve) Bn. The Kings at Oswestry.

DUKE OF LANCASTER'S OWN YEOMANRY
'France and Flanders, 1915–18'

1/1st Duke of Lancaster's Own Yeomanry.
   4.8.14 Manchester: attached Welsh Border Mtd. Bde. Aug. 'A' Squadron to East Lancs. (later 42nd) Div. Remainder of regiment to 58th Div. in Crowborough area in the autumn and in 1915 split up as divisional cavalry.
   'A' Squadron embarked for Egypt with 42nd Div. 19.9.14. Remained in Egypt until 29.1.17 then to 53rd Div. 23.8.17 to XXI Corps Cav. Regt. in Palestine until the end of the war.
   RHQ and 'C' Squadron to 23rd Div. at Aldershot on 27.6.15. 28.8.15 landed at Havre. Attached 1st Cav. Div. 20 April to 4 May 1916. 14.5.16 to III Corps Cav. Regt.
   'D' Squadron to 14th Div. at Aldershot in spring 1915. 23.5.15 landed at Havre. 14.5.16 to III Corps Cav. Regt.
   In May 1916 the III Corps Cav. Regt. was formed at Beaucourt with the above squadrons and 'C' Squadron Surrey Yeomanry. 24.7.17 RHQ and the two squadrons went to GHQ Troops, were dismounted and on 28 Aug. to Base Depot for infantry training. On 24.9.17 7 officers and 125 other ranks were absorbed by 12th Bn. Manchester Regt. in 52nd Bde. 17th Div. The battalion now became 12th (Duke of Lancaster's Own Yeo.) Bn. Manchester Regt. Remained unchanged until the end of the war.
2/1st Duke of Lancaster's Own Yeomanry.
   Formed 1914. In 1915 in newly formed Western Mtd. Bde By Mar. 1916 at Cupar, Fife and brigade became 21st Mtd. Bde. July 1916 became a cyclist unit in 14th Cyclist Bde. Oct. 1916 became 10th Cyclist Bde. still at Cupar and there until the end of 1917. About Jan. 1918 brigade moved to Lincolnshire and the unit was at Alford and Skegness. About May 1918 with brigade to Ireland and at Tralee until the end of the war.
3/1st Duke of Lancaster's Yeomantry.
   Formed in 1915 and in the summer affiliated to a reserve cav. regt. at the Curragh. Summer 1916 affiliated to 10th Reserve Cav. Regt. at the Curragh. Early 1917 absorbed by 6th Reserve Cav. Regt. at Tidworth.

LEICESTERSHIRE YEOMANRY
('Prince Albert's Own')
'France and Flanders, 1914–18'

1/1st Leicestershire Yeomanry.
   4.8.14 Leicester: North Midland Mtd. Bde. With brigade to Norfolk. Soon left brigade and landed in France on 3 Nov. 12.11.14 to 7th Cav. Bde. 3rd Cav. Div. Nov. 1917 to 8th Cav. Bde. 3rd Cav. Div. 14.3.18 withdrawn from 3rd Cav. Div. for conversion to a cyclist unit. This was changed for the unit to form a machine gun battalion with the North Somerset Yeomanry. After the German offensive the regiment was mounted again and returned to Cavalry Corps. 4.4.18 regiment split up sending one squadron to be absorbed in each regiment of the 3rd Cav. Bde. (4 Hussars, 5 and 16 Lancers).
2/1st Leicestershire Yeomanry.
   Formed in 1914. 1915 in 2/1st North Midlands Mtd. Bde. Oct. 1915 brigade to Norfolk joining 1st Mtd. Div. April 1916 brigade became 3rd Mtd. Bde. July 1916 became a cyclist unit in 3rd Cyclist Bde. 1st Cyclist Div., now in Holt area. Nov. 1916 mounted again, with other regts. of 3rd Cyclist Bde. which became 2nd Mtd. Bde. and joined new 1st Mtd. Div. (formerly 3rd and 2/2nd Mtd. Div.) at Stansted. By May 1917 at Leybourne (West Malling). Aug. 1917 became cyclist unit in 12th Cyclist Bde. Cyclist Div. By Jan. 1918 had moved to Canterbury and remained there until the end of the war.
3/1st Leicestershire Yeomanry.
   Formed 1915. In the summer affiliated to a reserve cavalry regiment at Aldershot. Summer 1916 affiliated to 12th Reserve Cav. Regt. at Aldershot. Early 1917 absorbed in 3rd Reserve Cav. Regt. at Aldershot.

LINCOLNSHIRE YEOMANRY
'Egypt, 1915–17'
'Palestine, 1917–18'
'France and Flanders, 1918'

1/1st Lincolnshire Yeomanry.
   4.8.14 Lincoln: North Midland Mtd. Bde. Sept. 1914 brigade to Norfolk joining 1st Mtd. Div. 27.10.15 embarked at Southampton for Salonika. Destination changed at sea to Alexandria and regiment arrived in Cairo by end of November. About April 1916 brigade became 22nd Mtd. Bde. and was with Western Frontier Force. Feb. 1917 brigade to Anzac Mtd. Div. July 1917 brigade to Yeomanry Mtd. Div. 7.4.18 regiment left 22nd Mtd. Bde. and with 1/1st East Riding Yeomanry formed 'D' Bn. M.G.C. 1.6.18 landed at Marseilles and to Etaples. 17.8.18 became 102nd Bn. M.G.C. With First Army until the end of the war.
2/1st Lincolnshire Yeomanry.
   Formed 1914. 1915 in 2/1st North Midland Mtd. Bde. Oct. 1915 brigade to Norfolk joining 1st Mtd. Div. April 1916 brigade became 3rd Mtd. Bde. July 1916 became a cyclist unit in 3rd Cyclist Bde. 1st Cyclist Div., now in Holt area. Nov. 1916 mounted again, with other regiments of 3rd Cyclist Bde. which became 2nd Mtd. Bde., and joined new 1st Mtd. Div. (formerly 3rd and 2/2nd Mtd. Div.) at Bishops Stortford. By May 1917 at Leybourne (West Malling). Aug. 1917 again became a cyclist unit in 12th Cyclist Bde. the Cyclist Div. to Tonbridge. Early in 1918 to Canterbury and remained there until the end of the war.
3/1st Lincolnshire Yeomanry.
   Formed 1915 and in the summer affiliated to a reserve cav. regt. at Aldershot. Summer 1916 affiliated to 12th Reserve Cav. Regt. at Aldershot. Early in 1917 absorbed in 1st Reserve Cav. Regt. at the Curragh.

CITY OF LONDON YEOMANRY
(Rough Riders)
'Gallipoli, 1915'
'Egypt, 1915–16'
'Macedonia, 1916–17'
'Palestine, 1917–18'
'France and Flanders, 1918'

1/1st City of London Yeomanry.
   4.8.14 Finsbury Square, London: London Mtd. Bde. To Hounslow. Sept. 1914 with brigade to 2nd Mtd. Div. at Streatley. Nov. 1914 brigade to North Walsham area. April 1915 to Egypt. Aug. 1915 to Gallipoli dismounted. Dec. 1915 returned to Egypt and mounted again. Jan.

1916 2nd Mtd. Div. broken up. Brigade to Suez Canal Defences and became 8th Mtd. Bde. Nov. 1916 to Salonika. June 1917 returned to Egypt and brigade joined Yeomanry Mtd. Div. on 21 July. 7.4.18 left 8th Mtd. Bde. and with 1/3rd County of London Yeomanry formed 'E' Bn. M.G.C. 1.6.18 landed at Marseilles and to Etaples. 19.8.18 became 103rd Bn. M.G.C. and was with First Army until the end of the war.

2/1st City of London Yeomanry.
Formed Aug. 1914 in London. Mar. 1915 to East Dereham in 2/1st London Mtd. Bde. 2/2nd Mtd. Div. 20.3.16 division became 3rd Mtd. Div. and soon after brigade became 12th Mtd. Bde. July 1916 became a cyclist unit and brigade became 4th Cyclist Bde. moving to 1st Cyclist Div. at North Walsham. Nov. 1916 1st Cyclist Div. broken up with 2/1st West Somerset Yeomanry formed 5th (West Somerset and City of London) Yeomanry Cyclist Regt. in 2nd Cyclist Bde.—independent—at Coltishall. Feb. 1917 replaced by 2/1st Hampshire Yeomanry and went to 5th Cyclist Bde. 1st Mtd. Div. at Littlebourne, near Canterbury. By July 1917 at Bridge, near Canterbury. 4.9.17 1st Mtd. became The Cyclist Div. In Jan. 1918 at Wingham, near Canterbury where it remained in 5th Cyclist Bde. until the end of the war.

3/1st City of London Yeomanry.
Formed 1915 and in the summer affiliated to a reserve cav. regt. in Eastern Command. Summer 1916 affiliated to 6th Reserve Cav. Regt. at Dublin. Early in 1917 absorbed by 1st Reserve Cav. Regt. at the Curragh.

1ST COUNTY OF LONDON YEOMANRY
(Middlesex Duke of Cambridge's Hussars)
'Gallipoli, 1915'
'Egypt, 1915–16'
'Macedonia, 1916–17'
'Palestine, 1917–18'

1/1st County of London Yeomanry.
4.8.14 Duke of York's H.Q., Chelsea: London Mtd. Bde. To Hounslow. Sept. 1914 with brigade to 2nd Mtd. Div. at Streatley. Nov. 1914 brigade to North Walsham area. April 1915 to Egypt. Aug. 1915 to Gallipoli, dismounted. Dec. 1915 returned to Egypt and mounted again. Jan. 1916 2nd Mtd. Div. broken up. Brigade to Suez Canal Defences and became 8th Mtd. Bde. Nov. 1916 to Salonika. June 1917 returned to Egypt and brigade joined Yeomanry Mtd. Div. on 21 July. 24.4.18 division became 1st Mtd. Div. 22.7.18 division became 4th Cav. Div. and brigade became 11th Cav. Bde. No further change until the end of the war.

2/1st County of London Yeomanry.
Formed in 1914 at Chelsea. Nov. 1914 Ranelagh Park. June 1915 Bylaugh Park (NE of East Dereham) in 2/1st London Mtd. Bde. 2/2nd Mtd. Div. Oct. 1915 Blickling Hall Summer 1916 became cyclist unit in 4th Cyclist Bde. 1st Cyclist Div. in North Walsham area (possibly in Kent during part of summer as cyclists). Nov. 1916 with 2/3 County of London Yeo. formed 6th (1st and 3rd County of London) Yeomanry Cyclist Regt. in 2nd Cyclist Bde. probably at Reepham. Mar. 1917 resumed identity and moved to Overstrand, still in 2nd Cyclist Bde. In autumn to Melton Constable. Here until May 1918 and then to Ireland with 2nd Cyclist Bde. Stationed at the Curragh until the end of the war.

3/1st County of London Yeomanry.
Formed April 1915 at Ranelagh. In summer affiliated to a reserve cav. regt. in Eastern Command. Summer 1916 affiliated to 6th Reserve Cav. Regt. at the Curragh. Early in 1917 absorbed by 2nd Reserve Cav. Regt. at the Curragh.

2ND COUNTY OF LONDON YEOMANRY
(Westminster Dragoons)
'Gallipoli, 1915'
'Egypt, 1915–17'
'Palestine, 1917–18'
'France and Flanders, 1918'

1/2nd County of London Yeomanry.
4.8.14 Elverton Street, Westminster: attached London Mtd. Bde. for training. Sept. 1914 to Egypt. 19.1.15 formed Yeomanry Mtd. Bde. with 1/1st Herts. Yeomanry Aug. 1915 to Gallipoli, dismounted, attached to 2nd Mtd. Div. and brigade became 5th Mtd. Dec. 1915 returned to Egypt, mounted again, and left 2nd Mtd. Div. In April 1916 was attached 6th Mtd. Bde. in Western Frontier Force. For the first eight months of 1917 the regiment was split up.

RHQ and 'C' Squadron on Northern Canal Defences.
'A' Squadron with 53rd Div. 14 Jan. to 14 Feb. and with 74th Div. 5 April to 23 Aug.
'B' Squadron was depot squadron at Zeitoun from 17 Jan. to Aug.

In Aug. 1917 the regiment concentrated and became XX Corps Cav. Regt. 'C' Squadron was at Zeitoun from July to Sept. In April 1918 left XX Corps and formed 'F' Bn. M.G.C. 1.6.18 landed in France. 19.8.18 became 104th Bn. M.G.C. and at the end of the war was with Second Army in Belgium.

2/2nd County of London Yeomanry.
Formed Aug. 1914 at Westminster. Early in 1915 to Feltham. Summer to Harlow. There are three versions of the history of this unit. The OFFICIAL HISTORY ORDER OF BATTLE VOLUME 2B says that the regiment joined 60th Div. at Harlow on 24.6.15 and went to 61st Div. in Chelmsford area on 24.1.16. To 59th Div. in Chelmsford area on 20.2.16 until April and there is no further mention. The official COMMANDERS HOME FORCES has a regimental index in some issues showing locations of units. In June 1916 this regiment is shown with 58th Div. The next six entries up to April 1918 list it as 'Overseas' and in Aug. 1918 as 'Tank Corps'. The regimental history 2ND COUNTY OF LONDON (WESTMINSTER DRAGOONS) YEOMANRY. THE FIRST TWENTY YEARS says that the regiment went to France, dismounted, at the end of 1915 for guard duties. That it returned to England in the summer of 1916 and went to Wool. Most rank and file were posted to the infantry while the officers and senior N.C.O.s were transferred to the Tank Corps. There are no campaign battle honours to support the overseas service. Perhaps a dismounted party went to France but the unit appears to have been absorbed in the Tank Corps.

3/2nd County of London Yeomanry.
Formed 1915 and in summer affiliated to a reserve cav. regt. in Eastern Command. 1916 with 9th Reserve Cav. Regt. at the Curragh. Early 1917 absorbed in 4th Reserve Cav. Regt. at Aldershot.

3RD COUNTY OF LONDON YEOMANRY
(Sharpshooters)
'Gallipoli, 1915'
'Egypt, 1915–16'
'Macedonia, 1916–17'
'Palestine, 1917–18'
'France and Flanders, 1918'

1/3rd County of London Yeomanry.
4.8.14 St. John's Wood London; London Mtd. Bde.

Subsequent record same as 1/1st City of London Yeomanry.

2/3rd County of London Yeomanry.
Formed 1914 in London. Mar. 1915 to Norfolk in 2/1st London Mtd. Bde. 2/2nd Mtd. Div. 20.3.16 division became 3rd Mtd. Div. and soon after brigade became 12th Mtd. Bde. July 1916 became a cyclist unit and brigade became 4th Cyclist Bde. moving to 1st Cyclist Div. in North Walsham area. Nov. 1916 1st Cyclist Div. broken up. With 2/1st County of London Yeomanry formed 6th (1st and 3rd County of London) Yeomanry Cyclist Regt. in 2nd Cyclist Bde., probably at Reepham. Mar. 1917 resumed identity and was at Worstead, near North Walsham. By July 1917 at Overstrand, still in 2nd Cyclist Bde. In 1918 at Coltishall. Here until May 1918 and then to Ireland with 2nd Cyclist Bde. Stationed at the Curragh and Athlone until the end of the war.

3/3rd County of London Yeomanry.
Formed 1915 and in the summer affiliated to a reserve cav. regt. in Eastern Comand. Summer 1916 affiiliated to 9th Reserve Cav. Regt. at the Curragh. Early in 1917 absorbed by 2nd Reserve Cav. Regt. at the Curragh.

LOTHIANS AND BORDER HORSE YEOMANRY
'France and Flanders, 1915'
'Macedonia, 1915–18'

1/1st Lothians and Border Horse.
4.8.14 Wemyss Place, Edinburgh: Lowland Mtd. Bde. To Cupar with brigade. Left brigade and in 1915 split up as divisional cavalry.
  RHQ and 'B' Squadron to 25th Div. at Aldershot in summer of 1915. 27.9.15 landed at Havre. 11.5.16 to V Corps Cav. Regt. (with two sqdns Glasgow Yeomanry). July 1917 dismounted and to base depot for infantry training. Sept. 1917 absorbed by 17th Royal Scots, 106th Bde. 35th Div.
  'A' Squadron to 26th Div. at Sutton Veny on 30.7.15 Sept. 1915 to France. Nov. 1915 to Salonika. 29.11.16 left 26th Div. and attached 8th Mtd. Bde. until 11.1.17. 11.5.17 to XII Corps Cav. Regt.
  'D' Squadron to 22nd Div. at Aldershot. Sept. 1915 to France. Nov. 1915 to Salonika. 29.11.16 left 22nd Div. and attached 8th Mtd. Bde. until 14.1.17. 11.5.17 to XII Corps Cav. Regt.
  The XII Corps Cavalry Regt. was formed at Salonika (a two squadron regiment) by 'A' and 'D' Squadrons and remained until the end of the war.

2/1st Lothians and Border Horse.
Formed 1914. 1915 with 2/1st Lowland Mtd. Bde. in Scotland. Mar. 1916 brigade at Dunbar and became 20th Mtd. Bde. July 1916 became a cyclist unit in 13th Cyclist Bde. Nov. 1916 brigade became 9th Cyclist Bde. By July 1917 at Haddington and remained here until about May 1918 and then to Ireland with 9th Cyclist Bde. Stationed at Londonderry and Enniskillen until the end of the war.

3/1st Lothians and Border Horse.
Formed 1915 and in the summer affiliated to a reserve cav. regt. at Aldershot. June 1916 affiliated to 2nd Reserve Cav. Regt. at Aldershot. Early in 1917 absorbed by 4th Reserve Cav. Regt. at Aldershot.

1st LOVAT'S SCOUTS YEOMANRY
'Gallipoli, 1915'
'Egypt, 1915–16'
'Macedonia, 1916–18'
'France and Flanders, 1916–18'

1/1st Lovat's Scouts.
  4.8.14 Beauly: Highland Mtd. Bde. 12.8.14 with Bde. to Blairgowrie, then to Huntingdon area. Nov. 1914 Bde. to Lincolnshire with regiment at Alford. April 1915 to north Norfolk. Aug. 1915 dismounted. 8.9.15 sailed from Devonport and arrived Alexandria on 18 Sept. 26.9.15 landed at Gallipoli and Bde. attached to 2nd Mtd. Div. Dec. 1915 returned to Egypt. Feb. 1916 Highland Mtd. Bde. in 2nd Dismounted Bde., Western Frontier Force. 27.9.16 with 1/2nd Lovat's Scouts and a company from 1/3rd Scottish Horse formed 10th (Lovat's Scouts) Bn. Cameron Highlanders at Cairo. 20.10.16 landed at Salonika and joined 82nd Bde. 27th Div. on 1 Nov. June 1918 left 27th Div. and went to France where it joined L. of C. Troops on 6.7.18.
  The Lovat's Scouts also formed 13 detachments for observation work which served in France from 1916 to 1918. These detachments were corps troops and provided observation posts to watch the enemy front. They may also have acted as snipers. The detachments became groups in Aug. 1917. No. 4 Group went to Italy about the end of 1917 and remained there as G.H.Q. Troops.

2/1st Lovat's Scouts.
Formed in 1914. Jan. 1915 in 2/1st Highland Mtd. Bde. April 1916 with Bde., now 1st Mtd. Bde. to 1st Mtd. Div. in Norfolk. Became cyclists in 1st Cyclist Bde. 1st Cyclist Div. at Somerleyton, near Lowestoft. Nov. 1916 1st Cyclist Div. broken up. 2/1st and 2/2nd Lovat's Scouts formed 1st (Lovat's Scouts) Yeomanry Cyclist Regt. in 1st Cyclist Bde. Mar. 1917 resumed identity still in 1st Cyclist Bde. at Gorleston. By July 1917 at Beccles and remained here until the end of the war in 1st Cyclist Bde.

3/1st Lovat's Scouts.
Formed July 1915 at Beauly and affiliated to a reserve cavalry regt. at Aldershot. June 1916 to Perth. Jan. 1917 disbanded; personnel to 2nd Line unit and 3rd (Reserve) Bn. Cameron Highlanders at Invergordon.

2ND LOVAT'S SCOUTS YEOMANRY
The record of the three units of this regiment is similar to that of the 1st Lovat's Scouts.

MONTGOMERYSHIRE YEOMANRY
'Egypt, 1916–17'
'Palestine, 1917–18'
'France and Flanders, 1918'

1/1st Montgomeryshire Yeomanry.
4.8.14 Welshpool: South Wales Mtd. Bde. 12.8.14 with brigade at Hereford. 29.8.14 Thetford then to Blickling and brigade joined 1st Mtd. Div. Sept. 1915 at Holt. Oct. 1915 to Cromer. Nov. 1915 dismounted. 4.3.16 sailed from Devonport for Egypt. 20.3.16 brigade joined with Welsh Border Mtd. Bde. to form 4th Dismounted Bde. in Western Frontier Force. 4.3.17 with 1/1st Welsh Horse at Helmia formed 25th (Montgomery & Welsh Horse Yeomanry) Bn. Royal Welsh Fusiliers in 231st Bde. 74th Div. May 1918 to France with 74th Div., no further change.

2/1st Montgomeryshire Yeomanry.
Formed at Welshpool in Sept. 1914. July 1915 to Dorchester in 2/1st South Wales Mtd. Bde. Sept. 1915 to Southwold, brigade in 1st Mtd. Div. By April 1916 at Rendlesham and brigade became 4th Mtd. Bde. Absorbed 2/1st Welsh Horse. July 1916 to Thorndon Park, Brentwood joining 2nd Mtd. Bde. of new 1st Mtd. Div. (formerly 3rd Mtd. Div.) Oct. 1916 became cyclist unit with 2/1st Denbighshire Yeomanry forming 3rd (Denbigh

& Montgomery) Yeomanry Cyclist Regt. at Worlingham (Beccles) in 1st Cyclist Bde. Mar. 1917 resumed identity at Worlingham in 1st Cyclist Bde. By Nov. 1917 at Gorleston and remained in this area until the end of the war.

3/1st Montgomeryshire Yeomanry.
June 1915 formed at Welshpool. July 1915 Brecon and then affiliated to 6th Reserve Cav. Regt. at the Curragh. June 1916 attached to 3rd Line Groups of Welsh Div. at Gobowen and then Oswestry. Jan. 1917 disbanded, personnel to 2nd Line unit and 4th (Reserve) Bn. Royal Welsh Fusiliers at Oswestry.

NORFOLK YEOMANRY
(The King's Own Royal Regiment)
'Gallipoli, 1915'
'Egypt, 1915–17'
'Palestine, 1917–18'
'France and Flanders, 1918'

1/1st Norfolk Yeomanry.
4.8.14 Cattle Market Street, Norwich: Eastern Mtd. Bde. Aug. 1914 with brigade to Woodbridge area in 1st Mtd. Div. July 1915 brigade moved nearer coast. Sept. 1915 dismounted and sailed in the 'Olympic' from Liverpool on 25 Sept. Landed at Anzac 10.10.15 and brigade was attached to 54th Div. Dec. 1915 to Egypt. 22.2.16 Eastern and South Eastern Mtd. Bdes. formed 3rd Dismtd. Bde. Suez Canal Defences till July 1916 then to Western Frontier Force. 7.2.17 became 12th (Norfolk Yeomanry) Bn. Norfolk Regt. in 230th Bde. 74th Div. May 1918 with 74th Div. to France landing at Marseilles on 7 May. 21.6.18 to 94th Bde. 31st Div. at Blaringhem. No further change.

2/1st Norfolk Yeomanry.
Formed 1914. Jan. 1915 in 2/1st Eastern Mtd. Bde. in Huntingdon area. Mar. 1916 brigade joined 4th Mtd. Div. in Wivenhoe area and became 13th Mtd. Bde. July 1916 became cyclist unit in 5th Cyclist Bde. 2nd Cyclist Div. in same area. Nov. 1916 2nd Cyclist Div. broken up and with 2/1st Suffolk Yeomanry formed 7th (Suffolk and Norfolk) Yeomanry Cyclist Regt. in 3rd Cyclist Bde. Mar. 1917 resumed identity still in 3rd Cyclist Bde. in Ipswich area. By July 1917 in Woodbridge until May 1918 then to Ireland with 3rd Cyclist Bde. then at Castlereagh and Gort until the end of the war.

3/1st Norfolk Yeomanry.
Formed in 1915 and in summer affiliated to a reserve cav. regt. in Eastern Command. Summer 1916 attached to 3rd Line Groups of East Anglian Div. Early 1917 disbanded, personnel to 2nd Line unit and 4th (Reserve) Bn. Norfolk Regt. at Halton Park.

NORTHAMPTONSHIRE YEOMANRY
'France and Flanders, 1914–17'
'Italy, 1917–18'

1/1st Northamptonshire Yeomanry.
4.8.14 Clare Street, Northampton. attached Eastern Mtd. Bde. for training. Oct. 1914 to 8th Div. near Winchester. 4.11.14 landed in France. April left 8th Div. and split up as divisional cavalry.
RHQ and 'B' Squadron to 6th Div. 14.4.15. To VI Corps Cav. Regt. 9.5.16.
'A' Squadron to 4th Div. 13.4.15. To VI Corps Cav. Regt. 11.5.16.
'C' Squadron to 5th Div. 12.4.15. To VI Corps Cav. Regt. 11.5.16.

The regiment concentrated in May 1916 as VI Corps Cav. Regt. Left VI Corps in summer of 1917 and seems to have become Fourth Army Troops and possibly attached to XV Corps for a time. 10.11.17 to Italy and became XIV Corps Cav. Regt. 18.4.18 XIV Corps became G.H.Q. British Force in Italy and unit became G.H.Q. Troops. 9.10.18 XIV Corps reformed and again became Corps Cav. Regt. till end of the war.

2/1st Northamptonshire Yeomanry.
Formed 1914. Nov. 1915 to April 1916 with 59th Div. in St. Albans area. RHQ and 'A' Squadron to 69th Div. in Yorkshire from 17.4.16 to 15.6.17. One squadron to 67th Div. in Kent from Oct. 1916 to June 1917. One squadron to France in winter 1916–17.
The three squadrons were as above in Mar. 1917 but during the year the squadron in France was absorbed in the Tank Corps (possibly Aug. 1917). One of the other two was absorbed in the 6th Reserve Cav. Regt. at Tidworth and the other one was disbanded.

3/1st Northamptonshire Yeomanry.
Formed in 1915 and in the summer affiliated to the 3rd Reserve Cav. Regt. at Canterbury. Early in 1917 absorbed in 6th Reserve Cav. Regt. at Tidworth.

NORTHUMBERLAND YEOMANRY
(Hussars)
'France and Flanders, 1914–18'

1/1st Northumberland Yeomanry.
4.8.14 Northumberland Road, Newcastle-on-Tyne: attached to Yorkshire Mtd. Bde. for training. Sept. 1914 to 7th Div. at Lyndhurst. 6.10.14 landed at Zeebrugge. April 1915 regiment split up as divisional cavalry.
RHQ and 'A' Squadron remained with 7th Div. 13.5.16 to XIII Corps Cav. Regt.
'B' Squadron to 1st Div. 13.4.15 and on 18.4.16 to XIII Corps Cav. Regt.
'C' Squadron to 8th Div. on 12.4.15 and on 13.5.16 to XIII Corps Cav. Regt.

In May 1916 the regiment concentrated and became XIII Corps Cav. Regt. About Aug. 1917 left XIII Corps and to VIII (or XIV) Corps. Nov. 1917 to III Corps. 8.10.18 to XII Corps as Corps Cav. Regt. until the end of the war.

2/1st Northumberland Yeomanry.
Formed at Newcastle Oct. 1914 and at Gosforth Park until May 1915 and then to Scarborough. April 1916 regiment split up.
RHQ and 'B' Squadron to 62nd Div. on Salisbury Plain and then East Anglia. Jan. 1917 left 62nd Div.
'A' Squadron remained at Scarborough.
'C' Squadron joined 59th Div. 28.3.16 and went to Ireland. Remained with 59th Div. until Jan. 1917.
Feb. 1917 regiment concentrated in Hertfordshire. 19.3.17 landed at Havre. 26.3.17 joined XIX Corps as Corps Cav. Regt. 28.8.17 to base depot at Etaples for infantry training. 25.9.17 absorbed by 9th Northumberland Fusiliers which became 9th (Northd. Hussars Yeomanry) Bn. Northd. Fus. in 103rd Bde. 34th Div. 26.5.18 to 183rd Bde. 61st Div. No further change.

3/1st Northumberland Yeomanry.
Formed Feb. 1915 at Gosforth Park and then to Stocksfield-on-Tyne. Summer affiliated to 5th Reserve Cav. Regt. at York. Jan. 1917 absorbed in 5th Reserve Cav. Regt. at Tidworth.

NOTTINGHAMSHIRE YEOMANRY
(Sherwood Rangers)
'Gallipoli, 1915'
'Egypt, 1915–16'
'Macedonia, 1916–17'
'Palestine, 1917–18'

1/1st Nottinghamshire Yeomanry (S.R.)
4.8.14 Retford: Notts. and Derby Mtd. Bde. Aug. with brigade to Diss area in 1st Mtd. Div. End Aug. with brigade to South Stoke area. In Nov. division moved to Norfolk coast with brigade in Holt area. April sailed from Avonmouth for Egypt. 18.8.15 landed at Suvla, dismounted. Dec. 1915 returned to Egypt. Jan. 1916 2nd Mtd. Div. broken up. Feb. 1916 to Salonika with brigade which became 7th Mtd. Bde. June 1917 7th Mtd. Bde. returned to Egypt. Ship carrying regiment torpedoed and landed at Mudros. 4.7.17 back in Egypt. Brigade attached to Desert Mtd. Corps. May 1918 brigade to new 2nd Mtd. Div. July 1918 became 14th Cav. Bde. 5th Cav. Div. No further change.

2/1st Nottinghamshire Yeomanry (S.R.)
Formed 1914 at Retford. Mar. 1915 2/1st Notts. and Derby Mtd. Bde. By June 1915 brigade in Kings Lynn area in 2/2nd Mtd. Div. Mar. 1916 division became 3rd Mtd. and brigade 9th Mtd. Bde. July 1916 division now became 1st Mtd. Div. and unit in 1st Mtd. Bde. at Thorndon Park, near Brentwood. Aug. 1917 became cyclist unit in 11th Cyclist Bde. The Cyclist Div. Remained in this formation until the end of the war in Canterbury area.

3/1st Nottinghamshire Yeomanry (S.R.).
Formed 1915 and in summer affiliated to a reserve cav. regt. at Aldershot. Summer 1916 affiliated to 1st Reserve Cav. Regt. at Aldershot. Early 1917 absorbed by 3rd Reserve Cav. Regt. at Aldershot.

NOTTINGHAMSHIRE YEOMANRY
(South Nottinghamshire Hussars)
'Gallipoli, 1915'
'Egypt, 1915–16'
'Macedonia, 1916–17'
'Palestine, 1917–18'
'France and Flanders, 1918'

1/1st Nottinghamshire Yeomanry (S.N.H.)
4.8.14 Derby Road, Nottingham: Notts. and Derby Mtd. Bde. 10.8.14 to Diss with brigade in 1st Mtd. Div. End Aug. with brigade to South Stoke area joining 2nd Mtd. Div. 18.11.14 with brigade to Norfolk, unit at Fakenham. 12 Dec. to Blakeney. 9.4.15 sailed from Avonmouth. 24.4.15 arrived Alexandria. 18.8.15 landed at Suvla, dismounted. Dec. 1915 returned to Egypt. Jan. 1916 2nd Mtd. Div. broken up. Feb. 1916 to Salonika with brigade which became 7th Mtd. Bde. June 1917 returned to Egypt with brigade. Brigade now attached to Desert Mounted Corps. April 1918 left 7th Mtd. Bde., dismounted, and with Warwickshire Yeomanry formed 'B' Bn. Machine Gun Corps. 26.5.18 sailed from Alexandria in 'Leasowe Castle' which was torpedoed on 27 May and sunk: survivors returned to Egypt. 18.6.18 sailed again from Alexandria and arrived Taranto on 21 June. By train to Etaples and on 19 August became 100th Bn. M.G.C.; it joined Fourth Army and remained there until the end of the war.

2/1st Nottinghamshire Yeomanry (S.N.H.)
20.9.14 formation began at Nottingham and was at Colwick Racecourse for the winter. 28.2.15 to Ollerton, now in 2/1st Notts. and Derby Mtd. Bde. June 1915 to Narford Park, near Swaffham: brigade now in 2/2nd Mtd. Div. In March division became 3rd Mtd. Div. and brigade 9th Mtd. Bde. July 1916 division became 1st Mtd. Div. and 9th Mtd. Bde. became 9th Cyclist Bde. and the regiments were converted to cyclists, now near Canterbury. By Nov. 1916 brigade was 5th Cyclist Bde. and remained near Canterbury during 1917. From Sept. to Dec. 1917 the 5th Cyclist Bde. was independent. During 1918 the unit remained at Littlebourne, near Canterbury, in 5th Cyclist Bde. of The Cyclist Div.

3/1st Nottinghamshire Yeomanry (S.N.H.)
Formed May 1915 at Ollerton. Sept. 1915 to Derby and affiliated to 14th Reserve Cav. Regt. at Aldershot. Oct. 1916 with 14th Reserve Cav. Regt. to Ireland. Feb. 1917 absorbed in 2nd Reserve Cav. Regt. at the Curragh.

OXFORDSHIRE YEOMANRY
(Queen's Own Oxfordshire Hussars)
'France and Flanders, 1914–19'

1/1st Oxfordshire Yeomanry.
4.8.14 Oxford: 2nd South Midland Mtd. Bde. 11.8.14 with brigade at Reading. 15.8.14 with 1st Mtd. Div. to Norfolk. 29.8.14 to Churn where brigade joined 2nd Mtd. Div. 19.9.14 and landed at Dunkirk on 22 Sept. to G.H.Q. Troops. 31.10.14 to 2nd Cav. Bde. 1st Cav. Div. 11.11.14 to 4th Cav. Bde. 2nd Cav. Div. No further change.

2/1st Oxfordshire Yeomanry.
Sept. 1914 formed at Oxford. Jan. 1915 in 2/2nd South Midland Mtd. Bde. April 1915 to Kings Lynn area and brigade joined 2/2nd Mtd. Div. July 1916 cyclist unit in 9th Cyclist Bde. in 1st Mtd. Div. (late 2/2nd Mtd.) 9th Cyclist Bde. became 5th Cyclist Bde. Now at Bridge near Canterbury. Feb. 1917 to 4th Cyclist Bde. at Ipswich. July 1917 at Wivenhoe. Nov. 1917 Frinton and then to Manningtree. About Jan. 1918 to Ireland with 4th Cyclist Bde. and stationed at Dublin until the end of the war.

3/1st Oxfordshire Yeomanry.
Formed in 1915 at Oxford. Summer affiliated to a reserve cav. regt. at Tidworth. Summer 1916 affiliated to 8th Reserve Cav. Regt. at the Curragh. Early in 1917 2nd Reserve Cav. Regt. at the Curragh.

PEMBROKE YEOMANRY
(Castlemartin)
'Egypt, 1916–17'
'Palestine, 1917–18'
'France and Flanders, 1918'

1/1st Pembroke Yeomanry.
4.8.14 Tenby: South Wales Mtd. Bde. 12.8.14 brigade concentrated at Hereford. End of Aug. to Thetford area joining 1st Mtd. Div. Then to Aylsham area with regiment at Haveringham and Heydon. Oct. 1915 probably to Cromer area. Nov. 1915 dismounted. Mar. 1916 sailed for Egypt. 20.3.16 South Wales Mtd. Bde. absorbed in 4th Dismounted Bde. 2.2.17 with 1/1st Glamorgan Yeomanry formed 24th (Pembroke and Glamorgan Yeo.) Bn. Welsh Regt. in 231st Bde. 74th Div. May 1918 to France and remained here until the end of the war in 74th Div.

2/1st Pembroke Yeomanry.
Formed 1914. Early 1915 at Carmarthen in 2/1st South Wales Mtd. Bde. then at Llandilo and Dorchester. Sept. 1915 brigade to Yoxford area joining 1st Mtd. Div. and

in 1916 brigade became 4th Mtd. Bde. July 1916 became a cyclist unit in 2nd Cyclist Bde. 1st Cyclist Div. Nov. 1916 division broken up and with 2/1st Glamorgan Yeomanry formed 2nd (Pembroke and Glamorgan) Yeomanry Cyclist Regt. in 1st Cyclist Bde. Mar. 1917 resumed identity now at Aldeburgh. July 1917 Benacre. By the end of the year at Lowestoft where it remained in 1st Cyclist Bde.

3/1st Pembroke Yeomanry.
Formed in 1915 at Carmarthen then to Brecon. Summer 1915 affiliated to a reserve cav. regt. in Ireland. Summer 1916 dismounted and attached to 3rd Line Groups of Welsh Div. at Oswestry. Early in 1917 disbanded, personnel to 2nd Line unit and 4th (Reserve) Bn. Welsh Regt. at Milford Haven.

SCOTTISH HORSE
'Gallipoli, 1915'
'Egypt, 1915–16'
'Macedonia, 1916–18'
'France and Flanders, 1918'

1/1st Scottish Horse.
4.8.14 Dunkeld. 12.8.14 Scone, Perth. 15 Aug. 1st and 2nd Regiments appear to have been attached for a short time to the Highland and West Riding Divs. T.F. at Bedford and Doncaster. By Nov. 1914 in Northumberland now in 1/1st Scottish Horse Mtd. Bde. From about Jan. 1915 brigade was attached to the 2/Northumnberlad Div. T.F. and employed on coast defence. 17.8.15 embarked, dismounted, in 'Transylvania' at Devonport. After leaving Malta re-equipped as infantry at sea. 2.9.15 landed at Suvla and brigade attached to 2nd Mounted Div. 28.12.15 landed in Egypt. Feb. 1916 1/1st Scottish Horse Mtd. Bde. absorbed in 1st Dismounted Bde. which was attached to 52nd Div. in Suez Canal Defences. 1.10.16 formed 13th (Scottish Horse Yeomanry) Bn. Black Watch at Abassia with 1/2nd Scottish Horse. To Salonika arriving on 21 Oct. 1.11.16 to 81st Bde. 27th Div. June 1918 to France via Taranto arriving Forges les Eaux on 24 June. 15.7.18 joined 149th Bde. 50th Div. at Martin Eglise: no further change.

1/2nd Scottish Horse.
4.8.14 Aberdeen. Subsequent record same as 1/1st Scottish Horse.

1/3rd Scottish Horse.
Formed Aug. 1914 and later joined 1/1st Scottish Horse Mtd. Bde. in Northumberland. Record same as 1/1st Scottish Horse until Oct. 1916 when the regiment formed 26th (Scottish Horse) Sqdn., Machine Gun Corps which remained with the E.E.F. and also sent a company to the Lovat Scouts who were forming the 10th Cameron Highlanders.

2/1st, 2/2nd and 2/3rd Scottish Horse.
Formed Aug. and Sept. 1914 at Dunkeld and Aberdeen and went to the Kettering area in 2/1st Scottish Horse Mtd. Bde. At the end of 1915 the brigade moved to Lincolnshire in the Alford area. In 1916 the brigade became the 19th Mtd. Bde. and in July the 12th Cyclist Bde.[1] when the regiments were converted to cyclist units. Remained in Lincolnshire until the end of 1917 and then went to Fife with the regiments at Ladybank (2/1st), St. Andrews (2/2nd) and Cupar (2/3rd). In April 1918 to Ireland with H.Q. and 2/1st at Limerick, 2/2nd at Lahinch and 2/3rd at Tulla. No further change.

3/1st, 3/2nd and 3/3rd Scottish Horse.
Formed at Dunkeld in 1915 and in summer affiliated to

[1] About Nov. 1916 became 8th Cyclist Bde.

a reserve cav. regt. at Aldershot. June 1916 returned to Dunkeld. Early in 1917 disbanded; personnel to 2nd Line units and 4th (Reserve) Bn. Black Watch at Ripon.

SHROPSHIRE YEOMANRY
'Egypt, 1916–17'
'Palestine, 1917–18'
'France and Flanders, 1918'

1/1st Shropshire Yeomanry.
4.8.14 Shrewsbury: Welsh Border Mtd. Bde. 20.8.14 Oswestry. 4.9.14 brigade joined 1st Mtd. Div. in East Anglia with regiment in Flixton area, near Bungay. 25.10.14 to Lowestoft till end of year then back to Flixton. Aug. 1915 to Benacre (south of Kessingland). 21.10.15 to Gorleston. Nov. 1915 dismounted. 4.3.16 embarked for Egypt in 'Arcadian' at Devonport. 14.3.16 arrived Alexandria. 20.3.16 Welsh Border Mtd. Bde. absorbed in 4th Dismtd. Bde. which served with Western Frontier Force. 2.3.17 with Cheshire Yeomanry formed 10th (Shropshire and Cheshire Yeomanry) Bn. K.S.L.I. at Cairo in 231st Bde. 74th Div. May 1918 to France with 74th Div. arriving at Marseilles on 7 May. No further change.

2/1st Shropshire Yeomanry.
Formed 1914. Early in 1915 in 2/1st Welsh Border Mtd. Bde. in Northumberland attached to 2/Northumberland Div. April 1916 for a short time in 1st Mtd. Div. in East Anglia and now 17th Mtd. Bde. Then to Morpeth area. July 1916 became a cyclist unit in 10th Cyclist Bde. Nov. 1916 brigade became 6th Cyclist Bde. Mar. 1917 at Newbiggin then to Woodhorn, near to Morpeth until end of year. Early in 1918 to Ireland with 6th Cyclist Bde. and stationed at the Curragh until the end of the war.

3/1st Shropshire Yeomanry.
Formed 1915 and in summer affiliated to a reserve cav. regt. in Ireland. Summer 1916 dismounted and attached to 3rd Line Groups of West Lancs. Div. at Oswestry. Early in 1917 disbanded: personnel to 2nd Line unit and 4th (Reserve) Bn. K.S.L.I. at (probably)Tenby.

NORTH SOMERSET YEOMANRY
'France and Flanders, 1914–18'

1/1st North Somerset Yeomanry.
4.8.14 Bath: 1st South Western Mtd. Bde. Oct. with brigade in Sussex but soon left brigade and landed in France on 3 Nov. 13.11.14 to 6th Cav. Bde. 3rd Cav. Div. 10.3.18 left 3rd Cav. Div. and it was proposed to convert the regiment to a cyclist unit. 12.3.18 another decision to form a machine gun battalion with Leicestershire Yeomanry. However, after the German offensive the regiment was mounted again and returned to Cavalry Corps. In April 1918 the regiment was broken up and sent a squadron to each regiment of 6th Cav. Bde. (1 Dgns. 3 D.G. and 10 Hussars) in 3rd Cav. Div.

2/1st North Somerset Yeomanry.
Formed 1914. Jan. 1915 2/1st South Western Mtd. Bde. May 1915 Calne area. Sept. 1915 Canterbury area. Mar. 1916 with brigade to Colchester area, brigade became 15th Mtd. Bde. and joined 4th Mtd. Div. July 1916 became a cyclist unit in 6th Cyclist Bde. 2nd Cyclist Div. Nov. 1916 2nd Cyclist Div. broken up: with 2/1st Wiltshire Yeomanry formed 10th (Wiltshire and North Somerset) Yeomanry Cyclist Regiment in 4th Cyclist Bde. in Ipswich area. Mar. 1917 resumed identity, at Ipswich still in 4th

Cyclist Bde. By July 1917 at Wivenhoe and in Nov. at Walton-on-the-Naze. Early in 1918 to Ireland with 4th Cyclist Bde. and stationed at Dublin until the end of the war.

3/1st North Somerset Yeomanry.
Formed in 1915 and in summer affiliated to a reserve cavalry regt. at Tidworth. Summer 1916 affiliated to 11th Reserve Cavalry Regt. at Tidworth. Early in 1917 absorbed in 6th Reserve Cavalry Regiment at Tidworth.

WEST SOMERSET YEOMANRY
'Gallipoli, 1915'
'Egypt, 1915–17'
'Palestine, 1917–18'
'France and Flanders, 1918'

1/1st West Somerset Yeomanry.
4.8.14 County Territorial Hall, Taunton. 2nd South Western Mtd. Bde. 13.8.14 Winchester. 15.8.14 with brigade to Colchester area, at Ardleigh. Oct. 1914 Great Bentley. Nov. Tendring. Sept. 1915 at Thorpe-le-Soken, dismounted and sailed from Liverpool in 'Olympic' 9.10.15 landed at Suvla and brigade attached to 11th Div., later to 2nd Mtd. and 53rd Divs. Dec. 1915 to Egypt. Feb. 1916 brigade absorbed in 2nd Dismounted Bde. in Western Frontier Force. 4.1.17 formed 12th (West Somerset Yeomanry) Bn. Somerset L.I. at Ismailia in 229th Bde. 74th Div. May 1918 to France with 74th Div. landing at Marseilles on 7 May. Remained in France with 74th Div. until the end of the war.

2/1st West Somerset Yeomanry.
Formed 1914 at Taunton. Jan. 1915 2/2nd South Western Mtd. Bde. May 1915 with brigade at Woodbury. Sept. 1915 to Essex. About May 1916 brigade, now 2nd Mtd. joined 1st Mtd. Div. in Norfolk. July 1916 1st Mtd. Div. became 1st Cyclist Div. Unit became cyclists in 1st Cyclist Bde. of this division, in Beccles area. Nov. 1916 1st Cyclist Div. broken up: with 2/1st City of London Yeomanry formed 5th (West Somerset and City of London) Yeomanry Cyclist Regiment in 2nd Cyclist Bde. —independent—in Norfolk. Mar. 1917 resumed identity and now at Elmham (north of East Dereham). Remained in Norfolk till about May 1918 then to Ireland with 2nd Cyclist Bde. Stationed at Athlone until end of war.

3/1st West Somerset Yeomanry.
Formed 1915 and in summer affiliated to a reserve cav. regt. at Tidworth. July 1916 attached to 3rd Line Groups of Wessex Div. at Winchester. Early in 1917 disbanded: personnel to 2nd Line unit and 4th (Reserve) Bn. Somerset L.I. at Bournemouth.

STAFFORDSHIRE YEOMANRY
(Queen's Own Royal Regiment)
'Egypt, 1915–17'
'Palestine, 1917–18'

1/1st Staffordshire Yeomanry.
4.8.14 Bailey Street, Stafford: North Midland Mtd. Bde. Sept. 1914 brigade to 1st Mtd. Div. in Diss area. 27.10.15. brigade embarked at Southampton for Salonika. Destination changed while at sea to Alexandria and regiment arrived in Cairo by the end of Nov. About April 1916 brigade became 22nd Mtd. Bde. and was in the Western Frontier Force. Feb. 1917 brigade to Anzac Mtd. Div. June 1917 brigade to Yeomanry Mtd. Div. April 1918 Yeomanry Mtd. Div. became 1st Mtd. Div. July 1918 formations changed designations to 12th Cav. Bde. 4th Cav. Div. No further change.

2/1st Staffordshire Yeomanry.
Formed 1914. 1915 in 2/1st North Midland Mtd. Bde. Oct. 1915 with brigade to 1st Mtd. Div. in Norfolk. About April 1916 brigade became 3rd Mtd. Bde. July 1916 division became 1st Cyclist Div. and regiment a cyclist unit in 3rd Cyclist Bde. of this division, now in Holt area. Nov. 1916 mounted again with other regiments of the brigade which became 2nd Mtd. Bde. and joined new 1st Mtd. Div. at Stansted. By May 1917 at Leybourne (West Malling) Aug. 1917 became a cyclist unit again in 12th Cyclist Bde. the Cyclist Div. End of 1917 at Tonbridge and then at Canterbury until the end of the war in Cyclist Div.

3/1st Staffordshire Yeomanry.
Formed 1915 and in summer affiliated to a reserve cav. regt. at Aldershot. Summer 1916 affiliated to 12th Reserve Cav. Regt. at Aldershot. Early in 1917 absorbed in 3rd Reserve Cav. Regt. at Aldershot.

SUFFOLK YEOMANRY
(The Duke of York's Own Loyal
Suffolk Hussars)
'Gallipoli, 1915'
'Egypt, 1915–17'
'Palestine, 1917–18'
'France and Flanders, 1918'

1/1st Suffolk Yeomanry.
4.8.14 Bury St. Edmunds: Eastern Mtd. Bde. 12.8.14 to Woodbridge with brigade in 1st Mtd. Div. July 1915 to Leiston. Sept. 1915 dismounted and sailed from Liverpool in 'Olympic' on 25 Sept. 10.10.15 landed at Anzac and brigade attached to 54th Div. Dec. 1915 to Egypt. 22.2.16 Eastern and South Eastern Mtd. Bdes. formed 3rd Dismounted Bde. which was on Suez Canal Defences till July 1916 then to Western Frontier Force. 5.1.17 formed 15th (Suffolk Yeomanry) Bn. Suffolk Regiment in 230th Bde. 74th Div. In May 1918 to France with 74th Div. landing at Marseilles on 7 May. No further change.

2/1st Suffolk Yeomanry.
Formed 1914. Jan. 1915 in 2/1st Eastern Mtd. Bde. at Ely. Mar. 1916 to 4th Mtd. Div. in Wivenhoe area: brigade became 13th Mtd. Bde. July 1916 became a cyclist unit in 5th Cyclist Bde, 2nd Cyclist Div. still in Colchester area. Nov. 1916 2nd Cyclist Div. broken up. With 2/1st Norfolk Yeomanry formed 7th (Norfolk and Suffolk) Yeomanry Cyclist Regt. in 3rd Cyclist Bde.— independent—at Ipswich. In Woodbridge area till May 1918 then to Ireland with 3rd Cyclist Bde. Stationed at Boyle and Collooney.

3/1st Suffolk Yeomanry.
Formed in 1915 and in summer affiliated to a reserve cav. regt. in Eastern Command. 1916 dismounted and attached to 3rd Line Groups of East Anglian Div. at Halton Park, Tring. Early in 1917 disbanded: personnel to 2nd Line unit and 4th (Reserve) Bn. Suffolk Regiment at Halton Park.

SURREY YEOMANRY
(Queen Mary's Regiment)
'France and Flanders, 1915'
'Egypt, 1915'
'Macedonia, 1916–18'

1/1st Surrey Yeomanry.
4.8.14 Melbourne House, King's Avenue, Clapham Park S.W. attached to South Eastern Mtd. Bde. for training.

Aug. 1914 to Kent. Later in year regiment split up as divisional cavalry.

'A' Squadron on 21 Nov. to 27th Div. at Winchester. 22.12.14 landed at Havre. 26.1.16 embarked at Marseilles and landed at Salonika on 11 Feb. 27.12.16 to XVI Corps Cav. Regt.

'B' Squadron on 22 Dec. to 28th Div. at Winchester. 18.1.15 landed at Havre. 4.11.15 embarked at Marseilles and landed at Alexandria on 11 Nov. 2.12.15 landed at Salonika. 27.12.16 to XVI Corps Cav. Regt.

'C' Squadron joined 29th Div. in Warwickshire in Jan. 1915. 17.3.15 embarked at Avonmouth. 2.4.15 landed at Alexandria. 26 June landed at Imbros and attached G.H.Q. M.E.F. until Feb. 1916 then to Egypt. 11.3.16 landed at Marseilles with 29th Div. 11 to 19 May in XV Corps Cav. Regt. 19.5.16 to III Corps Cav. Regt. with two squadrons Duke of Lancaster's Yeomanry. July 1917 dismounted and to base for infantry training. Sept. 1917 absorbed in 10th Royal West Surrey Regt. in 124th Bde. 41st Div. No further change.

The XVI Corps Cav. Regt. (a two squadron regt.) was formed at Salonika on 27.12.16 from 'A' and 'B' Squadrons and remained at Salonika until the end of the war.

2/1st Surrey Yeomanry.
Formed Sept. 1914 at Clapham and to Dorking. May 1915 Maresfield. Sept. Wrotham. Winter 1915-16 at Hastings possibly in 1/1st South Western Mtd. Bde. which became 2/1st Southern Mtd. Bde. Mar. 1916 with brigade to new 4th Mtd. Div. in Manningtree area: brigade became 16th Mtd. Bde. July 1916 division became 2nd Cyclist Div. and regiment became cyclist unit in 7th Cyclist Bde. at Woodbridge. Nov. 1916 division broken up and with 2/1st Sussex Yeomanry formed 8th (Surrey and Sussex) Yeomanry Cyclist Regt. in 3rd Cyclist Bde. at Ipswich. Mar. 1917 resumed identity and by July in Woodbridge area. Here till May 1918 and then to Ireland with 3rd Cyclist Bde. Stationed at Athlone and in Galway till end of war.

3/1st Surrey Yeomanry.
Formed Feb. 1915 at Clapham. June 1915 affiliated to 3rd Reserve Cav. Regt. at Canterbury. Early 1917 absorbed in 1st Reserve Cav. Regt. at the Curragh.

SUSSEX YEOMANRY

'Gallipoli, 1915'
'Egypt, 1916–17'
'Palestine, 1917–18'
'France and Flanders, 1918'

1/1st Sussex Yeomanry.
4.8.14 Church Street, Brighton: South Eastern Mtd. Bde. 11.8.14 to Canterbury with brigade and remained there until Sept. 1915. Sept. 1915 dismounted and sailed from Liverpool in 'Olympic' on 25 Sept. 8.10.15 landed at Cape Helles and brigade attached to 42nd Div. Dec. 1915 to Mudros. Feb. 1916 to Egypt. 1/1st South Eastern Mtd. Bde. absorbed in 3rd Dismounted Bde. On Suez Canal Defences until July and then to Western Frontier Force. 3.1.17 formed 16th (Sussex Yeomanry) Bn. Royal Sussex Regt. in 230th Bde. 74th Div. May 1918 to France with 74th Div. landing at Marseilles on 7 May. No further change.

2/1st Sussex Yeomanry.
Formed at Brighton in Sept. 1914 and remained here till May 1915. Then to Maresfield in 2/1st South Eastern Mtd. Bde. taking over horses from 2nd King Edward's Horse. Oct. 1915 to Canterbury with brigade which joined 4th Mtd. Div. in Mar. 1916 Brigade became 14th Mtd. Bde. July 1916 4th Mtd. became 2nd Cyclist Div. and regiment became a cyclist unit in 5th Cyclist Bde. at Great Bentley, Essex. Nov. 1916 2nd Cyclist Div. broken up and formed 8th (Surrey and Sussex) Yeomanry Cyclist Regt. at Ipswich in 3rd Cyclist Bde. Mar. 1917 resumed identity still in Ipswich and then to Woodbridge. May 1917 with brigade to Bromeswell Heath, Melton, near Woodbridge. Oct. 1917 to Grundisburgh area (west of Woodbridge). April 1918 to Ireland with 3rd Cyclist Bde. arriving Dublin on 21 April then to Clandeboye, Co. Down. Sept. 1918 to Boyle, Co. Roscommon where it remained.

3/1st Sussex Yeomanry.
Formed at Brighton in July 1915 and affiliated to 3rd Reserve Cav. Regt. at Canterbury. Summer 1916 to 3rd Line Groups, Home Counties Div. at Crowborough. Jan. 1917 disbanded: personnel to 2nd Line unit and 4th (Reserve) Bn. Royal Sussex Regt. at Tunbridge Wells.

WARWICKSHIRE YEOMANRY

'Gallipoli, 1915'
'Egypt, 1915–17'
'Palestine, 1917–18'
'France and Flanders, 1918'

1/1st Warwickshire Yeomanry.
4.8.14 St. John's, Warwick: 1st South Midland Mtd. Bde. 14.8.14 Bury St. Edmunds with brigade in 1st Mtd. Div. 31.8.14 Newbury and brigade joined 2nd Mtd. Div. Nov. with division to Norfolk; 16 Nov. Sheringham. 17 Dec. Norwich area. 11.4.15 sailed from Avonmouth; transport 'Wayfarer' with 763 horses on board torpedoed 60 miles N.W. of Scillies but towed to Queenstown. 24.4.15 arrived Alexandria. 18.8.15 to Gallipoli, dismounted. Dec. 1915 returned to Egypt. Jan. 1916 2nd Mtd. Div. broken up and brigade became 5th Mtd. Bde. which was independent. Feb. 1917 brigade to Imperial Mtd. Div. June 1917 division became Australian Mtd. Div. April 1918 left 5th Mtd. Bde. dismounted, and with South Notts. Huusars formed 'B' Bn. Machine Gun Corps. 26.5.18 sailed from Alexandria in 'Leasowe Castle' 27.5.18 ship torpedoed and sunk with a loss of 15 officers and 78 other ranks. Survivors returned to Egypt. Sailed again from Alexandria and landed at Taranto on 21 June. By train to Etaples and on 19 Aug. became 100th Bn. M.G.C. joined Fourth Army and remained there until the end of the war.

2/1st Warwickshire Yeomanry.
Sept. 1914 formed at Warwick. April 1915 at Cirencester in 2/1st South Midland Mtd. Bde. June 1915 to Kings Lynn area, brigade now in 2/2nd Mtd. Div. 14.7.15 at Holkham. Oct. 1915 to Fakenham. April 1916 brigade now 10th Mtd. Bde. and division now 3rd Mtd. Div. to Tunbridge Wells. June at Wrotham. July 1916 Division became 1st Mtd. Div. and regiment to 1st Mtd. Bde. at Thorndon Park, Brentwood. Aug. 1916 probably to Ashford, Kent for three weeks. Nov. 1916 at Epping. April 1917 back to Thorndon Park. Sept. 1917 became a cyclist unit and in Oct. attached to 214th Bde. 71st Div. at Colchester. This brigade was now formed into a special formation for Murmansk.[1] In Mar. 1918 all fit men of the brigade were drafted to France and the Murmansk

[1] 12.2.18 with brigade to 67th Div., still at Colchester.

operation cancelled. The unit may have left 67th Div. by September but appears to have remained in East Anglia.

3/1st Warwickshire Yeomanry.
Formed at Warwick, June 1915 and affiliated to 4th Reserve Cav. Regt. at Tidworth. Early in 1917 absorbed in 5th Reserve Cav. Regt. at Tidworth.

WELSH HORSE YEOMANRY

'Gallipoli, 1915'
'Egypt, 1915–17'
'Palestine, 1917–18'
'France and Flanders, 1918'

1/1st Welsh Horse.
Formed in Aug. 1914 in the southern counties of Wales under the administration of the Glamorgan T.F. Association with headquarters at Cardiff. Later in the year transferred to the Montgomeryshire T.F. Association with headquarters at Newtown. By early 1915 in 1/1st North Midland Mtd. Bde. of 1st Mtd. Div. in Diss area. About Feb. 1915 to 1/1st Eastern Mtd. Bde. 1st Mtd. Div. in Woodbridge area. Sept. 1915 dismounted and sailed from Liverpool in 'Olympic' on 25 Sept. 10.10.15 landed at Anzac and brigade attached to 54th Div. Dec. 1915 to Egypt. 22.2.16 Eastern and South Eastern Mtd. Bdes. formed 3rd Dismounted Bde. which was on Suez Canal Defences till July 1916 then to Western Frontier Force 4.3.17 with 1/1st Montgomeryshire Yeomanry formed 25th (Montgomeryshire and Welsh Horse Yeomanry) Bn. Royal Welsh Fusiliers at Helmieh, Cairo in 231st Bde. 74th Div. May 1918 to France with 74th Div. No further change.

2/1st Welsh Horse.
Formed at Newtown in 1914. July 1915 with 2/1st South Wales Mtd. Bde. in Dorchester area as a fourth regiment. Sept. 1915 with brigade to Yoxford area joining 1st Mtd. Div. In 1916 absorbed by 2/1st Montgomeryshire Yeomanry.

3/1st Welsh Horse.
Formed in 1915 and in summer affiliated to a reserve cav. regt. in Ireland. Summer 1916 attached to 3rd Line Groups of Welsh Div. at Oswestry. Early 1917 disbanded: personnel to 2/1st Montgomeryshire Yeomanry and 4th (Reserve) Bn. Royal Welsh Fusiliers at Oswestry.

WESTMORLAND AND CUMBERLAND YEOMANRY
'France and Flanders, 1915–18'

1/1st Westmorland and Cumberland Yeomanry.
4.8.14 Penrith: attached Welsh Border Mtd. Bde. for training. 1915 regiment split up as divisional cavalry.
RHQ and 'D' Squadron to 20th Div. at Larkhill in June 1915. 24.7.15 landed at Havre. 30 April to 14 May attached 2nd Cav. Div. 15.5.16 to XI Corps Cav. Regt.
'B' Squadron to 15th Div. at Marlborough on 23.6.15. July 1915 to France. 2 to 16 April attached 1st Cav. Div. 15.5.16 to XI Corps Cav. Regt.
'C' Squadron to 18th Div. on Salisbury Plain on 15.6.15. July 1915 to France. 30 May to 20 June 1916 attached to 1st Cav. Div. 15.5.16 to XI Corps Cav. Regt.
The regiment concentrated on 15.5.16 as XI Corps Cav. Regt. 21.7.17 left XI Corps, dismounted, and to base depot for infantry training. 22.9.17 21 officers and 239 other ranks absorbed in 7th Bn. Border Regt. which became 7th (Westmorland and Cumberland Yeo.) Bn. Border Regt.: in 51st Bde. 17th Div. No further change.

2/1st Westmorland and Cumberland Yeomanry.
Formed in 1914. By about July 1915 in newly formed Western Mtd. Bde. By April 1916 in area of Cupar, Fife. Brigade became 21st Mtd. Bde. July 1916 became cyclist unit in 14th Cyclist Bde. Oct. 1916 brigade became 10th Cyclist Bde., still at Cupar and there until the end of 1917. Then the brigade moved to Lincolnshire and the regiment was at Spilsby and Burgh-le-Marsh. About May 1918 with brigade to Ireland: stationed at Buttevant and Charleville until the end of the war.

3/1st Westmorland and Cumberland Yeomanry.
Formed in 1915 and affiliated to a reserve cavalry regiment in Ireland. Summer 1916 affiliated to 10th Reserve Cavalry Regiment at the Curragh. Early in 1917 absorbed in 2nd Reserve Cavalry Regiment at the Curragh. By 1918, after the 1st Line unit became infantry, the personnel joined the 5th (Reserve) Bn. Durham Light Infantry at Sutton-on-Hull.

ROYAL WILTSHIRE YEOMANRY
(Prince of Wales's Own Royal Regiment)
'France and Flanders, 1916–18'

1/1st Royal Wiltshire Yeomanry.
4.8.14 The Butts, London Road, Chippenham: 1st South Western Mtd. Bde. Oct. 1914 with Brigade to Sussex and in 1915 split up as divisional cavalry.
RHQ and 'D' Squadron joined 38th Div. at Winchester in 1915. 4.12.15 landed at Havre. 2 to 17 April 1916 attached to 1st Cav. Div. 1 to 20 May III Corps Cav. Regt. 21.5.16 to XV Corps Cav. Regt. (with 'A' and 'B' Squadrons South Irish Horse).
'A' Squadron to 40th Div. at Aldershot. 3.6.16 landed at Havre. 21.6.16 to IX Corps Cav. Regt. 19.11.16 to XV Corps Cav. Regt.
'B' Squadron to 41st Div. at Aldershot about Nov. 1915. 6.5.16 landed at Havre. 1 to 20 June attached to 2nd Cav. Div. 22.6.16 to IX Corps Cav. Regt. 25.11.16 to XV Corps Cav. Regt.
The regiment was reunited in Nov. 1916 when 'A' and 'B' Squadrons joined RHQ and 'D' Squadron in XV Corps Cav. Regt. 3.9.17 left XV Corps, was dismounted and went to No. 3 Infantry Base Depot at Rouen. 26.9.17 14 officers and 232 other ranks were absorbed in the 6th Wiltshire Regt. in 58th Bde. 19th Div. This unit now became 6th (Wiltshire Yeomanry) Bn. Wiltshire Regt. 13.5.18 reduced to training cadre and went to 30th Div. surplus personnel to 2nd Bn. 15.6.18 joined 42nd Bde. 14th Div. at Boulogne and crossed to England. 18.6.18 at Brookwood, Woking, reconstituted with newly formed 9th Dorsets. 4.7.18 landed at Boulogne and remained in 42nd 14th Div. 11.11.18 Belgium; Dottignies, N.E. of Roubaix.

2/1st Royal Wiltshire Yeomanry.
Formed in 1914. May 1915 in Calne area in 2/1st South Western Mtd. Bde. Sept. 1915 Canterbury. Mar 1916 Bde. joined 4th Mtd. Div. in Colchester area and became 15th Mtd. Bde. July 1916 4th Mtd. Div. became 2nd Cyclist Div. and unit became a cyclist bn. in 6th Cyclist Bde. At Tolleshunt d'Arcy, near Tiptree. Nov. 1916 Div. broken up: with 2/1st North Somerset Yeo. formed 10th (Wiltshire and North Somerset) Yeomanry Cyclist Regt. in 4th Cyclist Bde. at Ipswich. Mar. 1917 resumed identity, still in 4th Cyclist Bde. at Ipswich. July 1917 at Wivenhoe then to Frinton and Clacton. Early in 1918 to Ireland

with 4th Cyclist Bde. and at Dublin until the end of the war.

3/1st Royal Wiltshire Yeomanry.
Formed in 1915 and in the summer affiliated to a reserve cavalry regiment at Tidworth. Summer 1916 affiliated to 11th Reserve Cavalry Regiment at Tidworth. Early in 1917 absorbed in 3rd Reserve Cavalry Regiment at Aldershot. In 1918, as the 1st Line unit had become infantry, the personnel left the 3rd Reserve Cav. Regt. and joined the 4th (Reserve) Bn. Wiltshire Regt. at Larkhill.

WORCESTERSHIRE YEOMANRY
(The Queen's Own Worcestershire Hussars)
'Gallipoli, 1915'
'Egypt, 1915–17'
'Palestine, 1917–18'

1/1st Worcestershire Yeomanry.
4.8.14 Worcester: 1st South Midland Mtd. Bde. 11 Aug. Warwick. 14 Aug. Bury St. Edmunds with brigade in 1st Mtd. Div. 30 Aug. to Newbury where brigade joined 2nd Mtd. Div. 17.11.14 to Norfolk with division at Barningham then Kings Lynn. 11.4.15 sailed from Avonmouth. 22.4.15 arrived Alexandria. 18.8.15 landed at Suvla Bay. Nov. 1915 returned to Egypt. Jan. 1916 2nd Mtd. Div. broken up and brigade became 5th Mtd. Bde. which was independent. Feb. 1917 brigade to Imperial Mtd. Div. June 1917 division became Australian Mtd. Div. 5.5.18 left 5th Mtd. Bde. and became Corps Cav. Regt. of XX Corps until the end of the war.

2/1st Worcestershire Yeomanry.
Formed at Worcester Sept. 1914. April 1915 joined 2/1st South Midland Bde. at Cirencester. June 1915 to Kings Lynn area, brigade now in 2/2nd Mtd. Div. July 1915 at Holkham Hall. Mar. 1916 brigade became 10th Mtd. Bde. of 3rd Mtd. Div. July 1916 became a cyclist unit and moved to 8th Cyclist Bde. of 2nd Cyclist Div. at Tunbridge Wells. Nov. 1916 2nd Cyclist Div. broken up: with 2/1st Gloucestershire Yeomanry formed 12th (Gloucestershire and Worcestershire) Yeomanry Cyclist Regt. in 4th Cyclist Bde. at Ipswich. Mar. 1917 resumed identity. April 1917 to Wivenhoe. By Nov. at Frinton then to Manningtree. About April 1918 to Ireland with 4th Cyclist Bde. and stationed at Dublin until the end of the war.

3/1st Worcestershire Yeomanry.
Formed 1915 and in summer 1915 affiliated to a reserve cav. regt. at Tidworth. Summer 1916 affiliated to 4th Reserve Cav. Regt. at Tidworth. Early in 1917 absorbed in 5th Reserve Cav. Regt. at Tidworth.

YORKSHIRE DRAGOONS
(Queen's Own)
'France and Flanders, 1915–18'

1/1st Yorkshire Dragoons.
4.8.14 Doncaster: Yorkshire Mtd. Bde. 1915 regiment left brigade and split up as divisional cavalry.
RHQ and 'B' Squadron to 37th Div. on Salisbury Plain by June 1915. Landed at Havre 1.8.15. May 1916 to II Corps Cav. Regt.
'A' Squadron to 17th Div. in Winchester area in June 1915. Landed at Havre 16.7.15. May 1916 to II Corps Cav. Regt.
'C' Squadron to 19th Div. at Bulford 26.6.15. Landed at Havre 20.7.15. 21 April to 9 May 1916 attached 3rd Cav. Div. May 1916 to II Corps Cav. Regt.

The regiment concentrated at Hazebrouck on 12 May 1916 as II Corps Cav. Regt. Oct. 1917 to Cav. Corps Troops. 6.12.17 to Lucknow Cav. Bde. 4th Cav. Div. Feb. 1918 4th Cav. Div. broken up and the regiment was dismounted to become a cyclist battalion. 16.3.18 to II Corps as corps cyclist battalion until the end of the war.

2/1st Yorkshire Dragoons.
Formed in 1914. 1915 in 2/1st Yorkshire Mtd. Bde. in Yorkshire. Mar. 1916 in Beverley area and brigade became 18th Mtd. Bde. July 1916 became a cyclist unit in 11th Cyclist Bde. Nov. 1916 brigade became 7th Cyclist Bde. and now in Bridlington area. Mar. 1917 at Barmston. July 1917 to end of year at Burton Agnes. Jan. to April 1918 Bridlington. May 1918 to Ireland with 7th Cyclist Bde. and stationed at Fermoy.

3/1st Yorkshire Dragoons.
Formed 1915 and in summer affiliated to 5th Reserve Cav. Regt. at York. Early in 1917 absorbed in 6th Reserve Cav. Regt. at Tidworth.

YORKSHIRE HUSSARS YEOMANRY
(Alexandra, Princess of Wales's Own)
'France and Flanders, 1915–18'

1/1st Yorkshire Hussars.
4.8.14 York: Yorkshire Mtd. Bde. 1915 regiment left brigade and split up as divisional cavalry.
RHQ and 'A' Squadron to 50th Div. in Northumberland on 4 April. 18.4.15 landed at Havre. 10.5.16 to XVII Corps Cav. Regt.
'B' Squadron to 46th Div. in Luton area. 28.2.15 landed at Havre. 5.5.16 to XVII Corps Cav. Regt.
'C' Squadron to 49th Div. in Yorkshire. 16.4.15 landed at Havre. 8.5.16 to XVII Corps Cav. Regt.
Early in May 1916 the regiment concentrated to form XVII Corps Cav. Regt. 26.8.17 left XVII Corps, dismounted, and went to Etaples for infantry training. 13.11.17 400 all ranks absorbed in 9th Bn. West Yorkshire Regt. of 32nd Bde. 11th Div. Unit became 9th (Yorkshire Hussars Yeomanry) Bn. West Yorkshire Regt. No further change.

2/1st Yorkshire Hussars.
Formed 1914. 1915 in 2/1st Yorkshire Mtd. Bde. in Yorkshire. Mar. 1916 in Beverley area and brigade became 18th Mtd Bde. July 1916 became cyclist unit in 11th Cyclist Bde. Nov. 1916 brigade became 7th Cyclist Bde. now in Bridlington area. Mar. 1917 Driffield. July to end of year Barmston then to Bridlington. May 1918 to Ireland with 7th Cyclist Bde, stationed at Fermoy and Fethard until the end of the war.

3/1st Yorkshire Hussars.
Formed in 1915 and in the summer affiliated to 5th Reserve Cav. Regt. at York. Early in 1917 absorbed in 5th Reserve Cav. Regt. at Tidworth. In 1918 lost its connection with 5th Reserve Cav. Regt., when the 1st Line unit became infantry, and joined 5th (Reserve) Bn. West Yorkshire Regt. at Rugeley, Cannock Chase.

EAST RIDING OF YORKSHIRE YEOMANRY
'Egypt, 1915–17'
'Palestine, 1917–18'
'France and Flanders, 1918'

1/1st East Riding Yeomanry.
4.8.14 Railway Street, Beverley: Yorkshire Mtd. Bde. Left brigade in 1915 and attached to 2/Northumbrian Div. near Newcastle. May 1915 to North Midland Mtd.

Bde. 1st Mtd. Div. in Norfolk, replacing 1/1st Welsh Horse. 27.10.15 brigade embarked at Southampton for Salonika. Destination changed while at sea to Alexandria and regiment arrived in Cairo by the end of Nov. About April 1916 brigade became 22nd Mtd. Bde. and was in the Western Frontier Force. Feb. 1917 brigade to Anzac Mtd. Div. June 1917 brigade to Yeomanry Mtd. Div. 7.4.18 left, 22nd Mtd. Bde., dismounted, and with 1/1st Lincolnshire Yeomanry formed 'D' Bn. Machine Gun Corps. 1.6.18 landed at Marseilles and to Etaples. Aug. 1918 became 102nd (Lincolnshire and East Riding Yeomanry) Bn. Machine Gun Corps. To First Army until the end of the war.

2/1st East Riding Yeomanry.
Formed 1914. 1915 in 2/1st Yorkshire Mtd. Bde. in Yorkshire. Mar. 1916 in Beverley area and brigade became 18th Mtd. Bde. July 1916 became a cyclist unit in 11th Cyclist Bde. Nov. 1916 brigade became 7th Cyclist Bde. now in Bridlington area. Remained at Bridlington until May 1918 and then to Ireland with 7th Cyclist Bde. Stationed at Bandon and Fermoy until the end of the war.

3/1st East Riding Yeomanry.
Formed in 1915 and in the summer affiliated to 5th Reserve Cav. Regt. at York. Early in 1917 absorbed in 1st Reserve Cav. Regt. at the Curragh.

Appendix I to Part I

ANALYSIS OF THE SERVICE OF CAVALRY REGIMENTS IN THE GREAT WAR, 1914–18

26   Regiments went to France in 1914 and remained there until the end of the war in 1918.
      1st and 2nd Life Guards, Royal Horse Guards.
      2nd, 3rd, 4th, 5th, 6th and 7th Dragoon Guards, 1st, 2nd and 6th Dragoons.
      3rd, 4th, 8th, 10th, 11th, 15th, 18th, 19th and 20th Hussars.
      5th, 9th, 12th, 16th and 17th Lancers.

2   Regiments went to Mesopotamia in 1915 and 1917 remaining there until the end of the war.
      7th and 14th Hussars.

1   Regiment went to France in 1914 and then to Mesopotamia in 1916 until the end of the war.
      13th Hussars.

1   Regiment went to France in 1914 and returned to India in 1917.
      1st Dragoon Guards.

1   Regiment remained in India throughout the war.
      21st Lancers.

—
31
—

All regiments were horsed throughout the war with the exception of the three Household Cavalry Regiments. They were converted to machine gun battalions in 1918.

Appendix II to Part I

ANALYSIS OF THE SERVICE AND EMPLOYMENT OF YEOMANRY REGIMENTS IN THE GREAT WAR, 1914-18

PART 1 First Line Units.

18   Regiments went dismounted to Gallipoli in 1915 (12) and Egypt in 1916 (1). They formed twelve infantry battalions in 1917 for the 74th (Yeomanry) Division which went to France in 1918.
     Ayr, Cheshire, Denbigh, 1st Devon, North Devon, Fife and Forfar, Glamorgan, East Kent, West Kent, Lanark, Montgomery, Norfolk, Pembroke, Shropshire, West Somerset, Suffolk, Sussex and Welsh Horse.

9   Regiments went to Egypt, mounted, in 1915 and seven of them served in Gallipoli (dismounted). Three went to Salonika for 1916-17. They were all dismounted in Egypt in 1918 and formed five machine gun battalions which went to France.
     Bucks., Berks., Lincoln, City of London, 2nd Co. of London, 3rd Co. of London, South Notts. Hussars, Warwick and East Riding.

7   Regiments went to Egypt, mounted, in 1915 and six of them served in Gallipoli (dismounted). Two went to Salonika for 1916-17 and back to Egypt. They all remained, mounted, in Palestime until the end of the war.
     Dorset, Gloucester, Herts., 1st Co. of London, Sherwood Rangers, Stafford and Worcester.

7   Regiments went to France in 1915-16 as squadrons of divisional cavalry and became corps cavalry regiments in 1916. They were absorbed in infantry battalions in 1917.
     Hampshire, Lancashire Hussars, Duke of Lancaster's, Glasgow, Westmorland and Cumberland, Wiltshire and Yorkshire Hussars.

4   Regiments went to France in 1914-15 and joined cavalry brigades. In 1918 they were absorbed in cavalry regiments.
     Bedford, Essex, Leicester and North Somerset.

4   Regiments went to Gallipoli, dismounted, in 1915 and then to Egypt. Converted to infantry in 1916 and went to Salonika. To France in 1918.
     1st and 2nd Lovat's Scouts and 1st and 2nd Scottish Horse.

3   Regiments went to France in 1914-15 as divisional cavalry and became corps cavalry regiments in 1916. They remained as corps troops until the end of the war, two in France (one as cyclists) and one in Italy.
     Northampton, Northumberland and Yorkshire Dragoons.

2   Regiments went to France in 1915 as squadrons of divisional cavalry and then to Salonika. Here, in 1916, they became corps cavalry regiments and remained at Salonika.
     Lothians & Border Horse and Surrey.

1   Regiment went to France, mounted, in 1914 and served throughout the war.
     Oxfordshire.

1   Regiment went to Egypt, mounted, in 1915 and to Gallipoli, dismounted. Then back to Egypt and to Salonika in 1916 until the end of the war.
     Derbyshire.

1   Regiment went to Gallipoli, dismounted, in 1915. Then to Egypt and in 1916 converted to a machine gun squadron.
     3rd Scottish Horse.

57

NOTES

1. There were 55 yeomanry regiments before the war and two more were raised in Aug. 1914.
2. A few single squadrons served away from their regiments but they have not been shown above.
3. Thirty-one yeomanry regiments took part in the Gallipoli campaign. Thirteen went to Egypt with the 2nd Mounted Division in April 1915. They were dismounted in Aug. and each regiment left a squadron headquarters and the officers and men of two troops to look after the horses. The strength of these parties was about 100 for a regiment. The other eighteen regiments which took part in the campaign came out from England dismounted.

PART 2. Second Line Units

35   Regiments were converted to cyclists in 1916 (33) and 1917 (2) and went to Ireland in 1918.
     Ayr, Berks., Cheshire, 1st Devon, North Devon, Dorset, Essex, Fife and Forfar, Gloucester, Hampshire, East Kent, West Kent, Lanark, Lancashire Hussars, Duke of Lancaster's, 1st Co. of London, 3rd Co. of London, Lothians & Border Horse, Norfolk, Oxford, 1st, 2nd and 3rd Scottish Horse, Shropshire, North Somerset, West Somerset, Suffolk, Surrey, Sussex, Westmorland & Cumberland, Wiltshire, Worcester, Yorkshire Dragoons, Yorkshire Hussars and East Riding.

16   Regiments were converted to cyclists in 1916 (9) and 1917 (7) and remained in England until the end of the war.
     Bucks., Denbigh, Derbyshire, Glamorgan, Herts Leicester, Lincoln, City of London, 1st and 2nd Lovat's Scouts, Montgomery, Sherwood Rangers, South Notts. Hussars, Pembroke, Stafford and Warwickshire.

3   Regiments were absorbed in reserve cavalry regiments in 1917 and 1918.
     Bedford, Glasgow and Northampton.

1   Regiment was absorbed in the Tank Corps in 1916.
     2nd Co. of London.

1   Regiment went to France in 1917 as a corps cavalry regiment and was absorbed in an infantry battalion.
     Northumberland Hussars.

1   Regiment was absorbed by another 2nd Line unit in 1916.
     Welsh Horse.

57

All the above were formed as mounted units soon after the outbreak of war and remained mounted until the conversions which began in 1916.

Appendix III to Part I

OUTLINE HISTORIES OF YEOMANRY FORMATIONS

1. DIVISIONS

1ST MOUNTED DIVISION
Formed in Aug. 1914. July 1916 became 1ST CYCLIST DIVISION. Nov. 1916 broken up. The division was in East Anglia all the time.

2ND MOUNTED DIVISION
Formed in Aug. 1914 in Berkshire and in Nov. went to East Anglia. April 1915 to Egypt. Aug. 1915 to Gallipoli, dismounted: each regiment left a squadron headquarters and two troops (about 100 men) behind in Egypt to look after the horses. Dec. 1915 returned to Egypt and broken up in January 1916.

2/2ND MOUNTED DIVISION
Formed in Mar. 1915 from 2nd Line units and went to East Anglia in place of 2nd Mounted Division. Mar. 1916 became 3RD MOUNTED DIVISION and in Aug. 1ST MOUNTED DIVISION. Sept. 1917 all regiments converted to cyclists and became THE CYCLIST DIVISION. It remained in Kent until the end of the war.

4TH MOUNTED DIVISION
Formed in East Anglia in Mar. 1916. Aug. 1916 became 2ND CYCLIST DIVISION and remained in East Anglia until it was broken up in Nov., 1916.

YEOMANRY MOUNTED DIVISION
Formed in Palestine in June 1917. April 1918 became 1ST MOUNTED DIVISION and six of the nine yeomanry regiments were replaced by Indian cavalry regiments. July 1918 became 4TH CAVALRY DIVISION.

2ND MOUNTED DIVISION
Another 2ND MOUNTED DIVISION was formed in Egypt in May 1918 but it included only two yeomanry regiments. It became 5th Cav. Div. in Aug. 1918 and remained in Palestine.

74th (YEOMANRY) DIVISION
Formed in Egypt in Mar. 1917 with 18 dismounted yeomanry regiments (see page 34). Went to France in May 1918 where it remained.

2. MOUNTED BRIGADES

a. Pre-War Formations

MOUNTED BRIGADES

EASTERN
4.8.14 Belchamp Hall, Sudbury. Essex, Norfolk and Suffolk Yeomanry. Attached for Training. Bedford, Herts. and Northampton Yeomanry.
In East Anglia till Sept. 1915 then dismounted. Oct./Dec. Gallipoli. Feb. 1916 absorbed in 3rd Dismounted Bde. in Egypt.

HIGHLAND
4.8.14 Academy Street, Inverness. Fife & Forfar Yeo. 1st & 2nd Lovat's Scouts.
Huntingdon, Lincolnshire and Norfolk. Aug. 1915 dismounted. Sept./Dec. Gallipoli. Feb. 1916 absorbed in 2nd Dismounted Bde. in Egypt.

LONDON
4.8.14 Duke of York's H.Q. Chelsea. City of London, 1st & 3rd County of London Yeomanry. Attached for Training. 2nd Co. of London Yeomanry.
East Anglia. April 1915 Egypt. Aug./Dec. 1915 Gallipoli then Egypt. Became 8TH MOUNTED BDE. Nov. 1916/June 1917 Salonkia. 1917–18 Palestine. July 1918 became 11TH CAVALRY BDE.

LOWLAND
4.8.14 Dublin St., Edinburgh. Ayr, Lanark and Lothians & Border Horse. Attached for training. Glasgow Yeo.
Scotland. Sept. 1915 dismounted Oct./Dec. 1915 Gallipoli. Egypt. Feb. 1916 absorbed in 1st Dismounted Bde.

NORTH MIDLAND
4.8.14 Magazine Square, Leicester. Leicester, Lincoln, and Staffordshire Yeomanry.
East Anglia until Oct. 1915. 1915–17 Egypt. Mar. 1916 became 22ND MTD. BDE. 1917–18 Palestine July 1918 became 12TH CAVALRY BDE.

NOTTS. & DERBY
4.8.14 Derby Road, Nottingham. Sherwood Rangers, S. Notts. Hussars, Derbyshire Yeomanry.
East Anglia. April 1915 Egypt. Aug./Dec. Gallipoli. Egypt. 1916–17 Salonika. Became 7TH MTD. BDE. 1917–18 Palestine. July 1918 became 14TH CAVALRY BDE.

SOUTH EASTERN
4.8.14 Russell Square, London. East Kent, West Kent, and Sussex Yeomanry. Attached for Training. Surrey Yeo.
Kent. Sept. 1915 dismounted. Oct./Dec. 1915 Gallipoli. Egypt. Feb. 1916 absorbed in 3rd Dismounted Bde.

1ST SOUTH MIDLAND
4.8.14 St. John's, Warwick. Gloucester, Warwick and Worcestershire Yeomanry.
East Anglia. April 1915 Egypt. Aug./Dec. 1915 Gallipoli. 1916–17 Egypt. Became 5TH MOUNTED BDE. 1917–18 Palestine. Aug. 1918 became 13TH CAV. BDE.

2ND SOUTH MIDLAND
4.8.14 Lonsdale Road, Oxford. Berks., Bucks. and Oxford Yeomanry.
East Anglia. April 1915 Egypt. Aug./Dec. 1915 Gallipoli. 1916–17 Egypt. Became 6TH MOUNTED BDE. 1917–18 Palestine. July 1918 became 10TH CAVALRY BDE.

SOUTH WALES
4.8.14 The Barracks, Carmarthen. Glamorgan, Montgomery and Pembroke Yeomanry.

East Anglia. Nov. 1915 dismounted. Mar. 1916 Egypt and absorbed in 4th Dismounted Bde.

1ST SOUTH WESTERN
4.8.14 Butcher Row, Salisbury. Hampshire, North Somerset and Wiltshire Yeomanry. Attached for Training. Dorset Yeomanry.
Sussex. 1915 regiments left: may have provided H.Q. for 2/1st Southern Mtd. Bde.

2ND SOUTH WESTERN
4.8.14 Goldsmith Street, Exeter. R. 1st Devon, R. N. Devon and West Somerset Yeomanry.
East Anglia. Sept. 1915 dismounted Oct./Dec. 1915 Gallipoli. Egypt. Feb. 1916 absorbed in 2nd Dismounted Bde.

WELSH BORDER
4.8.14 High Street, Shrewsbury. Cheshire, Denbigh and Shropshire Yeomanry. Attached for Training. Lancs. Hussars, Dule of Lancaster's and Westmorland & Cumberland Yeo.
East Anglia. Nov. 1915 dismounted. Mar. 1916 Egypt and absorbed in 4th Dismounted Bde.

YORKSHIRE
4.8.14 St. Leonards, York. Yorkshire Dragoons, Yorkshire Hussars and East Riding Yeomanry. Attached for Training. Northumberland Yeomanry.
Regiments left the brigade in 1915 and it ceased to exist.

SCOTTISH HORSE
Formed in August 1914.
1st, 2nd and 3rd Scottish Horse.

NOTES

1. The location of brigade headquarters and the regiments in the brigade before the war are shown above after the date 4.8.14.
2. The numbering 1/1st etc. was added to the titles of brigades in Jan. 1915.

b. Second Line Formations

In 1915 most of the 2nd Line Yeomanry Regiments formed fifteen mounted brigades with the same titles and composition as the pre-war 1st Line formations. Two new ones were also formed: 2/1st Southern and 2/1st Western Mounted Brigades.

On 31 March 1916 orders were issued for the numbering of mounted brigades. By now most of the 2nd Line mounted brigades had moved to East Anglia, replacing the 1st Line ones as they went overseas.

The following table shows the numbering of 2nd Line mounted brigades ordered on 31 Mar. 1916 together with their allotment and locations at the time.

Brigade	Number	Allotment	Location
2/1st Highland	1st	1st Mtd. Div.	East Anglia
2/2nd South Western	2nd	do.	do.
2/1st North Midland	3rd	do.	do.
2/1st S. Wales	4th	do.	do.
2/1st Notts. & Derby	9th	3rd Mtd. Div.	do.
2/1st S. Midland	10th	do.	do.
2/2nd S. Midland	11th	do.	do.
2/1st London	12th	do.	do.
2/1st Eastern	13th	4th Mtd. Div.	do.
2/1st South Eastern	14th	do.	Kent
2/1st South Western	15th	do.	East Anglia
2/1st Southern	16th	do.	do.
2/1st Welsh Border	17th	Northern Command	Northumberland
2/1st Yorkshire	18th	do.	Yorkshire
2/1st Scottish Horse	19th	do.	Lincolnshire
2/1st Lowland	20th	Scottish Command	Dunbar
2/1st Western	21st	do.	Cupar

There was a major reorganization of the yeomanry in July 1916 when most of the 2nd Line regiments were converted to cyclists—only twelve regiments remained mounted. Most of the brigades became cyclist brigades and eight of them were in the two cyclist divisions; the others were independent formations.

There were further changes in Nov. 1916 when the two cyclist divisions were broken up and the brigades became independent. At the same time there were changes in the composition of the brigades and in their numbering. The three remaining mounted brigades formed the Mounted Division.

In September 1917 the Mounted Division became The Cyclist Division and the Mounted brigades became the three cyclist brigades of the division.

By the summer of 1918 there were twelve cyclist brigades. Three with The Cyclist Division in Kent (5th, 11th and 12th): one in East Anglia (1st) and eight in Ireland (2nd, 3rd, 4th, 6th, 7th, 8th, 9th and 10th). There were no further changes until the end of the war.

Part II

BRITISH INFANTRY REGIMENTS IN THE GREAT WAR
1914-1918

Introduction to Part II

This work gives, in brief, an outline history of the infantry battalions of the British Army in the Great War, 1914–18. It is based on an earlier version of 1929 which included the Cavalry and Yeomanry as well as the Infantry. The Cavalry and Yeomanry portion was considerably revised and expanded to appear as a separate volume in 1969—*Historical Records of British Cavalry and Yeomanry Regiments in the Great War, 1914–18*. The Infantry portion of the 1929 book has also been revised and enlarged to make this book which tells the story of 1,761 battalions.

The account of each pre-war battalion starts with its station on 4th August 1914 and its place in the order of battle if it was serving in a formation. The entry for a wartime battalion opens with the date and place of formation with its brigade and division. This is followed by moves in the United Kingdom, date of going overseas and destination. Changes in allotment to formations and moves between theatres of war, with any other information, are noted. Finally, each battalion's account closes with its brigade and division and location at the end of the war; the day of the armistice in 1918. The armistice dates in the various theatres of war were: Macedonia 30th September, Palestine and Mesopotamia 31st October, Italy 4th November and France 11th November 1918. The date of the end of the war for battalions stationed in the United Kingdom is taken as 11th November. Moves within the United Kingdom have been given, when possible, as this information is not easily obtainable and very few units at home kept war diaries.

A completely new organization was created for the vast expansion of the army by thirty divisions, called the New Armies or, popularly at the time, Kitchener's Army. The authority for the formation of the first six divisions was Army Order 324 of 21st August 1914, headed Augmentation of the Army. Paragraph 3 of the Order reads:

'The new battalions will be raised as additional battalions of the regiments of Infantry of the Line and will be given numbers following consecutively on the existing battalions of their regiments. They will be further distinguished by the word "Service" after the number . . .'

The title Service seems to date from the South African War when the companies raised by the Volunteers for attachment to their Regular Battalions in South Africa were called Service Companies. (For details of the New Army battalions see Appendix II to Part II).

In the summer of 1916 a general pool of infantry reserves was constituted, known as the Training Reserve and all the Second Reserve and Local Reserve battalions were absorbed in the 112 battalions of the Training Reserve. But the wartime reserve battalions of the Irish Regiments were not incorporated in the new organization. In October 1917 forty-six Graduated and twenty-three Young Soldier battalions of the Training Reserve were affiliated to twenty-three Infantry Regiments in groups of three. The Graduated Battalions were numbered 51st and 52nd and the Young Soldier Battalions 53rd in the regiments (see Appendix III to Part II).

While the augmentation of the Regular Army was taking place the Territorial Force was also being considerably increased. The fourteen pre-war divisions were recruited up to war establishment and some new units formed to complete the order of battle. In the early months of the war all Territorial units formed a second-line and early in 1915 they were formed into another fourteen divisions. These divisions were not numbered until August 1915 but they are usually referred to by their numbers in this work from when they were formed. In 1914 each Territorial Force unit was ordered to form a third-line as a reserve unit to train and supply reinforcements to the 1st and 2nd Line. The Territorial units were given fractional designations e.g. the pre-war 7th Battalion of the Lancashire Fusiliers became three battalions called 1/7th, 2/7th and 3/7th (see Appendix IV to Part II for particulars of Third Line Territorial battalions).

Between 1915 and 1918 a number of other new battalions were added to most infantry regiments, these included dismounted Yeomanry, Territorial battalions, garrison battalions, labour battalions, and others. In June 1918 about thirty new battalions were formed on the East Coast but after a brief existence most of them were disbanded. They are recorded under their regiments but the disbanded ones are not included in Appendix I to Part II.

This Record has been compiled from information collected over a wide field: the sources are given on page 121. I have also used my notes made during many years of research on the War Diaries while they were with the Historical Section, Committee of Imperial Defence, with War Office Records at Droitwich and Hayes and with the Public Record Office at Ashridge and, finally, at Chancery Lane. I have always had the most willing assistance from the staff of the various establishments storing the diaries.

I am most grateful to Miss R. E. B. Coombs and Mr. David Nash of the Imperial War Museum and to Mr. D. W. King, O.B.E., F.L.A., Chief Librarian (now retired), and Mr. C. A. Potts, Ministry of Defence Library (Central and Army), for their help when I was working in these two fine libraries.

Nearly all the details given have documentary support but, in a few cases, they are the result of deduction, particularly in the case of home service units. Where there was any doubt the qualifying words 'about', 'by', 'in the early part of' and so on have been used. There are occasional slight variations in the style of the battalion histories because, as the work progressed, fresh sources of information were found and minor changes were made to improve the layout. The titles of regiments are as shown in the Army List for August 1914.

E.A.J.

January 1976.

British Infantry Regiments in the Great War 1914-1918

FOOT GUARDS

GRENADIER GUARDS

1st Battalion.
 4.8.14 Warley: London District. Sept. 1914 to 20th Bde. 7th Div. at Lyndhurst. 7.10.14 landed at Zeebrugge. 4.8.15 to 3rd Guards Bde. Guards Div. 11.11.18 3rd Guards Bde. Guards Div. France; Maubeuge.
2nd Battalion.
 4.8.14 Chelsea: 4th (Guards) Bde. 2nd Div. 15.8.14 landed at Havre. 20.8.15 to 1st Guards Bde. Guards Div. 11.11.18 1st Guards Bde. Guards Div. France; N.E. of Maubeuge.
3rd Battalion.
 4.8.14 Wellington Barracks: London District. 27.7.15 landed at Havre. 19.8.15 to 2nd Guards Bde. Guards Div. 11.11.18 2nd Guards Bde. Guards Div. France; near Maubeuge.
4th Battalion.
 Formed at Marlow 14.7.15. To France. 19.8.15 to 3rd Guards Bde. Guards Div. 8.2.18 to 4th Guards Bde. 31st Div. 20.5.18 4th Guards Bde. to G.H.Q. Reserve. 11.11.18 4th Guards Bde. France; Criel Plage, S.W. of Le Treport.
5th (Reserve) Battalion.
 Formed at Kensington in Aug. 1914 as 4th (Reserve) Bn. 15.8.14 to Chelsea Barracks. 14.7.15 became 5th (Reserve) Bn. Remained at Chelsea.
1st Provisional Battalion was formed at Aldershot on 7.8.18 for duty at the Senior Officers School.

COLDSTREAM GUARDS

1st Battalion.
 4.8.14 Aldershot: 1st (Guards) Bde. 1st Div. Aug. 1914 to France. 25.8.15 to 2nd Guards Bde. Guards Div. 11.11.18 2nd Guards Bde. Guards Div. France; near Maubeuge.
2nd Battalion.
 4.8.14 Windsor: 4th (Guards) Bde. 2nd Div. 13.8.14 landed at Havre. 20.8.15 to 1st Guards Bde. Guards Div. 11.11.18 1st Guards Bde. Guards Div. France; N.E. of Maubeuge.
3rd Battalion.
 4.8.14 Chelsea Barracks: 4th (Guards) Bde. 2nd Div. 13.8.14 landed at Havre. 20.8.15 to 1st Guards Bde. Guards Div. 8.2.18 to 4th Guards Bde. 31st Div. 20.5.18 4th Guards Bde. to G.H.Q. Reserve. 11.11.18 4th Guards Bde. France; Criel Plage, S.W. of Le Treport.
4th Battalion. (Pioneers).
 Formed at Windsor on 17.7.15 as Guards Pioneer Bn. but soon became 4th Bn. 15.8.15 to France and joined Guards Div. 11.11.18 Pioneer Bn. Guards Div. France; near Maubeuge.
5th (Reserve) Battalion.
 Formed at Windsor in Aug. 1914 as 4th (Reserve) Bn. and in July 1915 became 5th (Reserve) Bn. Stationed at Windsor throughout the war. Provided drafts of 16,860 all ranks.
1st Provisional Battalion was formed at Aldershot on 7.8.18 for duty at the Senior Officers School.

SCOTS GUARDS

1st Battalion.
 4.8.14 Aldershot: 1st (Guards) Bde. 1st Div. 14.8.14 landed at Havre. 25.8.15 to 2nd Guards Bde. Guards Div. 11.11.18 2nd Guards Bde. Guards Div. France; Maubeuge.
2nd Battalion.
 4.8.14 Tower of London: London District. Sept. 1914 to 20th Bde. 7th Div. at Lyndhurst. 7.10.14 landed at Zeebrugge. 9.8.15 to 3rd Guards Bde. Guards Div. 11.11.18 3rd Guards Bde. Guards Div. France; Maubeuge.
3rd (Reserve) Battalion.
 Formed at Chelsea Barracks 18.8.14. 31.8.14 to Esher. 2.10.14 to Wellington Barracks until the end of the war. Provided drafts of 11,201 all ranks.

IRISH GUARDS

1st Battalion.
 4.8.14 Wellington Barracks: 4th (Guards) Bde. 2nd Div. 13.8.14 landed at Havre. 20.8.15 to 1st Guards Bde. Guards Div. 11.11.18 1st Guards Bde. Guards Div. France; Assevent, N.E. of Maubeuge.
2nd Battalion.
 18.7.15 formed at Warley Barracks. 17.8.15 landed at Havre, and joined 2nd Guards Bde. Guards Div. 8.2.18 to 4th Guards Bde. 31st Div. 20.5.18 4th Guards Bde. to G.H.Q. Reserve. 11.11.18 4th Guards Bde. G.H.Q. Troops. France; Criel Plage, S.W. of Le Treport.
3rd (Reserve) Battalion.
 Formed in 1914 as 2nd (Reserve) Bn. at Warley Barracks. July 1915 became 3rd (Reserve) Bn. and remained at Warley.

WELSH GUARDS

1st Battalion.
 Regiment raised by Royal Warrant of 26 Feb. 1915 and battalion was at White City. 28.4.15 Sandown Park. 4.6.15 Wellington Barracks. 18.8.15 landed at Havre to 3rd Guards Bde. Guards Div. 11.11.18 3rd Guards Bde. Guards Div. France; Maubeuge.
2nd (Reserve) Battalion.
 Formed at Wellington Barracks Aug. 1915. Sept. & Oct. 1915 at Marlow then to Tower of London till June 1916. 12.6.16 to Tadworth. 24.10.16 Orpington. 15.5.17 Tadworth. 5.9.17 to Ranelagh Club, Barnes till end of the war.

4TH (FOOT GUARDS) BATTALION GUARDS MACHINE GUN REGIMENT

Early in 1918 the four machine gun companies of divisions were formed into machine gun battalions. The four companies in the Guards Division became the 4th Bn. Machine Gun Guards on 1.3.18. By a Royal Warrant of 10th May 1918 the Guards Machine Gun Regiment was formed and the Guards Division unit became the 4th (Foot Guards) Battalion of the new regiment. It remained with the Guards Division until the end of the war when it was in the Maubeuge area. The three Household Cavalry regiments formed the 1st, 2nd and 3rd Battalions of the Guards Machine Gun Regiment.

INFANTRY

THE ROYAL SCOTS (LOTHIAN REGIMENT)

1st Battalion.
4.8.14 Allahabad. 16.11.14 landed at Devonport and joined 81st Bde. 27th Div. at Winchester. 20.12.14 landed at Havre. 29.11.15 sailed from Marseilles. 8.12.15 arrived at Salonika. 30.9.18 81st Bde. 27th Div. Bulgaria; Izlis, N.W. of Doiran.

2nd Battalion.
Plymouth: 8th Bde. 3rd Div. 14.8.14 landed at Boulogne. 11.11.18 8th Bde. 3rd Div. France; near Solesmes.

3rd (Reserve) Battalion.
4.8.14 Glencorse, Edinburgh. Aug. 1914 to Weymouth. May 1915 to Edinburgh until end of 1917 and then to Ireland. Stationed at Mullingar until the end of the war.

1/4th Battalion (Queen's Edinburgh Rifles) T.F.
4.8.14 Forrest Hill, Edinburgh: Lothian Bde. Coast Defences, Scottish Command. 24.4.15 to Scottish Rifles Bde. Lowland Div. which became 156 Bde. 52nd Div. 24.5.15 embarked at Liverpool. 4.6.15 arrived Alexandria. 14.6.15 landed at Gallipoli. 6.7.15 formed composite bn. with 1/7th. 8.1.16 left Gallipoli for Egypt and on 20.1.16 resumed identity. 17.4.18 arrived Marseilles. 11.11.18 156th Bde. 52nd Div. Belgium; Herchies, N.W. of Mons.

1/5th Battalion (Queen's Edinburgh Rifles) T.F.
4.8.14 Forrest Hill, Edinburgh: Lothian Bde. Coast Defences, Scottish Command. 11.3.15 to 88th Bde. 29th Div. at Leamington. 20.3.15 embarked at Avonmouth. 2.4.15 arrived Alexandria. 25.4.15 landed at Gallipoli. 18.10.15 to Mudros. 7.1.16 to Egypt. 10.3.16 embarked at Port Said for France and landed at Marseilles 22.3.16. 24.4.16 left 29th Div. to L. of C. 15.6.16 amalgamated with 1/6th Bn. to form 5/6th Bn. 29.7.16 joined 14th Bde. 32nd Div. at Bethune. 11.11.18 14th Bde. 32nd Div. France; Avesnelles, near Avesnes.

1/6th Battalion T.F.
4.8.14 33, Gilmore Place, Edinburgh: Lothian Bde. Coast Defences, Scottish Command. After supplying drafts to 4th and 8th Bns. was at Selkirk and Peebles in 1915. Aug. 1915 to Edinburgh. 5.9.15 embarked at Devonport. 14.9.15 arrived Alexandria. 20.11.15 to 27.2.16 with Western Frontier Force. 8 to 16 May 1916 Alexandria to Marseilles. 15.6.16 amalgamated with 1/5th Bn. (see above).

1/7th Battalion T.F.
4.8.14 Dalmeny Street, Leith: attached Lothian Bde. 24.4.15 to Scottish Rifles Bde. Lowland Div. Subsequent record same as 1/4th Bn. (Note 1).

1/8th Battalion T.F.
4.8.14 Haddington: Lothian Bde. Coast Defences, Scottish Command. 5.11.14 landed at Havre. 11.11.14 to 22nd Bde. 7th Div. at Merris. 19.8.15 to 51st Div. as Pioneer Bn. 11.11.18 Pioneer Bn. 51st Div. France; Estrun, north of Cambrai.

1/9th (Highlanders) Battalion T.F.
4.8.14 89 East Claremont Street, Edinburgh: Lothian Bde. Coast Defences, Scottish Command. 26.2.15 landed at Havre and to 81st Bde. 27th Div. 24.11.15 to 14th Bde. 5th Div. 25.1.16 to Third Army Troops. 1.3.16 to 154th Bde. 51st Div. 6.2.18 to 183rd Bde. 61st Div. 1.6.18 to 46th Bde. 15th Div. 11.11.18 46th Bde. 15th Div. Belgium; Pipaix, east of Tournai.

1/10th (Cyclist) Battalion T.F.
4.8.14 Linlithglow: Army Troops. To East Linton and on coast defence duty at North Berwick until April 1918 and then to Ireland where it was stationed at Claremorris, the Curragh and Port Arlington. By the end of 1916 over 90 per cent of the original personnel had gone overseas.

2/4th Battalion (Queen's Edinburgh Rifles) T.F.
Formed at Edinburgh Sept. 1914. Feb. 1915 to Penicuik. May 1915 to Peebles. Nov. 1915 to 195th Bde. 65th Div. at Cambusbarron and amalgamated with 2/5th and 2/6th Bns. to form No. 19 Bn. Jan. 1916 became 2/4th Bn. again. Mar. 1916 with 65th Div. to Essex. Jan. 1917 to Ireland with 65th Div., at Fermoy and in Aug. 1917 absorbed in bns. of 195th Bde.

2/5th Battalion (Queen's Edinburgh Rifles) T.F.
Formed at Edinburgh Sept. 1914 and here till May 1915 and then to Peebles. In Nov. 1915 amalgamated with 2/4th and 2/6th Bns. at Cambusbarron to form No. 19 Bn.

2/6th Battalion T.F.
Formed at Edinburgh Mar. 1915. May 1915 to Peebles. In Nov. 1915 amalgamated with 2/4th and 2/5th Bns. to form No. 19 Bn. at Cambusbarron.

2/7th Battalion T.F.
Formed at Leith Aug. 1914 here till Mar. 1915 then to Peebles. Nov. 1915 to 194th Bde. 65th Div. at Larbert. Mar. 1916 with 65th Div. to Essex. Jan. 1917 with 65th Div. to Ireland and stationed in Dublin. Sept. 1917 to the Curragh. About Mar. 1918 disbanded, Category A and B men for drafts remainder to 4th (Reserve) Bn.

2/8th Battalion T.F.
Formed at Haddington Sept. 1914. May 1915 to Peebles. Nov. 1915 to 194th Bde. 65th Div. at Falkirk and became No. 16 Bn. until Jan. 1916. Mar. 1916 with 65th Div. to Essex. Jan. 1917 to Ireland with 65th Div. and stationed at Dublin. In summer of 1917 disbanded and absorbed in 194th Bde.

2/9th (Highlanders) Battalion T.F.
Formed at Edinburgh Sept. 1914. May 1915 to Peebles. Nov. 1915 to Tillicoultry in 195th Bde. 65th Div. becoming No. 20 Bn. till Jan. 1916. Mar. 1916 with 65th Div. to Essex. Jan. 1917 to Ireland with 65th Div. stationed at Tralee. By July 1917 at Limerick. Mar. 1918 65th Div. broken up and to Moore Park, near Fermoy, and disbanded in Mar. 1918.

2/10th (Cyclist) Battalion T.F.
Formed at Linlithglow in Sept. 1914. Oct. Bathgate. From 1915 on coast defence duty at Berwick and Coldingham. June 1918 to Ireland at Dundalk and then reorganized as an infantry battalion. July 1918 to England at Aldershot. 17 to 25 Aug. 1918 Newcastle to Archangel and remained in North Russia until June 1919. (for 3rd line unit see note 2).

3/4th, 3/5th, 3/6th, 3/7th and 3/8th Battalions T.F.
All formed at Peebles May to July 1915 except 3/8th which was in Dec. 1914. Nov. 1915 to Loanhead (4), Galashiels (5), Selkirk (6), Innerleithen (7) and 3/8th still at Peebles. 8.4.16 became reserve bns. May 1916 Stobs Camp. 1.9.16 amalgamated in 4th (Reserve) Bn. in Lowland Reserve Bde. T.F. at Catterick. June 1917 absorbed 9th (Reserve) Bn. Nov. 1917 to Edinburgh and joined Edinburgh Special Reserve Bde. April 1918 to Haddington and by end of the war at Cupar. (Forth Garrison).

3/9th Battalion T.F.
Formed at Peebles in June 1915. Nov. 1915 to Selkirk. 8.4.16 became 9th (Res.) Bn. May 1916 Stobs Camp. 1.9.16 in Lowland Res. Bde. T.F. at Catterick. June 1917 absorbed in 4th (Reserve) Bn. at Catterick.

11th (Service) Battalion.
Formed at Edinburgh Aug. 1914—K1—to 27th Bde. 9th Div. in Bordon area near Aldershot. May 1915 landed in

France. 11.11.18 27th Bde. 9th Div. Belgium; near Courtrai.

12th (Service) Battalion.
Formed at Edinburgh Aug. 1914—K1—subsequent record same as 11th Bn.

13th (Service) Battalion.
Formed at Edinburgh Sept. 1914—K2—to 45th Bde. 15th Div. at Aldershot. Nov. 1914 Bramshott. Feb. 1915 Basingstoke in billets. Mar. 1915 Chiseldon. July 1915 landed in France. 11.11.18 45th Bde. 15th Div. Belgium; Blicquy, S.W. of Ath.

14th (Reserve) Battalion.
Formed at Weymouth Nov. 1914 as a service bn. of K4 in 102nd Bde. of original 34th Div. 10.4.15 became a 2nd res. Bn. May 1915 Stobs Camp. Oct. 1915 Richmond in 12th Res. Bde. April 1916 South Queensferry. 1.9.16 became 54th Training Reserve Bn. at Kirkcaldy in 12th Reserve Bde.

15th (Service) Battalion. (1st Edinburgh).
Raised in Edinburgh Sept. 1914 by the Lord Provost and City. Mar. 1915 Troon. June 1915 Ripon and 101st Bde. 34th Div. 10.8.15 taken over by the War Office. Sept. 1915 to Sutton Veny. 8.1.16 landed at Havre. 16.5.18 reduced to cadre. 17.6.18 cadre to 39th Div. 14.8.18 disbanded in France.

16th (Service) Battalion. (2nd Edinburgh).
Raised in Edinburgh Dec. 1914 by Lt. Col. G. McCrae, MP. June 1915 to Ripon and 101st Bde. 34th Div. 10.8.15 taken over by the War Office. Subsequent record same as 15th Bn.

17th (Service) Battalion. (Rosebery).
Raised in Edinburgh Feb. 1915 by Lord Rosebery and a local committee as a bantam bn. April 1915 Glencorse. May 1915 Selkirk. June 1915 Masham and 106th Bde. 35th Div. 3.7.15 taken over by the War Office. Aug. 1915 Chiseldon. 1.2.16 landed at Havre. 11.11.18 106th Bde. 35th Div. Belgium; west of Grammont.

18th (Reserve) Battalion.
Formed at Edinburgh in June 1915 with depot companies of 15th, 16th and 17th Bns. as a local reserve battalion. Oct. 1915 to Ripon and in April 1916 to Dundee. 1.9.16 became 77th Training Reserve Bn. at Dundee in 18th Reserve Bde.

19th (Labour) Battalion.
Formed at Blairgowrie in April 1916 and to France in May. April 1917 transferred to Labour Corps (1st & 2nd Labour Coys.).

1st Garrison Battalion.
Formed at Edinburgh in Aug. 1915. Oct. 1915 to Stobs and at end of month to Mudros. Feb. 1916 to Egypt and was in Egypt and Cyprus until the end of the war.

2nd (Home Service) Garrison Battalion.
Formed at Leith in Aug. 1916. Aug. 1917 became 1st Bn. Royal Defence Corps.

NOTES

1. On 22 May 1915 a troop train carrying Battalion H.Q. and A and D Companies of the 1/7th Royal Scots from Larbert to Liverpool crashed into a local train near Gretna Green and within a minute the London to Glasgow express ran into the wreckage. 227 officers and men were killed and 246 injured. The remaining two companies in another train embarked at Liverpool on 24 May for Alexandria.
 This was the worst railway accident in Great Britain. A memorial to the dead was unveiled on 12 May 1916 at Leith Rosebank Cemetery by Lord Rosebery who had been the Honorary Colonel of the battalion.
2. The Third Line Depot of the 10th Bn., sometimes known as 3/10th Bn., was abolished in Mar. 1916. Personnel to 1st and 2nd Lines and M.G.C.

THE QUEEN'S (ROYAL WEST SURREY REGIMENT).

1st Battalion.
4.8.14 Bordon: 3rd Bde. 1st Div. 13.8.14 landed at Havre. 8.11.14 to I Corps Troops. 21.7.15 to 5th Bde. 2nd Div. 15.12.15 to 100th Bde. 33rd Div. 5.2.18 to 19th Bde. 33rd Div. 11.11.18 19th Bde. 33rd Div. France; Berlaimont.

2nd Battalion.
4.8.14 Pretoria. 27.8.14 sailed from Cape Town. 19.9.14 landed at Southampton and joined 22nd Bde. 7th Div. at Lyndhurst. 6.10.14 landed at Zeebrugge. 20.12.15 to 91st Bde. 7th Div. 18 to 24 Nov. 1917 to Italy. 4.11.18 91st Bde. 7th Div. Italy; west of Udine.

3rd (Reserve) Battalion.
4.8.14 Guildford. Aug. 1914 to Chattenden on Thames-Medway Defences. Nov. 1914 Rochester. Feb. 1916 to Sittingbourne until the end of the war in Sittingbourne Special Reserve Brigade.

1/4th Battalion T.F.
4.8.14 Croydon: Surrey Bde. Home Counties Div. Aug. 1914 Maidstone. Sept. and Oct. Canterbury. 29.10.14 embarked at Southampton and sailed for India with Home Counties Div. 3.12.14 landed at Bombay and remained in India until the end of the war. Home Counties Div. broken up on arrival in India.

1/5th Battalion T.F.
4.8.14 Guildford. Surrey Bde. Home Counties Div. Aug. 1914 Maidstone. Sept. and Oct. Canterbury. 29.10.14 embarked at Southampton and sailed for India with Home Counties Div. 2.12.14 landed at Bombay and Home Counties Div. broken up. 7.12.15 arrived Basra in 34th Indian Bde. 11.1.16 to 12th Indian Bde. 12th Indian Div. May 1916 Bde. to 15th Indian Div. 31.10.18 12th Indian Bde. 15th Indian Div. Mesopotamia; near Hilla, south of Baghdad.

2/4th Battalion T.F.
Formed at Croydon in Aug. 1914. Nov. 1914 to Windsor in 2/Surrey Bde. 2/Home Counties Div. 24.4.15 to 160th Bde. 53rd Div. at Cambridge. (Joined 53rd Div. as a composite bn. with 2/5th Bn. but became 2/4th again after two months). 18.7.15 sailed from Devonport. 9.8.15 landed at Gallipoli. 13–19 Dec. 1915 to Egypt. 18–22 June 1918 Alexandria to Taranto. 29.6.18 to 101st Bde. 34th Div. at Proven. 11.11.18 101st Bde. 34th Div. Belgium; near Courtrai.

2/5th Battalion T.F.
Formed at Guildford in Sept. 1914. Nov. 1914 to Windsor in 2/Surrey Bde. 2/Home Counties Div. May 1915 about 400 men to 2/4th Bn. in 53rd Div. to form composite bn. About Nov. 1915 to Reigate. July 1916 to Westbere and in Nov. to Margate. April 1917 Westbere. Sept. 1917 all available men posted as drafts and remainder absorbed in 200th Bde. In Aug. 1915 2/Home Counties Div. became 67th Div.

3/4th Battalion T.F.
Formed at Windsor in June 1915 from balance of 2/4th Bn. which had joined 53rd Div. as composite bn. July 1915 to 200th Bde. 67th Div. at Tunbridge Wells. Oct. 1915 Reigate. July 1916 Westbere. Nov. 1916 Ramsgate. April 1917 Westbere. 1.6.17 landed at Havre, attached to 9th, 4th and 12th Divs. 9.8.17 to 62nd Bde. 21st Div. 11.2.18 disbanded at Moislains personnel to 1st, 6th, 7th and 8th Bns.

3/5th Battalion T.F.
Formed at Guildford 1.6.15. Sept. Windsor. Oct. Purfleet. End of 1915 Cambridge. 8.4.16 became 5th (Reserve) Bn. and to Crowborough. 1.9.16 absorbed in 4th (Reserve) Bn.

4/4th Battalion T.F.
Formed at Croydon July 1915. Sept. Windsor. Oct. Purfleet. Early 1916 Crowborough. 8.4.16 became 4th (Reserve) Bn. 1.9.16 absorbed 5th (Reserve) Bn. By Oct. 1916 at Tunbridge Wells where it remained in Home Counties Res. Bde. T.F.

6th (Service) Battalion.
Formed at Guildford Aug. 1914—K1—37th Bde. 12th Div. at Purfleet. Nov. Hythe. Feb. 1915 Aldershot. May 1915 landed at Boulogne. 11.11.18 37th Bde. 12th Div. France; Rumegies, east of Orchies.

7th (Service) Battalion.
Formed at Guildford Sept. 1914—K2—55th Bde. 18th Div. at Purfleet. April with brigade to Colchester. May 1915 to Salisbury Plain. 27.7.15 landed at Boulogne. 11.11.18 55th Bde. 18th Div. France; Pommereuil, east of Le Cateau.

8th (Service) Battalion.
Formed at Guildford Sept. 1914—K3—72nd Bde. 24th Div. at Shoreham. Dec. 1914 Worthing. April 1915 Shoreham. June 1915 to Aldershot (Blackdown). 31.8.15 landed at Boulogne. 7.2.18 to 17th Bde. 24th Div. 11.11.18 17th Bde. 24th Div. France; Bavai.

9th (Reserve) Battalion.
Formed at Gravesend Oct. 1914 as a service bn. of K4 in 93rd Bde. of original 31st Div. Mar. 1915 Wrotham. 10.4.15 became a 2nd Res. Bn. and Bde. became 5th Reserve Bde. May 1915 Colchester. Sept. 1915 Shoreham. 1.9.16 absorbed in Training Reserve Bns. of 5th Reserve Bde. at Shoreham.

10th (Service) Battalion (Battersea).
Raised on 3.6.15 by the Mayor and Borough of Battersea and joined 124th Bde. 41st Div. and by Feb. 1916 was in Stanhope Lines, Aldershot. 6.5.16 landed at Havre. Nov. 1917 to Italy. 5.3.18 back in France. 11.11.18 124th Bde. 41st Div. Belgium; Tenbosch, near Nederbrakel.

11th (Service) Battalion (Lambeth).
Raised on 16.6.15 by the Mayor and Borough of Lambeth. By Feb. 1916 at Aldershot (Wellington Lines) in 123rd Bde. 41st Div. 5.5.16 landed at Havre. Nov. 1917 to Italy. 6.3.18 back in France. 11.11.18 123rd Bde. 41st Div. Belgium; west of Nederbrakel.

12th (Reserve) Battalion.
Formed at Brixton in Oct. 1915 as a local reserve bn. from depot coys. of 10th and 11th Bns. To Northampton in 23rd Reserve Bde. May 1916 to Aldershot. 1.9.16 became 97th Training Reserve Bn. at Aldershot in 23rd Reserve Bde.

13th, 14th and 15th (Labour) Battalions.
Formed in July, Aug. and Sept. 1916 at Balmer (13) and Crawley (14 and 15). Went to France. 1.6.17 transferred to Labour Corps as 93rd and 94th, 95th and 96th and 97th and 98th Labour Coys.

16th (Home Service) Battalion.
Formed at Farnham 11.11.16 and to 213th Bde. 71st Div. Mar. 1917 with division to Colchester. Nov. 1917 to 214th Bde. 71st Div. 12.2.18 214th Bde. to 67th Div. and still at Colchester. By the end of Oct. 1918 had left 67th Div. and probably remained at Colchester.

17th and 18th (Labour) Battalions.
Formed at Crawley Nov. 1916. By Mar. 1917 at Purfleet. June 1917 transferred to Labour Corps becoming Eastern Command Labour Centre.

19th Battalion T.F.
On 1.1.17 the 69th Provisional Bn. at Lowestoft in 225th Bde. became the 19th Bn. The 69th Provisional Bn. was formed at Tunbridge Wells in June 1915 from Home Service personnel of T.F. Bns. It remained at Lowestoft in 225th Bde. until the end of the war.

A 20th Bn. was formed at Cromer on 1.6.18 and absorbed by the 21st Middlesex Regt. on 3.7.18.

51st (Graduated) Battalion.
On 27.10.17 the 245th Graduated Bn. (formerly 28th Training Reserve Bn. from 8th Northamptons) at Thoresby in 208th Bde. 69th Div. became the 51st Bn. Jan. 1918 at Sheffield. April 1918 left 69th Div. and (?) to 192nd Bde. 64th Div. at Norwich. By July 1918 in 204th Bde. 68th Div. at Bury St. Edmunds where it remained.

52nd (Graduated) Battalion.
On 27.10.17 the 255th Graduated Bn. (formerly 29th Training Reserve Bn. from 9th East Kent Regt.) at Colchester in 214th, then 213th, Bde. 71st Div. became the 52nd Bn. 18.2.18 to 192nd Bde. 64th Div. at Norwich. By Nov. 1918 at Cromer.

53rd (Young Soldier) Battalion.
On 27.10.17 the 25th Young Soldier Bn. (formerly 10th Royal Sussex) at St. Albans in 4th Reserve Bde. became the 53rd Bn. No further change.

THE BUFFS (EAST KENT REGIMENT)

1st Battalion.
4.8.14 Fermoy: 16th Bde. 6th Div. 19 Aug. Cambridge. 10.9.14 landed at St. Nazaire. 11.11.18 16th Bde. 6th Div. France; Bohain.

2nd Battalion.
4.8.14 Wellington, Madras. 16.11.14 sailed from Bombay. 23.12.14 landed at Plymouth and joined 85th Bde. 28th Div. at Winchester. 17.1.15 embarked for Havre at Southampton. 25–30 Oct. 1915 Marseilles to Alexandria. Nov. 1915 to Salonika. 30.9.18 85th Bde. 28th Div. Macedonia, north of Lake Doiran.

3rd (Reserve) Battalion.
4.8.14 Canterbury. 8 Aug. 1914 to Dover where it remained throughout the war. (Dover Garrison).

1/4th Battalion T.F.
4.8.14 Canterbury: Kent Bde. Home Counties Div. To Dover and then back to Canterbury with Kent Bde. 30.10.14 sailed from Southampton for India where the Home Counties Div. was broken up. 26.7.15 sailed for Aden. Feb. 1916 returned to India where it remained.

1/5th (The Weald of Kent) Battalion T.F.
4.8.14 Drill Hall, Ashford: Kent Bde. Home Counties Div. To Dover and then back to Canterbury with Kent Bde. Later to Sandwich. 30.10.14 sailed from Southampton for India, where the division was broken up. Dec. 1915 landed at Basra in 35th Indian Bde. which joined 7th Indian Div. Feb. 1916 35th Ind. Bde. became corps troops and the bn. formed a composite unit with two coys. 1/4 Hampshire until May. 12.5.16 35th Indian Bde. to 14th Indian Div. 31.10.18 35th Indian Bde. 14th Indian Div. Mesopotamia, Shahraban, N.E. of Baghdad.

2/4th Battalion T.F.
Formed at Canterbury in Sept. 1914. Nov. 1914 at Ascot in 202nd Bde. 67th Div. May 1915 to Ashford and remained here and other parts of Kent in 67th Div. until disbanded in Nov. 1917. (Note 1).

2/5th (The Weald of Kent) Battalion T.F.
Formed at Ashford in Sept. 1914. Subsequent record same as 2/4th Bn.

3/4th and 3/5th Battalions T.F.
Formed at Canterbury and Ashford in July and Mar. 1915. Dec. 1915 to Cambridge. 8.4.16 became Reserve Bns. 1.9.16 4th Bn. absorbed 5th Bn. which later in 1916 was at Tunbridge. By Nov. 1917 at Crowborough. Nov. 1918 Tunbridge Wells in Home Counties Res. Bde. T.F.

6th (Service) Battalion.
Formed at Canterbury Aug. 1914—K1—to Colchester and Purfleet in 37th Bde. 12th Div. Nov. 1914 to Shorncliffe. Feb. 1915 to Aldershot. June 1915 landed at Boulogne. 11.11.18 37th Bde. 12th Div. France; Rumegies, east of Orchies.

7th (Service) Battalion.
Formed at Canterbury Sept. 1914—K2—to Purfleet in 55th Bde. 18th Div. April Colchester. May 1915 to Salisbury Plain. July 1915 landed at Boulogne. 11.11.18 55th Bde. 18th Div. France; Pommereuil, east of Le Cateau.

8th (Service) Battalion.
Formed at Canterbury 12.9.14—K3—to Shoreham in 72nd Bde. 24th Div. Dec. 1914 to billets in Worthing. April 1915 returned to Shoreham. June 1915 to Blackdown, near Aldershot. 1.9.15 landed at Boulogne. 18.10.15 to 17th Bde. 24th Div. 13.2.18 disbanded at Hancourt; personnel to 1st and 6th Bns.

9th (Reserve) Battalion.
Formed at Dover in Oct. 1914 as a service bn. of K4 in 95th Bde. of original 32nd Div. 10.4.15 became a 2nd reserve bn. and Bde. became 7th Reserve Bde. May 1915 Purfleet. Sept. 1915 Shoreham. April 1916 Dover. 1.9.16 became 29th Training Reserve Bn. at Dover in 7th Reserve Bde.

10th (Royal East Kent & West Kent Yeomanry) Battalion T.F.
Formed at Sollum, Egypt on 1.2.17 from two dismounted Yeomanry regiments—East Kent and West Kent Yeomanry. In 230th Bde. 74th Div. May 1918 to France with 74th Div. landing at Marseilles on 7.5.18. 11.11.18 230th Bde. 74th Div. Belgium; Tournai.

1st (Home Service) Garrison Battalion.
Formed at Dover on 29.4.16 and in Aug. 1917 became 2nd Bn. Royal Defence Corps at Dover.

NOTE

1. In April 1915 the 202nd (2/Kent) Bde. 67th (2/Home Counties) Div. T.F. formed the Kent Composite Bn. Each battalion of the brigade (2/4th and 2/5th Buffs and 2/4th and 2/5th R. West Kent) contributed one company. This battalion joined the 160th Bde. 53rd Div. at Cambridge on 24.4.15 and on 14.6.15 it became the 2/4th R. West Kent.

THE KING'S OWN
(ROYAL LANCASTER REGIMENT)

1st Battalion.
4.8.14 Dover: 12th Bde. 4th Div. To Cromer then Neasden, Middlesex. 23.8.14 landed at Boulogne. 12th Bde. in 36th Div. from 4.11.15 to 3.2.16 11.11.18 12th Bde. 4th Div. France; Querenaing, S.W. of Valenciennes.

2nd Battalion.
4.8.14 Lebong, India. 19.11.14 sailed for U.K. 22.12.14 landed at Plymouth and joined 83rd Bde. 28th Div. at Winchester. 16.1.15 arrived at Havre. Oct. 1915 to Egypt. Early Dec. 1915 to Salonika. 30.9.18 83rd Bde. 28th Div. Macedonia; north of Lake Doiran.

3rd (Reserve) Battalion.
4.8.14 Lancaster. Aug. to Saltash for a few days then to Sunderland[1] and in 1915 to Plymouth again until 1917. By Nov. 1917 at Harwich where it remained. (Harwich Garrison).

1/4th Battalion T.F.
4.8.14 Ulverston: North Lancs. Bde. West Lancs. Div.

[1] But part of the battalion may have remained at Saltash.

14.8.14 to Slough on railway guard duty. Nov. 1914 to Sevenoaks. April 1915 N. Lancs. Bde. to 51st Div. at Bedford and became 154th Bde. May 1915 landed at Boulogne. 6.1.16 to 164th Bde. 55th Div. in Hallencourt area. 11.11.18 164th Bde. 55th Div. Belgium; near Ath.

1/5th Battalion T.F.
4.8.14 Lancaster: North Lancs. Bde. West Lancs. Div. 14.8.14 to Didcot on railway guard duties. Nov. 1914 to Sevenoaks. 15.2.15 landed at Havre. 3.3.15 to 83rd Bde. 28th Div. 21.10.15 to 2nd Bde. 1st Div. 7.1.16 to 166th Bde. 55th Div. in Hallencourt area. 11.11.18 166th Bde. 55th Div. Belgium; near Ath.

2/4th Battalion T.F.
Formed at Blackpool Feb. 1915. 18.1.16 amalgamated with 3/4th Bn. 8.4.16 became 4th (Reserve) Bn. at Oswestry. 1.9.16 absorbed 5th (Reserve) Bn. and at Oswestry until 1918. By June 1918 at Dublin where it remained.

2/5th Battalion T.F.
Formed at Lancaster Sept. 1914. Nov. 1914 to Blackpool. Feb. 1915 to North Lancs. Bde. 55th Div. at Sevenoaks. April 1915 to 170th (2/N. Lancs.) Bde. 57th Div. July 1916 to Aldershot. Feb. 1917 landed in France. 11.11.18 170th Bde. 57th Div. France; Lezennes, east of Lille.

3/4th Battalion T.F.
Formed June 1915 and amalgamated with 2/4th 18.1.16.

3/5th Battalion T.F.
Formed June 1915. 8.4.16 became 5th (Reserve) Bn. at Oswestry 1.9.16 absorbed by 4th (Reserve) Bn.

6th (Service) Battalion.
Formed at Lancaster Aug. 1914—K1—to Tidworth in 38th Bde. 13th Div. Feb. 1915 to Aldershot. July 1915 Gallipoli. Jan. 1916 to Egypt. Feb. 1916 to Mesopotamia. 31.10.18 38th Bde. 13th Div. Mesopotamia; near Delli Abbas, N.E. of Baghdad.

7th (Service) Battalion.
Formed at Lancaster Sept. 1914—K2—to Tidworth Pennings in 56th Bde. 19th Div. Dec. 1914 to billets in Andover. Feb. 1915 Clevedon. Mar. 1915 Tidworth. July 1915 landed in France. 22.2.18 disbanded in France; personnel to 1/4th and 1/5th Bns. and 6th Entrenching Bn.

8th (Service) Battalion.
Formed at Lancaster Oct. 1914—K3—to Codford in 76th Bde. 25th Div. Nov. 1914 to Boscombe in billets. May 1915 Odiham, Aldershot. 27.9.15 landed in France. 15.10.15 with 76th Bde. to 3rd Div. 11.11.18 76th Bde. 3rd Div. France; near Solesmes.

9th (Service) Battalion.
Formed at Lancaster Oct. 1914—K3—to Eastbourne in 65th Bde. 22nd Div. Nov. 1914 to Seaford and in Dec. to billets in Eastbourne. April 1915 Seaford. June 1915 to Aldershot. Sept. 1915 landed in France. Oct. 1915 to Salonika landing on 7 Nov. 30.9.18 Macedonia; north of Lake Doiran.

10th (Reserve) Battalion.
Formed at Saltash Oct. 1914 as a service bn. of K4 in 99th Bde. of original 33rd Div. Dec. 1914 Kingsbridge. 10.4.15 became a 2nd reserve bn. May 1915 Swanage. Aug. 1915 Wareham in 10th Reserve Bde. 1.9.16 became 43rd Training Reserve Bn. at Wareham in 10th Reserve Bde.

11th (Service) Battalion.
Formed at Lancaster Aug. 1915 as a bantam bn. and to Aldershot in 120th Bde. 40th Div. in Blackdown area. 2.3.16 absorbed 12th South Lancs. Regt. 3.6.16 landed in France. 7.2.18 disbanded in France; personnel to 6th Entrenching Bn.

12th (Reserve) Battalion.
Formed at Lancaster Jan. 1916 as a 2nd reserve bn. April 1916 to Prees Heath in 17th Reserve Bde. 1.9.16 became 76th Training Reserve Bn. at Prees Heath in 17th Reserve Bde.

12th Battalion T.F.
On 1.1.17 the 41st Provisional Bn. at Westgate (formerly in 9th Provisional Bde.) became the 12th Bn. The previous 12th Bn.—see above—had become a T.R. unit. The 41st Provisional Bn. had been formed in 1915 from Home Service personnel of T.F. Bns. Jan. 1917 to 218th Bde. 73rd Div. at Coggeshall. Summer 1917 at Witham and back at Coggeshall in the winter. The 73rd Div. was broken up in Mar. 1918 and the Bn. was disbanded on 29.3.18.

THE NORTHUMBERLAND FUSILIERS

1st Battalion.
4.8.14 Portsmouth: 9th Bde. 3rd Div. 14.8.14 landed at Havre. 11.11.18 9th Bde. 3rd Div. France; La Longueville, east of Bavai.

2nd Battalion.
4.8.14 Sabathu, India. 20.11.14 sailed from Karachi. 22.12.14 landed at Plymouth, to Winchester in 84th Bde. 28th Div. 18.1.15 landed at Havre. 24.10.15 sailed from Marseilles. 29.10.15 Alexandria to 21 Nov. 24.11.5 landed at Salonika. June 1918 left 28th Div. for France. Itea to Taranto 26–27 June. 16.7.18 to 150th Bde. 50th Div. at Martin Eglise. 11.11.18 150th Bde. 50th Div. France; Dourlers, north of Avesnes.

3rd (Reserve) Battalion.
4.8.14 Newcastle-on-Tyne. Aug. 1914 to East Boldon, near Sunderland where it remained (Tyne Garrison).

1/4th Battalion T.F.
4.8.14 Hexham: Northumberland Bde. Northumbrian Div. On Tyne Defences till April 1915 and then to France. 14.5.15 formation became 149th Bde. 50th Div. 15.7.18 reduced to cadre and to Dieppe area (L. of C.). 16.8.18 to 118th Bde. 39th Div. at Havre. 10.11.18 disbanded.

1/5th Battalion T.F.
4.8.14 Walker, Newcastle-on-Tyne: Northumberland Bde. Northumbrian Div. Subsequent record same as 1/4th Bn.

1/6th Battalion T.F.
4.8.14 St. George's Drill Hall, Northumberland Road, Newcastle-on-Tyne: Northumberland Bde. Northumbrian Div. Subsequent record same as 1/4th Bn.

1/7th Battalion T.F.
4.8.14 Alnwick: Northumberland Bde. Northumbrian Div. On Tyne Defences till April 1915 and then to France. 14.5.15 formation became 149th Bde. 50th Div. 12.2.18 to 42nd Div. as Pioneer Bn. 11.11.18 Pioneer Bn. 42nd Div. France; near Hautmont.

2/4th, 2/5th and 2/6th Battalions T.F.
2/4th and 2/5th formed at Blythe Nov. 1914. 2/6th at Newcastle 28.12.14. Jan. 1915 all to 188th Bde. 63rd Div. at Swalwell Camp, near Newcastle. Nov. Bde. to York. July 1916 63rd Div. broken up, brigade remained at York. Nov. 1916 to 217th Bde. 72nd Div. at Clevedon. Jan. 1917 to Northampton. May 1917 to Ipswich. 2/5th and 2/6th disbanded in Dec. 1917 and 2/4th in May 1918.

2/7th Battalion T.F.
Formed at Alnwick 26.9.14. Jan. 1915 to 188th Bde. 63rd Div. at Swalwell Camp near Newcastle. Nov. 1915 bde. to York. Jan. 1917 to Egypt as a garrison bn.

3/4th, 3/5th, 3/6th and 3/7th Battalions T.F.
Formed in June 1915 at Hexham (4), Newcastle (5, 6) and Alnwick (7). 8.4.16 at Catterick became Reserve Bns. 1.9.16 at Redcar 5th, 6th and 7th Bns. absorbed by 4th Bn. End 1916 Catterick. After Mar. 1917 to Atwick, Hornsea. Early 1918 South Dalton and by June 1918 Rowlston, Hornsea where it remained. In Northumbrian Res. Inf. Bde. T.F.

8th (Service) Battalion.
Formed at Newcastle Aug. 1914—K1—to Grantham in 34th Bde. 11th Div. April 1915 to Witley. July 1915 to Mediterranean. 7.8.15 landed at Gallipoli. Jan. 1916 to Egypt. July 1916 to France. 11.11.18 34th Bde. 11th Div. France; Grosse Naie, S.W. of Aulnois.

9th (Service) Battalion.
Formed at Newcastle Sept. 1914—K2—to Wareham area in 52nd Bde. 17th Div. Dec. 1914 Wimborne. Mar. 1915 Wool. June 1915 Hursley. July 1915 to France. 3.8.17 to 104th Bde. 34th Div. 25.9.17 absorbed 2/1st Northumberland Yeomanry and became 9th (Northumberland Hussars Yeomanry) Bn. 26.5.18 to 183rd Bde. 61st Div. 11.11.18 183rd Bde. 61st Div. France; south of Valenciennes, at Bermerain.

10th (Service) Battalion.
Formed at Newcastle Sept. 1914—K3—to Bullswater, near Frensham in 68th Bde. 23rd Div. Dec. 1914 to North Camp, Aldershot. Feb. 1915 to Ashford, Kent. May 1915 to Bramshott. Aug. 1915 to France. Nov. 1917 to Italy. 4.11.18 68th Bde. 23rd Div. Italy; Porcia.

11th (Service) Battalion.
Formed at Newcastle Sept. 1914—K3—subsequent record same as 10th Bn.

12th (Service) Battalion.
Formed at Newcastle Sept. 1914—K3—to Halton Park in 62nd Bde. 21st Div. Nov. 1914 to billets in Aylesbury area. May 1915 Halton Park. Aug. 1915 Witley. Sept. 1915 to France. 10.8.17 amalgamated with 13th Bn. to form 12/13th Bn. 11.11.18 62nd Bde. 21st Div. France; near Berlaimont.

13th (Service) Battalion.
Formed at Newcastle Sept. 1914—K3—subsequent record same as 12th Bn.

14th (Service) Battalion (Pioneers).
Formed at Newcastle Sept. 1914—K3—Army Troops, 21st Div. at Halton Park and Aylesbury area. Jan. 1915 became Pioneer Bn. 21st Div. Aug. 1915 Witley. Sept. 1915 to France. 11.11.18 Pioneer Bn. 21st Div. France; near Berlaimont.

15th (Reserve) Battalion.
Formed at Darlington in Oct. 1914 as a serivce bn. of K4 in 89th Bde. of original 30th Div. 10.4.15 became a 2nd reserve bn. and Bde. became 1st Reserve Bde. Nov. 1915 to Rugeley, Cannock Chase. 1.9.16 absorbed in Training Res. Bns. of 1st Reserve Bde. at Rugeley.

16th (Service) Battalion (Newcastle).
Raised at Newcastle Sept. 1914 by the Newcastle & Gateshead Chamber of Commerce. Nov. 1914 Alnwick then Cramlington. June 1915 to 96th Bde. 32nd Div. at Catterick. 21.8.15 to Codford St. Mary. 22.11.15 landed at Boulogne. 7.2.18 disbanded at Elverdinghe: personnel to T.F. Bns. in 50th Div.

17th (Service) Battalion (N.E.R., Pioneers).
Raised by North Eastern Railway at Hull in Sept. 1914 11.1.15 became a Pioneer Bn. At Hull till June 1915 then to 32nd Div. as Pioneer Bn. at Catterick. 21.8.15 to Codford St. Mary. 1.9.15 taken over by the War Office. 21.11.15 landed at Havre. 19.10.16 to G.H.Q. Railway Construction Troops. 2.9.17 rejoined 32nd Div. at Ghyvelde. 15.11.17 to G.H.Q. Railway Construction again. 31.5.18 to 52nd Div. as Pioneer Bn. 11.11.18 Pioneer Bn. 52nd Div. Belgium; Sirault, N.W. of Mons.

18th (Service) Battalion. (1st Tyneside Pioneers).
Raised at Newcastle by the Lord Mayor and City 14.10.14. 21.12.14 to Rothbury. 8.2.15 became a Pioneer Bn. April 1915 to Cramlington. July 1915 to Kirkby Malzeard as Pioneer Bn. 34th Div. 30.8.15 Windmill Hill, Salisbury Plain. End Sept. 1915 to Sutton Veny. 8.1.16 landed at Havre. 18.5.18 reduced to cadre. 17.6.18 to 116th Bde. 39th Div. 29.7.18 118th Bde. 16.8.18 to 66th Div. 20.9.18 with 197th Bde. to L. of C. 11.11.18 197th Bde. France; Haudricourt, south of Aumale. (Taken over by War Office 15.8.15).

19th (Service) Battalion. (2nd Tyneside Pioneers).
Raised at Newcastle by the Lord Mayor and City 16.11.14. 13.1.15 to Morpeth. 4.5.15 Cramlington. 8.2.15 became a Pioneer Bn. 16.6.15 to Masham as Pioneer Bn. 35th Div. Aug. 1915 taken over by the War Office and to Perham Down. 29.1.16 landed at Havre. 11.11.18 Pioneer Bn. 35th Div. Belgium; Waermaerde, east of Courtrai.

20th (Service) Battalion. (1st Tyneside Scottish).
Raised at Newcastle by the Lord Mayor and City 14.10.14. Mar. 1915 Alnwick. June 1915 102nd Bde. 34th Div. End Aug. 1915 to Salisbury Plain. 15.8.15 taken over by the War Office. Jan. 1916 to France. 3.2.18 disbanded in France.

21st (Service) Battalion. (2nd Tyneside Scottish).
Raised at Newcastle by the Lord Mayor and City 26.9.14. Subsequent record same as 20th Bn.

22nd (Service) Battalion. (3rd Tyneside Scottish).
Raised at Newcastle by the Lord Mayor and City 5.11.14. Mar. 1915 Alnwick. June 1915 102nd Bde. 34th Div. End Aug. 1915 to Salisbury Plain. 15.8.15 taken over by the War Office. Jan. 1916 to France. 17.5.18 reduced to cadre. 18.6.18 to England with 16th Div. 18.6.18 absorbed new 38th Bn. at Margate and rejoined 16th Div. at Aldershot in 48th Bde. July 1918 to France. 11.11.18 48th Bde. 16th Div. Belgium; south of Tournai.

23rd (Service) Battalion. (4th Tyneside Scottish).
Raised at Newcastle by the Lord Mayor and City 16.11.14. Mar. 1915 Alnwick. June 1915 102nd Bde. 34th Div. End Aug. 1915 to Salisbury Plain. 15.8.15 taken over by the War Office. Jan. 1916 to France. 17.5.18 reduced to cadre. 17.6.18 to 116th Bde. 39th Div. 16.8.18 to 66th Div. 20.9.18 with 197th Bde. to L. of C. 11.11.18 197th Bde. France; near Aumale.

24th (Service) Battalion. (1st Tyneside Irish).
Raised at Newcastle by the Lord Mayor and City 14.11.14. Mar. 1915 Woolsington. June 1915 103rd Bde. 34th Div. 27.8.15 taken over by War Office. End Aug. 1915 to Salisbury Plain. Jan. 1916 to France. 10.8.17 amalgamated with 27th Bn. to form 24/27th. 26.2.18 disbanded in France.

25th (Service) Battalion. (2nd Tyneside Irish).
Raised at Newcastle by the Lord Mayor and City 9.11.14. Mar. 1915 Woolsington. June 1915 103rd Bde. 34th Div. 27.8.15 taken over by the War Office. End Aug. 1915 to Salisbury Plain. Jan. 1916 to France. 3.2.18 to 102nd Bde. 34th Div. 16.5.18 reduced to cadre. Subsequent record same as 23rd Bn.

26th (Service) Battalion. (3rd Tyneside Irish).
Raised at Newcastle by the Lord Mayor and City Nov. 1914. Mar. 1915 Woolsington Park. June 1915 to 103rd Bde. 34th Div. 27.8.15 taken over by the War Office. Subsequent record same as 20th Bn.

27th (Service) Battalion. (4th Tyneside Irish).
Raised at Newcastle by the Lord Mayor and City Jan. 1915. Mar. 1915 to Woolsington Park. Subsequent record same as 24th Bn.

28th (Reserve) Battalion.
Formed at Cramlington in July 1915 from depot coys. of 18th and 19th Bns. as a local reserve bn. Nov. 1915 Ripon in 19th Reserve Bde. Dec. 1915 Harrogate. 1.9.16 absorbed in Training Reserve Bns. of 19th Reserve Bde.

29th (Reserve) Battalion. (Tyneside Scottish).
Formed at Alnwick in July 1915 from depot coys. of 20th to 23rd Bns. as a local reserve bn. Jan. 1916 Barnard's Castle in 20th Reserve Bde. April 1916 Hornsea 1.9.16 became 84th Training Reserve Bn. at Hornsea in 20th Reserve Bde.

30th (Reserve) Battalion. (Tyneside Irish).
Formed at Woolsington in July 1915 from depot coys. of 24th to 27th Bns. as a local reserve bn. Nov. 1915 Richmond, Yorks. in 29th Reserve Bde. Dec. 1915 Catterick. April 1916 Hornsea. 1.9.16 became 85th Training Reserve Bn. at Hornsea in 20th Reserve Bde.

31st (Reserve) Battalion.
Formed at Catterick Nov. 1915 from depot coys. of 16th Bn. as a local reserve bn. in 20th Reserve Bde. April 1916 to Hornsea. 1.9.16 became 86th Training Reserve Bn. at Hornsea in 20th Reserve Bde.

32nd (Reserve) Battalion.
Formed at Ripon Nov. 1915 from depot coys. of 17th Bn. as a local reserve bn. in 19th Reserve Bde. Dec. 1915 Harrogate. June 1916 Usworth, Washington. 1.9.16 became 80th Training Reserve Bn. in 19th Reserve Bde. at Newcastle.

33rd (Reserve) Battalion. (Tyneside Scottish).
Formed at Hornsea June 1916 from the 29th (R) Bn. as a local reserve bn. 1.9.16 absorbed in Training Reserve Bns. of 20th Reserve Bde. at Hornsea.

34th (Reserve) Battalion. (Tyneside Irish).
Formed at Hornsea June 1916 from the 30th (R) Bn. as a local reserve bn. 1.9.16 absorbed in Training Reserve Bns. of 20th Reserve Bde. at Hornsea.

35th Battalion T.F.
On 1.1.17 the 21st Provisional Bn. at Herne Bay in 227th Bde. became the 35th Bn. The Bn. had been formed about June 1915 from Home Service personnel of T.F. Bns. Remained at Herne Bay until early in 1918 and then to Westleton where it remained.

36th Battalion T.F.
On 1.1.17 the 22nd Provisional Bn. at St. Osyth in 222nd Bde. became the 36th Bn. The Bn. had been formed about June 1915 from Home Service personnel of T.F. Bns. After Mar. 1917 to Ramsgate and by April 1918 at Margate. 27.4.18 became a Garrison Guard Bn. and went to France in May 1918 joining 178th Bde. 59th Div. The title 'Garrison Guard' was dropped by July 1918. 11.11.18 178th Bde. 59th Div. Belgium; N.E. of Tournai.

37th (Home Service) Battalion.
Formed at Margate on 27.4.18 and replaced 36th Bn. in 222nd Bde. Remained at Margate.

A 38th Bn. was formed at Margate on 1.6.18 and absorbed by the 22nd Bn. on 18.6.18.

1st Garrison Battalion.
Formed in Aug. 1915 and went to Malta.

2nd Garrison Battalion.
Formed at Newcastle in Oct. 1915 and went to India in Feb. 1916.

3rd (Home Service) Garrison Battalion.
Formed at Sunderland about Mar. 1916 and was in Ireland in 1917 and 1918 at Belfast.

51st (Graduated) Battalion.
On 27.10.17 the 238th Graduated Bn. (formerly the new 4th Training Reserve Bn.) at Welbeck in 206th Bde. 69th Div. became the 51st Bn. Early in 1918 to Middlesbrough and later to Guisborough where it remained.

52nd (Graduated) Battalion.
On 27.10.17 the 276th Graduated Bn. (formerly 3rd Training Reserve Bn. from 10th North Stafford) at Canterbury in 200th Bde. 67th Div. became the 52nd Bn. 5.3.18 to 206th Bde. 69th Div. at Barnards Castle and by June 1918 at Guisborough where it remained.

53rd (Young Soldier) Battalion.
On 27.10.17 the 5th Young Soldier Bn. (formerly 10th Leicesters) at Rugeley, Cannock Chase in 1st Reserve Bde. became 53rd Bn. About Oct. 1918 to Clipstone.

NOTE
Woolsington Hall, where the Tyneside Irish Bns. were stationed in the spring of 1915, is north-west of Newcastle-on-Tyne.

THE ROYAL WARWICKSHIRE REGIMENT

1st Battalion.
4.8.14 Shorncliffe: 10th Bde. 4th Div. 22.8.14 landed in France. 11.11.18 10th Bde. 4th Div. France; S.E. of Valenciennes.

2nd Battalion.
4.8.14 Malta. 19.9.14 landed in England and joined 22nd Bde. 7th Div. at Lyndhurst. 6.10.14 landed at Zeebrugge. 24.11.17 arrived in Italy. 4.11.18 22nd Bde. 7th Div. Italy; west of Udine.

3rd (Reserve) Battalion.
4.8.14 Warwick. Aug. 1914 Portsmouth then Isle of Wight. By Nov. 1917 at Dover where it remained (Dover Garrison).

4th (Extra Reserve) Battalion
4.8.14 Warwick. Record same as 3rd Bn.

1/5th Battalion T.F.
4.8.14 Thorp Street, Birmingham: Warwickshire Bde. South Midland Div. Aug. to Chelmsford area. 22.3.15 landed at Havre. 13.5.15 formation became 143rd Bde. 48th Div. Nov. 1917 to Italy. 4.11.18 143rd Bde. 48th Div. Austria; N.E. of Trent.

1/6th Battalion T.F.
4.8.14 Thorp Street, Birmingham: Warwickshire Bde. South Midland Div. Subsequent record same as 1/5th Bn.

1/7th Battalion T.F.
4.8.14 Coventry: Warwickshire Bde. South Midland Div. Subsequent record same as 1/5th Bn.

1/8th Battalion T.F.
4.8.14 Aston Manor, Birmingham: Warwickshire Bde. South Midland Div. Aug. to Chelmsford area. 22.3.15 landed at Havre. 13.5.15 formation became 143rd Bde. 48th Div. Nov. 1917 to Italy. 11.9.18 left 48th Div. for France and joined 75th Bde. 25th Div. in St. Riquier area on 19.9.18. 11.11.18 75th Bde. 25th Div. France; near Landrecies.

2/5th Battalion T.F.
Formed in Birmingham Oct. 1914. Feb. 1915 to 2/1st Warwickshire Bde. 2/1st South Midland Div. in Northampton area. Mar. 1915 with division to Chelmsford area. Aug. 1915 formation became 182nd Bde. 61st Div. Mar. 1916 with division to Salisbury Plain. 21.5.16 landed in France. 20.2.18 disbanded, personnel to 2/6th Bn. and 24th Entrenching Bn.

2/6th Battalion T.F.
Formed in Birmingham Oct. 1914. Subsequent record same as 2/5th Bn. but served until the end of the war. 11.11.18 182nd Bde. 61st Div. France; south of Valenciennes.

2/7th Battalion T.F.
Formed at Coventry Oct. 1914. Subsequent record same as 2/6th Bn.

2/8th Battalion T.F.
Formed at Birmingham Oct. 1914. Subsequent record same as 2/5th Bn. but on disbandment personnel to 2/7th Bn. and 25th Entrenching Bn.

3/5th and 3/6th Battalions T.F.
Formed at Birmingham May 1915. To Weston-super-Mare. 8.4.16 became 5th and 6th (Reserve) Bns. To Ludgershall. 1.9.16 5th (Res.) absorbed 6th (Res.) Bn. in South Midland Res. Bde. T.F. at Ludgershall. Winter 1916–17 at Cheltenham. By Mar. 1917 at Catterick. Summer 1917 to Northumberland where it remained in the Blyth area until the end of the war (Tyne Garrison).

3/7th and 3/8th Battalions T.F.
Formed at Coventry and Birmingham May 1915. To Weston-super-Mare. 8.4.16 became 7th and 8th (Reserve) Bns. To Ludgershall. 1.9.16 7th (Res.) Bn. absorbed 8th (Res.) Bn. in South Midland Reserve Bde. T.F. at Ludgershall. Subsequent record same as 5th Bn.

9th (Service) Battalion.
Formed at Warwick Aug. 1914—K1—on Salisbury Plain in 39th Bde. 13th Div. Jan. 1915 Basingstoke. Feb. 1915 13th Div. at Blackdown, Aldershot. 24.6.15 sailed from Avonmouth. July 1915 landed at Gallipoli. Jan. 1916 to Mudros and then to Egypt. 16.2.16 embarked at Suez. 28.2.16 landed at Basra. July 1918 with 39th Bde. to North Persia Force. 31.10.18 39th Bde. Transcaspia; Krasnovodsk.

10th (Service) Battalion.
Formed at Warwick Sept. 1914—K2—on Salisbury Plain in 57th Bde. 19th Div. Dec. 1914 billets for the winter. Mar. 1915 19th Div. concentrated around Tidworth. 17.7.15 landed in France. 11.11.18 57th Bde. 19th Div. France; west of Bavai.

11th (Service) Battalion.
Formed at Warwick Oct. 1914—K3—Army Troops attached 24th Div. on South Downs. April 1915 joined 112th Bde. 37th Div. on Salisbury Plain. 30.7.15 landed in France. 7.2.18 disbanded in France; Wardrecques area.

12th (Reserve) Battalion.
Formed at Parkhurst, Isle of Wight as a service bn. of K4 in 97th Bde. of original 32nd Div. Jan. 1915 Newport. 10.4.15 became a 2nd reserve bn. May 1915 Wool 8th Reserve Bde. 1.9.16 absorbed in Training Reserve Bns. of 8th Reserve Bde. at Wool.

13th (Reserve) Battalion.
Formed at Golden Hill, Isle of Wight as a service bn. of K4 in 97th Bde. of original 32nd Div. Feb. 1915 Totland Bay. 10.4.15 became a 2nd reserve bn. May 1915 Swanage, in 8th Reserve Bde. Oct. 1915 Blandford. 1.9.16 became 33rd Training Reserve Bn. in 8th Reserve Bde. at Wool.

14th (Service) Battalion. (1st Birmingham).
Raised at Birmingham by the Lord Mayor and a local committee in Sept. 1914. 5.10.14 to Sutton Coldfield. 25.6.15 to Wensley Dale and 95th Bde. 32nd Div. 5.8.15 to Codford, Salisbury Plain. 21.11.15 landed at Boulogne. 28.12.15 to 13th Bde. 5th Div. 29 Nov–6 Dec. 1917 to Italy. 1–6 April 1918 returned to France. 5.10.18 became Pioneer Bn. 5th Div. 11.11.18 Pioneer Bn. 5th Div. France; Pont-sur-Sambre.

15th (Service) Battalion. (2nd Birmingham).
Raised at Birmingham by the Lord Mayor and a local committee in Sept. 1914. 5.10.14 to Sutton Coldfield. June 1915 to Wensley Dale and 95th Bde. 32nd Div. Aug. 1915 to Codford, Salisbury Plain. 21.11.15 landed at Boulogne. 26.12.15 to 14th Bde. 5th Div. 14.1.16 to 13th Bde. 5th Div. 10–16 Dec. 1917 to Italy. 1–6 April 1918 returned to France. 6.10.18 disbanded near Ytres: personnel to 14th and 16th Bns.

16th (Service) Battalion. (3rd Birmingham).
Raised at Birmingham by the Lord Mayor and a local committee in Sept. 1914. At Moseley, Birmingham. Mar. 1915 to Malvern. June 1915 to Wensley Dale and 95th Bde. 32nd Div. Aug. 1915 to Codford, Salisbury Plain. 21.11.15 landed in France 26.12.15 to 15th Bde. 5th Div. 13.12.17 to Italy. 8.4.18 returned to France. 4.10.18 to 13th Bde. 5th Div. 11.11.18 13th Bde. 5th Div. France; near Le Quesnoy.

17th (Reserve) Battalion.
Formed at Sutton Coldfield in June 1915 from depot coys. of 14th, 15th and 16th Bns. Nov. 1915 to Chisledon in 22nd Reserve Bde. 1.9.16 became 92nd Training Reserve Bn. at Chisledon in 22nd Reserve Bde.

18th Battalion T.F.
On 1.1.17 the 81st Provisional Bn. at Bath in 215th Bde. 72nd Div. became the 18th Bn. The Bn. had been formed in April 1915 from Home Service personnel of T.F. Bns. Jan. 1917 to Bedford. May 1917 to Ipswich. 19.1.18 disbanded.

1st Garrison Battalion.
Formed at Weymouth in Aug. 1915. Aug. 1915 to Egypt where it remained.

51st (Graduated) Battalion.
On 27.10.17 the 262nd Graduated Bn. (formerly 93rd Training Reserve Bn. from 15th Gloucesters) at Ipswich in 216th Bde. 72nd Div. became the 51st Bn. In Jan. 1918 the 72nd Div. was broken up and the Bn. went to 205th Bde. 68th Div. at Lowestoft. By June 1918 at Henham Park, near Southwold, where it remained.

52nd (Graduated) Battalion.
On 27.10.17 the 274th Graduated Bn. (formerly 94th Training Reserve Bn. from 16th Gloucesters) at Chelmsford in 220th Bde. 73rd Div. became the 52nd Bn. In Mar. 1918 the 73rd Div. was broken up and the Bn. went to 205th 68th Div. at Lowestoft. By June 1918 at Henham Park where it remained.

53rd (Young Soldier) Battalion.
On 27.10.17 the 95th Young Soldier Bn. (formerly 11th D.C.L.I.) at Chisledon in 22nd Reserve Bde. became the 53rd Bn. The 22nd Reserve Bde. ceased to exist on 31.10.17 and the Bn. soon went to Larkhill in 8th Reserve Bde. where it remained.

THE ROYAL FUSILIERS
(CITY OF LONDON REGIMENT)

1st Battalion.
4.8.14 Kinsale: 17th Bde. 6th Div. Aug. 1914 Cambridge. Sept. 1914 landed at St. Nazaire. 14.10.15 17th Bde. to 24th Div. 11.11.18 17th Bde. 24th Div. France; Bavai.

2nd Battalion.
4.8.14 Calcutta. Jan. 1915 landed in England and to Stockingford, near Nuneaton joining 86th Bde. 29th Div. Mar. 1915 embarked at Avonmouth. 28.3.15 Alexandria. 11.4.15. Lemnos. 25.4.15 landed at Gallipoli. 8.1.16 Egypt. Mar. 1916 landed at Marseilles. 11.11.18 86th Bde. 29th Div. Belgium; St. Genois, S.E. of Courtrai.

3rd Battalion.
4.8.14 Lucknow. Dec. 1914 arrived England and to 85th Bde. 28th Div. near Winchester. Jan. 1915 landed at Havre. Oct. 1915 to Egypt. Dec. 1915 Salonika. 3/4 July 1918 Greece to Taranto. 9.7.18 arrived France. 15.7.18 to 149th Bde. 50th Div. at Martin Eglise. 11.11.18 149th Bde. 50th Div. France; Dourlers, north of Avesnes.

4th Battalion.
4.8.14 Parkhurst, Isle of Wight: 9th Bde. 3rd Div. 13.8.14 landed at Havre. 11.11.18 9th Bde. 3rd Div. France; near Bavai.

5th and 6th (Reserve) Battalions.
4.8.14 Hounslow. Aug. 1914 to Dover where 5th Bn. remained (Dover Garrison). 6th to Carrickfergus end of 1917.

7th (Extra Reserve) Battalion.
4.8.14 Artillery Place, Finsbury. To Falmouth. 24.7.16 landed at Havre. 27.7.16 to 190th Bde. 63rd Div. 11.11.18 190th Bde. 63rd Div. Belgium; Harveng, south of Mons.

8th (Service) Battalion.
Formed at Hounslow 21.8.14—K1—to 36th Bde. 12th Div. at Colchester. Nov. 1914 Hythe. Feb. 1915 Aldershot. May 1915 to France. 6.2.18 disbanded in France.

9th (Service) Battalion.
Formed at Hounslow 21.8.14—K1—subsequent record same as 8th Bn. till Feb. 1918. 11.11.18 36th Bde. 12th Div. France; east of Orchies.

10th (Service) Battalion.
Raised by the Lord Mayor and City of London 21.8.14—K2—although a locally raised unit it was in K2 and for a time had an unofficial second title 'Stockbrokers'. It was recruited from business staffs in the City. Sept. 1914 to 54th Bde. 18th Div. Oct. 1914 Army Troops. 18th Div. Mar. 1915 to 111th Bde. 37th Div. on Salisbury Plain. 30.7.15 landed at Boulogne. 11.11.18 111th Bde. 37th Div. France; south of Le Quesnoy.

11th (Service) Battalion.
Formed at Hounslow 6.9.14—K2—to Colchester in 54th Bde. 18th Div. May 1915 Salisbury Plain. July 1915 to France. 11.11.18 54th Bde. 18th Div. France; near Le Cateau.

12th (Service) Battalion.
Formed at Hounslow 13.9.14—K3—to South Downs in 73rd Bde. 24th Div. Nov. 1914 to April 1915 in billets at Shoreham and Brighton. June 1915 Pirbright. 1.9.15 landed in France. 18.10.15 to 17th Bde. 24th Div. 13.2.18 disbanded in France; personnel to 1st, 10th and 11th Bns.

13th (Service) Battalion.
Formed at Hounslow 13.9.14—K3—to South Downs, Army Troops, attd. 24th Div. Dec. 1914 to billets in Worthing. Mar. 1915 to 111th Bde. 37th Div. at Ludgershall. 30.7.15 landed at Boulogne. 4.2.18 to 112th Bde. 37th Div. 11.11.18 112th Bde. 37th Div. France; south of Le Quesnoy.

14th and 15th (Reserve) Battalions.
Formed at Dover in Oct. 1914 as service bns. of K4 in 95th Bde. of original 32nd Div. 10.4.15 became 2nd reserve bns. and Bde. became 7th Reserve Bde. May 1915 Purfleet. Sept. 1915 Shoreham. Mar. 1916 Dover. 1.9.16 became 31st and 32nd Training Reserve Bns. at Dover in 7th Reserve Bde.

16th (Reserve) Battalion.
Formed at Falmouth in Oct. 1914 as a service bn. of K4 in 103rd Bde. of original 34th Div. 10.4.15 became a 2nd res. bn. May 1915 Purfleet. Sept. 1915 Shoreham in 5th Reserve Bde. 1.9.16 became 22nd Training Reserve Bn. (absorbing 9th R. West Kent) at Shoreham in 5th Reserve Bde.

17th (Service) Battalion. (Empire).
Raised in London by the British Empire Committee on 31.8.14. 12.9.14 to Warlingham, Surrey. June 1915 to Clipstone Camp, Notts. to 99th Bde. 33rd Div. 1.7.15 taken over by the War Office. Aug. 1915 to Tidworth. 17.11.15 landed at Boulogne. 25.11.15 with 99th Bde. to 2nd Div. 13.12.15 to 5th Bde. 2nd Div. 6.2.18 to 6th Bde. 2nd Div. 11.11.18 6th Bde. 2nd Div. France; Preux-au-Sart, N.E. of Le Quesnoy.

18th (Service) Battalion. (1st Public Schools).
Raised at Epsom by the Public Schools and University Mens' Force on 11.9.14. June 1915 to Clipstone Camp, Notts. in 98th Bde. 33rd Div. 1.7.15 taken over by the War Office. Aug. 1915 Tidworth. Nov. 1915 landed in France. 27.11.15 to 19th Bde. 33rd Div. 26.2.16 to G.H.Q. Troops. 24.4.16 disbanded and many of the men were commissioned.

19th and 21st (Service) Battalions. (2nd & 4th Public Schools).
Raised at Epsom on 11.9.14 by the P.S. & U.M.F. Subsequent record similar to the 18th Bn., but 21st Bn. was at Ashstead from Oct. 1914 to Mar. 1915. In Nov. 1915 they remained in 98th Bde. To G.H.Q. Troops on 27 and 28 Feb. 1916 and both disbanded on 24.4.16 and many of the men were commissioned.

20th (Service) Battalion. (3rd Public Schools).
Raised at Epsom on 11.9.14 like the other P.S. Bns. Subsequent record similar to 18th Bn. but was at Leatherhead from Oct. 1914 to Mar. 1915. Nov. 1915 landed in France. 27.11.15 to 19th Bde. 33rd Div. 16.2.18 disbanded in France.

22nd (Service) Battalion. (Kensington).
Raised by the Mayor and Borough of Kensington on 11.9.14 at the White City. Oct. 1914 to Horsham. June 1915 to Clipstone Camp, Notts. in 99th Bde. 33rd Div. 1.7.15 taken over by the War Office. Aug. 1915 to Tidworth. Nov. 1915 landed at Boulogne. 25.11.15 with 99th Bde. to 2nd Div. 26.2.18 disbanded at Metz-en-Couture.

23rd (Service) Battalion. (1st Sportsman's).
Raised in London by E. Cunliffe-Owen on 25.9.14—recruits enrolled at Hotel Cecil in the Strand. To Hornchurch. June 1915 to Clipstone Camp, Notts. in 99th Bde. 33rd Div. 1.7.15 taken over by the War Office. Aug. 1915 to Kandahar Barracks, Tidworth. 17.11.15 landed at Boulogne. 25.11.15 99th Bde. to 2nd Div. 11.11.18 99th Bde. 2nd Div. France; near Le Quesnoy.

24th (Service) Battalion. (2nd Sportsman's).
Raised in London by E. Cunliffe-Owen on 20.11.14. June 1915 to Clipstone Camp, Notts. in 99th Bde. 33rd Div. 1.7.15 taken over by the War Office. Nov. 1915 landed at Boulogne. 25.11.15 99th Bde. to 2nd Div. 13.12.15 to 5th Bde. 2nd Div. 11.11.18 5th Bde. 2nd Div. France; north of Le Quesnoy.

25th (Service) Battalion. (Frontiersmen).
Raised in London by the Legion of Frontiersmen on 12.2.15. 10.4.15 embarked at Plymouth for East Africa. 4.5.15 arrived at Mombasa. Left East Africa for England about the end of 1917. Disbanded at Putney on 29.6.18.

26th (Service) Battalion. (Bankers).
Raised by the Lord Mayor and City of London 17.7.15 from Bank Clerks and Accountants. To Marlow. Nov. 1915 to Aldershot to 124th Bde. 41st Div. 4.5.16 embarked for France. Nov. 1917 to Italy. Mar. 1918 returned to France. 11.11.18 124th Bde. 41st Div. Belgium; north of Renaix.

27th (Reserve) Battalion.
Formed at Horsham Aug. 1915 from depot coys. of 17th, 22nd and 32nd Bns. as a local reserve bn. Nov. 1915 Oxford in 24th Reserve Bde. April 1916 Edinburgh. 1.9.16 became 103rd Training Reserve Bn. at Edinburgh in 24th Reserve Bde.

28th and 29th (Reserve) Battalions.
Formed at Epsom Aug. 1915 from depot coys. of 18th and 19th Bns. (28) and 20th and 21st Bns. (29) as local reserve bns. Nov. 1915 Oxford. Mar. 1916 Edinburgh. 1.9.16 became 104th and 105th Training Reserve Bns. at Edinburgh in 24th Reserve Bde.

30th and 31st (Reserve) Battalions.
Formed at Romford in Aug. 1915 and at Colchester in Sept. 1915 from depot coys. of 23rd and 24th Bns. (30) and 10th and 26th Bns. (31) as local reserve bns. Nov. 1915 Leamington in 24th Reserve Bde. Jan. 1916 Oxford (30) and Abingdon (31). April 1916 Edinburgh. 1.9.16 became 106th and 107th Training Reserve Bns. at Edinburgh in 24th Reserve Bde.

32nd (Service) Battalion. (East Ham).
Raised by the Mayor and Borough of East Ham on 18.10.15. Dec. 1915 to 124th Bde. 41st Div. at Aldershot. 5.5.16 embarked for France. Nov. 1917 to Italy. Mar. 1918 returned to France. 18.3.18 disbanded in France.

33rd (Labour) Battalion.
Formed at Seaford on 5.3.16. June 1916 to France: First Army Troops. April 1917 became 99th and 100th Labour Coys. Labour Corps.

34th (Labour) Battalion.
Formed at Falmer on 9.4.16. June 1916 to France. April 1917 became 101st and 102nd Labour Coys. Labour Corps.

35th (Labour) Battalion.
Formed at Falmer May 1916. June 1916 to France. April 1917 became 103rd and 104th Labour Coys. Labour Corps.

36th (Labour) Battalion.
Formed at Falmer May 1916. June 1916 to France. April 1917 became 105th and 106th Labour Coys. Labour Corps.

37th (Labour) Battalion.
Formed at Falmer 6.6.16. To France and July 1916 Fourth Army Troops. April 1917 became 107th and 108th Labour Coys. Labour Corps.

38th (Service) Battalion.
Formed at Plymouth on 20.1.18 from Jewish volunteers. 5.2.18 embarked at Southampton for Cherbourg and then across France and Italy to Taranto. Alexandria on 1.3.18. 11.6.18 to 31st Bde. 10th Div. until 25.7.18. In Sept. attached to Australian and New Zealand Mtd. Div. in Chaytor's Force. In Palestine until the end of the war.

39th (Service) Battalion.
Formed at Plymouth on 21.1.18 from Jewish volunteers. April 1918 to Egypt. In Sept. with 38th Bn. in Chaytor's Force.

40th (Service) Battalion.
Formed at Plymouth in Jan. 1918 from Jewish volunteers. Aug. 1918 to Egypt where it remained.

41st and 42nd (Reserve) Battalions.
Formed at Plymouth to provide drafts for the 38th, 39th and 40th Bns.

43rd and 44th (Garrison) Battalions.
Formed in France in May and Sept. 1918 from Garrison Guard Coys. for duty at the five Army Headquarters.

(45th and 46th (Service) Battalions were formed in London in April 1919 and went to North Russia. They were disbanded in December 1919.)

51st (Graduated) Battalion.
On 27.10.17 the 259th Graduated Bn. (formerly 106th Training Reserve Bn. from 30th Royal Fus.) at Ipswich in 215th Bde. 72nd Div. became the 51st Bn. By Mar. 1918 in 204th Bde. 68th Div. at Newmarket where it remained.

52nd (Graduated) Battalion.
On 27.10.17 the 265th Graduated Bn. (formerly 107th Training Reserve Bn. from 31st Royal Fus.) at Ipswich in 217th Bde. 72nd Div. became the 52nd Bn. Feb. 1918 in 204th Bde. 68th Div. at Newmarket where it remained.

53rd (Young Soldier) Battalion.
On 27.10.17 the 104th Young Soldier Bn. of the Training Reserve (formerly 28th Royal Fus.) at Catterick became the 53rd Bn. and went to 2nd Reserve Bde. at Cannock Chase. Oct. 1918 to Clipstone.

THE KING'S (LIVERPOOL REGIMENT)

1st Battalion.
4.8.14 Talavera Barracks, Aldershot: 6th Bde. 2nd Div. 13.8.14 landed at Havre. 11.11.18 6th Bde. 2nd Div. France; Preux-au-Sart, N.E. of Le Quesnoy.

2nd Battalion.
4.8.14 Peshawar. Remained in India throughout the war.

3rd (Reserve) Battalion.
4.8.14 Seaforth, Liverpool. Aug. 1914 Hightown. July 1915 Pembroke Dock. End 1917 to Ireland at Cork.

4th (Extra Reserve) Battalion.
4.8.14 Seaforth, Liverpool. To Edinburgh?. 6.3.15 landed at Havre and to Sirhind Bde. Lahore Div. at Robecq. 10.11.15 attached 137th Bde. 46th Div. 3.12.15 attached 56th and 58th Bdes. 19th Div. 27.2.16 to 98th Bde. 33rd Div. 11.11.18 98th Bde. 33rd Div. France; Sassegnies, N.W. of Avesnes.

1/5th Battalion T.F.
4.8.14 65, St. Anne Street, Liverpool: Liverpool Bde. West Lancashire Div. Autumn 1914 Canterbury. 22.2.15 landed at Havre and to 6th Bde. 2nd Div. 15.12.15 to 99th Bde. 2nd Div. 7.1.16 to 165th Bde. 55th Div. 11.11.18 165th Bde. 55th Div. Belgium, Ath.

1/6th (Rifle) Battalion T.F.
4.8.14 Princes Park Barracks, Upper Warwick Street, Liverpool: Liverpool Bde. West Lancashire Div. Autumn 1914 Canterbury. 25.2.15 landed at Havre and to 15th Bde. 5th Div. at Bailleul. 18.11.15 to Third Army Troops. 26.1.16 to 165th Bde. 55th Div. 11.11.18 165th Bde. 55th Div. Belgium, west of Ath.

1/7th Battalion T.F.
4.8.14 99 Park Street, Bootle: Liverpool Bde. West Lancs. Div. Autumn to Canterbury. 8.3.15 landed at Havre. and to 6th Bde. 2nd Div. at Vendin-lez-Bethune. 4.9.15 to 5th Bde. 2nd Div. 11.11.15 to 22nd Bde. 7th Div. 7.1.16 to 165th Bde. 55th Div. 11.11.18 165th Bde. 55th Div. Belgium; Ligne, west of Ath.

1/8th (Irish) Battalion T.F.
4.8.14 75 Shaw Street, Liverpool: Liverpool Bde. West Lancs. Div. Autumn 1914 Canterbury. Feb. 1915 to North Lancs. Bde. at Sevenoaks. 18.4.15 with North Lancs. Bde. to Highland Div. at Bedford and bde. became 3rd Highland. 3.5.15 landed at Boulogne. 12.5.15 formation became 154th Bde. 51st Div. 7.1.16 to 165th Bde. 55th Div. 31.1.18 to 171st Bde. 57th Div. absorbing 2/8th Bn. 11.11.18 171st Bde. 57th Div. France; Hellemmes, east of Lille.

1/9th Battalion T.F.
4.8.14 57 Everton Road, Liverpool: South Lancs. Bde. West Lancs. Div. 13.8.14 to Edinburgh—Brigade was on Forth Defences. Oct. 1914 to Tunbridge Wells. 13.3.15 landed at Havre and to 2nd Bde. 1st Div. 12.11.15 to 3rd Bde. 1st Div. 7.1.16 to 165th Bde. 55th Div. 1.2.18 to 172nd Bde. 57th Div. absorbing 2/9th Bn. 11.11.18 172nd Bde. 57th Div. France; Hellemmes, east of Lille.

1/10th (Scottish) Battalion T.F.
4.8.14 7 Fraser Street, Liverpool: South Lancs. Bde. West Lancs. Div. Aug. 1914 Edinburgh—Brigade was on Forth Defences. 10.10.14 Tunbridge Wells. 2.11.14 landed at Havre and to 9th Bde. 3rd Div. 6.1.16 to 166th Bde. 55th Div. 11.11.18 166th Bde. 55th Div. Belgium; Villers Notre Dame, west of Ath.

7th (Isle of Man) Volunteer Battalion.
4.8.14 Douglas: attached West Lancs. Div. This was the only surviving Volunteer Bn. after the formation of the Territorial Force in 1908. A service company was formed in 1915 and posted to the 16th Bn. King's at Hoylake in Mar. 1915. In Oct. 1915 it was transferred to the 3rd Cheshire at Birkenhead and became the 1st Manx (Service) Coy. On 12.1.16 the company joined the 2nd Cheshire at Salonika and became A Coy. of that Bn. A second service coy. was formed at Bidstone Camp, near Birkenhead on 27.11.15. This coy. was later broken up and used for drafts for France.

2/5th Battalion T.F.
Formed at Liverpool Sept. 1914. Nov. to Blackpool. Feb. 1915 to Canterbury in 171st Bde. 57th Div. July 1916 to Bourley, Aldershot. Sept. 1916 Woking. Feb. 1917 landed in France. 1.2.18 disbanded in France; personnel to 2/6, 2/7th, 11th and 12th Bns.

2/6th (Rifle) Battalion T.F.
Formed at Liverpool 10.9.14. 10.11.14 Blackpool. 8.2.15 to Canterbury in 171st Bde. 57th Div. 15.3.15 Margate. 13.7.15 Upstreet Camp. 15.7.16 Bourley, Aldershot. 27.9.16 Inkerman Barracks, Woking. 14.2.17 landed at Boulogne. 11.11.18 171st Bde. 57th Div. France; Faubourg de Fives, Lille.

2/7th Battalion T.F.
Formed at Bootle about Oct. 1914. Nov. 1914 Blackpool. Feb. 1915 Canterbury in 171st Bde. 57th Div. July 1916 Tweseldown, Aldershot. Sept. 1916 Woking. Feb. 1917 landed in France. 11.11.18 171st Bde. 57th Div. France; Faubourg de Fives, Lille.

2/8th (Irish) Battalion T.F.
Formed at Liverpool about Oct. 1914. Nov. 1914 Blackpool. Feb. 1915 Canterbury in 171st Bde. 57th Div. July 1916 Tweseldown, Aldershot. Sept. 1916 Woking. Feb. 1917 landed in France. 31.1.18 absorbed by 1/8th Bn. in France.

2/9th Battalion T.F.
Formed at Liverpool about Oct. 1914. Nov. 1914 Blackpool. Feb. 1915 to Kent?, Ashford in 172nd Bde. 57th Div. July 1916 to Mytchett, Aldershot. Sept. 1916 Blackdown. Feb. 1917 landed in France. 1.2.18 absorbed by 1/9th Bn. in France.

2/10th (Scottish) Battalion T.F.
Formed at Liverpool about Oct. 1914. Nov. 1914 Blackpool. Feb. 1915 to Kent?, Ashford in 172nd Bde. 57th Div. July 1916 to Mytchett. Aldershot. Sept. 1916 Blackdown. Feb. 1917 landed in France. 20.4.18 to 55th Div. 30.4.18 absorbed by 1/10 Bn.

3/5th and 3/6th Battalions T.F.
Formed at Liverpool in May 1915 and in autumn to Blackpool. Early 1916 to Oswestry and on 8.4.16 became 5th and 6th Res. Bns. 1.9.16 became 5th Reserve Bn. in West Lancs. Reserve Bde. at Oswestry. No further change.

3/7th, 3/8th and 3/9th Battalions T.F.
Formed May 1915 and in autumn to Blackpool. Early 1916 to Oswestry and on 8.4.16 became 7th, 8th and 9th Res. Bns. 1.9.16 became 7th Reserve Bn. in West Lancs. Reserve Bde. at Oswestry. No further change.

3/10th Battalion T.F.
Formed at Liverpool in May 1915 and in autumn to Blackpool. Early 1916 to Oswestry and on 8.4.16 became 10th Reserve Bn. 1.9.16 West Lancs. Reserve Bde. at Oswestry. No further change.

11th (Service) Battalion. (Pioneers).
Formed 23.8.14 at Seaforth Liverpool—K1—to Barrosa Barracks, Aldershot: Army Troops 14th Div. 28.11.14 to Farnham in billets. 11.1.15 became Pioneer Bn. 14th Div. 24.3.15 to Watts Common, Farnborough. 30.5.15 landed

at Boulogne. 27.4.18 .Reduced to cadre at Molingham, S.E. of Aire. 17.6.18 cadre to England to Brookwood. 19.6.18 absorbed in 15th Loyal N. Lancs.

12th (Service) Battalion.
Formed Sept. 1914 at Seaforth, Liverpool—K2—to Aldershot; Army Troops 20th Div. Jan. 1915 to 61st Bde. 20th Div. Feb. 1915 Witley. April 1915 Salisbury Plain. 27.7.15 landed at Boulogne. 11.11.18 61st Bde. 20th Div. France; St. Waast-la-Vallee, west of Bavai.

13th (Service) Battalion.
Formed Oct. 1914 at Seaforth, Liverpool—K3—to Salisbury Plain; Army Troops 25th Div. Nov. 1914 to Bournemouth in billets. Feb. 1915 to 76th Bde. 25th Div. May 1915 to Aldershot. 27.9.15 landed at Havre. 15.10.15 76th Bde. to 3rd Div. 23.10.15 to 8th Bde. 3rd Div. 4.4.16 to 9th Bde. 3rd Div. 11.11.18 9th Bde. 3rd Div. France; Le Grand Sart, east of Le Quesnoy.

14th (Service) Battalion.
Formed Oct. 1914 at Seaforth, Liverpool—K3—65th Bde. 22nd Div. on South Downs at Seaford and in Dec. to Eastbourne in billets. April 1915 Seaford. June 1915 Aldershot. 5.9.15 landed at Boulogne. 28.10.15 sailed from Marseilles. 5.11.15 arrived Salonika. 11.6.18 left 22nd Div. for France via Itea-Taranto. 26.6.18 Forges-les-Eaux. 23.7.18 to 66th Div. 13.8.18 absorbed by 18th Bn. in 199th Bde. 66th Div.

15th (Reserve) Battalion.
Formed at Formby in Nov. 1914 as a service bn. of K4 in 105th Bde. of original 35th Div. 10.4.15 became a 2nd reserve bn. July 1915 Kinmel. Aug. 1915 Prees Heath in 11th Reserve Bde. 1.9.16 became 49th Training Reserve Bn. at Prees Heath in 11th Reserve Bde.

16th (Reserve) Battalion.
Formed Dec. 1914 at Hoylake as a service bn. of K4 in 105th Bde. of original 35th Div. 10.4.15 became a 2nd reserve bn. July 1915 Kinmel. Aug. 1915 Prees Heath in 11th Reserve Bde. 1.9.16 absorbed in Training Reserve Bns. of 11th Reserve Bde. at Prees Heath.

17th (Service) Battalion. (1st City).
Raised in Liverpool by Lord Derby on 29.8.14 Sept. in old watch factory at Prescot. 30.4.15 to Belton Park, Grantham in 89th Bde. 30th Div. 27.8.15 taken over by the War Office. Sept. 1915 to Larkhill. 7.11.15 landed at Boulogne. 14.5.18 reduced to cadre at Buysscheure, N.E. of St. Omer. 16.6.18 to 66th Div. 30.6.18 to England with 75th Bde. 25th Div. at Mytchett, Aldershot. Reformed on East Coast and returned to Aldershot. 9.9.18 75th Bde. Bde. left 25th Div. and renumbered 236th for service in North Russia. 11.10.18 sailed from Glasgow for Murmansk and then on to Archangel where it remained until Sept. 1919.

18th (Service) Battalion. (2nd City).
Raised in Liverpool by Lord Derby on 29.8.14. To Hooton Park Racecourse then Knowsley Park. 30.4.15 to Belton Park, Grantham in 89th Bde. 30th Div. 27.8.15 taken over by the War Office. Sept. 1915 to Larkhill. Nov. 1915 landed at Boulogne. 25.12.15 to 21st Bde. 30th Div. 24.9.17 1/1 Lancashire Hussars (16 officers and 290 other ranks) joined battalion: previously VIII Corps Cavalry Regt. Became 18th (Lancashire Hussars Yeomanry) Bn. 11.2.18 to 89th Bde. 30th Div. 14.5.18 reduced to cadre at Le Paradis, N.E. of St. Omer. 19.6.18 to 66th Div. 13.8.18 absorbed 14th Bn. and reformed. 19.9.18 to 199th Bde. 66th Div. 11.11.18 199th Bde. 66th Div. Belgium; Vieux Sart, east of Avesnes.

19th (Service) Battalion. (3rd City).
Raised in Liverpool by Lord Derby on 29.8.14. Nov. to Knowsley Park. 30.4.15 to Belton Park, Grantham in 89th Bde. 30th Div. 27.8.15 taken over by the War Office. Sept. 1915 to Larkhill. Nov. 1915 landed at Boulogne. 14.5.18 reduced to cadre at Buysscheure, N.E. of St. Omer. 19.6.18 to 66th Div. and absorbed by 14th Bn.

20th (Service) Battalion. (4th City).
Raised in Liverpool by Lord Derby on 16.10.14. To Tournament Hall, Knotty Ash and then Knowsley Park. 30.4.15 to Belton Park, Grantham in 89th Bde. 30th Div. 27.8.15 taken over by the War Office. Sept. 1915 to Larkhill. Nov. 1915 landed at Boulogne. 8.2.18 disbanded at Chauny, east of Noyon.

21st and 22nd (Reserve) Battalions.
Formed at Knowsley Park Aug. 1915 as local reserve bns. from depot coys. of 17th and 18th Bns. (21) and 19th and 20th Bns. (22). May 1916 Formby in 16th Reserve Bde. 1.9.16 became 67th and 68th Training Reserve Bns. in 16th Reserve Bde. at Altcar.

23rd and 24th (Works) Battalions.
Formed May and June 1916. 23rd at Prescot. In Mar. 1917 at Prescot and Hereford. April 1917 23rd Bn. became 1st Labout Bn. No record of 24th Bn. May have become 27th Bn.

25th Battalion T.F.
On 1.1.17 43rd Provisional Bn. became 25th Bn. at Sheringham in 223rd Bde. 43rd Bn. had been formed in 1915 with Home Service personnel of T.F. Bns. By July 1917 at Sidestrand. 7.5.18 landed at Calais as a Garrison Guard Bn. and to 59th Div. at Estree Cauchie. 16.6.18 to 176th Bde. 59th Div. July 1918 title of Garrison Guard dropped. 11.11.18 176th Bde. 59th Div. Belgium: Velaines N.E. of Tournai.

26th Battalion T.F.
On 1.1.17 44th Provisional Bn. in 218th Bde. 73rd Div., moving to Kelvedon, Essex, became 26th Bn. This bn. had been formed in 1915 with Home Service personnel of T.F. Bns. The 73rd Div. was broken up early in 1918 and the bn. was disbanded at Kelvedon on 29.3.18.

27th (Works) Battalion.
Could have been a renumbering of 24th Bn. April 1917 became 2nd Labour Bn.

27th (Home Service) Battalion.
Formed on 27.4.18 at Sidestrand to replace 25th Bn. in 223rd Bde. Remained at Sidestrand.

A 28th Battalion was formed at Clacton about 22 June 1918 but it was broken up early in July to reconstitute the 17th Bn. which had been reduced to cadre in May 1918.

1st Garrison Battalion.
Formed on 19.8.15 at Seaforth, Liverpool and went to Egypt in Sept. 1915 and remained there.

2nd Garrison Battalion.
Formed in Nov. 1915 at Pembroke Dock. Mar. 1916 to Egypt and may have been at Mudros later in the year. Jan. 1917 to Salonika and on L. of C. 28.8.17 to 228th Bde. attd. 28th Div. 30.9.18 228th Bde. 28th Div. Macedonia; Paprit, north of Salonika.

3rd (Home Service) Garrison Battalion.
Formed at Pembroke Dock April 1916. Aug. 1917 became 3rd Bn. Royal Defence Corps.

1st and 2nd Dock Battalions.
Formed in Aug. 1915 and in (?) 1918 at Liverpool where they remained.

51st (Graduated) Battalion.
On 27.10.17 the 217th Graduated Bn. (formerly 60th Training Reserve Bn. from 20th Welsh Regt.) at Fermoy in 195th Bde. 65th Div. became the 51st Bn. Early in 1918 the 65th Div. was broken up and the battalion returned to England and joined 203rd Bde. 68th Div. at Yarmouth by 11.3.18. May 1918 at Benacre Park and in June at Herringfleet where it remained.

52nd (Graduated) Battalion.
On 27.10.17 the 233rd Graduated Bn. (formerly 75th Training Reserve Bn. from 12th East Lancs. Regt.) at Herringfleet in 205th Bde. 68th Div. became the 52nd Bn. Then to Lowestoft and in spring to Saxmundham. About June 1918 to Henham Park where it remained.

53rd (Young Soldier) Battalion.
On 27.10.17 the 72nd Young Soldier Bn. of the Training Reserve (formerly 21st Bn. Lancs. Fusiliers) at Prees Heath became the 53rd Bn. and moved to Kinmel and the 14th Reserve Bde. where it remained.

THE NORFOLK REGIMENT

1st Battalion.
4.8.14 Holywood, Belfast: 15th Bde. 5th Div. Aug. 1914 landed at Havre. Dec. 1917 to Italy. April 1918 returned to France, arriving Doullens 8 April. 11.11.18 15th Bde. 5th Div. France; Jolimetz, S.E. of Le Quesnoy.

2nd Battalion.
4.8.14 Belgium: 18th Indian Bde. 6th (Poona) Div. 6.11.14 sailed from Bombay. 15.11.14 landed at Sanniya, Mesopotamia. 29.4.16 captured at Kut al Amara. While the bn. was besieged in Kut a composite English Bn. was formed on 4 Feb. at El Orah, on the Tigris, composed of drafts and recovered wounded from 2nd Norfolk and 2nd Dorset. It had two coys. from each regt. and was nicknamed the Norsets. It was broken up on 21.7.16. 16.7.16 2nd Bn. was reconstituted with two coys. from the Composite Bn. and reinforcements. Feb. 1917 to 37th Indian Bde. 14th Indian Div. 31.10.18 37th Indian Bde. 14th Indian Div. Mesopotamia; Imam Abbas, near Mirjana, N.E. of Baghdad.

3rd (Reserve) Battalion.
4.8.14 Norwich. 9.8.14 to Felixstowe where it remained throughout the war, (Harwich Garrison).

1/4th Battalion T.F.
4.8.14 Drill Hall, St. Giles, Norwich: Norfolk & Suffolk Bde. East Anglian Div. Aug. 1914 Colchester. May 1915 Watford and formation became 163rd Bde. 54th Div. 29.7.15 embarked at Liverpool. 5.8.15 arrived Mudros. 10.8.15 landed at Suvla Bay. 19.12.15 arrived Alexandria. 31.10.18 163rd Bde. 54th Div. Palestine; Beirut.

1/5th Battalion T.F.
4.8.14 East Dereham: Norfolk & Suffolk Bde. East Anglian Div. Subsequent record same as 1/4th Bn.

1/6th (Cyclist) Battalion T.F.
4.8.14 Cattle Market Street, Norwich. Aug. 1914 to coast defence in Norfolk and remained in Norfolk until 1918 attached to various formations (Mounted Div. Cyclist Bdes., etc.) and at North Walsham, Thetford, Sidestrand and Worstead and other places near the coast. Early in 1918 to Ireland and stationed at Tralee, Castle Mayo and Randalstown.

2/4th Battalion T.F.
Formed at Norwich in Sept. 1914. Nov. 1914 to Peterborough in 208th Bde. 69th Div. July 1915 Bury St. Edmunds. July 1916 to Harrogate. Oct. 1916 to Doncaster By April 1917 Thoresby and in autumn to Doncaster. June 1918 disbanded, personnel to 4th Reserve Bn.

2/5th Battalion T.F.
Formed at East Dereham, Oct. 1914. Subsequent record similar to 2/4th Bn. Disbanded in May 1918.

2/6th (Cyclist) Battalion T.F.
Formed in Oct. 1914 at Bridlington where it remained until 1917 then at Filey and Hunmanby. In 1918 to Bridlington again.

3/4th and 3/5th Battalions T.F.
Formed at Norwich and East Dereham early in 1915. Aug. 1915 to Windsor Great Park. Oct. 1915 to Halton Park, Tring. 8.4.16 became 4th and 5th Reserve Bns. 1.9.16 4th Bn. absorbed 5th Bn. in East Anglian Res. Bde. at Halton Park. By Nov. 1917 Crowborough and to Hastings late in 1918.

3/6th (Cyclist) Battalion T.F.
Formed at Norwich May 1915 and disbanded in March 1916.

7th (Service) Battalion.
Formed at Norwich Aug. 1914—K1—to Shorncliffe in 35th Bde. 12th Div. Jan. 1915 to billets at Romney and Littlestone. Feb. 1915 to Malplaquet Barracks, Aldershot. 31.5.15 landed at Boulogne. 11.11.18 35th Bde. 12th Div. France; Landas, east of Orchies.

8th (Service) Battalion.
Formed at Norwich Sept. 1914—K2—to Shorncliffe in 53rd Bde. 18th Div. Oct. 1914 Colchester. April 1915 Codford. 25.7.15 landed at Boulogne. 12.2.18 disbanded at Elverdinghe. 15 officers and 300 men to 9th Bn. 5 officers and 100 men to 7th Bn.

9th (Service) Battalion.
Formed at Norwich Sept. 1914—K3—to Shoreham in 71st Bde. 24th Div. Jan. 1915 billets in Brighton. Feb. 1915 Shoreham. June 1915 Blackdown, Aldershot. 30.8.15 landed at Boulogne. 11.10.15 71st Bde. to 6th Div. 11.11.18 71st Bde. 6th Div. France; Bohain.

10th (Reserve) Battalion.
Formed at Walton-on-the-Naze Oct. 1914 as a service bn. of K4 in 94th Bde. of original 31st Div. Mar. 1915 Felixstowe. 10.4.15 became a 2nd reserve bn. and Bde. became 6th Reserve Bde. May 1915 Colchester. Mar. 1916 Parkeston, Harwich. 1.9.16 became 25th Training Reserve Bn. at Parkeston in 6th Reserve Bde.

11th Battalion T.F.
On 1.1.17 the 61st Provisional Bn. at Guildford in 212th Bde. 71st Bde. became the 11th Bn. The battalion had been formed about July 1915 at Lowestoft with Home Service personnel of T.F. Bns. Mar. 1917 to Colchester. 20.12.17 disbanded.

12th (Norfolk Yeomanry) Battalion T.F.
Formed in Egypt on 11.2.17 from the dismounted Norfolk Yeomanry in 230th Bde. 74th Div. 1.5.18 sailed from Alexandria and arrived Marseilles on 7 May. 21.6.18 to 94th Bde. 31st Div. at Blaringham. 11.11.18 94th Bde. 31st Div. Belgium; Avelghem.

1st Garrison Battalion.
Formed at Seaford in Sept. 1915 and went to India in Dec. 1915.

THE LINCOLNSHIRE REGIMENT

1st Battalion.
4.8.14 Portsmouth: 9th Bde. 3rd Div. 14.8.14 landed at Havre. 14.11.15 to 62nd Bde. 21st Div. 11.11.18 62nd Bde. 21st Div. France; Aymeries, north of Aulnoye.

(The Bermuda Rifle Volunteer Corps sent a contingent of 2 officers and 125 men which served with the 1st Bn. from June 1915 to the end of the war. Their casualties, in killed and wounded, were over seventy-five per cent of their strength).

2nd Battalion.
4.8.14 Bermuda. Sept. to Halifax, Nova Scotia. 3.10.14 sailed for U.K. and landed at Devonport. To Hursley Park, near Winchester to 25th Bde. 8th Div. 6.11.14 landed at Havre. 4.2.18 to 62nd Bde. 21st Div. joining 1st Bn. 11.11.18 62nd Bde. 21st Div. France; Aymeries, north of Aulnoye.

3rd (Reserve) Battalion.
4.8.14 Lincoln. Aug. 1914 to Grimsby until early in 1918 and then to Ireland where it was at Cork.

1/4th Battalion T.F.
4.8.14 Drill Hall, Lincoln: Lincoln & Leicester Bde. North Midland Div. 11.8.14 to Belper. 15.8.14 Luton. 1.3.15 landed at Havre. May 1915 formation became 138th Bde. 46th Div. 7.1.16 sailed from Marseilles for Egypt arriving Alexandria 13 Jan. 4.2.16 embarked at Alexandria. 9.2.16 arrived Marseilles. 31.1.18 to 177th Bde. 59th Div. absorbing 2/4th Bn. 8.5.18 reduced to cadre. 2.6.18 to 49th Bde. 16th Div. 17.6.18 102nd Bde. 34th Div. 27.6.18 117th Bde. 39th Div. 27.7.18 118th Bde. 39th Div. 28.9.18 116th Bde. 39th Div. 8.11.18 disembodied.

1/5th Battalion T.F.
4.8.14 Infantry Drill Hall, Grimsby: Lincoln & Leicester Bde. North Midland Div. Subsequent record same as 1/4th Bn. until May 1918. 11.11.18 138th Bde. 46th Div. France; Sains du Nord, S.E. of Avesnes.

2/4th Battalion T.F.
Formed at Lincoln 13.9.14. July 1915 St. Albans in 177th Bde. 59th Div. April 1916 to Ireland; Dublin and Fermoy Jan. 1917 returned to England at Fovant. Feb. 1917 to France. 31.1.18 absorbed by 1/4th Bn.

2/5th Battalion T.F.
Formed at Grimsby 6.2.15. Subsequent record same as 2/4th Bn. to Jan. 1918. Remained in 177th Bde. 59th Div. until 8.5.18 and then reduced to cadre. 29.5.18 to 21st Bde. 30th Div. 28.6.18 to 66th Div. 31.7.18 absorbed by 1/5th Bn.

3/4th and 3/5th Battalions T.F.
Formed at Lincoln and Grimsby on 1.6.15 and 17.4.15. 8.4.16 became 4th and 5th Reserve Bns. at Grantham. 1.9.16 4th Bn. absorbed 5th Bn. in North Midland Reserve Bde. at Saltfleet where it remained.

6th (Service) Battalion.
Formed at Lincoln Aug. 1914—K1—to Belton Park, Grantham in 33rd Bde. 11th Div. April 1915 Frensham. 1.7.15 sailed from Liverpool. 12.7.15 Alexandria. 18.7.15 Mudros. 20 to 31 July at Cape Helles. 7.8.15 landed at Suvla Bay. 21.12.15 Imbros. 2.2.16 Alexandria. 2.7.16 embarked at Alexandria. 8.7.16 landed at Marseilles. 11.11.18 33rd Bde. 11th Div. Belgium; near Aulnois, north of Maubeuge.

7th (Service) Battalion.
Formed at Lincoln Sept. 1914—K2—to Wool in 51st Bde. 17th Div. June 1915 Winchester. 14.7.15 landed at Boulogne. 11.11.18 51st Bde. 17th Div. France; Aulnoye, south of Maubeuge.

8th (Service) Battalion.
Formed at Lincoln Sept. 1914—K3—to Halton Park, Tring in 63rd Bde. 21st Div. Dec. 1914 to Leighton Buzzard in billets. April 1915 Halton Park. Aug. 1915 Witley. 10.9.15 landed at Boulogne. 8.7.16 with 63rd Bde. to 37th Div. 11.11.18 63rd Bde. 37th Div. France; Neuville, S.W. of Le Quesnoy.

9th (Reserve) Battalion.
Formed at Lincoln Nov. 1914 as a service bn. of K4 in 91st Bde. of original 30th Div. 10.4.15 became a 2nd reserve bn. and Bde. became 3rd Reserve Bde. April 1915 Lichfield. Nov. 1915 Brocton, Cannock Chase. 1.9.16 became 11th Training Reserve Bn. at Brocton in 3rd Reserve Bde.

10th (Service) Battalion. (Grimsby).
Raised at Grimsby on 9.9.14 by the Mayor and Town. Dec. 1914 to Brocklesby. June 1915 to Ripon in 101st Bde. 34th Div. 10.8.15 taken over by the War Office. Aug. 1915 to Perham Down. Sept. 1915 Sutton Veny. 9.1.16 landed in France. 3.2.18 to 103rd Bde. 34th Div. 18.5.18 reduced to cadre. 17.6.18 to 116th Bde. 39th Div. 16.8.18 to 66th Div. 20.9.18 with 197th Bde. to L. of C. near Aumale.

11th (Reserve) Battalion.
Formed at Lincoln Oct. 1915 from depot coys. of 10th Bn. as a local reserve bn. Jan. 1916 Harrogate in 19th Reserve Bde. July 1916 Durham. 1.9.16 became 82nd Training Reserve Bn. in 19th Reserve Bde. at Newcastle.

12th (Labour) Battalion.
Formed July 1916 at Brocklesby. Aug. 1916 to France and worked on L. of C. April 1917 transferred to Labour Corps as 16th and 17th Labour Coys.

13th Battalion T.F.
On 1.1.17 the 28th Provisional Bn. at Bath in 215th Bde. 72nd Div. became the 13th Bn. The battalion had been formed in 1915 from home service personnel of T.F. Bns. Jan. 1917 to Bedford. May 1917 Ipswich. About July 1917 left 72nd Div. and was disbanded at Ipswich on 31.10.17.

1st Garrison Battalion.
Formed Sept. 1915 and went to India in Oct. 1915.

2nd (Home Service) Garrison Battalion.
Formed May 1916 at North Coates, near Grimsby. Aug. 1917 became 4th Bn. Royal Defence Corps at Grimsby.

THE DEVONSHIRE REGIMENT

1st Battalion.
4.8.14 Jersey. 21.8.14 landed at Havre. 14.9.14 to 8th Bde. 3rd Div. 30.9.14 to 14th Bde. 5th Div. 12.1.16 to 95th Bde. 5th Div. 27.11.17 entrained for Italy, arrived 4 Dec. 3 to 7.4.18 returned to France. 11.11.18 95th Bde. 5th Div. France; Le Quesnoy.

2nd Battalion.
4.8.14 Cairo. 13.9.14 sailed for U.K. 1.10.14 arrived Southampton and to Hursley Park, near Winchester in 23rd Bde. 8th Div. 6.11.14 landed at Havre. 11.11.18 23rd Bde. 8th Div. Belgium; Tertre, west of Mons.

3rd (Reserve) Battalion.
4.8.14 Exeter. 8 Aug. to Plymouth. 28 Aug. returned to Exeter. May 1915 to Devonport where it remained. (Plymouth Garrison).

1/4th Battalion T.F.
4.8.14 Exeter: Devon & Cornwall Bde., Wessex Div. 5 Aug. to Plymouth. 9 Aug. to Salisbury Plain with Wessex Div. 9.10.14 embarked at Southampton for India. 11.11.14 arrived Karachi. 2.3.16 landed at Basra in 41st Indian Bde. 5.5.16 to 37th Indian Bde. 14th Indian Div. Feb. 1917 to Amara for Tigris Defences and L. of C. 31.10.18 Mesopotamia; Baquaba, N.E. of Baghdad.

1/5th (Prince of Wales's) Battalion T.F.
4.8.14 Millbay, Plymouth: Devon & Cornwall Bde. Wessex Div. 5 Aug. to Plymouth. 9 Aug. to Salisbury Plain with Wessex Div. 9.10.14 embarked at Southampton for India. 11.11.14 arrived Karachi. 22.3.17 embarked at Bombay for Egypt. 4.4.17 landed at Suez. 25.6.17 to 232nd Bde. 75th Div. 26.5.18 sailed for France and arrived Marseilles 1 June. To 185th Bde. 62nd Div. 11.11.18 185th Bde. 62nd Div. France; Sous-le-Bois, Maubeuge.

1/6th Battalion T.F.
4.8.14 Barnstaple: Army Troops attached Wessex Div. 5 to 9 Aug. Plymouth then to Salisbury Plain with Wessex Div. 16.9.14 to Devon & Cornwall Bde. 9.10.14 embarked at Southampton for India. 11.11.14 arrived Karachi. 30.12.15 embarked at Karachi in 36th Indian Bde. 5.1.16 landed at Basra. 12.5.16 Bde. to 14th Indian Div. Sept. 1916 to Tigris Defences and L. of C. 31.10.18 Mesopotamia; Basra.

1/7th (Cyclist) Battalion T.F.
4.8.14 Exeter: unalloted. After a week at Totnes on

mobilization to Seaton Carew, north of West Hartlepool, on coast defence. 1916 and 1917 at Bawdsey, Suffolk attached to various cyclist bdes. early in 1918 to 11th Cyclist Bde. Cyclist Div. at Canterbury where it remained.

2/4th Battalion T.F.
Formed at Exeter 16.9.14. Oct. 2/Devon & Cornwall Bde. 2/Wessex Div. 12.12.14 embarked at Southampton for India arriving early Jan. 1915. 15.10.17 sailed from Bombay for Egypt. 25.10.17 landed at Suez. 13.12.17 to 234th Bde. 75th Div. July 1918 left 75th Div. and disbanded in Egypt on 17.8.18.

2/5th (Prince of Wales's) Battalion T.F.
Formed at Plymouth 16.9.14. 5.9.15 sailed from Devonport for Egypt and arrived 17.9.15. June 1916 disbanded in Egypt.

2/6th Battalion T.F.
Formed at Barnstaple 16.9.14. Oct. 2/Devon & Cornwall Bde. 2/Wessex Div. 12.12.14 embarked at Southampton for India arriving early in Jan. 1915. 14.9.17 landed at Basra. To L. of C. 31.10.18 Mesopotamia; Amara.

2/7th (Cyclist) Battalion T.F.
Formed at Totnes Oct. 1914. 1916 Sevenoaks. 1917 Margate attd. 5th Cyclist & 222nd Bdes. 1918 Southminster attd. 67th Div. and Nov. 1918 at Maldon.

3/4th, 3/5th and 3/6th Battalions T.F.
Formed 25.3.15 at Exeter, Plymouth and Barnstaple. Autumn 1915 to Bournemouth. 8.4.16 became 4th, 5th and 6th Reserve Bns. at Bournemouth. 1.9.16 5th and 6th Reserve Bns. absorbed by 4th Bn. at Hursley Park, Winchester. Oct. 1916 Bournemouth. Mar. 1917 Sutton Veny. Early 1918 at Larkhill. April 1918 to Ireland; stationed at Belfast, Londonderry and Clonmany, Donegal. Sept. 1916 to April 1918 in Wessex Reserve Bde.

3/7th (Cyclist) Battalion T.F.
Formed in 1915—perhaps only a Third Line Depot—and abolished in Mar. 1916.

8th (Service) Battalion.
Formed at Exeter 19.8.14—K1—to Rushmoor Camp, Camp, Aldershot as Army Troops, 14th Div. Nov. 1914 Barossa Barracks, Aldershot. Dec. 1914 billets in villages south of Farnham. Mar. 1915 to Aldershot. May 1915 left 14th Div. 26.7.15 landed at Havre. 4.8.15 to 20th Bde. 7th Div. at Carvin. Nov. 1917 to Italy arriving Legnago on 22 Nov. 4.11.18 20th Bde. 7th Div. Italy; Cisterna, east of Gradisca.

9th (Service) Battalion.
Formed at Exeter 15.9.14—K2—to Rushmoor Camp, Aldershot as Army Troops, 20th Div. Oct. 1914 Bisley. Nov. 1914 Tournai Barracks, Aldershot. Feb. 1915 Haslemere. April 1915 Bordon left 20th Div. 28.7.15 landed at Havre. 8.8.15 to 20th Bde. 7th Div. at Calonne-sur-la-Lys. Nov. 1917 to Italy. Sept. 1918 left 7th Div. to France, arriving St. Riquier 16 Sept. and joined 7th Bde. 25th Div. at Canchy. 11.11.18 7th Bde. 25th Div. France; Landregies.

10th (Service) Battalion.
Formed at Exeter 25.9.14—K3—to Stockton Camp, Salisbury Plain in 79th Bde. 26th Div. Nov. 1914 billets at Bath. April 1915 Sutton Veny. 23.9.15 landed at Boulogne. Nov. 1915 to Salonika. 30.9.18 79th Bde. 26th Div. Macedonia; east of Strumica.

11th (Reserve) Battalion.
Formed at Exeter in Nov. 1914 as a service bn. of K4 in 100th Bde. of original 33rd Div. Dec. 1914 billets in Torquay. 10.4.15 became a 2nd reserve bn. May 1915 Wareham in 10th Reserve Bde. 1.9.16 became 44th Training Reserve Bn. at Wareham in 10th Reserve Bde.

12th (Labour) Battalion.
Formed at Devonport May 1916. To France June 1916—Fourth Army Troops. April 1917 became 152nd and 153rd Labour Coys.

13th (Works) Battalion.
Formed at Saltash June 1916. To Plymouth. April 1917 became 3rd Labour Bn.

14th (Labour) Battalion.
Formed at Plymouth Aug. 1916. To France Oct. 1916—Third Army Troops. April 1917 became 154th and 155th Labour Coys.

15th Battalion T.F.
On 1.1.17 86th Provisional Bn. at Herne Bay in 227th Bde. became 15th Bn. It had been formed in Aug. 1915 from Home Service personnel. of the TF. Bns. In 1918 to Aldeburgh where it remained.

16th (Royal 1st Devon & Royal North Devon Yeomanry) Battalion T.F.
Formed at Moascar, Egypt on 4.1.17 from the two dismounted Devon Yeomanry regiments and went to 229th Bde. 74th Div. 7.5.18 landed at Marseilles. 11.11.18 229th Bde. 74th Div. Belgium; east of Tournai.

1st Garrison Battalion.
Formed at Weymouth on 8.8.15 27.9.15 sailed from Devonport for Egypt and in 1917 was in Palestine.

2nd (Home Service) Garrison Battalion.
Formed at Exeter July 1916. To Plymouth and Falmouth and in Aug. 1917 became 5th Bn. Royal Defence Corps.

51st (Graduated) Battalion.
On 27.10.17 206th Inf. Bn. (Graduated) of the Training Reserve—formerly 33rd Bn.—at North Walsham in 192nd Bde. 64th Div. became 51st Bn. To Norwich for the winter and by May 1918 at Holt where it remained.

52nd (Graduated) Battalion.
On 27.10.17 210th Inf. Bn. (Graduated) of the Training Reserve—formerly 37th Bn.—at Taverham in 193rd Bde. 64th Div. became 52nd Bn. To Norwich for the winter. 26.2.18 to 192nd Bde. 64th Div. By May 1918 at Cromer where it remained.

53rd (Yong Soldier) Battalion.
On 27.10.17 35th Young Soldier Bn. at Sutton Mandeville in 8th Reserve Bde. became 53rd Bn. Jan. 1918 to Rollestone where it remained.

Locations of places on Salisbury Plain mentioned above.
Larkhill   4 miles N.W. of Amesbbury.
Rollestone   4 miles west of Amesbury.
Stockton   11 miles N.W. of Salisbury.
Sutton Mandeville   9 miles west of Salisbury.
Sutton Veny   3 miles S.E. of Warminster.

THE SUFFOLK REGIMENT

1st Battalion.
4.8.14 Khartoum. 23.10.14 landed at Liverpool and to Lichfield 17.11.14 Felixstowe. Dec. Hursley Park, Winchester to 84th Bde. 28th Div. 18.1.15 landed at Havre. 24.10.15 embarked at Marseilles. 30.10.15 Alexandria. 23 to 29 Nov. 1915 Alexandria to Salonika. 30.9.18 84th Bde. 28th Div. Macedonia; north of Lake Doiran.

2nd Battalion.
4.8.14 Curragh: 14th Bde. 5th Div. 17.8.14 landed at Havre. 30.9.14 to G.H.Q. (after heavy casualties at Le Cateau). 25.10.14 to 8th Bde. 3rd Div. 22.10.15 to 76th Bde. 3rd Div. 11.11.18 76th Bde. 3rd Div. France; La Longueville, east of Bavai.

3rd (Reserve) Battalion.
4.8.14 Bury St. Edmunds. 9.8.14 to Felixstowe where it remained. (Harwich Garrison).

1/4th Battalion T.F.
4.8.14 Portman Road, Ipswich: Norfolk & Suffolk Bde.,

East Anglian Div. 6.8.14 Felixstowe then Shenfield and Braxted to Severalls, near Colchester. 9.11.14 landed at Havre, having left East Anglian Div. 4.11.14 Jullundur Bde. Lahore Div. at Vieille Chapelle. 15.11.15 to 46th Bde. 15th Div. 27.2.16 to 98th Bde. 33rd Div. 15.2.18 to 58th Div. as Pioneer Bn. 11.11.18 Pioneer Bn. 58th Div. Belgium; Wiers, west of Peruwelz.

1/5th Battalion T.F.
4.8.14 Bury St. Edmunds: Norfolk & Suffolk Bde. East Anglian Div. Aug. to Felixstowe then Mile End, near Colchester. 18.5.15 to Watford, formation now 163rd Bde. 54th Div. 30.7.15 sailed from Liverpool. 6.8.15 Mudros. 9.8.15 Imbros. 10.8.15 landed at Suvla Bay. 7.12.15 Mudros. 19.12.15 Alexandria. 31.10.18 163rd Bde. 54th Div. Palestine; near Beirut.

1/6th (Cyclist) Battalion T.F.
4.8.14 Ipswich: unallotted. 5.8.14 to Saxmundham where it remained most of the war. Early 1918 at Wickham Market. Attached to 1st Mounted Div. in 1914-15. 68th Div. in 1917 and 1918 and finally to 227th Bde.

2/4th Battalion T.F.
Formed at Ipswich in Oct. 1914. Nov. 1914 Peterborough in 208th Bde. 69th Div. May 1915 Cambridge and by Aug. Bury St. Edmunds. Disbanded Dec. 1915.

2/5th Battalion T.F.
Formed at Bury St. Edmunds Oct. 1914 and to Peterborough in 208th Bde. 69th Div. May 1915 Cambridge and by Aug. Bury St. Edmunds. July 1916 to Harrogate. Oct. 1916 Doncaster. April 1917 Thoresby Park. 18.9.17 to 202nd Bde. 67th Div. at Canterbury and disbanded there in April 1918.

2/6th (Cyclist) Battalion T.F.
Formed at Ipswich Sept. 1914. Nov. 1914 to Louth, Lincs. From early in 1915 to the end of the war was stationed at various places on the coast between Skegness and Sutton-on-Sea.

3/4th and 3/5th Battalions T.F.
Formed at Ipswich and Bury St. Edmunds in April 1915. Aug. 1915 Windsor Great Park. Oct. 1915 Halton Park, Tring. 8.4.16 became 4th and 5th Reserve Bns. 1.9.16 4th Bn. absorbed 5th Bn. in East Anglian Res. Bde. 23.7.17 absorbed 1st Res. Bn. Cambridgeshire Regt. becoming the Cambridge and Suffolk Reserve Bn. Autumn 1917 to Crowborough. By Nov. 1918 at Hastings.

3/6th (Cyclist) Battalion T.F.
Formed at Ipswich in May 1915 and disbanded in Mar. 1916.

7th (Service) Battalion.
Formed at Bury St. Edmunds 20.8.14—K1—to Shorncliffe in 35th Bde. 12th Div. Feb. 1915 to Blenheim Barracks, Aldershot. 30.5.15 landed at Boulogne. 19.5.18 reduced to cadre: 11 officers and 408 men to 1/1st Cambridge. 24.5.18 cadre to 39th Div. 16.8.18 to 66th Div. 20.9.18 to L. of C. with 197th Bde. 11.11.18 197th Bde. France; Haudricourt, south of Aumale.

8th (Service) Battalion.
Formed at Bury St. Edmunds 9.9.14—K2—to Shorncliffe in 53rd Bde. 18th Div. Oct. 1914 to Colchester. May 1915 Codford, Salisbury Plain. 25.7.15 landed at Boulogne. 7.2.18 disbanded at Rousbrugge: personnel to 2nd, 4th and 7th Bns.

9th (Service) Battalions.
Formed at Bury St. Edmunds Sept. 1914—K3—to Shoreham, 71st Bde. 24th Div. Dec. 1914 billets in Brighton. Mar. 1915 Shoreham. June 1915 Blackdown. 30.8.15 landed at Boulogne. 11.10.15 71st Bde. to 6th Div. 16.2.18 disbanded at Courcelles-le-Comte.

10th (Reserve) Battalion.
Formed at Felixstowe in Oct. 1914 as a service bn. of K4 in 94th Bde. of original 31st Div. Mar. 1915 Bury St. Edmunds. 10.4.16 became a 2nd reserve bn. and Bde. became 6th Res. Bde. May 1915 Colchester. Mar. 1916 Harwich. 1.9.16 became 26th Training Reserve Bn. at Harwich in 6th Reserve Bde.

11th (Service) Battalion. (Cambridgeshire).
Raised at Cambridge 25.9.14 by the Cambridge and Isle of Ely T.F. Association. May 1915 to Ripon and 101st Bde. 34th Div. 1.7.15 taken over by the War Office. Aug. 1915 to Perham Down and Warminster later. 9.1.16 landed at Boulogne. 26.5.18 to 183rd Bde. 61st Div. 11.11.18 183rd Bde. 61st Div. France; Bermerain.

12th (Service) Battalion. (East Anglian).
Formed at Bury St. Edmunds July 1915 as a bantam bn. Nov. 1915 to Bordon and 121st Bde. 40th Div. Dec. Pirbright. 6.6.16 landed at Havre. 6.5.18 reduced to cadre. 16.6.18 to 14th Div. 17.6.18 to England and Pirbright and reconstituted with newly formed 16th Bn., joined 43rd Bde. and landed at Boulogne on 5.7.18. 11.11.18 43rd Bde. 14th Div. Belgium; Molembaix, north of Tournai.

13th (Reserve) Battalion. (Cambridgeshire).
Formed at Cambridge Sept. 1915 with depot coys. of 11th Bn. as a local reserve bn. Nov. 1915 to Trowbridge. Feb. 1916 Leamington. July 1916 Richmond Park. 1.9.16 became 108th Training Reserve Bn. in 26th Reserve Bde. at Wimbledon.

14th Battalion T.F.
On 1.1.17 64th Provisional Bn. at Weybourne in 223rd Bde. became 14th Bn. The 64th Provisional Bn. had been formed in June 1915 with home service personnel of the T.F. Bns. By July 1917 at Sheringham and to April 1918, then Holt. By Nov. 1918 at Cley in 223rd Bde.

15th (Suffolk Yeomanry) Battalion T.F.
Formed in Egypt on 5.1.17 from dismounted Suffolk Yeomanry. To 230th Bde. 74th Div. May 1918 to France landing at Marseilles on 7 May. 11.11.18 230th Bde. 74th Div. Belgium; Tournai.

A 16th Bn. appears to have been formed at Pirbright on 1.6.18 and was absorbed in the 12th Bn. on 18.6.18.

1st (Reserve) Garrison Battalion.
Formed 14.3.16 at Gravesend and remained during the war at Tilbury, Gravesend and Isle of Grain. (Thames and Medway Garrison).

2nd (Home Service) Garrison Battalion.
Formed 5.5.16 at Harwich. Early 1917 at Felixstowe and in Aug. 1917 became 6th Bn. Royal Defence Corps.

PRINCE ALBERT'S
(SOMERSET LIGHT INFANTRY)

1st Battalion.
4.8.14 Colchester: 11th Bde. 4th Div. 17 Aug. Harrow. 22.8.14 landed at Havre. 11.11.18 11th Bde. 4th Div. France; moving from Haspres to Curgies, south of Valenciennes.

2nd Battalion.
4.8.14 Quetta. Remained in India throughout the war.

3rd (Reserve) Battalion.
4.8.14 Taunton. 8 Aug. to Devonport until Nov. 1917 then to Ireland. Stationed at Londonderry, to April 1918, then Belfast.

1/4th Battalion T.F.
4.8.14 Lower Bristol Road, Bath: South-Western Bde. Wessex Div. To war station at Plymouth and after a few days to Durrington, Salisbury Plain. 9.10.14 sailed from Southampton and arrived Bombay 9.11.14; division broken up. 21.1.16 landed at Basra in 37th Indian Bde. which was attached to 3rd Indian Div. 5.5.16 to 41st

Indian Bde. on L. of C. Bde. broken up. Mar. 1918 to 56th Indian Bde. Sept. 1918 Bde. to 14th Indian Div. 31.10.18 56th Indian Bde. 14th Indian Div. Mesopotamia; Tekrit, north of Baghdad.

1/5th Battalion T.F.
4.8.14 County Territorial Hall, Taunton: South-Western Bde. Wessex Div. To war station at Plymouth for a few days then to Salisbury Plain. 9.10.14 sailed from Southampton and arrived Bombay 9.11.14; division broken up. 26.4.17 sailed from Bombay and 11.5.17 landed at Suez. To 233rd Bde. 75th Div. 31.10.18 233rd Bde. 75th Div. Palestine; Kalkiliah, south of Haifa.

2/4th Battalion T.F.
Formed at Bath Sept. 1914. Salisbury Plain then billets in Bath; 135th Bde. 45th Div. 12.12.14. sailed for India, arrived 23 Jan. and division was broken up. Aug. 1915 to Andaman Islands. Jan. 1916 returned to India. 25.9.17 landed at Suez to 232nd Bde. 75th Div. 2.5.18 left 75th Div. for France and sailed from Port Said 23.5.18 for Marseilles (1.6.18). 19.6.18 to 34th Div. at Berthen and on 5.7.18 became Pioneer Bn. 11.11.18 Pioneer Bn. 34th Div. Belgium; Wevelghem, west of Courtrai.

2/5th Battalion T.F.
Formed at Taunton Sept. 1914. Salisbury Plain then Bath. In 135th Bde. 45th Div. 12.12.14 sailed for India where division was broken up. Remained in India.

3/4th and 3/5th Battalions T.F.
Formed at Bath and Taunton in Mar. 1915. Autumn 1915 Bournemouth. 8.4.16 became 4th and 5th Reserve Bns. 1.9.16 4th Bn. absorbed 5th Bn. at Hursley Park, Winchester in Wessex Res. Bde. Oct. 1916 to Bournemouth. Mar. 1917 Sutton Veny and end 1917 to Larkhill. April 1918 to Oswestry and West Lancs. Res. Bde. until the end of the war.

6th (Service) Battalion.
Formed at Taunton Aug. 1914—K1—to Aldershot in 43rd Bde. 14th Div. 21.5.15 landed at Boulogne. 14.4.18 formed composite bn. with 5th Bn. Oxford & Bucks. L.I. 27.4.18 reduced to cadre. 18.6.18 to 16th Div. at Boulogne and to England. 20.6.18 reconstituted at Cromer by absorbing 13th Bn. D.C.L.I. 4.7.18 to 49th Bde. 16th Div. at Aldershot. 1.8.18 landed at Boulogne. 11.11.18 49th Bde. 16th Div. Belgium; Bruyelle, south of Tournai. (Nov. 1914 to Feb. 1915 Witley Camp, Godalming).

7th (Service) Battalion.
Formed at Taunton 13.9.14—K2—to Woking in 61st Bde. 20th Div. Feb. 1915 Witley Camp, near Godalming. Mar. 1915 Amesbury. April 1915 Larkhill. 24.7.15 landed at Boulogne. 11.11.18 61st Bde. 20th Div. France; Feignies, north of Maubeuge.

8th (Service Battalion.
Formed at Taunton 20.10.14—K3—to Halton Park, near Tring in 63rd Bde. 21st Div. Nov. 1914 to billets in Leighton Buzzard. April 1915 Halton Park. Aug. 1915 Witley Camp. 10.9.15 landed at Havre. 8.7.16 with 63rd Bde. to 37th Div. 11.11.18 63rd Bde. 37th Div. France; Neuville, N.E. of Solesmes.

9th (Reserve) Battalion.
Formed at Plymouth Oct. 1914 as a service bn. of K4 in 98th Bde. of original 33rd Div. Dec. 1914 St. Austell. 10.4.15 became a 2nd reserve bn. May 1915 Wareham. Aug. 1915 Swanage. Oct. 1915 Blandford in 10th Reserve Bde. July 1916 Swanage. 1.9.16 became 45th Training Reserve Bn. at Swanage in 10th Reserve Bde.

10th (Home Service) Battalion.
Formed at Weston-super-Mare on 6.11.16 in 216th Bde. 72nd Div. Jan. 1917 to Bedford. Mar. 1917 to Ipswich. By July 1917 had left 72nd Div. and was disbanded at Ipswich on 30.11.17.

11th Battalion T.F.
On 1.1.17 the 85th Provisional Bn. at Whitstable in 227th Bde. became the 11th Bn. The battalion had been formed at Yeovil in April 1915 from Home Service personnel of the T.F. Bns. in the South-Western Bde. Oct. 1917 Herne Bay. Mar. 1918 Wrentham, Suffolk. 27.4.18 became a Garrison Guard Bn. 6.5.18 landed in France and went to 177th Bde. 59th Div. By 16.7.18 the title 'Garrison Guard' had been discontinued. 11.11.18 177th Bde. 59th Div. Belgium; Pecq, north of Tournai.

12th (West Somerset Yeomanry) Battalion T.F.
Formed at Ismaila, Egypt on 4.1.17 from dismounted West Somserset Yeomanry in 229th Bde. 74th Div. 30.4.18 left Alexandria for France with 74th Div. and landed at Marseilles on 7 May. 11.11.18 229th Bde. 74th Div. Belgium; moving from Havinnes to Escalette, east of Tournai.

13th (Home Service) Battalion.
Formed at Wrentham, Suffolk on 27.4.18 to replace 11th Bn. in 227th Bde. Remained at Wrentham in 227th Bde.

1st Garrison Battalion.
Formed at Plymouth in Jan. 1917 and went to India Feb. 1917.

THE PRINCE OF WALES'S OWN (WEST YORKSHIRE REGIMENT)

1st Battalion.
4.8.14 Lichfield: 18th Bde. 6th Div. 7 Aug. Dunfermline 13 Aug. Cambridge. 10.9.14 landed at St. Nazaire. 11.11.18 18th Bde. 6th Div. France; Fresnoy, N.E. of St. Quentin.

2nd Battalion.
4.8.14 Malta. 14.9.14 embarked for U.K. 25.9.14 landed at Southampton and to 23rd Bde. 8th Div. At Hursley Park, Winchester. 5.11.14 landed at Havre. 11.11.18 23rd Bde. 8th Div. Belgium; Tertre, west of Mons.

3rd (Reserve) Battalion.
4.8.14 York. Aug. 1914 to Whitley Bay where it remained throughout the war (Tyne Garrison).

4th (Extra Reserve) Battalion.
4.8.14 York. Aug. 1914 Falmouth. Dec. 1915 Redcar. April 1916 West Hartlepool where it remained (Tees Garrison).

1/5th Battalion T.F.
4.8.14 York: 1st West Riding Bde. West Riding Div. 10 Aug. Selby. End Aug. Strensall. End Oct. to York for the winter. About Mar. 1915 Gainsborough. 15.4.15 landed at Boulogne. 15.5.15 formation became 146th Bde. 49th Div. 11.11.18 146th Bde. 49th Div. France; Evin-Malmaison, north of Douai.

1/6th Battalion T.F.
4.6.14 Belle Vue Barracks, Bradford: 1st West Riding Bde. West Riding Div. Subsequent record same as 1/5th Bn.

1/7th Battalion. (Leeds Rifles) T.F.
4.8.14 Carlton Barracks, Leeds: 1st West Riding Bde. West Riding Div. Subsequent record same as 1/5th Bn.

1/8th Battalion. (Leeds Rifles) T.F.
4.8.14 Carlton Barracks, Leeds: 1st West Riding Bde. West Riding Div. Subsequent record same as 1/5th Bn. until 1918. 30.1.18 to 185th Bde. 62nd Div. absorbing 2/8th Bn. to form 8th Bn. 11.11.18 185th Bde. 62nd Div. France; Mont Plaisir, west of Maubeuge.

2/5th Battalion T.F.
Formed at York 28.9.14. 1.3.15 to Matlock in 185th Bde. 62nd Div. May 1915 Thoresby Park. Oct 1915 Retford. Nov. 1915 Newcastle. Jan. 1916 Salisbury Plain. June 1916 Somerleyton, near Lowestoft. Oct. 1916 to Bedford.

Jan. 1917 landed at Havre. 13.8.18 disbanded in Vauchelles area.

2/6th Battalion T.F.
Formed at Bradford 12.9.14. Subsequent record similar to 2/5th Bn. but disbanded on 31.1.18.

2/7th Battalion (Leeds Rifles) T.F.
Formed at Leeds 15.9.14. Subsequent record same as 2/5h but reduced to cadre on 16.6.18. Cadre to England and absorbed by 18th Bn. York & Lancaster Regt. at Pirbright on 19.6.18.

2/8th Battalion. (Leeds Rifles) T.F.
Formed at Leeds 14.9.14. Subsequent record same as 2/5th Bn. but on 1.2.18 absorbed by 1/8th Bn. to form 8th Bn.

3/5th and 3/6th Battalions T.F.
Formed at York and Bradford on 25.3.15. 8.4.16 became reserve bns. at Clipstone. 1.9. 165th Bn. absorbed 6th Bn. in West Riding Res. Bde. T.F. at Clipstone. Oct. 1917 to Rugeley, Cannock Chase. Summer 1918 to Suffolk and by Nov. 1918 at Southend.

3/7th and 3/8th Battalions T.F.
Formed at Leeds on 25.3.15. 8.4.16 became reserve bns. at Clipstone. 1.9.16 7th Bn. absorbed 8th Bn. in West Riding Res. Bde. at Clipstone. Autumn 1917 to Rugeley, Cannock Chase. 1918 to Ireland and in Nov. 1918 at Clonmaney, Co. Donegal in 27th Res. Bde.

9th (Service) Battalion.
Formed at York on 25.8.14—K1—to Belton Park, Grantham in 32nd Bde. 11th Div. April 1915 to Witley Camp, Godalming. 3.7.15 sailed from Liverpool. 10.7.15 arrived Mudros. 6.8.15 landed at Suvla Bay. 20.12.15 to Mudros. 7.2.16 arrived Egypt. 1.7.16 landed at Marseilles. 13.11.17 absorbed 400 all ranks of Yorkshire Hussars becoming 9th (Yorkshire Hussars Yeomanry) Bn. 11.11.18 32nd Bde. 11th Div. France; Bettignies, north of Maubeuge.

10th (Service) Battalion.
Formed at York on 3.9.14—K2—to Wareham in 50th Bde. 17th Div. May 1915 Romsey. 14.7.15 landed at Boulogne. 11.11.18 50th Bde. 17th Div. France; Fontaine, S.W. of Maubeuge.

11th (Service) Battalion.
Formed at York on 10.9.14—K3—to Frensham in 69th Bde. 23rd Div. 1.12.14 to Oudenarde Barracks, Aldershot. Feb. 1915 to Folkestone and Maidstone. May 1915 Bramshot. 26.8.15 landed at Havre. 14.11.17 arrived in Italy. 4.11.18 69th Bde. 23rd Div. Italy; near Porcia. west of Pordenone.

12th (Service) Battalion.
Formed 16.9.14—K3—to Halton Park. Tring in 63rd Bde. 21st Div. Nov. to billets in Leighton Buzzard area. May 1915 to Halton Park. Aug. 1915 Witley Park, Godalming. Sept. 1915 landed at Havre. 16.11.15 to 9th Bde. 3rd Div. 17.2.18 disbanded. Formed 10th Entrenching Bn. with 8th E. Yks.

13th (Reserve) Battalion.
Formed at York in Oct. 1914 as a service bn. of K4 in 90th Bde. of original 30th Div. 10.4.15 became a 2nd reserve bn. and Bde. became 2nd Reserve Bde. May 1915 Harrogate. Oct. 1915 Rugeley, Cannock Chase. 1.9.16 became 8th Training Reserve Bn. at Rugeley in 2nd Reserve Bde.

14th (Reserve) Battalion.
Formed at Falmouth in Nov. 1914 as a service bn. of K4 in 103rd Bde. of original 34th Div. Jan. 1915 Penzance. 10.4.15 became a 2nd reserve bn. May 1915 Lichfield. Nov. 1915 Brocton, Cannock Chase in 3rd Reserve Bde. 1.9.16 absorbed in Training Reserve Bns. of 3rd Reserve Bde. at Brocton.

15th (Service) Battalion. (1st Leeds).
Raised at Leeds in Sept. 1914 by the Lord Mayor and City: at Colsterdale. June 1915 to Ripon in 93rd Bde. 31st Div. 10.8.15 taken over by the War Office. Aug. 1915 to Fovant, Salisbury Plain. Dec. 1915 to Egypt. Mar. 1916 to France. 7.12.17 amalgamated with 17th Bn. at Acq to form 15th/17th Bn. 11.11.18 93rd Bde. 31st Div. Belgium; Renaix.

16th (Service) Battalion. (1st Bradford).
Raised at Bradford in Sept. 1914 by the Lord Mayor and City. Jan. 1915 Skipton. May 1915 to Ripon in 93rd Bde. 31st Div. Subsequent record similar to 15th Bn. but it was disbanded in France on 15.2.18.

17th (Service) Battalion. (2nd Leeds).
Raised at Leeds in Dec. 1914 by the Lord Mayor and City as a bantam bn. Jan. 1915 Ilkley. May 1915 Skipton. June 1915 to 106th Bde. 35th Div. at Masham, Yorks. 27.8.15 taken over by the War Office. Aug. 1915 to Salisbury Plain. 1.2.16 landed at Havre. 16.11.17 left 35th Div. for XIX Corps on railway work. 7.12.17 amalgamated with 15th Bn.

18th (Service) Battalion. (2nd Bradford).
Raised 22.1.15 at Bradford by the Lord Mayor and City. Subsequent record similar to 16th Bn. Disbanded in France, 15.12.18.

19th and 20th (Reserve) Battalions.
Formed in Aug. 1915 and Clipstone from depot coys. of 15th and 17th Bns. and 16th and 18th Bns. as local reserve bns. 1.9.16 became 88th and 89th Training Reserve Bns. of 21st Reserve Bde. in Blyth area.

21st (Service) Battalion. (Wool Textile Pioneers).
Raised in the West Riding 24.9.15 by the Lord Mayor and City of Leeds. June 1916 to France and joined 4th Div. on 21.6.16 as pioneer Bn. 11.11.18 Pioneer Bn. 4th Div. France; Montignies area, east of Valenciennes. (Note 1).

22nd (Labour) Battalion.
Formed April 1916 at Millington, near Pocklington. May 1916 to France and to Fifth Army Troops. May 1917 became 18th and 19th Labour Coys, Labour Corps.

A 23rd Battalion was formed at Aldeburgh in June 1918 and was absorbed in the 13th Bn. Yorkshire Regt. in a few weeks.

1st Garrison Battalion.
Formed in August 1915 at ? Sheffield and went to Malta.

2nd (Home Service) Garrison Battalion.
Formed Mar. 1916. Stationed at Witley Bay and in Aug. 1917 became 7th Bn. Royal Defence Corps.

51st (Graduated) Battalion.
On 27.10.17 the 242nd Graduated Bn. (formerly new 10th Training Reserve Bn.) at Clipstone in 207th Bde. 69th Div. became 51st Bn. By May 1918 at Thoresby and in autumn returned to Clipstone.

52nd (Graduated) Battalion.
On 27.10.17 the 277th Graduated Bn. (formerly 9th Training Reserve Bn. from 11th South Staffords) at Canterbury in 200th Bde. 67th Div. became 52nd Bn. Feb. 1918 to 207th Bde. 69th Div. at Clipstone. By May 1918 at Thoresby and in autumn returned to Clipstone.

53rd (Young Soldier) Battalion.
On 27.10.17 the 6th Young Soldier Bn. of the Training Reserve (formerly 13th West Yorks. Regt.) became the 53rd Bn. at Rugeley, Cannock Chase in 2nd Reserve Bde. Later to Brocton. In the autumn to Clipstone.

NOTE

1. 21st Bn. was at Halifax on formation and went to Skipton in Feb. 1916.

THE EAST YORKSHIRE REGIMENT.

1st Battalion.
4.8.14 York: 18th Bde. 6th Div. 8 Aug. Edinburgh. 14 Aug. Cambridge. 10.9.14 landed at St. Nazaire. 26.11.15 to 64th Bde. 21st Div. at Armentieres. 11.11.18 64th Bde. 21st Div. France; Berlaimont.

2nd Battalion.
4.8.14 Kamptee. Dec. 1914 landed in England and to Hursley Park, Winchester in 83rd Bde. 28th Div. 16.1.15 landed at Havre. 26.10.15 sailed from Marseilles. 3.11.15 Alexandria. 28.11.15 sailed from Alexandria. 3.12.15 landed at Salonika. 30.9.15 83rd Bde. 28th Div. Macedonia; north of Lake Doiran.

3rd (Reserve) Battalion.
4.8.14 Beverley. Aug. 1914 to Hedon, nr. Hull. April 1916 to Withernsea where it remained. (Humber Garrison).

1/4th Battalion T.F.
4.8.14 Londesborough Barracks, Hull: York & Durham Bde. Northumbrian Div. To South Holderness then Darlington. Oct. 1914 to Newcastle. 17.4.15 landed at Boulogne. 12.5.15 formation became 150th Bde. 50th Div. 15.7.18 reduced to cadre. To L. of C. in Dieppe area. 16.8.18 to 116th Bde. 39th Div. at Etaples. 7.11.18 demobilized at Cucq.

5th (Cyclist) Battalion T.F.
4.8.14 Park Street, Hull. To Louth. May 1915 Withernsea and Newbiggin. (Tyne Garrison).

2/4th Battalion T.F.
Formed Darlington Sept. 1914 and in Darlington with 1/4th Bn. Nov. 1914 Hull. Feb. 1915 Darlington in 189th Bde. 63rd Div. July 1915 Cramlington near Newcastle. Nov. 1915 Retford. July 1916 63rd Div. broken up and 189th Bde. to Catterick. Nov. 1916 to Bermuda where it remained.

3/4th Battalion T.F.
Formed at Hull 19.6.15 to South Dalton. 8.4.16 became Reserve Bn. 1.9.16 in Northumbrian Res. Bde. T.F. at Catterick. 1917 at Hornsea and by Nov. 1918 at South Dalton after Hornsea till autumn of 1918. (Humber Garrison).

6th (Service) Battalion. (Pioneers).
Formed at Beverley 27.8.14—K1—to Belton Park, Grantham in 32nd Bde. 11th Div. Dec. 1914 became Pioneer Bn. 11th Div. April 1915 Witley Camp, Godalming. 1.7.15 sailed from Avonmouth. 16.7.15 arrived Mudros. 7.8.15 landed at Suvla Bay. 17.12.15 to Mudros. 4.2.16 landed at Alexandria. 10.7.16 landed at Marseilles. 11.11.18 Pioneer Bn. 11th Div. France; Hergies, north of Bavai.

7th (Service) Battalion.
Formed at Beverley 16.9.14—K2—to Wareham in 50th Bde. 17th Div. May 1915 Romsey. 14.7.15 landed at Boulogne. 11.11.18 50th Bde. 17th Div. France; Aulnoye.

8th (Service) Battalion.
Formed at Beverley 22.9.14—K3—to Halton Park, Tring in 62nd Bde. 21st Div. Dec. 1914 billets in Wendover area. May 1915 Halton Park. Aug. 1915 Witley Camp, Godalming. 9.9.15 landed at Boulogne. 16.11.15 to 8th Bde. 3rd Div. 17.2.18 disbanded. Formed 10th Entrenching Bn. with 12th W. Yks.

9th (Reserve) Battalion.
Formed at York 9.11.14 as a service bn. of K4 in 90th Bde. of original 30th Div. 10.4.15 became a second reserve bn. in 2nd Reserve Bde. (formerly 90th). May 1915 York to Harrogate. Sept. 1915 Rugeley, Cannock Chase. 1.9.16 became 7th Training Reserve Bn. in 2nd Reserve Bde. at Rugeley.

10th (Service) Battalion. (1st Hull).
Raised at Hull on 29.8.14 by Lord Nunburnholme and East Riding T.F. Assn. Nov. 1914 to Hornsea. June 1915 to Ripon and 92nd Bde. 31st Div. 11.9.15 taken over by the War Office. Oct. 1915 Salisbury Plain. 15.12.15 sailed from Devonport. 30.12.15. arrived Port Said. Mar. 1916 to France. 11.11.18 92nd Bde. 31st Div. Belgium; near Flobecq, east of Renaix.

11th (Service) Battalion. (2nd Hull).
Raised at Hull on 2.9.14 by Lord Nunburnholme and East Riding T.F. Assn. Subsequent record similar to 10th Bn. but taken over by the War Office on 1.9.15. 11.11.18 92nd Bde. 31st Div. Belgium; near Flobecq, east of Renaix.

12th (Service) Battalion. (3rd Hull).
Raised at Hull by on 11.8.14 Lord Nunburnholme and East Riding T.F. Assn. Subsequent record similar to 10th Bn. but taken over by the War Office on 1.9.15 and disbanded in France on 8.2.18 at Ecoivres.

13th (Service) Battalion. (4th Hull).
Raised at Hull on 3.11.14 by Lord Nunburnholme and East Riding T.F. Assn. Subsequent record similar to 10th Bn. but taken over by the War Office on 27.8.15 and disbanded in France on 8.2.18 at Ecurie.

14th (Reserve) Battalion. (Hull).
Formed at Lichfield in Aug. 1915 as a local reserve bn. from depot coys. of 10th, 11th, 12th and 13th Bns. To Clipstone Jan. Apr. 1916 Seaton Delaval. 1.9.16 became 90th Training Reserve Bn. in 21st Reserve Bde. in Blyth area.

15th (Reserve) Battalion.
Formed at Seaton Delaval in Feb. 1916 by 14th Bn. as a local reserve bn. 1.9.16 absorbed by 15th York & Lancs. Regt. which formed 91st Training Reserve Bn. in 21st Reserve Bde.

1st Garrison Battalion.
Formed at Sheffield in Oct. 1915. Nov. 1915 Lichfield. Feb. 1916 to India.

2nd (Home Service) Garrison Battalion.
Formed at Hull April 1916 and in Aug. 1917 became 8th Bn. Royal Defence Corps.

THE BEDFORDSHIRE REGIMENT

1st Battalion.
4.8.14 Mullingar: 15th Bde. 5th Div. 16.8.14 landed in France. Dec. 1917 to Italy. April 1918 to France. 11.11.18 15th Bde. 5th Div. France; Louvignies.

2nd Battalion.
4.8.14 Roberts Heights, Pretoria. 19.9.14 landed at Southampton and to 21st Bde. 7th Div. at Lyndhurst. 7.10.14 landed at Zeebrugge. 19.12.15 21st Bde. to 30th Div. and Bn. to 89th Bde. 11.2.18 to 90th Bde. 30th Div. 22.5.18 to 54th Bde. 18th Div. 11.11.18 54th Bde. 18th Div. France; Louvignies.

3rd (Reserve) Battalion.
4.8.14 Bedford. Aug. 1914 to Felixstowe and remained in area Felixstowe–Harwich throughout the war. (Harwich Garrison).

4th (Extra Reserve) Battalion.
4.8.14 Bedford. Aug. 1914 to Felixstowe and remained in area Felixstowe–Harwich until July 1916. 25.7.16 landed at Havre and went to 190th Bde. 63rd Div. 11.11.18 190th Bde. 63rd Div. France; Harmignies, S.E. of Mons.

1/5th Battalion T.F.
4.8.14 Gwyn Street, Bedford: East Midland Bde. East Anglian Div. Aug. 1914 to Romford and then Bury St. Edmunds. May 1915 to St. Albans and formation became 162nd Bde. 54th Div. 26.5.15 sailed from Plymouth.

10.8.15 arrived Mudros. 11.8.15 landed at Suvla Bay. 4.12.15 Mudros and on to Egypt. 31.10.18 162nd Bde. 54th Div. Palestine; Beirut.

2/5th Battalion.
Formed at Bedford Sept. 1914. To Newmarket. Jan. 1915 207th Bde. 69th Div. By June 1916 Harrogate. Oct. 1916 Darlington. May 1917 Carburton Camp in The Dukeries. Oct. 1917 Clipstone. 18.3.18 disbanded at Clipstone.

3/5th Battalion T.F.
Formed at Bedford June 1915. Aug. 1915 Windsor Great Park. Oct. 1915 Halton Park, Tring. 8.4.16 became 5th (Reserve) Bn. 1.9.16 in East Anglian Reserve Bde. T.F. at Halton Park. 11.7.17 combined with 1st (Reserve) Bn. Hertford Regt. Autumn 1917 Crowborough and about Aug. 1918 to Hastings.

6th (Service) Battalion.
Formed at Bedford Aug. 1914—K1—Army Troops attached 9th Div. at Aldershot. Mar. 1915 to 112th Bde. 37th Div. on Salisbury Plain. 30.7.15 landed at Havre. 20.5.18 reduced to cadre—700 all ranks to 1/1st Hertford Regt.—cadre to 39th Div. 4.8.18 disbanded in France.

7th (Service) Battalion.
Formed at Bedford Sept. 1914—K2—Army Troops attached 15th Div. at Aldershot. 25.2.15 to 54th Bde. 18th Div. at Colchester May 1915 to Salisbury Plain. July 1915 to France. 25.5.18 reduced to cadre—personnel to 2nd Bn.—cadre to 89th Bde. 30th Div. 19.6.18 to 197th Bde. 66th Div. 31.7.18 cadre absorbed in 2nd Bn.

8th (Service) Battalion.
Formed at Bedford Sept. 1914—K3—to South Downs, near Shoreham in 71st Bde. 24th Div. Billets in Brighton for winter. June 1915 Blackdown. Aug. 1915 landed in France. 11.10.15 71st Bde. to 6th Div. 17.11.15 to 16th Bde. 6th Div. 16.2.18 disbanded in France.

9th (Reserve) Battalion.
Formed at Felixstowe in Oct. 1914 as a service bn. of K4 in 94th Bde. of original 31st Div. Feb. 1915 Mill Hill. 10.4.15 became a 2nd reserve bn. and 94th Bde. became 6th Reserve Bde. May 1915 Colchester. 1.9.16 absorbed in Training Reserve Bns. of 6th Reserve Bde. at Harwich.

10th (Reserve) Battalion.
Formed at Dovercourt in Nov. 1914 as a service bn. of K4 in 106th Bde. of original 35th Div. Jan. 1915 White City. 10.4.15 became a 2nd reserve bn. May 1915 Colchester in 6th Reserve Bde. Mar. 1916 Dovercourt. 1.9.16 became 27th Training Reserve Bn. in 6th Reserve Bde. at Dovercourt.

11th Battalion T.F.
On 1.1.17 the 68th Provisional Bn. at Pakefield, near Lowestoft in 225th Bde. became the 11th Bn. It had been formed at Southwold in June 1915 from Home Personnel of T.F. Bns. Remained at Pakefield in 225th Bde. until the end of the war.

12th and 13th (Transport Workers) Battalions.
Formed in Dec. 1916 and Mar. 1917 at Croydon where they remained, sending working parties to ports as required.

1st Garrison Battalion.
Formed in Dec. 1915 at Bedford and went to India in Feb. 1916.

2nd Garrison Battalion.
Formed in Dec. 1916 at Bedford and went to India in Feb. 1917.

3rd Garrison Battalion.
Formed in Jan. 1917 at Bedford and went to India and Burma.

51st (Graduated) Battalion.
On 27.10.17 the 219th Graduated Bn. (formerly 25th Training Reserve Bn. from 10th Norfolks) at Colchester in 212th Bde. 71st Div. became the 51st Bn. Feb. 1918 to 193rd Bde. 64th Div. at Norwich. May 1918 at Taverham and in autumn 1918 returned to Norwich.

52nd (Graduated) Battalion.
On 27.10.17 the 252nd Graduated Bn. (formerly 26th Training Reserve Bn. from 10th Suffolks) at Colchester in 213th Bde. 71st Div. became the 52nd Bn. Feb. 1918 to 193rd Bde. 64th Div. at Norwich. May 1918 at Taverham and in autumn 1918 returned to Norwich.

53rd (Young Soldier) Battalion.
On 27.10.17 the 27th Young Soldier Bn. of the Training Reserve (formerly 10th Bedfords) at Clipstone in 2nd Reserve Bde. became the 53rd Bn. About Jan. 1918 to Cannock Chase where it remained.

THE LEICESTERSHIRE REGIMENT

1st Battalion.
4.8.14 Fermoy: 16th Bde. 6th Div. 19 Aug. Cambridge. 10.9.14 landed at St. Nazaire. 17.11.15 to 71st Bde. 6th Div. 11.11.18 71st Bde. 6th Div. France; Rue de Vaux, Bohain.

2nd Battalion.
4.8.14 Ranikhet: Garhwal Bde. Meerut Div. 12.10.14 landed at Marseilles. 10 to 17 Nov. Marseilles to Alexandria. In Egypt to 28th Indian Bde. 23 Nov.—6 Dec. Suez to Basra. 28th Indian Bde. to 7th Indian Div. 22.1.18 landed at Suez and to Palestine. 31.10.18 28th Indian Bde. 7th Indian Div. Syria; Shaikh Bedaur, near Tripoli.

3rd (Reserve) Battalion.
4.8.14 Leicester. Aug. 1914 Portsmouth. May 1915 Hull and remained in Hull area to the end of the war (Humber Garrison).

1/4th Battalion T.F.
4.8.14 Oxford Street, Leicester: Lincoln & Leicester Bde., North Midland Div. To Luton area. Nov. Bishop's Stortford area. 3.3.15 landed at Havre. 12.5.15 formation became 138th Bde. 46th Div. 21.1.16 embarked at Marseilles for Egypt but disembarked next day as move was cancelled. 11.11.18 138th Bde. 46th Div. France; Sains du Nord, S.E. of Avesnes.

1/5th Battalion T.F.
4.8.14 Drill Hall, Loughborough: Lincoln & Leicester Bde. North Midland Div. Subsequent record same as 1/4th Bn. but landed at Havre on 28.2.15.

2/4th Battalion T.F.
Formed at Leicester Sept. 1914. Jan. 1915 to Luton area in 2/1st Lincoln & Leicester Bde. 2/North Midland Div. July 1915 to St. Albans area. Aug. 1915 formation became 177th Bde. 59th Div. April 1916 to Ireland. Jan. 1917 to Fovant area. 24 Feb. 1917 landed in France. 8.5.18 reduced to Trg. Cadre and to England with 16th Div. 20.6.18 cadre absorbed by 14th Leicester at Aldeburgh.

2/5th Battalion T.F.
Formed at Loughborough Sept. 1914. Record same as 2/4th Bn. to 3.2.18 and then disbanded.

3/4th & 3/5th Battalions T.F.
Formed 1915, April 1916 became 4th & 5th Reserve Bns. and 1.9.16 became 4th Reserve Bn. stationed at Grantham and Catterick (1916) and North Coates and Louth (1917–18). In North Midland Res. Bde. T.F.

6th (Service) Battalion.
Formed Aug. 1914 at Leicester—K1—Army Troops attached 9th Div. at Aldershot. April 1915 to 110th Bde. 37th Div. on Salisbury Plain. 29.7.15 landed in France. 7.7.16 110th Bde. to 21st Div. 11.11.18 110th Bde. 21st Div. France; Berlaimont.

7th (Service) Battalion.
Formed Sept. 1914 at Leicester—K2—Army Troops attached 15th Div. at Aldershot. April 1915 to 110th Bde. 37th Div. Subsequent record same as 6th Bn.

8th (Service) Battalion.
Formed Sept. 1914 at Leicester—K3—Army Troops attached 23rd Div. in Aldershot area. April 1915 to 110th Bde. 37th Div. on Salisbury Plain. 29.7.15 landed in France. 7.7.16 110th Bde. to 21st Div. 28.6.18 reduced to Training Cadre, surplus to 7th Bn. 29.6.18 to 25th Div. at Boulogne and to England. 7.7.18 cadre formed 14th West Riding Regt. at Clacton.

9th (Service) Battalion.
Formed at Leicester Sept. 1914—K3—Army Troops attached 23rd Div. at Aldershot. April 1915 to 110th Bde. 37th Div. at Perham Down on Salisbury Plain. 29.7.15. landed in France. 7.7.16 110th Bde. to 21st Div. 20.2.18 disbanded at Moislains; personnel to 6th, 7th, 8th and 11th Bns. and VII Corps Reinforcement Camp.

10th (Reserve) Battalion.
Formed at Portsmouth Nov. 1914 as a service bn. of K4 in 96th Bde. of original 32nd Div. 10.4.15 became a 2nd reserve bn. June 1915 to Barnards Castle. Nov. 1915 to Rugeley, Cannock Chase in 1st Reserve Bde. 1.9.16 became 5th Training Reserve Bn. at Rugeley in 1st Reserve Bde.

11th (Service) Battalion. (Midland Pioneers).
Raised at Leicester in Oct. 1915 by the Mayor and local committee. Stationed in Leicester. Mar. 1916 landed in France. 1.4.16 to 6th Div. as Pioneer Bn. 11.11.18 Pioneer Bn. 6th Div. France; Bohain.

12th (Reserve) Battalion.
Formed at Leicester in Mar. 1916 as a local reserve bn. from the depot coys. of the 11th Bn. in 19th Reserve Bde July 1916 to Newcastle-on-Tyne area. 1.9.16 became 83rd Training Reserve Bn. in 19th Reserve Bde.

13th (Labour) Battalion.
Formed in autumn of 1916 and from Oct. 1916 to April 1917 in France with Third Army Troops. April 1917 transferred to the Labour Corps as 20th and 21st Labour Companies.

14th (Service) Battalion.
Formed at Aldeburgh June 1918 absorbing cadre of 2/4th Bn. 26.6.18 joined 47th Bde. 16th Div. at Aldershot. 30.7.18 landed in France. 11.11.18 47th Bde. 16th Div. Belgium; south of Tournai.

1st (Home Service) Garrison Battalion.
Formed at Easington May 1916 where it remained. Aug. 1917 became 9th Bn. Royal Defence Corps.

51st (Graduated) Battalion.
On 27.10.17 the 261st Graduated Bn. (formerly 10th Training Reserve Bn. from 15th Yorkshire Regt.) at Ipswich in 216th Bde. 72nd Div. became the 51st Bn. Jan. 1918 to 207th Bde. 69th Div. at Clipstone. April 1918 Thoresby Park. In the autumn to 208th Bde. 69th Div. at Welbeck.

52nd (Graduated) Battalion.
On 27.10.17 the 267th Graduated Bn. (formerly 15th Training Reserve Bn. from 13th Lancs. Fusiliers) at Witham, Essex in 218th Bde. 73rd Div. became the 52nd Bn. Jan. 1918 to 207th Bde. 69th Div. at Clipstone. April 1918 Thoresby Park. In the autumn to 208th Bde. 69th Div. at Welbeck.

53rd (Young Soldier) Battalion.
On 27.10.17 the 12th Young Soldier Bn. of the Training Reserve (formerly 13th Sherwood Foresters) at Rugeley, Cannock Chase in 1st Training Reserve Bde. became the 53rd Bn. By Nov. 1918 was at Clipstone.

THE ROYAL IRISH REGIMENT

1st Battalion.
4.8.14 Nasirabad. 13.10.14 embarked at Bombay. 18.11.14 arrived at Devonport and to Winchester in 82nd Bde. 27th Div. 20.12.14 landed at Havre. 28.11.15 sailed from Marseilles. 5.12.15 arrived Salonika. 3.11.16 to 30th Bde. 10th Div. 2.9.17 sailed for Egypt arriving 6.9.17. 31.10.18 30th Bde. 10th Div. Palestine; Burka, N.W. of Nablus.

2nd Battalion.
4.8.14 Devonport: 8th Bde. 3rd Div. 14.8.14 landed at Boulogne. 24.10.14 to Army Troops on L. of C. 14.3.15 to 12th Bde. 4th Div. at Le Bizet. 26.7.15 to 11th Bde. 4th Div. 22.5.16 to 22nd Bde. 7th Div. 14.10.16 to 49th Bde. 16th Div. at Kemmel. 23.4.18 to 188th Bde. 63rd Div. 11.11.18 188th Bde. 63rd Div. France; Spiennes, south of Mons.

3rd (Reserve) Battalion.
4.8.14 Clonmel. Aug. 1914 Dublin. Sept. 1916 Templemore, Co. Tipperary. End 1917 Dublin. April 1918 to England and in Irish Reserve Bde. at Larkhill.

4th (Extra Reserve) Battalion.
4.8.14 Kilkenny. Aug. 1914 Queenstown. May 1915 to England at Gosport. Sept. 1915 returned to Ireland at Fermoy. May 1916 Queenstown. April 1918 to England and in Irish Reserve Bde. at Larkhill.

5th (Service) Battalion. (Pioneers).
Formed at Clonmel 29.8.14—K1—in 29th Bde. 10th Div. at Fermoy and Longford. May 1915 to England at Basingstoke. About June 1915 became Pioneer Bn. 10th Div. 7.7.15 embarked at Liverpool. 22.7.15 Mudros. 7.8.15 landed at Suvla Bay. 30.9.15 Mudros. 6.10.15 landed at Salonika. 10 to 16 Sept. 1917 Salonika to Alexandria. 1.4.18 to 52nd Div. 10.4.18 embarked at Alexandria. 17.4.18 arrived Marseilles. 31.5.18 to L. of C. 14.7.18 to 50th Div. at Arques la Bataille, near Martin Eglise, S.E. of Dieppe. 11.11.18 Pioneer Bn. 50th Div. France; Semousies, north of Avesnes.

6th (Service) Battalion.
Formed at Clonmel 6.9.14—K2—47th Bde. 16th Div. Mar. 1915 joined by one coy. (250 all ranks) from Guernsey Militia. At Fermoy till Sept. 1915 and then to Aldershot. Dec. 1915 landed at Havre. 9.2.18 disbanded in France at Saulcourt, near Epehy. Personnel to 2nd and 7th Bns.

7th (South Irish Horse) Battalion.
Formed in France on 1.9.17 from the dismounted 1st and 2nd South Irish Horse. The two regiments had been the Corps Cavalry Regiments of I and XVIII Corps and were dismounted in Aug. 1917 for training as infantry. 14.10.17 to 49th Bde. 16th Div. at Ervillers. 18.4.18 reduced to cadre. 26.6.18 reformed with 500 all ranks from R. Dublin Fus., 250 from R. Munster Fus. and 85 from R. Irish Regt. 4.7.18 to 21st Bde. 30th Div. at Hellbroucq. 11.11.18 21st Bde. 30th Div. Belgium; Ellezelles, east of Renaix.

8th (Service) Battalion.
On 25.5.18 2nd Garrison Guard Bn. Royal Irish Regt. (see below) in 178th Bde. 59th Div. in France became 8th (Garrison) Bn. 20.6.18 to 121st Bde. 40th Div. at Tilques. 13.7.18 'Garrison' deleted from title. 11.11.18 121st Bde. 40th Div. France; Lannoy, south of Roubaix.

1st Garrison Battalion.
Formed at Dublin 2.8.15. 28.8.15 landed at Holyhead. 6.9.15 sailed from Devonport. 24.9.15 Mudros. Oct. 1915 working parties sent to Suvla Bay. 5.2.16 arrived in Egypt where it remained.

2nd (Home Service) Garrison Battalion.
Formed at Dublin Mar. 1916. In Dublin until April 1918 when it became 2nd Garrison Guard Bn. on 18.4.18 and went to France joining 178th Bde. 59th Div. 25.5.18 became 8th Garrison Bn. (see above).

ALEXANDRA, PRINCESS OF WALES'S OWN (YORKSHIRE REGIMENT)

1st Battalion.
4.8.14 Bariam, Punjab. Remained in India throughout the war.

2nd Battalion.
4.8.14 Guernsey. 28.8.14 Southampton and to Lyndhurst in 21st Bde. 7th Div. 6.10.14 landed at Zeebrugge. 20.12.15 21st Bde. to 30th Div. at Fienvillers. 11.5.18 to 32nd Bde. 11th Div. at Mazingarbe absorbing 6th Bn. (21 officers and 640 men). 11.11.18 32nd Bde. 11th Div. France; Goegnies Chaussee, north of Maubeuge.

3rd (Reserve) Battalion.
4.8.14 Richmond: 8 Aug. to West Hartlepool where it remained. (Tees Garrison).

1/4th Battalion T.F.
4.8.14 Northallerton: York & Durham Bde. Northumbrian Div. To Newcastle for a week and then to Hammersknott Park, Darlington. Oct. 1914 Newcastle. 18.4.15 landed at Boulogne. 14.5.15 formation became 150th Bde. 50th Div. 16.7.18 reduced to cadre and to Dieppe area on L. of C. 16.8.18 to 116th Bde. 39th Div. at Cucq, near Etaples. 6.11.18 dismobilized.

1/5th Battalion T.F.
4.8.14 Scarborough: York & Durham Bde. Northumbrian Div. 5 to 12 Aug. Hull then Hammersknott Park, Darlington. 16.10.14 to Billets at Newcastle. 17.5.15 landed at Boulogne. 14.5.15 formation became 150th Bde. 50th Div. 15.7.18 reduced to cadre and to Dieppe area on L. of C. 16.8.18 to 116th Bde. 39th Div. at Cucq, near Etaples. 6.11.18 demobilized.

2/4th Battalion T.F.
Formed at Northallerton on 4 Sept. 1914. Early 1915 to Benton, Newcastle in 189th Bde. 63rd Div. July 1915 Cramlington. Nov. 1915 Gainsborough July 1916 63rd Div. broken up and 189th Bde. to Catterick. 9.11.16 to 220th Bde. 73rd Div. at Blackpool. Jan. 1917 to Chelmsford. Reduced in strength from July 1917 and disbanded 21.12.17.

2/5th Battalion T.F.
Formed at Scarborough Sept. 1914. Subsequent record same as 2/4th Bn. but disbanded 29 Mar. 1918.

3/4th and 3/5th Battalions T.F.
Formed at Northallerton and Scarborough in April and Mar. 1915. April 1916 to Redcar and became 4th and 5th (Reserve) Bns. 1.9.16 4th Bn. absorbed 5th Bn. Autumn 1916 to Catterick and by July 1917 at Sutton-on-Hull. From 1.9.16 in Northumbrian Res. Bde. T.F. April 1918 to Hornsea where it remained. (Humber Garrison).

6th (Service) Battalion.
Formed at Richmond 25.8.14—K1—to Belton Park, Grantham in 32nd Bde. 11th Div. April 1915 to Witley Camp, Godalming. 3.7.15 sailed from Liverpool. 10.7.15 Mudros. 6.8.15 landed at Suvla Bay. 18.12.15 Imbros. 7.2.16 landed at Alexandria. June 1916 with 11th Div. to France landing at Marseilles on 1.7.16. 15.5.18 reduced to cadre, personnel to 2nd Bn. (see above). Cadre to 66th Div. 19 to 29 June and joined 75th Bde. 25th Div. at Boulogne on 30.6.18, landed at Folkestone same day and to Mytchett, Aldershot. July 1918 to Margate and reconstituted absorbing the new 19th Bn. End of Aug. returned to Mytchett and on 9 Sept. 75th Bde. became 236th Bde. for service in North Russia. 17.10.18 sailed from Dundee and landed at Murmansk on 27.11.18.

7th (Service) Battalion.
Formed at Richmond in Sept. 1914—K2—to Wareham in 50th Bde. 17th Div. May 1915 Romsey. 14.7.15 landed at Boulogne. 19.2.18 disbanded, personnel to 6th, 12th and 13th Bns.

8th (Service) Battalion.
Formed at Richmond 22.9.14—K3—to Frensham in 69th Bde. 23rd Div. 1914 Aldershot. Feb. 1915 Folkestone and Maidstone. May 1915 Bramshott. 26.8.15 landed at Boulogne. 13.11.17 arrived in Italy. 4.11.18 69th Bde. 23rd Div. Italy; Palse, west of Pordenone.

9th (Service) Battalion.
Formed at Richmond 26.9.14—K3—to Frensham in 69th Bde. 23rd Div. Subsequent record similar to 8th Bn. until Sept. 1918 when it returned to France, arriving 17.9.18 and joined 74th Bde. 25th Div. 11.11.18 74th Bde. 25th Div. France; Bousies, N.W. of Landrecies.

10th (Service) Battalion.
Formed at Richmond 30.9.14—K3—to Berkhamsted in 62nd Bde. 21st Div. Oct. 1914 Halton Park. Nov. 1914 billets in Aylesbury. May 1915 Halton Park. Aug. 1915 Witley Camp. Godalming. 10.9.15 landed at Boulogne. 10.2.18 disbanded at Moislains, personnel to 2nd, 4th and 5th Bns.

11th (Reserve) Battalion.
Formed at West Hartlepool in Oct. 1914 as a service bn. of K4 in 89th Bde. of original 30th Div. and to Darlington. 10.4.15 became a second reserve bn. (89th Bde. became 1st Reserve Bde.) Oct. 1915 to Rugeley, Cannock Chase. 1.9.16 absorbed in Training Reserve Bns. of 1st Reserve Bde. at Rugeley.

12th (Service) Battalion. (Tees-side Pioneers).
Raised at Middlesbrough 21.12.14 by the Mayor and Town. To Gosforth. Aug. 1915 to Cannock Chase. 27.8.15 taken over by the War Office. Sept. 1915 to Badajoz Barracks, Aldershot as Pioneer Bn. 40th Div. 2.6.16 landed at Boulogne. 5.5.18 reduced to cadre. 26.6.18 cadre absorbed by 17th Worcestershire Regt. at La Belle Hotesse, S.W. of Hazebrouck.

13th (Service) Battalion.
Formed at Richmond July 1915 as a bantam bn. To Aldershot in 121st Bde. 40th Div. 2.4.16 absorbed 18th Sherwood Foresters at Woking. 6.6.16 landed at Havre. 6.5.18 reduced to cadre at St. Momelin. 3 to 17 June 34th Div. then to 30th Div. 30.6.18 joined 75th Bde. 25th Div. and to England. July 1918 reformed at Aldeburgh, absorbing newly formed 23rd West Yorkshire Regt. Subsequent record same as 6th Bn.

14th (Reserve) Battalion.
Formed at Darlington Sept. 1915 as a local reserve bn. from depot coys. of 12th Bn. To Newcastle. 1.9.16 became 81st Training Reserve Bn. in 19th Reserve Bde. at Newcastle.

15th (Reserve) Battalion.
Formed in Mar. 1916 as a second reserve bn. To Rugeley. 1.9.16 became 10th Training Reserve Bn. in 2nd Reserve Bde. at Rugeley, Cannock Chase.

16th (Labour) Battalion.
Formed at Brocklesby, Lincs. in June 1916. 12.7.16 landed at Havre. Employed at Havre on L. of C. until April 1917 and then became 22nd and 23rd Labour Coys., Labour Corps.

17th (Home Service) Battalion.
Formed at Blackpool Nov. 1916 in 220th Bde. 73rd Div. Jan. 1917 to Chelmsford and disbanded 15.12.1917.

18th Battalion T.F.
On 1.1.17 24th Provisional Bn. at Clacton in 222nd Bde. became 18th Bn. The 24th Provisional Bn. had been formed at Newcastle in June 1915 from Home Service personnel of the T.F. Bns. April 1917 to Margate where it remained in the 222nd Bde. until the end of the war.
A 19th Battalion was formed at Margate in June 1918 and was absorbed by the 6th Bn. early in July 1918.

1st Garrison Battalion.
Formed at Pontefract in Oct. 1915. Sailed for India on 24.12.15 and remained in India.

2nd (Home Service) Garrison Battalion.
Formed at Richmond May 1916. Mar. 1917 at Hartlepool and Aug. 1917 became 10th Bn. Royal Defence Corps.

THE LANCASHIRE FUSILIERS

1st Battalion.
4.8.14 Karachi. Oct. to Aden. Dec. sailed for England. 2.1.15 landed at Avonmouth and went to Nuneaton joining 86th Bde. 29th Div. 16.3.15 sailed from Avonmouth 29.3.15 Alexandria. 10.4.15 Mudros. 25.4.15 landed at Gallipoli. 2.1.16 left Gallipoli for Egypt arriving Alexandria. 8 Jan. Mar. 1916 to France landing Marseilles 29.3.16. 11.11.18 86th Bde. 29th Div. Belgium; Moen, S.E. of Courtrai.

2nd Battalion.
4.8.14 Dover: 12th Bde. 4th Div. 20.8.14 landed at Boulogne. 4.11.15 12th Bde. to 36th Div. and returned to 4th Div. on 3.2.16 11.11.18 12th Bde. 4th Div. France; Artres, south of Valenciennes.

3rd (Reserve) Battalion.
4.8.14 Bury. 8.8.14 Hull. Nov. 1916 to Withernsea where it remained. (Humber Garrison).

4th (Extra Reserve) Battalion.
4.8.14 Bury. 8.8.14 Barrow-in-Furness. Oct. 1916 to Barry, South Wales, where it remained. (Severn Garrison)

1/5th Battalion T.F.
4.8.14 Castle Armoury, Bury: Lancashire Fusiliers Bde. East Lancs. Div. 20 Aug. to Turton (Bde. camp). 9.9.14 embarked at Southampton. 25.9.14 arrived Alexandria. 5.5.15 landed at Gallipoil. 26.5.15 formation became 125th Bde. 42nd Div. 28.12.15 Mudros. 15.1.16 arrived. Alexandria. Feb. 1917 to France, landing Marseilles 27.2.17. 11.11.18 125th Bde. 42nd Div. France; Hautmont, near Maubeuge.

1/6th Battalion T.F.
4.8.14 Rochdale: Lancashire Fusiliers Bde. East Lancs. Div. 20 Aug. to Turton (Bde. camp). 9.9.14 embarked at Southampton. 25.9.14 arrived Alexandria. 5.5.15 landed at Gallipoli. 26.5.15 formation became 125th Bde. 42nd Div. 27.12.15 Mudros. 16.1.16 Alexandria. Feb. 1917 to France, landing Marseilles 28.2.17. 19.2.18 to 197th Bde. 66th Div. at Marcelcave absorbing 2/6th Bn. to form 6th Bn. 9.4.18 reduced to cadre. 22.7.18 to 199th Bde. 13.8.18 reconstituted absorbing 12th Bn. from Salonika at Haudricourt. 22.9.18 to 198th Bde. 11.11.18 198th Bde. 66th Div. France; St. Hilaire-sur-Helpe, west of Avesnes.

1/7th Battalion T.F.
4.8.14 Drill Hall, Cross Lane, Salford: Lancashire Fusiliers Bde. East Lancs. Div. Subsequent record same as 1/5th Bn.

1/8th Battalion T F.
4.8.14 Drill Hall, Cross Lane, Salford: Lancashire Fusiliers Bde. East Lancs. Div. Subsequent record same as 1/5th Bn.

2/5th Battalion T.F.
Formed at Bury 9.9.14 Oct. to Mossborough, near St. Helens and then to billets in Southport, 197th Bde. 66th Div. 17.4.15 to Bedford joining 3rd Highland Bde. Highlrnd Div. 4.5.15 landed at Boulogne. 12.5.15 formation became 154th Bde. 51st Div. 7.1.16 to 164th Bde. 55th Div. 11.11.18 164th Bde. 55th Div. Belgium; Ath.

2/6th Battalion T.F.
Formed at Mossborough 29.9.14. Oct. to billets in Southport, 197th Bde. 66th Div. May 1915 to Crowborough. Oct. 1915 Tunbridge Wells. March 1916 Meanee Barracks, Colchester. 26.2.17 landed at Havre. 21.1.18 absorbed by 1/6th Bn. at Marcelcave to form 6th Bn.

2/7th Battalion T.F.
Formed at Salford Aug. 1914. Sept. Mossborough. Oct. billets in Southport. 197th Bde. 66th Div. May 1915 Crowborough. Oct. 1915 Tunbridge Wells. Mar. 1916 Hyderabad Barracks, Colchester. 28.2.17 landed at Havre. April 1918 reduced to cadre. 30.6.18 returned to England in 74th Bde. 25th Div. and to Aldershot. 9.7.18 disbanded and formed 24th Bn.

2/8th Battalion T.F.
Formed at Mossborough 29.9.14. Subsequent record same as 2/7th Bn. till April 1918. Reduced to cadre 22.4.18 and disbanded at Haudricourt 31.7.18.

3/5th Battalion T.F.
Formed at Bury 11.10.14. At Bury till May 1915 then to 197th Bde. 66th Div. at Crowborough. Mar. 1916 to Colchester. 1.3.17 landed at Havre. 14.2.18 disbanded at St. Jans-ter-Biezen, near Poperinghe.

3/6th, 3/7th and 3/8th Battalions T.F.
All formed in Mar. 1915 at Rochdale and Salford. 1915 to Codford. April 1916 to Witley and on 8.4.16 became Reserve Bns. 1.9.16 6th Bn. absorbed 7th and 8th Bns. in East Lancs. Reserve Bde. Oct. 1916 Southport. Jan. 1917 Ripon. July 1917 Scarborough. April 1918 to Bridlington where it remained.

4/5th Battalion.
Formed at Southport spring 1915. To Codford. April 1916 to Witley. 8.4.16 became 5th (Reserve) Bn. 1.9.16 in East Lancs. Reserve Bde. Oct. 1916 Southport Jan. 1917 Ripon. July 1917 Scarborough where it remained.

9th (Service) 5Baattlion.
Formed at Bury 31.8.14—K1—to Belton Park, Grantham in 34th Bde. 11th Div. April 1915 to Witley, Godalming. July 1915 to Egypt, from Devonport 5 July, Alexandria 17 July. 24 July Imbros. 6.8.15 landed at Suvla Bay 18.12.15 Mudros. Jan. 1916 to Egypt arriving Alexandria 31.1.16. July 1916 to July 1916 to France, arriving Marseilles 10 July. 12.2.18 disbanded at Allouagne.

10th (Service) Battalion.
Formed at Bury Sept. 1914—K2—to Bovington in 52nd Bde. 17th Div. 1 June 1915 Hursley. 15.7.15 landed at Boulogne. 11.11.18 52nd Bde. 17th Div. France; Beaufort, south of Maubeuage.

11th (Service) Battalion.
Formed at Codford Sept. 1914—K3—Army Troops, 25th Div. at Codford but soon to 74th Bde. 25th Div. Dec. 1914 to billets at Boscombe. April 1915 Hursley. May 1915 Malplaquet Barracks, Aldershot. 25.9.15 landed at Boulogne. 12.8.18 disbanded near Dieppe.

12th (Service) Battalion.
Formed at Bury Sept. 1914—K3—to Seaford in 65th Bde. 22nd Div. Dec. 1914 to billets at Eastbourne. April 1915 Seaford. June 1915 Aldershot. 5.9.15 landed at Boulogne. Nov. 1915 to Salonika, arriving 5 Nov. July 1918 returned to France, crossing Itea–Taranto 8/9, arriving Forges-les-Eaux 16 July. To 66th Div. 13.8.18 absorbed by 6th Bn. at Haudricourt.

13th (Reserve) Battalion.
Formed at Hull 5.12.14 as a service bn. of K4, to Chesterfield. April 1915 Lichfield. 10.4.15 became a second

64 British Regiments 1914-1918

reserve bn. Nov. 1915 Rugeley. Dec. 1915 Brocton. 1.9.16 became 15th Training Reserve Bn. in 3rd Reserve Bde. at Brocton, Cannock Chase.

There was no 14th Battalion.

15th (Service) Battalion. (1st Salford).
Raised at Salford on 11.9.14 by Mr. Montague Barlow, M.P. and the Salford Brigade Committee. 28.12.14 to Conway, North Wales. 21.6.15 to Catterick Bridge and 96th Bde. 32nd Div. 13.8.15 Codford, Salisbury Plain. 27.8.15 taken over by the War Office. 22.11.15 landed at Boulogne. 11.11.18 96th Bde. 32nd Div. France; Sambreton, south of Landrecies.

16th (Service) Battalion. (2nd Salford).
Raised at Salford on 5.11.14 by Mr. Montague Barlow, M.P. and the Salford Brigade Committee. 11.2.15 to Conway. Subsequent record similar to 15th Bn. 11.11.18 96th Bde. 32nd Div. France; La Folie, south of Landrecies.

17th (Service) Battalion. (1st South-East Lancashire).
Raised at Bury on 3.12.14 by Lieut. Col. G. E. Wike and a committee as a bantam bn. 16.3.15 to Chadderton, near Oldham. June 1915 to Masham, Yorks. and 104th Bde. 35th Div. 27.8.15 taken over by the War Office. Aug. 1915 to Cholderton, Salisbury Plain. 29.1.16 landed at Havre. Early 1917 ceased to be a bantam bn. 11.11.18 104th Bde. 35th Div. Belgium, Grammont.

18th (Service) Battalion. (2nd South-East Lancashire).
Raised at Bury on 13.1.15 by Lieut. Col. G. E. Wike, and a committee as a bantam bn. 8.4.15 to Garswood Park, Ashton-in-Makerfield. June 1915 to Masham, Yorks. and 104th Bde. 35th Div. Subsequent record similar to 17th Bn. 11.11.18 104th Bde. 35th Div. Belgium; Paricke, west of Grammont.

19th (Service) Battalion. (3rd Salford) (Pioneers).
Raised at Salford on 15.1.15 by Mr. Montague Barlow, M.P. and the Salford Brigade Committee. Mar. 1915 to Conway. June 1915 to Catterick Bridge and 96th Bde. 32nd Div. 25.8.15 to Codford, Salisbury Plain. 27.8.15 taken over by the War Office. 22.11.15 landed at Havre. 5.1.16 to 14th Bde. 32nd Div. 29.7.16 to G.H.Q. Troops and became a Pioneer Bn. 7.8.16 to 49th Div. as Pioneer Bn. 11.11.18 Pioneer Bn. 49th Div. France; Odomez, north of Valenciennes.

20th (Service) Battalion. (4th Salford).
Raised at Salford on 23.3.15 by Mr. Montague Barlow, M.P. and the Salford Brigade Committee as a bantam bn. July 1915 to Conway. Aug. 1915 to Cholderton, Salisbury Plain. in 104th Bde. 35th Div. 27.8.15 taken over by the War Office 30.1.16 landed at Havre. 16.2.18 disbanded at St. Jean, near Ypres.

21st (Reserve) Battalion. (Salford).
Formed at Conway in Aug. 1915 as a local reserve bn. from depot coys. of 15th, 16th and 19th Bns. Nov. 1915 to Prees Heath in 17th Reserve Bde. 1.9.16 became 72nd Training Reserve Bn. at Prees Heath in 17th Reserve Bde.

22nd (Reserve) Battalion.
Formed at Ashton-in-Makerfield, Lancs. in Aug. 1915 as a local reserve bn. from depot coys. of 17th, 18th and 20th Bns. Nov. 1915 to Prees Heath in 17th Reserve Bde. 1.9.16 became 73rd Training Reserve Bn. at Prees Heath in 17th Reserve Bde.

23rd (Service) Battalion.
Formed in France in May 1918 at Habarcq, near Arras as 4th Provisional Garrison Bn. and to 176th Bde. 59th Div. 25.5.18 became 23rd Garrison Bn. Lancashire Fusiliers. 19.6.18 to 121st Bde. 40th Div. July 1918 'Garrison' omitted from title. 11.11.18 121st Bde. 40th Div. France; Lannoy, south of Roubaix.

On 9.7.18 the 2/7th Bn. wasre constituted at Aldershot as the 24th Bn. It then went to Cromer where it remained.

THE ROYAL SCOTS FUSILIERS

1st Battalion.
4.8.14 Gosport: 9th Bde. 3rd Div. 14.8.14 landed at Havre. 5.4.16 to 8th Bde. 3rd Div. 11.11.18 8th Bde. 3rd Div. France; Romeries, N.E. of Solesmes.

2nd Battalion.
4.8.14 Gibraltar. Sept. 1914 arrived in England and to 21st Bde. 7th Div. at Lyndhurst. About 6 Oct. landed at Zeebrugge. 19.12.15 with 21st Bde. to 30th Div. and then to 90th Bde. 30th Div. 7.4.18 to 120th Bde. 40th Div. 26.4.18 to South African Bde. 9th Div. 13.9.18 to 28th Bde. 9th Div. 11.11.18 28th Bde. 9th Div. Belgium; Cuerne, N.E. of Courtrai.

3rd (Reserve) Battalion.
4.8.14 Ayr. Aug. 1914 to Gourock-Clyde Defences. April 1916 to Greenock where it remained (Clyde Garrison).

1/4th Battalion T.F.
4.8.14 Kilmarnock: South Scottish Bde. Lowland Div. Aug. 1914 to Stirling. 11.5.15 formation became 155th Bde. 52nd Div. May 1915 to Mediterranean, sailing from Liverpool 21 May and arriving Mudros on 29 May. 7.6.15 landed at Gallipoli. Jan. 1916 to Egypt. April 1918 to France, arriving Marseilles on 17 April. 11.11.18 155th Bde. 52nd Div. France; Jurbise, north of Mons.

1/5th Battalion T.F.
4.8.14 Ayr: South Scottish Bde. Lowland Div. Subsequent record same as 1/4th Bn.

The Ardeer Company T.F.
4.8.14 Ardeer. Very little information is available about this company. It was formed in 1913 by Nobel's Explosives Co. to guard their factory at Ardeer in the event of war. In 1913 and 1914 it went to annual camp with the 4th Bn. Royal Scots Fusiliers. On, or before, mobilization it was on guard duty at the explosives factory at Ardeer. It appears to have been disbanded in Nov. 1914 so that all ranks could go back to their important work in the factory, having handed over the guard duties to a company of the Scottish Rifles. However, the company is still shown in the Army List for Nov. 1918 with five officers. It was not reformed after the war.

2/4th Battalion T.F.
Formed at Kilmarnock in Oct. 1914. Jan. 1915 194th Bde. 65th Div. Summer 1915 at Rumbling Bridge, Kinross. Nov. 1915 at Falkirk and with 2/5th Bn. and 2/5th Border Regt. formed No. 13 Bn. in 194th Bde. Jan. 1916 resumed identity and absorbed 2/5th Bn. Mar. 1916 Chelmsford. Jan. 1917 to Ireland at Ballykinler and Dublin. Aug. 1917 at Oughterard, Galway. Nov. 1917 at Dublin later to the Curragh. 65th Div. was broken up in Mar. 1918 and the battalion was disbanded at the Curragh on 15.5.18.

2/5th Battalion T.F.
Formed at Ayr in Oct. 1914. Subsequent record same as 2/4th Bn. which absorbed it in Jan. 1916.

3/4th and 3/5th Battalions T.F.
Formed at Kilmarnock and Ayr in May 1915. End 1915 (?) Ripon. 8.4.16 became 4th and 5th Reserve Bns. and to Catterick. 1.9.16 4th Bn. absorbed 5th Bn. at Catterick in Lowland Reserve Bde. T.F. Nov. 1917 at Edinburgh. Dec. 1917 to Kinross where it remained. (Forth Garrison).

6th (Service) Battalion.
Formed at Ayr Aug. 1914—K1—to Bordon in 27th Bde. 9th Div. Feb. 1915 to Bramshott. 11.5.15 landed at Boulogne. 7.5.16 to 45th Bde. 15th Div. and amalgamated with 7th Bn. to form 6/7TH BATTALION. 21.2.18 to 59th Div. as Pioneer Bn. 10.5.18 reduced to training cadre. 18.6.18 joined 47th Bde. 16th Div. at Boulogne and

went to England. 20.6.18 to Deal and on 2.7.18 absorbed by 18th Scottish Rifles.

7th (Service) Battalion.
Formed at Ayr Sept. 1914—K2—to Aldershot in 45th Bde. 15th Div. Nov. 1914 Bramshott. Feb. 1915 Basingstoke in billets. Mar. 1915 Chiseldon–Draycott Camp. 9.7.15 landed at Boulogne. 13.5.16 amalgamated with 6th Bn. (see above).

8th (Service) Battalion.
Formed at Ayr 1.10.14—K3—to Codford St. Mary, Salisbury Plain in 77th Bde. 26th Div. Nov. 1914 Bristol in billets. April 1915 Sutton Veny. 20.9.15 landed at Boulogne. Nov. 1915 to Salonika. 30.9.18 77th Bde. 26th Div. Macedonia; near Strumica, N.W. of Lake Doiran.

9th (Reserve) Battalion.
Formed at Gourock 23.10.14 as a service bn. of K4. 10.4.15 became a second reserve bn. May 1915 to Paisley. Aug. 1915 Stobs. Oct. 1915 Catterick. April 1916 Inverkeithing in 12th Reserve Bde. 1.9.16 became 55th Training Reserve Bn. in 12th Reserve Bde. at Inverkeithing.

10th (Works) Battalion.
Formed June 1916 at Ayr? To Dumbarton where it remained until April 1917 when it became 4th Labour Bn., Labour Corps.

11th Battalion T.F.
On 1.1.17 the 11th Provisional Bn. at Deal in 221st Bde. became 11th Bn. The Bn. had been formed in the summer of 1915 from Home Service personnel of the T.F. Bns. 27.4.18 became a Garrison Guard Bn. and went to France on 5 May. 12.5.18 to 178th Bde. 59th Div. July Garrison Guard designation dropped. 11.11.18 178th Bde. 59th Div. Belgium; Velaines, north of Tournai.

12th (Ayr & Lanark Yeomanry) Battalion T.F.
Formed in Egypt 14.1.17 from the dismounted Ayrshire and Lanarkshire Yeomanry in 229th Bde. 74th Div. May 1918 to France. 21.6.18 to 94th Bde. 31st Div. 11.11.18 94th Bde. 31st Div. Belgium, near Renaix.

13th (Home Service) Battalion.
Formed 27.4.18 at Deal to replace 11th Bn. in 221st Bde. and to Ramsgate. About July 1918 to Sandwich where it remained.

1st Garrison Battalion.
Formed at Gailes Oct. 1915 and to India in Feb. 1916. 2nd (Home Service) Garrison Battalion was formed early in 1916 and soon after absorbed in 1st Garrison Bn.

THE CHESHIRE REGIMENT

1st Battalion.
4.8.14 Londonderry: 15th Bde. 5th Div. 16.8.14 landed at Havre. Dec. 1917 to Italy. April 1918 returned to France. 11.11.18 15th Bde. 5th Div. France; near Le Quesnoy.

2nd Battalion.
4.8.14 Jubbulpore. 24.12.14 arrived at Devonport and joined 84th Bde. 28th Div. at Winchester. 17.1.15 landed at Havre. Oct. 1915 to Egypt. Nov. 1915 to Salonika. 30.9.18 84th Bde. 28th Div. Macedonia; north of Lake Doiran. (see Note 1).

3rd (Reserve) Battalion.
4.8.14 Chester. Aug. 1914 to Birkenhead on Mersey Defences. Dec. 1917 to Newcastle-on-Tyne. May 1918 to Seaton Carew. Sept. 1918 to West Hartlepool where it remained (Tees Garrison).

1/4th Battalion T.F.
4.8.14 Grange Road West, Birkenhead: Cheshire Bde. Welsh Div. Aug. 1914 Shrewsbury and Church Stretton and end of month to Northampton. Dec. 1914 to Cambridge. May 1915 to Bedford. 13.5.15 formation became 159th Bde. 53rd Div. July 1915 sailed from Devonport for Alexandria. 9.8.15 landed at Gallipoli. Dec. 1915 to Egypt. 31.5.18 left 53rd Div. and went to France via Alexandria and Taranto. 1.7.18 joined 102nd Bde. 34th Div. at Proven. 11.11.18 102nd Bde. 34th Div. Belgium; west of Courtrai.

1/5th (Earl of Chester's) Battalion T.F.
4.8.14 The Drill Hall, Volunteer Street, Chester: Cheshire Bde. Welsh Div. Aug. 1914 Shrewsbury then Northampton. Dec. 1914 Cambridge. Feb. 1915 left Welsh Div. and landed at Havre. 15 Feb. 19.2.15 14th Bde. 5th Div. 29.11.15 became Pioneer Bn. 5th Div. 13.2.16 to 56th Div. as Pioneer Bn. 11.11.18 Pioneer Bn. 56th Div. Belgium. Athis, north of Bavai.

1/6th Battalion T.F.
4.8.14 The Armoury, Stockport: Cheshire Bde. Welsh Div. Aug. 1914 Shrewsbury then Northampton. Nov. 1914 left Welsh Div. and landed in France 10 Nov. To G.H.Q. Troops and on 17.12.14 to 15th Bde. 5th Div. 1.3.15 to G.H.Q. Troops. 9.1.16 to 20th Bde. 7th Div. 29.2.16 to 118th Bde. 39th Div. 28.5.18 to 75th Bde. 25th Div. 17.6.18 absorbed 16 offrs. and 492 men from 11th Bn. which had been reduced to cadre. 8.7.18 to 21st Bde. 30th Div. near Watten. 11.11.18 21st Bde. 30th Div. Belgium; Anseroeuil, near Renaix.

1/7th Battalion T.F.
4.8.14 The Drill Hall, Macclesfield: Cheshire Bde. Welsh Div. Subsequent record similar to 1/4th Bn.

2/4th Battalion T.F.
Formed at Birkenhead 9.9.14. Winter at Aberystwyth. Mar. 1915 at Northampton in 204th Bde. 68th Div. Aug. 1915 Bedford. 8.12.15 absorbed by 2/7th Bn.

2/5th (Earl of Chester's) Battalion T.F.
Formed at Chester 28.11.14. 18.2.15 to Cheshire Bde. Welsh Div. at Cambridge replacing 1/5th Bn. 22.4.15 to 204th Bde. 68th Div. at Northampton. Aug. 1915 Bedford. Summer 1916 Lowestoft area. 1917 Westleton, near Yoxford. Later to Bury St. Edmunds where it was disbanded on 21.4.18.

2/6th Battalion T.F.
Formed at Stockport 7.9.14. 22.11.14 to Cheshire Bde. Welsh Div. at Northampton replacing 1/6th Bn. Dec. 1914 Cambridge. 22.4.15 to 204th Bde. 68th Div. at Northampton. Aug. 1915 Bedford. 22.11.15 absorbed 2/5th Bn. Welsh Regt. Sept. 1916 in Lowestoft area. Mar. 1917 Yarmouth. July 1917 Southwold where it was disbanded on 11.9.17.

2/7th Battalion T.F.
Formed at Macclesfield on 10.10.14. Mar. 1915 at Northampton in 204th Bde. 68th Div. Aug. 1915 Bedford. 8.12.15 absorbed 2/4th Bn. Sept. 1916 in Lowestoft area. May 1917 Wrentham, south of Lowestoft. In this area until 31.3.18 when it was disbanded at Southwold.

3/4th Battalion T.F.
Formed at Birkenhead on 15.3.15. To Oswestry. 8.4.16 became 4th (Reserve) Bn. 1.9.16 absorbed 5th, 6th and 7th (Reserve) Bns. in Welsh Reserve Bde. T.F. By April 1918 at Kinmel and in Aug. 1918 to Whitstable where it remained.

3/5th, 3/6th and 3/7th Battalions T.F.
Formed at Chester, Stockport and Macclesfield in Mar. 1915. To Oswestry. 8.4.16 became Reserve Bns. 1.9.16 absorbed by 4th (Reserve) Bn. at Oswestry.

8th (Service) Battalion.
Formed at Chester 12.8.14—K1—to Tidworth in 40th Bde. 13th Div. Oct. 1914 to Chiseldon. Feb. 1915 to Pirbright, Aldershot. June 1915 to Egypt. July 1915 Gallipoli. Jan. 1916 Egypt. Feb. 1916 to Mesopotamia.

31.10.18 40th Bde. 13th Div. Mesopotamia; north of Baghdad.

9th (Service) Battalion.
Formed at Chester 13.9.14—K2—to Salisbury Plain in 56th Bde. 19th Div. Dec. 1914 to billets in Basingstoke. Mar. 1915 Salisbury Plain. 19.7.15 landed at Boulogne. 7.2.18 to 56th Bde. 19th Div. 11.11.18 56th Bde. 19th Div. France; west of Bavai.

10th (Service) Battalion.
Formed at Chester 10.9.14—K3—to Codford St. Mary in 75th Bde. 25th Div. Nov. 1914 to billets in Bournemouth. May 1915 to Aldershot. 26.9.15 landed in France, 26.10.15 to 7th Bde. 25th Div. 21.6.18 reduced to cadre: personnel to 9th Bn. End June 1918 to England at Aldershot with 25th Div. July 1918 to North Walsham and absorbed by 15th South Wales Borderers.

11th (Service) Battalion.
Formed at Chester 17.9.14—K3—to Codford St. Mary in 75th Bde. 25th Div. Nov. 1914 to billets in Bournemouth. May 1915 to Aldershot. 26.9.15 landed in France. 17.6.18 reduced to cadre: personnel to 1/6th Bn. 23.6.18 cadre to 39th Div. and disbanded in France on 3.8.18.

12th (Service) Battalion.
Formed at Chester Sept. 1914—K3—Army Troops attached 22nd Div. at Seaford. Dec. 1914 to billets in Eastbourne. Feb. 1915 to 66th Bde. 22nd Div. June 1915 to Aldershot. 6.9.15 landed at Boulogne. Nov. 1915 to Salonika. 30.9.18 66th Bde. 22nd Div. Macedonia; near Lake Doiran.

13th (Service) Battalion.
Raised at Port Sunlight by Gershom Stewart, M.P. on 1.9.14. To Chester. Oct. 1914 to Salisbury Plain joining 74th Bde. 25th Div. To billets in Bournemouth for the winter. May 1915 to Aldershot. 25.9.15 landed in France. 16.2.18 disbanded in France. (see Note 2).

14th (Reserve) Battalion.
Formed at Birkenhead in Oct. 1914 as a service bn. of K4 in 105th Bde. of original 35th Div. 10.4.15 became a 2nd reserve bn. July 1915 to Kinmel. Aug. 1915 Prees Heath in 11th Reserve Bde. 1.9.16 became 59th Training Reserve Bn. at Prees Heath in 11th Reserve Bde.

15th (Service) Battalion. (1st Birkenhead).
Raised in Birkenhead 18.11.14 by Alfred Bigland, M.P. as a Bantam Bn. To Hoylake. June 1915 to Masham, Yorkshire in 105th Bde. 35th Div. Aug. 1915 to Salisbury Plain and taken over by the War Office on 15.8.15. Jan. 1916 landed at Havre. 11.11.18 105th Bde. 35th Div. Belgium; Audenhove, N.E. of Renaix.

16th (Service) Battalion. (2nd Birkenhead).
Raised in Birkenhead 3.12.14 by Alfred Bigland, M.P. as a Bantam Bn. To Bebington. June 1915 to Masham, Yorkshire in 105th Bde. 35th Div. Aug. 1915 to Salisbury Plain and taken over by the War Office on 15.8.15. Jan. 1916 landed at Havre. 6.2.18 disbanded in Belgium.

17th (Reserve) Battalion.
Formed at Bebington 10.8.15 as a local reserve bn. from depot coys. of 15th and 16th Bns. To Prees Heath in 17th Reserve Bde. 1.9.16 became 74th Training Reserve Bn. at Prees Heath in 17th Reserve Bde.

18th and 19th (Labour) Battalions.
Formed at Oldham in Mar. and April 1916. April and May 1916 to France. April 1917 transferred to Labour Corps as 56th and 57th and 58th and 59th Labour Companies.

20th (Labour) Battalion.
Formed at Chester June 1916. July 1916 to France. April 1917 transferred to Labour Corps as 60th and 61st Labour Coys.

21st (Labour) Battalion.
Formed at Chester Aug. 1916 Oct. 1916 to France. April 1917 transferred to Labour Corps as 62nd and 63rd Labour Coys.

22nd (Labour) Battalion.
Formed at Chester Dec. 1916. Dec. 1916 to France. April 1917 transfered to Labour Corps as 64th and 65th Labour Coys.

23rd Battalion T.F.
On 1.1.17 46th Provisional Bn. at Happisburgh, Norfolk in 224th Bde. became the 23rd Bn. The 46th Provisional Bn. had been formed in June 1915 from Home Service personnel of T.F. Bns. At Happisburgh until end of 1917 and then to Bacton. April 1918 at Happisburgh and on 27.4.18 became a Garrison Guard Bn. 21.5.18 landed at Calais and went to 178th Bde. 59th Div. 19.6.18 to 121st Bde. 40th Div. The title 'Garrison Guard' now discontinued. 11.11.18 121st Bde. 40th Div. France; near Roubaix.

24th (Home Service) Battalion.
Formed at Mundesley on 27.4.18 to replace the 23rd Bn. in 224th Bde. Remained at Mundesley.

1st Garrison Battalion.
Formed at Chester 1.8.15. Sept. 1915 to Gibraltar.

2nd Garrison Battalion.
Formed at Bebington Oct. 1915. Mar. 1916 to Egypt. At the end of the war was on Palestine L. of C.

3rd (Home Service) Garrison Battalion.
Formed in Nov. 1915 and in Nov. at Ramsay, Isle of Man. July 1916. Gretna. Nov. 1916 Liverpool. Aug. 1917 became 11th Bn. Royal Defence Corps.

51st (Graduated) Battalion.
On 27.10.17 the 213th Graduated Bn. (formerly 59th Training Reserve Bn. from 13th S.W.B.) at the Curragh in 194th Bde. 65th Div. became the 51st Bn. In Mar. 1918 the 65th Div. was broken up and the Bn. remained at the Curragh.

52nd (Graduated) Battalion.
On 27.10.17 the 221st Graduated Bn. (formerly 61st Training Reserve Bn. from 21st Welsh Regt.) at the Curragh in 196th Bde. 65th Div. became the 52nd Bn. In Mar. 1918 the 65th Div. was broken up and the Bn. remained at the Curragh.

53rd (Young Soldier) Battalion.
On 27.10.17 the 62nd Training Reserve Bn. (formerly 12th R.W.F.) at Kinmel, Rhyl in 14th Reserve Bde. became the 53rd Bn. No further change.

NOTES

1. The 1st Manx (Service) Company joined the 2nd Bn. at Salonika on 12.1.16 and became "A" company. It was formed in the Isle of Man in Mar. 1915—see 7th (Isle of Man) Volunteer Bn. The King's Liverpool Regiment on page 51.
2. The 13th Bn. differed from other locally raised units in two respects. It had no second title, although there is a reference to the "Wirral Battalion" in the regimental history and it was allotted to a division (25th) of the Third New Army—K3.

THE ROYAL WELSH FUSILIERS

1st Battalion.
4.8.14 Malta. 3.9.14 sailed for England and on arrival joined 22nd Bde. 7th Div. at Lyndhurst. 7.10.14 landed at Zeebrugge. Nov. 1917 to Italy. 4.11.18 22nd Bde. 7th Div. Italy; west of Udine.

2nd Battalion.
4.8.14 Portland. 11.8.14 landed at Rouen as L. of C. Troops. 22.8.14 to 19th Bde. at Valenciennes. 12.10.14 19th Bde. attached 6th Div. 31.5.15 Bde. attached to 27th

Div. 19.8.15 Bde. to 2nd Div. 25.11.15 Bde. to 33rd Div. 6.2.18 to 115th Bde. 38th Div. 11.11.18 115th Bde. 38th Div. France; Aulnoye.

3rd (Reserve) Battalion.
4.8.14 Wrexham, but at Pembroke Docks. 9 Aug. returned to Wrexham. May 1915 to Litherland, Liverpool. Nov. 1917 to Ireland and at Limerick to the end of the war.

1/4th (Denbighshire) Battalion T.F.
4.8.14 Wrexham: North Wales Bde. Welsh Div. To Conway till end of Aug. and then to Northampton. 6.11.14 landed at Havre. 7.12.14 to 3rd Bde. 1st Div. at Bailleul. 1.9.15 to 47th Div. as Pioneer Bn. at Les Brebis. 11.11.18 Pioneer Bn. 47th Div. Belgium; Bizencourt, N.E. of Tournai.

1/5th (Flintshire) Battalion T.F.
4.8.14 Drill Hall, Flint: North Wales Bde. Welsh Div. To Conway till end of Aug. then to Northampton. Dec. 1914 Cambridge. May 1915 Bedford. 13.5.15 formation became 158th Bde. 53rd Div. 19.7.15 sailed from Devonport for Imbros. 9.8.15 landed at Suvla Bay. Dec. 1915 to Egypt. 3.8.18 amalgamated with 1/6th to form 5/6TH BATTALION. 31.10.18 158th Bde. 53rd Div. moving back from Palestine to Egypt.

1/6th (Carnarvonshire & Anglesey) Battalion T.F.
4.8.14 Carnarvon: North Wales Bde. Welsh Div. Subsequent record same as 1/5th Bn.

1/7th (Merioneth & Montgomery) Battalion T.F.
4.8.14 Newtown, Montgomery: North Wales Bde. Welsh Div. Subsequent record same as 1/5th Bn. but to 160th Bde. 53rd Div. on 24.6.18.

2/4th (Denbighshire) Battalion. T.F.
Formed at Wrexham Sept. 1914. 22.11.14 to Welsh Div. at Northampton. Dec. 1914 to Cambridge. 22.4.15 to 203rd Bde. 68th Div. at Northampton. July 1915 to Bedford. Nov. 1916 to Aldeburgh. May 1917 to Henham Park, Halesworth. Oct. 1917 to Yarmouth and disbanded by Mar. 1918.

2/5th (Flintshire) Battalion T.F.
Formed at Wrexham Sept. 1914. April 1915 to 203rd Bde. 68th Div. at Northampton. July 1915 Bedford. Nov. 1916 Westleton May 1917 to Henham Park, Halesworth. Oct. 1917 to Yarmouth and disbanded on 16.3.18.

2/6th (Carnarvonshire & Anglesey) Battalion T.F.
Formed at Carmarthen Sept. 1914. April 1915 to 203rd Bde. 68th Div. at Northampton. July 1915 Bedford. Nov. 1916 to Southwold. April 1917 to Henham Park, Halesworth. Disbanded 8.9.17.

2/7th (Meroneth & Montgomery) Battalion T.F.
Formed at Newtown Sept. 1914. Subsequent record same as 2/6th Bn. but at Wrentham for winter 1916–17. Nov. 1916 absorbed 2/1st Brecknockshire Bn. Disbanded 12.9.17.

3/4th, 3/5th, 3/6th and 3/7th Battalions T.F.
Formed in Mar. (3/4 and 3/5) and May (3/6) and June 1915 (3/7) at pre-war stations of 1st Line Bns. 8.4.16 became (Reserve) Bns. 1.9.16 4TH (RESERVE) BATTALION absorbed the other three units in Welsh Reserve Bde. at Oswestry. Mar. 1918 to Kinmel. July 1918 to Herne Bay to end.

8th (Service) Battalion.
Formed at Wrexham Aug. 1914—K1—to 40th Bde. 13th Div. Salisbury Plain. Autumn to Chiseldon in billets? Feb. 1915 to Blackdown. July 1915 to Mudros. 16–30 July at Helles then back to Mudros. 4.8.15 landed at Anzac. Jan. 1916 to Egypt. Feb. 1916 to Mesopotamia, leaving Suez 14 Feb. Basra 28 Feb. 31.10.18 40th Bde. 13th Div. Mesopotamia; dispersed about Kirkuk and Kifri, north of Baghdad.

9th (Service) Battalion.
Formed at Wrexham 9.9.14—K2—to 58th Bde. 19th Div. at Tidworth. Dec. to billets at Basingstoke. Mar. 1915 Tidworth. 19.7.15 landed at Boulogne. 11.11.18 58th Bde. 19th Div. France; Eth, west of Bavai.

10th (Service) Battalion.
Formed at Wrexham 16.9.14—K3—to 76th Bde. 25th Div. at Codford St. Mary, Salisbury Plain. Nov. 1914 to billets at Bournemouth. 29.4.15 to Romsey. 3.6.15 to Barrosa Barracks, Aldershot. 27.9.15 landed at Boulogne. 15.10.15 76th Bde. to 3rd Div. 8.2.18 disbanded.

11th (Service) Battalion.
Formed at Wrexham 18.9.14—K3—to 67th Bde. 22nd Div. at Seaford. Dec. billets at St. Leonards. April 1915 Seaford. June 1915 Aldershot. Early Sept. 1915 to France. 30.10.15 sailed from Marseilles. 5.11.15 arrived Salonika. 30.9.18 67th Bde. 22nd Div. Macedonia; N.W. of Lake Doiran.

12th (Reserve) Battalion.
Formed at Wrexham Oct. 1914 as a service bn. of K4 in 104th Bde. of original 35th Div. 10.4.15 became a second reserve bn. and to Kinmel. 1.9.16 became 62nd Training Reserve Bn. in 14th Reserve Bde. at Kinmel. (Feb. 1915 Tenby .To Kinmel in June).

13th (Service) Battalion. (1st North Wales).
Raised at Rhyl 3.9.14 by Denbigh & Flint T.F. Associations and transferred to Welsh National Executive Committee on 10.10.14 Nov. 1914 to Llandudno in 128th Bde. 43rd Div. 28.4.15 formation became 113th Bde. 38th Div. Aug. 1915 to Winchester. Dec. 1915 to France. 11.11.18 113th Bde. 38th Div. France; Wattignies, N.E. of Avesnes.

NOTE ON THE LOCALLY RAISED BATTALIONS

At a meeting in Cardiff on 29th September 1914 the Welsh National Executive Committee (W.N.E.C.) was appointed with the task of raising a Welsh Army Corps under the same conditions as the other locally raised units in England and Scotland. The force was later reduced to one division—the 38th. The 13th and 15th Bns. of the Royal Welsh Fusiliers, which had already been raised were taken over by the committee and the 14th, 16th, 17th and 19th were soon added. An official authority states that these four battalions were raised in Cardiff but other sources say that they were raised in North Wales. The latter seems the more likely and is how they are shown here.

14th (Service) Battalion.
Raised at Llandudno by the W.N.E.C. on 2.11.14 in 128th Bde. 43rd Div. 29.4.15 formation became 113th Bde. 38th Div. Aug. 1915 to Winchester. Early Dec. 1915 to France. 11.11.18 113th Bde. 38th Div. France; Dimont, N.E. of Avesnes.

15th (Service) Battalion. (1st London Welsh).
Raised in London on 20.10.14. 5.12.14 to Llandudno and 128th Bde. 43rd Div. Subsequent record same as 14th Bn. but disbanded in France on 27.2.18.

16th (Service) Battalion.
Raised at Llandudno by W.N.E.C. from 13th Bn. about Nov. 1914. Subsequent record same as 14th Bn. but on 11.11.18 at Dimechaux, N.E. of Avesnes.

17th (Service) Battalion. (2nd North Wales).
Raised at Llandudno 2.2.15 in 128th Bde. 43rd Div. 29.4.15 formation became 113th Bde. 38th Div. 14.7.15 to 115th Bde. 38th Div. Subsequent record same as 16th Bn.

18th (Reserve) Battalion. (2nd London Welsh).
Raised in London as a service bn. in Feb. 1915 and at Grays Inn. June 1915 to Bangor and 38th Div. Aug. 1915 to Kinmel and became a local reserve bn. in 14th Reserve

Bde. 1.9.16 with 20th Bn. became 63rd Training Reserve Bn. at Kinmel in 14th Reserve Bde.

19th (Service) Battalion.
Raised in Mar. 1915 by the W.N.E.C. as a bantam bn. and at Deganwy in 38th Div. until Aug. 1915. Sept. 1915 to Aldershot in 110th Bde. 40th Div. Early in June 1916 to France. 6.2.18 disbanded in France.

20th, 21st and 22nd (Reserve) Battalions.
Formed in North Wales probably as second reserve bns. By April 1916 at Kinmel in 14th Reserve Bde. 1.9.16 20th Bn. with 18th Bn. formed 63rd Training Reserve Bn. and 21st and 22nd formed 64th Training Reserve Bn. both in 14th Reserve Bde. at Kinmel.

23rd Battalion T.F.
On 1.1.17 47th Provisional Bn. at Mundesley in 224th Bde. became 23rd Bn. The Bn. had been formed in the summer of 1915 with Home Service personnel of T.F. Bns. June 1917 to Bacton. Sept. 1917 to Hemsby, Norfolk where it remained in 224th Bde.

24th (Denbighshire Yeomanry) Battalion T.F.
Formed in Egypt 1.3.17 from dismounted Denbighshire Yeo. in 231st Bde. 74th Div. Early May 1918 to France. 21.6.18 to 94th Bde. 31st Div. 11.11.18 94th Bde. 31st Div. Belgium; moving from Avelghem to Renaix.

25th (Montgomery & Welsh Horse Yeomanry) Battalion T.F.
Formed at Helmia, Egypt 4.3.17 from dismounted Montgomery and Welsh Horse Yeomanry in 231st Bde. 74th Div. Early May 1918 to France. 11.11.18 231st Bde. 74th Div. Belgium; north of Ath.

26th (Service) Battalion.
On 16.7.18 4th Garrison Guard Bn. in 176th Bde. 59th Div. became 26th Bn. 11.11.18 176th Bde. 59th Div. Belgium; Delpre, N.E. of Tournai.

1st Garrison Battalion.
Formed at Wrexham July 1915. To Gibraltar in Sept. 1915 and remained there.

2nd Garrison Battalion.
Formed at Garswood Park, near Wigan 21.10.15. Sailed from Devonport 6.3.16 for Egypt where it remained.

3rd (Reserve) Garrison Battalion.
Formed at Wrexham Feb. 1916. Nov. 1916 Abergele then Rhyl and Gobowen. June 1917 Oswestry. Nov. 1917 to Ireland and at Cork. Mar. 1918 to Crosshaven where it remained.

4th Garrison Battalion.
Formed at Bebington 15.4.16. June 1916 to France and was Third Army Troops. 1918 became 4th Garrison Guard Bn. 16.5.18 to 176th Bde. 59th Div. 16.7.18 became 26th Bn. (see above).

5th (Home Service) Garrison Battalion.
Formed at Wrexham Aug. 1916. To Barrow-in-Furness. Aug. 1917 became 12th Bn. Royal Defence Corps.

6th Garrison Battalion.
Formed at Aintree Sept. 1916. Jan. 1917 to Egypt where it remained.

A 7th Garrison Battalion was formed in Jan. 1917 but disbanded in Feb. 1917.

THE SOUTH WALES BORDERERS

1st Battalion.
4.8.14 Bordon: 3rd Bde. 1st Div. 13.8.14 landed at Havre. 11.11.18 3rd Bde. 1st Div. France; Fresnoy le Grand, north of Le Quesnoy.

2nd Battalion.
4.8.14 Tientsin. 23.9.14 landed at Lao Shan Bay for operations in conjunction with Japanese against Tsingtao. 4.12.14 embarked at Hong Kong and landed at Plymouth 12.1.15. To Rugby and 87th Bde. 29th Div. 17.3.15 sailed from Avonmouth. 29.3.15 arrived Alexandria. 11.4.15 Mudros. 25.4.15 landed on Gallipoli. 11.1.16 Egypt. 15.3.16 arrived Marseilles. 11.11.18 87th Bde. 29th Div. Belgium; near Lessines.

3rd (Reserve) Battalion.
4.8.14 Brecon. 8 Aug. Pembroke Dock. Nov. 1914 to Mar. 1915 detachment of four coys. at Edinburgh. June 1915 to Hightown, near Liverpool where it remained (Mersey Garrison).

1/1st Brecknockshire Battalion T.F.
4.8.14 Brecon: South Wales Bde. Army Troops attd. Welsh Div. 5 Aug. Pembroke Dock. 28.9.14 Dale. 29.10.14 sailed from Southampton with Home Counties Div. Arrived Bombay 3.12.14 transhipped and sailed for Aden arriving 16.12.14. Aug. 1915 to India, Bombay 11 Aug., and remained in India.

2/1st Brecknockshire Battalion T.F.
Formed at Brecon Sept. 1914. April 1915 Dale. End 1915 to Bedford attached 68th Div. Nov. 1916 absorbed by 2/7th Bn. R. Welsh Fusiliers at Wrentham, near Southwold.

3/1st Brecknockshire Battalion T.F.
Formed about April 1915 and in Milford Haven till 1917. 8.4.16 became 1st (Reserve) Bn. 1.9.16 in Welsh Reserve Bde. Aug. 1917 combined with 1st (Reserve) Bn. Monmouthshire Regt. at Gobowen.

4th (Service) Battalion.
Formed at Brecon Aug. 1914—K1—to Park House Camp, near Tidworth in 40th Bde. 13th Div. Oct. Chisledon. Dec. 1914 to Cirencester in billets. Mar. 1915 Woking. 29.6.15 sailed from Avonmouth for Mudros (12 July). 15.7.15 landed on Gallipoli. 8.1.16 Mudros. 30.1.16 Egypt. 15.2.16 embarked at Suez. 4.3.16 arrived Basra. 31.10.18 40th Bde. 13th Div. Mesopotamia; north of Kirkuk.

5th (Service) Battalion (Pioneers).
Formed at Brecon Sept. 1914—K2—to Park House Camp, near Tidworth. 58th Bde. 19th Div. Dec. 1914 to Basingstoke in billets. 10.1.15 became Pioneer Bn. 19th Div. Jan. 1915 to Burnham, Somerset, billets. Mar. 1915 Bulford, April Perham Down. 16.7.15 landed at Havre. 11.11.18 Pioneer Bn. 19th Div. France; Hergies, north of Bavai.

6th (Service) Battalion (Pioneers).
Formed at Brecon 12.9.14—K3 to Codford in 76th Bde. 25th Div. Nov. 1914 Bournemouth in billets. Feb. 1915 became Pioneer Bn. 25th Div. April 1915 Hursley Park. May 1915 Tournay Barracks, Aldershot. 25.9.15 landed at Havre. 2.7.18 to 30th Div. as Pioneers. 11.11.18 Pioneer Bn. 30th Div. Belgium; Amougies, west of Renaix.

7th (Service) Battalion.
Formed at Brecon 14.9.14—K3—to Seaford in 67th Bde. 22nd Div. Dec. 1914 to St. Leonards in billets. April 1915 Seaford. End May Aldershot. 6.9.15 landed at Boulogne. 10.10.15 sailed from Marseilles and arrived Salonika 9 Nov. 30.9.18 67th Bde. 22nd Div. Macedonia; Hasanli, N.W. of Lake Doiran.

8th (Service) Battalion.
Formed at Brecon 19.9.14—K3—to Seaford in 67th Bde. 22nd Div. Dec. 1914 to Hastings in billets. April 1915 Seaford. end May Aldershot. 6.9.15 landed at Boulogne. 30.10.15 sailed from Marseilles and arrived Salonika about 12 Nov. 30.6.18 to 65th Bde. 22nd Div. 30.9.18 65th Bde. 22nd Div. Macedonia; N.W. of Lake Doiran.

9th (Reserve) Battalion.
Formed at Pembroke Dock on 31.10.14 as a service bn. of K4. and on 1.1.15 to 104th Bde. of original 35th Div.

10.4.15 became a second reserve bn. and to Kinmel Park in 13th Reserve Bde. 1.9.16 became 57th Bn. Training Reserve at Kinmel Park in 13th Reserve Bde.

10th (Service) Battalion. (1st Gwent).
Raised at Brecon by the Welsh National Executive Committee in Oct. 1914. End of the year to Colwyn Bay in 130th Bde. 43rd Div. 29.4.15 formation became 115th Bde. 38th Div. July 1915 to Hursley Park, Winchester then Hazeley Down. 4.12.15 landed at Havre. 11.11.18 115th Bde. 38th Div. France; near Aulnoye.

11th (Service) Battalion. (2nd Gwent).
Raised at Brecon by the W.N.E.C. on 5.12.14. Jan. 1915 to Colwyn Bay. 29.4.15 formation became 115th Bde. 38th Div. Aug. 1915 to Hazeley Down, Winchester. 4.12.15 landed at Havre. 27.2.18 disbanded in France.

12th (Service) Battalion. (3rd Gwent).
Raised at Newport by the W.N.E.C. in Mar. 1915 as a bantam bn. July 1915 to Prees Heath in the Welsh Bantam Bde. Sept. 1915 to Aldershot and Bde. became 119th Bde. 40th Div. Dec. 1915 to Blackdown 2.6.16 landed in France at Havre. 10.2.18 disbanded in France.

NOTE
For particulars of the formation of locally raised battalions in Wales see the note at the bottom of page 67 under Royal Welsh Fusiliers.

13th (Reserve) Battalion.
Formed at St. Asaph in July 1915 as a local reserve bn. from depot coys. of 10th and 11th Bns. Sept. 1915 to Kinmel Park in 13th Reserve Bde. 1.9.16 became 59th Training Reserve Bn. in 13th Reserve Bde. at Kinmel Park.

14th (Reserve) Battalion.
Formed at Prees Heath in Sept. 1915 as a local reserve Bn. from depot coy. of 12th Bn. Oct. 1915 Conway. About Jan. 1916 to Kinmel Park in 14th Reserve Bde. 1.9.16 became 65th Training Reserve Bn. in 14th Reserve Bde. at Kinmel Park.

15th (Service) Battalion.
Formed at North Walsham in June 1918. July 1918 absorbed cadre of 10th Cheshire Regt. About Sept. 1918 to Aldershot and possibly disbanded before the end of the war.

51st (Graduated) Battalion.
On 27.10.17 the 230th Graduated Bn. (formerly 58th Training Reserve Bn. from 12th Welsh Regt.) at Aldeburgh in 204th Bde. 68th Div. became the 51st Bn. By April 1918 at Stowlangtoft, Suffolk where it remained in 68th Div.

52nd (Graduated) Battalion.
On 27.10.17 the 282nd Graduated Bn. (formerly 57th Training Reserve Bn. from 9th S.W.B.) at Patrickbourne. Canterbury. in 201st Bde. 67th Div. became the 52nd Bn, Jan. 1918 at Broadstairs. By April 1918 at Foxhall Heath, near Ipswich where it remained in 67th Div.

53rd (Young Soldier) Battalion.
On 27.10.17 the 59th Young Soldier Bn. at Kinmel Park in 14th Reserve Bde. became the 53rd Bn. No further change.

THE KING'S OWN SCOTTISH BORDERERS

1st Battalion.
4.8.14 Lucknow. 2.11.14 sailed from Bombay and was in Egypt 17 Nov. to 14 Dec. arriving Plymouth 28.12.14. To Warley and in mid Jan. to Rugby joining 87th Bde. 29th Div. 18.3.15 sailed from Avonmouth for Egypt arriving 30 Mar. 16.4.15 to Mudros. 25.4.15 landed at Gallipoli. 8.1.16 left Gallipoli for Alexandria. 18.3.16 landed Marseilles. 11.11.18 87th Bde. 29th Div. Belgium; Celles, S.W. Renaix.

2nd Battalion.
4.8.14 Dublin: 13th Bde. 5th Div. 15.8.14 landed at Havre. Dec. 1917 to Italy. 7.4.18 arrived back in France. 11.11.18 13th Bde. 5th Div. France; near Le Quesnoy.

3rd (Reserve) Battalion.
4.8.14 Dumfries. 9 Aug. to Portland and Weymouth. About April 1915 to Edinburgh (Portobello and Craigmillar). Dec. 1917 to Ireland and stationed at Templemore and from May 1918 at Claremorris.

1/4th (The Border) Battalion T.F.
4.8.14 Galashiels: South Scottish Bde. Lowland Div. To Cambusbarron, near Stirling. 11.5.15 formation became 155th Bde. 52nd Div. 24.5.15 sailed from Liverpool. 4.6.15 arrived Alexandria. 14.6.15 to Gallipoli. 8.1.16 to Mudros. 31.1.16 Alexandria. 17.4.18 arrived Marseilles. 11.11.18 155th Bde. 52nd Div. Belgium; Sirault; N.W. Mons.

1/5th (Dumfries & Galloway) Battalion T.F.
4.8.14 Dumfries: South Scottish Bde. Lowland Div. 11.8.14 to Bannockburn, near Stirling. 11.5.15 formation became 155th Bde. 52nd Div. 21.5.15 sailed from Liverpool. 29.5.15 Mudros. 6.6.15 landed at Gallipoli. 7.1.16 Mudros. 4.2.16 Alexandria. 17.4.18 arrived Marseilles. 28.6.18 to 103rd Bde. 34th Div. 11.11.18 103rd Bde. 34th Div. France; Halluin.

2/4th (The Border) Battalion T.F.
Formed in Sept. 1914 at Galashiels. Jan. 1915 to 194th Bde. 65th Div. Aug. 1915 at Hawick. Nov. 1915 formed No. 14 Bn. in 194th Bde. with 2/5th Bn. Jan. 1916 absorbed in 2/5th Bn.

2/5th (Dumfries & Galloway) Battalion T.F.
Formed in Sept. 1914 at Dumfries. Jan. 1915 to 194th Bde. 65th Div. Aug. 1915 to Rumbling Bridge and Milnathort. Nov. 1915 to Falkirk area and with 2/4th Bn. formed No. 14 Bn. in 194th Bde. Jan. 1916 absorbed 2/4th Bn.[1] Feb. 1916 to Chelmsford. Jan. 1917 to Ireland to Ballykinler. July 1917 at the Curragh. Disbanded 15 May 1918.

3/4th and 3/5th Battalions T.F.
Formed in Jan. and Mar. 1915 at Galashiels and Dumfries. Early 1916 to Ripon. 8.4.16 became 4th and 5th (Reserve) Bns. 1.9.16 4th Bn. absorbed 5th Bn. at Catterick in Lowland Reserve Bde. Oct. 1917 to Dunfermline where it remained. (Forth Garrison).

6th (Service) Battalion.
Formed at Berwick-on-Tweed in Aug. 1914—K1—to Bordon in 28th Bde. 9th Div. Mar. 1915 Bramshott. 12.5.15 landed at Boulogne. 6.5.16 to 27th Bde. 9th Div. 11.11.18 27th Bde. 9th Div. Belgium; near Courtrai.

7th (Service) Battalion.
Formed at Berwick-on-Tweed in Sept. 1914—K2—to Bordon in 46th Bde. 15th Div. Feb. 1915 to Winchester in billets. April 1915 to Salisbury Plain—Park House and Chisledon. 10.7.17 landed at Boulogne. 28.5.16 amalgamated with 8th Bn. in Bethune to form 7/8TH BATTALION. 11.11.18 46th Bde. 15th Div. Belgium; Tongres-Notre-Dame, south of Ath.

8th (Service) Battalion.
Formed at Berwick-on-Tweed in Sept. 1914—K2—subsequent record same as 7th Bn.

9th (Reserve) Battalion.
Formed at Portland in Nov. 1914 as a service bn. of K4 in 102nd Bde. of original 34th Div. Feb. 1915 to Dorchester. 10.4.15 became a second reserve bn. June 1915 to Stobs. Oct. 1915 to Catterick. in 12th Reserve Bde. April 1916 to

[1] Resumed identity as 2/5th Bn.

Kinghorn. 1.9.16 became 53rd Training Reserve Bn. at Kinghorn in 12th Reserve Bde.

10th (Service) Battalion.
On 11.6.18 9th Garrison Guard Bn. (formed in France in 1918) became 10th (Garrison) Bn. in 120th Bde. 40th Div. in Lederzeele area. By 13 July title of Garrison dropped and became a Service Bn. 11.11.18 120th Bde. 40th Div. Belgium; near Pecq, east of Roubaix.

THE CAMERONIANS (SCOTTISH RIFLES).

1st Battalion.
4.8.14 Glasgow: 15.8.14 landed at Havre, L. of C. Troops. 22.8.14 joined 19th Bde. forming at Valenciennes. 12.10.14 19th Bde. attached 6th Div. 31.5.15 Bde. attached to 27th Div. 19.8.15 Bde. to 2nd Div. 25.11.15 19th Bde. to 33rd Div. 11.11.18 19th Bde. 33rd Div. France; Sart-Bara, near Berlaimont.

2nd Battalion.
4.8.14 Malta. 15.9.14 sailed for England and arrived Southampton 22.9.14. To Hursley Park to 23rd Bde. 8th Div. 5.11.14 landed at Havre. 3.2.18 to 59th Bde. 20th Div. 11.11.18 59th Bde. 20th Div. France; Jenlain, north of Le Quesnoy.

3rd (Reserve) Battalion.
4.8.14 Hamilton. Aug. 1914 to Nigg, Cromarty until early in 1918 then to Invergordon, in Cromarty Garrison.

4th (Extra Reserve) Battalion.
4.8.14 Hamilton. Aug. 1914 to Gourock. April 1916 Greenock. By 1917 on coast defence in East Lothian at Haddington. In Edinburgh Special Reserve Bde. June 1918 to Redford Barracks, Edinburgh. (Forth Garrison).

1/5th Battalion T.F.
4.8.14 261 W Princes Street, Glasgow: Scottish Rifle Bde. Lowland Div. Aug. to Larbert. Nov. 1914 left Lowland Div. and went to France landing at Havre. on 5.11.14. 19.11.14 to 19th Bde. 6th Div. 31.5.15 Bde attached to 27th Div. 19.8.15 19th Bde. to 2nd Div. 25.11.15 19th Bde. to 33rd Div. 29.5.16 amalgamated with 1/6th Bn. to form 5/6TH BATTALION. 11.11.18 19th Bde. 33rd Div. France; Sart-Bara, near Berlaimont.

1/6th Battalion T.F.
4.8.14 Muirhall, Hamilton: Scottish Rifle Bde. Lowland Div. Aug. to Falkirk area. Mar. 1915 left Lowland Div. and went to France landing at Havre 21 Mar. 24.3.15 to 23rd Bde. 8th Div. at Estaires. 2.6.15 to 154th Bde. 51st Div. 12.1.16 to Div. Troops to be trained as Pioneers. 25.2.16 to 100th Bde. 33rd Div. 29.2.16 amalgamated with 1/5th Bn. (see above).

1/7th Battalion T.F.
4.8.14 Victoria Road, Glasgow: Scottish Rifle Bde. Lowland Div. Aug. to Grangemouth. 11.5.15 formation became 156th Bde. 52nd Div. May 1915 to Mediterranean embarking Liverpool on 24 May, arriving Alexandria 4 June. 14.6.15 landed at Gallipoli. 1.7.15 formed a composite bn. with 1/8th Bn. 9.1.16 at Mudros 21.2.16 resumed identity. April 1918 to France arriving Marseilles 17 April. 11.11.18 156th Bde. 52nd Div. France; Jurbise, north of Mons.

1/8th Battalion T.F.
4.8.14 149 Cathedral Street, Glasgow: Scottish Rifle Bde. Lowland Div. Aug. to Larbert. 11.5.15 formation became 156th Bde. 52nd Div. May 1915 to Mediterranean, embarking Devonport 18 May arriving Mudros 29 May. 14.6.15 landed at Gallipoli. Subsequent record same as 1/7th Bn. until 28.6.18 when the bn. was transferred to 103rd Bde. 34th Div. 11.11.18 103rd Bde. 34th Div. France; Halluin.

2/5th Battalion T.F.
Formed in Glasgow Sept. 1914. Jan. 1915 in 195th Bde. 65th Div. By Aug. 1915 at Cambusbarron, near Stirling. In Nov. 1915 with 2/8th Bn. formed No. 17 Bn. in 195th Bde. Jan 1916 resumed identity and absorbed 2/8th Bn. Mar. 1916 to Billericay and by July 1916 at Terling, Essex. Jan. 1917 to Ireland, to Moore Park, near Fermoy. Jan. 1918 at Tralee and disbanded on 15 May 1918.

2/6th Battalion T.F.
Formed at Hamilton Sept. 1914. Jan. 1915 in 195th Bde. 65th Div. By Aug. 1915 at Cambusbarron near Stirling. In Nov. 1915 with 2/7th Bn. formed No. 18 Bn. in 195th Bde. Jan. 1916 resumed identity and absorbed 2/7th Bn. Mar. 1916 to Billericay and by July 1916 at Terling, Essex. Jan. 1917 to Ireland, to Kilworth. Jan. 1918 in Galway and disbanded on 15 May 1918.

2/7th Battalion T.F.
Formed in Glasgow Sept. 1914. Subsequent record same as 2/6th Bn.

2/8th Battalion T.F.
Formed in Glasgow Sept. 1914. Subsequent record same as 2/5th Bn.

3/5th Battalion T.F.
Formed in Glasgow Nov. 1914. By Nov. 1915 at Ripon. 8.4.16 became 5TH (RESERVE) BATTALION and to Catterick. 1.9.16 absorbed 6th, 7th and 8th (Reserve) Bns. in Lowland Reserve Bde. at Catterick. Autumn 1917 at Galashiels and Hawick. Dec. 1917 to Leven where it remained. (Forth Garrison).

3/6th, 3/7th and 3/8th Battalions T.F.
Formed at Hamilton (6) April 1915 and Glasgow (7 & 8) Mar. 1915. To Ripon. 8.4.16 became 6th, 7th and 8th (Reserve) Bns. To Catterick. 1.9.16 absorbed by 5th (Reserve) Bn.

9th (Service) Battalion.
Formed at Hamilton Aug. 1914—K1—to 28th Bde. 9th Div. at Bordon. 12.5.15 landed at Boulogne. 6.5.16 to 27th Bde. 9th Div. 5.2.18 to 43rd Bde. 14th Div. 21.4.18 to South African Bde. 9th Div. 12.9.18 to 28th Bde. 9th Div. 11.11.18 28th Bde. 9th Div. Belgium; Cuerne, N.E. of Courtrai.

10th (Service) Battalion.
Formed at Hamilton Sept. 1914—K2—to 46th Bde. 15th Div. at Bordon. Feb. 1915 to Winchester in billets. April 1915 to Salisbury Plain, Park House and Chiseldon. 10.7.15 landed at Boulogne. 11.11.18 46th Bde. 15th Div. Belgium; moving to Tongres-Notre-Dame, south of Ath.

11th (Service) Battalion.
Formed at Hamilton Oct. 1914—K3—to 77th Bde. 26th Div. at Codford St. Mary, Salisbury Plain. Nov. 1914 to Bristol in billets. Feb. 1915 Warminster. April 1915 Sutton Veny. 20.9.15 landed at Boulogne. Nov. 1915 to Salonika landing 24 Nov. 30.9.18 77th Bde. 26th Div. Macedonia; Strumica, N.W. of Lake Doiran.

12th (Reserve) Battalion.
Formed at Nigg Oct. 1914 as a service bn. of K4 in 101st Bde. of original 34th Div. Feb. 1915 to Tain. 10.4.15 became a second reserve bn. May 1915 Stobs. By Dec. 1915 at Catterick in 12th Reserve Bde. April 1916 Kinghorn. 1.9.16 became 56th Training Reserve Bn. in 12th Reserve Bde. at Kinghorn.

13th (Service) Battalion.
Formed at Hamilton July 1915 as a bantam bn. Sept. 1915 to 120th Bde. 40th Div. at Aldershot. Feb. 1916 absorbed by 14th H.L.I. at Aldershot.

14th (Labour) Battalion.
Formed June 1916 and to France in July on L. of C.

April 1917 became Nos. 3 and 4 Coys. of Labour Corps.
15th Battalion T.F.
On 1.1.17 10th Provisional Bn. at Deal in 221st Bde. became 15th Bn. The 10th Provisional Bn. had been formed in the summer of 1915 from Home Service personnel of the T.F. Bns. Early 1918 at Walmer and returned to Deal by April 1918 where it remained in 221st Bde.
16th and 17th (Transport Workers) Battalions.
Formed at Paisley in Dec. 1916 and at Hamilton in Feb. 1917 for duty at ports. 16th Bn. remained at Paisley but 17th Bn. moved to Motherwell in 1918.
18th (Service) Battalion.
Formed at Aldershot 1.6.18 and moved to Deal. 20.6.18 absorbed cadre of 6/7th Royal Scots Fusiliers. 2.7.18 to 48th Bde. 16th Div. at Aldershot. 31.7.18 to France. 11.11.18 48th Bde. 16th Div. Belgium; south of Tournai.
There may have been a 19th (Transport Workers) Bn. and A.C.I. 1220 of 2 Nov. 1918 ordered the formation of 20th (Transport Workers) Bn.
1st Garrison Battalion.
Formed at Hamilton Feb. 1916 and went to India at the end of the month.

THE ROYAL INNISKILLING FUSILIERS

1st Battalion.
4.8.14 Trimulgherry, India. Early Dec. sailed for England arriving Avonmouth 10.1.15. To Rugby and 87th Bde. 29th Div. Mar. 1915 to Mediterranean, Mudros in April. 25.4.15 landed at Gallipoli. 8/9 Jan. 1916 evacuated Gallipoli and went to Egypt. 18.3.16 arrived Marseilles. 5.2.18 to 109th Bde. 36th Div. 11.11.18 109th Bde. 36th Div. France; Roncq, north of Tourcoing.
2nd Battalion.
4.8.14 Dover: 12th Bde. 4th Div. 8–18 Aug. Norfolk. 22.8.14 landed at Havre. 6.12.14 to G.H.Q. Troops. 26.1.15 to 5th Bde. 2nd Div. 22.7.15 to Third Army Troops. 18.11.15 to 14th Bde. 5th Div. 24.12.15 to 96th Bde. 32nd Div. 3.2.18 to 109th Bde. 36th Div. 11.11.18 109th Bde. 36th Div. France; Roncq, north of Tourcoing.
3rd (Reserve) Battalion.
4.8.14 Omagh. Aug. to Lough Swilly. Sept. 1914 Londonderry. About April 1918 absorbed 4th and 12th Bns. and to Oswestry in West Lancs. Reserve Bde. where it remained.
4th (Extra Reserve) Battalion.
4.8.14 Enniskillen. Aug. to Lough Swilly. Oct. 1914 Buncrana. 1916 Clonmany then back to Buncrana. About April 1918 absorbed by 3rd Bn. at Oswestry.
5th (Service) Battalion.
Formed at Omagh Aug. 1914—K1—31st Bde. 10th Div. at Dublin. Early 1915 Kildare. April 1915 Basingstoke. July 1915 to Mediterranean—Mudros. 7.8.15 landed at Gallipoli. Oct. 1915 to Salonika. Sept. 1917 to Egypt and Palestine. 28.5.18 left 10th Div. and went to France, embarking Alexandria 17 June, Taranto 22 June arriving Serqueux 29.6.18. 19.7.18 to 198th Bde. 66th Div. at Abancourt. 11.11.18 198th Bde. 66th Div. France; near Avesnes.
6th (Service) Battalion.
Formed at Omagh Aug. 1914—K1—31st Bde. 10th Div. at Dublin. Early 1915 Kildare. April 1915 Basingstoke. July 1915 to Mediterranean—Mudros. 7.8.15 landed at Gallipoli. Oct. 1915 to Salonika. Sept. 1917 to Egypt and Palestine. 2.5.18 left 10th Div. and went to France landing at Marseilles on 1.6.18. 7.6.18 to 43rd Bde. 14th Div. 18.6.18 to 103rd Bde. 34th Div. 29.6.18 to L. of C. 16.7.18 to 151st Bde. 50th Div. at Martin Eglise. 11.11.18 151st Bde. 50 the Div. France; near Monceau, N.W. of Avesnes.
7th (Service) Battalion.
Formed at Omagh Oct. 1914—K2—49th Bde. 16th Div. at Tipperary. Aug. 1915 Finner Camp. Sept. 1915 Woking. Feb. 1916. to France. 23.8.17 amalgamated with 8th Bn. to form 7TH/8TH BATTALION. 22.4.18 reduced to training cadre, personnel to 2nd Royal Irish Regt. 17.6.18 to 102nd Bde. 34th Div. 26.6.18 to G.H.Q. Troops and reformed with 18 officers and 857 men from 8th Rifle Brigade. 3.7.18 to 89th Bde. 30th Div. 11.11.18 89th Bde. 30th Div. Belgium; N.W. of Lessines.
8th (Service) Battalion.
Formed at Omagh Oct. 1914—K2—49th Bde. 16th Div. at Tipperary. Subsequent record same as 7th Battalion.
9th (Service) Battalion. (Co. Tyrone).
Raised at Omagh in Sept. 1914 from the Tyrone Volunteers and included two companies of Volunteers who had already joined the 5th and 6th Bns. To Finner Camp in 3rd Bde. Ulster Div. 2.11.14 formation became 109th Bde. 36th Div. Jan. 1915 to Randalstown. July 1915 Ballycastle. Early Sept. 1915 to Bordon area. Oct. 1915 to France. 11.11.18 109th Bde. 36th Div. France; Roncq, north of Tourcoing.
10th (Service) Battalion. (Derry).
Raised at Omagh in Sept. 1914 from Derry Volunteers. To Finner Camp in 3rd Bde. Ulster Div. 2.11.14 formation became 109th Bde. 36th Div. May 1915 Randalstown. July 1915 to Seaford. Early Sept. 1915 to Bordon area. Oct. 1915 to France. 21.1.18 disbanded in France, 7 officers and 150 men to 2nd Bn.
11th (Service) Battalion. (Donegal and Fermanagh).
Raised at Omagh in Sept. 1914 from Donegal and Fermanagh Volunteers. To Finner Camp in 3rd Bde. Ulster Div. 2.11.14 formation became 109th Bde. 36th Div. Nov. 1914 to Enniskillen. Jan. 1915 Randalstown. July 1915 to Seaford. Early Sept. 1915 to Bordon area. Oct. 1915 to France. 21.2.18 disbanded in France, 20 officers and 400 men to 9th Bn.
12th (Reserve) Battalion.
Formed at Enniskillen April 1915 from depot coys. of 9th, 10th and 11th Bns. June 1915 to Ballyshannon. Aug. 1915 to Newtownards. Dec. 1915 to Enniskillen, now in 15th Reserve Bde. 1916 to Finner Camp. About April 1918 absorbed by 3rd Bn. at Oswestry.
Further particulars about the raising of the 9th, 10th and 11th Battalions are given below.
13th (Service) Battalion.
On 11.6.18 the 11th Garrison Guard Bn. in France became the 13th (Garrison) Bn. in 119th Bde. 40th Div. near St. Omer. 13.7.18 word Garrison omitted from title. 11.11.18 119th Bde. 40th Div. France; south of Roubaix.

THE 36TH (ULSTER) DIVISION

The First and Second New Armies formed in August, 1914 each contained an Irish Division, the 10th and 16th. These divisions were composed of service battalions from all the Irish Infantry Regiments.
In September 1914 the Ulster Division was formed from the Ulster Volunteer Force which raised thirteen battalions for the three Irish Regiments based in Ulster; Royal Inniskilling Fusiliers, Royal Irish Rifles and Royal Irish Fusiliers. These battalions were clothed and administered by their raisers in the same way as the locally raised New Army battalions in Great Britain. They also had a second title showing their local origin.
On 28 October 1914 the division was numbered 36th

THE GLOUCESTERSHIRE REGIMENT

1st Battalion.
  4.8.14 Bordon: 3rd Bde. 1st Div. 13.8.14 landed at Havre. 11.11.18 3rd Bde. 1st Div. France; Fresnoy-le-Grand.

2nd Battalion.
  4.8.14 Tientsin. Sept. sailed for U.K. 8.11.14 landed at Southampton, to Winchester joining 81st Bde. 27th Div. 18.12.14 landed at Havre. End Nov. 1915 to Salonika, landing on 12 Dec. 3.11.16 to 82nd Bde. 27th Div. 10.9.18 82nd Bde. 27th Div. Macedonia; north of Lake Doiran.

3rd (Reserve) Battalion.
  4.8.14 Bristol. Aug. 1914 to Abbey Wood, Woolwich. May 1915 Gravesend. May 1916 Sittingbourne. Remained in Sittingbourne-Maidstone area until the end of the war. (Thames and Medway Garrison).

1/4th (City of Bristol) Battalion T.F.
  4.8.14 Queen's Road, Clifton, Bristol: Gloucester and Worcester Bde. South Midland Div. Aug. 1914 to Swindon and end of month to Maldon, Essex. 30.3.15 landed at Boulogne. 15.5.15 formation became 144th Bde. 48th Div. End Nov. 1917 to Italy. 4.11.18 144th Bde. 48th Div. Austria: Baselge di Pine, N.E. of Trent.

1/5th Battalion T.F.
  4.8.14 The Barracks, Gloucester: South Midland Bde. South Midland Div. Aug. 1914 to war station in Isle of Wight for a few days then rejoined div. at Swindon. End Aug. to Chelmsford. 29.3.15 landed at Boulogne. 15.5.15 formation became 145th Bde. 48th Div. End Nov. 1917 to Italy. 11.9.18 left 48th Div. and returned to France. 17.9.18 to 75th Bde. 25th Div. in St. Riquier area. 11.11.18 75th Bde. 25th Div. France; Preux, north of Landrecies.

1/6th Battalion T.F.
  4.8.14 St. Michael's Hill, Bristol: Gloucester & Worcester Bde. South Midland Div. Subsequent reocrd similar to 1/4th Bn. but location on 4.11.18 was Cire, east of Trent.

2/4th (City of Bristol) Battalion T.F.
  Formed at Bristol in Sept. 1914. Jan. 1915 to Northampton in 183rd Bde. 61st Div. April 1915 to Chelmsford. Feb. 1916 to Salisbury Plain. 24.5.16 landed in France. 20.2.18 disbanded in France.

2/5th Battalion T.F.
  Formed at Gloucester in Sept. 1914. 1.2.15 to Northampton in 184th Bde. 61st Div. April 1915 to Chelmsford. 19 Feb. 1916 to Park House Camp, near Tidworth. 25.5.16 landed at Havre. 11.11.18 184th Bde. 61st Div. France; Maresches, south of Valenciennes.

2/6th Battalion T.F.
  Formed at Bristol in Sept. 1914. Subsequent record similar to 2/4th Bn.

3/4th, 3/5th and 3/6th Battalions T.F.
  Formed in 1915 and for winter 1915/16 at Weston-super-Mare. 8.4.16 became 4th, 5th and 6th Reserve Bns. 1.9.16 4th Bn. absorbed 5th and 6th Bns. in South Midlands Res. Bde. T.F. at Ludgershall. Winter 1916/17 at Cheltenham. Mar. 1917 at Catterick. July 1917 Horton, Northumberland. Oct. 1917 to Seaton Delaval where it remained. (Tyne Garrison).

7th (Service) Battalion.
  Formed at Bristol Aug. 1914—K1—39th Bde. 13th Div. To Tidworth. Jan. 1915 Basingstoke in billets. Feb. 1915 Blackdown, Aldershot. June 1915 sailed from Avonmouth. July 1915 landed at Gallipoli. Jan. 1916 to Egypt. Feb. 1916 to Mesopotamia. July 1918 39th Bde. to North Persia Force. 31.10.18 39th Bde. North Persia; Bijar.

8th (Service) Battalion.
  Formed at Bristol Sept. 1914—K2—To Perham Down in 57th Bde. 19th Div. Dec. 1914 in winter billets. Mar. 1915 Tidworth. 18.7.15 landed in France. 11.11.18 57th Bde. 19th Div. France; west of Bavai.

9th (Service) Battalion.
  Formed at Bristol Sept. 1914—K3—To Codford St. Mary in 78th Bde. 26th Div. Nov. 1914 to billets in Cheltenham. April 1915 Longbridge Deverill area. 21.9.15 landed in France. Nov. 1915 to Salonika. 4.7.18 left 26th Div. for France via Itea and Taranto arriving Serqueux on 17 July. 21.7.18 to 198th Bde. 66th Div. 22.9.18 became Pioneer Bn. 66th Div. 11.11.18 Pioneer Bn. 66th Div. France; east of Avesnes.

10th (Service) Battalion.
  Formed at Bristol Sept. 1914—K3—Army Troops attached 26th Div. on Salisbury Plain. Nov. 1914 to billets in Cheltenham. April 1915 Salisbury Plain. 8.8.15 landed in France. 17.8.15 to 1st Bde. 1st Div. 14.2.18 disbanded in France: personnel to 13th Entrenching Bn.

11th (Reserve) Battalion.
  Formed at Abbey Wood, Woolwich in Oct. 1914 as a service bn. of K4 in 106th Bde. of original 35th Div. Nov. 1914 to Cheltenham. 10.4.15 became a 2nd reserve bn. May 1915 Belhus Park, near Grays, Essex. Sept. 1915 Seaford in 4th Reserve Bde. 1.9.16 became 16th Training Reserve Bn. in 4th Reserve Bde. at Seaford.

12th (Service) Battalion. (Bristol).
  Raised at Bristol by the Citizens' Recruiting Committee on 30.8.14. June 1915 to Wensley Dale joining 95th Bde. 32nd Div. 23.6.15 taken over by the War Office. Aug. 1915 to Salisbury Plain. 21.11.15 landed in France. 26.12.15 with 95th Bde. to 5th Div. Nov. 1917 to Italy with 5th Div. April 1918 returned to France with 5th Div. 19.10.18 disbanded in France.

13th (Service) Battalion. (Forest of Dean) (Pioneers).
  Raised by Lieut. Col. H. Webb, M.P. Dec. 1914 at Malvern. 12.7.15 taken over by the War Office. Aug. 1915 to Winchester as Pioneer Bn. 39th Div. Sept. 1915 to Aldershot. 3.3.16 landed in France. 6.5.18 reduced to cadre. 16.6.18 cadre to 66th Div. 20.9.18 to L. of C. with 197th Bde. 11.11.18 197th Bde. France; near Aumale.

14th (Service) Battalion. (West of England).
  Raised at Bristol by the Citizens' Recruiting Committee as a Bantam Bn. 22.4.15. June 1915 to Masham, Yorkshire in 105th Bde. 35th Div. 23.6.15 taken over by the War Office. Aug. 1915 to Salisbury Plain. 30.1.16 landed at Havre. 11.2.18 disbanded in France. 12 officers and 250 other ranks to 13th Bn.

15th (Reserve) Battalion.
  Formed in Aug. 1915 from depot coys. of 12th and 14th Bns. at Sutton Coldfield as a local reserve bn. To Chiseldon in 22nd Reserve Bde. 1.9.16 became 93rd Training Reserve Bn. at Chiseldon in 22nd Reserve Bde.

16th (Reserve) Battalion.
  Formed in Nov. 1915 from depot coys. of 13th Bn. at Chiseldon as a local reserve bn. in 22nd Reserve Bde. 1.9.16 became 94th Training Reserve Bn. at Chiseldon in 22nd Reserve Bde.

17th Battalion T.F.
  On 1.1.17 the 82nd Provisional Bn. at Walton-on-the-Naze in 226th Bde. became the 17th Bn. The 82nd Provisional Bn. had been formed in June 1915 from Home Service personnel of T.F. Bns. After Mar. 1917 to Clacton where it remained until the summer of 1918. It was in the Clacton area in 226th Bde. until the end of the war when it was at St. Osyth.

18th (Service) Battalion.
  Formed at Clacton on 20.6.18 from cadre of 5th Oxford &

Bucks. L.I. 2.7.18 to Aldershot and 49th Bde. 16th Div. 1.8.18 landed in France. 11.11.18 49th Bde. 16th Div. Belgium; south of Tournai.

THE WORCESTERSHIRE REGIMENT

1st Battalion.
  4.8.14 Cairo. 30 Sept.–16 Oct. Alexandria to Liverpool and joined 24th Bde. 8th Div. at Hursley Park, Winchester. 6.11.14 landed at Havre. 18.10.15 24th Bde. to 23rd Div. 15.7.16 24th Bde. returned to 8th Div. 11.11.18 24th Bde. 8th Div. Belgium; Harchies, east of Conde.
2nd Battalion.
  4.8.14 Aldershot: 5th Bde. 2nd Div. 14.8.14 landed at Boulogne. 20.12.15 to 100th Bde. 33rd Div. 11.11.18 100th Bde. 33rd Div. France; Petit Maubeuge, N.W. of Avesnes.
3rd Battalion.
  4.8.14 Tidworth: 7th Bde. 3rd Div. 16.8.14 landed at Rouen. 18.10.15 7th Bde. to 25th Div. 10.11.17 to 74th Bde. 25th Div. 22.6.18 to 57th Bde. 19th Div. absorbing 10th Bn. 11.11.18 57th Bde. 19th Div. France; west of Bavai.
4th Battalion.
  4.8.14 Meiktila, Burma. 1.2.15 landed at Avonmouth and to Banbury joining 88th Bde. 29th Div. Mar. to Leamington. 21.3.15 sailed from Avonmouth for Egypt. 25.4.15 landed at Gallipoli. 14.1.16 back in Egypt. 15.3.16 sailed from Alexandria 20.3.16 Marseilles. 11.11.18 88th Bde. 29th Div. Belgium; west of Lessines.
5th & 6th (Reserve) Battalions.
  4.8.14 Worcester. Aug. 1914 to Plymouth. Autumn 1917 to Harwich until the end of the war. (Harwich Garrison).
1/7th Battalion T.F.
  4.8.14 Kidderminster: Gloucester & Worcester Bde. South Midland Div. Aug. 1914 to Swindon then Maldon, Essex. 31.3.15 landed at Boulogne. 13.5.15 formation became 144th Bde. 48th Div. Nov. 1917 to Italy. 4.11.18 144th Bde. 48th Div. Austria; Pergine, east of Trent.
1/8th Battalion T.F.
  4.8.14 Worcester. Subsequent record same as 1/7th Bn. until Sept. 1918 when returned to France arriving St. Riquier on 17.9.18 joining 75th Bde. 25th Div. 11.11.18 75th Bde. 25th Div. France; Preux, north of Landrecies.
2/7th Battalion T.F.
  Formed at Kidderminster Sept. 1914. Jan. 1915 to 2/1st Gloucester & Worcester Bde. 2/1st South Midland Div. in Northampton area. Mar. 1915 to Chelmsford area. Aug. 1915 formation became 183rd Bde. 61st Div. Mar. 1916 to Salisbury Plain. 25.5.16 landed at Havre. 6.2.18 disbanded at Germaine: personnel to 2/8th and 10th Bns.
2/8th Battalion T.F.
  Formed at Worcester Sept. 1914. Subsequent record same as 2/7th Bn. till 11.2.18 when to 182nd Bde. 61st Div. 11.11.8 182nd Bde. 61st Div. France; south of Valenciennes.
3/7th & 3/8th Battalions T.F.
  Formed at Worcester April 1915. April 1916 at Weston-super-Mare then to Salisbury Plain and became 7th & 8th Reserve Bns. Sept. 1916 amalgamated to 7th Reserve Bn. Oct. 1916 Cheltenham area and then to Catterick. Early summer 1917 to Blyth, Northumberland. 1918 Newcastle-on-Tyne. In South Midland Res. Bde. T.F. (Tyne Garrison).
9th (Service) Battalion.
  Formed at Worcester, Aug. 1914—K1—39th Bde. 13th Div. on Salisbury Plain. Jan. 1915 Basingstoke. Feb. 1915 with 13th Div. to Blackdown, Aldershot. 24.6.15 sailed from Avonmouth. 13.7.15 landed at Gallipoli. 24.1.16 landed in Egypt. 16 Feb.–10 Mar. to Mesopotamia. July 1918 39th Bde. to North Persia Force. 31.10.18 39th Bde. North Persia; Resht.
10th (Service) Battalion.
  Formed at Worcester Sept. 1914—K2—57th Bde. 19th Div. on Salisbury Plain. Dec. 1914 billets. Mar. 1915 19th Div. in Tidworth area. 19.7.15 landed at Boulogne. 22.6.18 reduced to Training Cadre at Hautvillers, personnel to 3rd Bn. 28.6.18 cadre to 121st Bde. 40th Div. and on 10 July absorbed by 17th Bn.
11th (Service) Battalion.
  Formed at Worcester Sept. 1914—K3—78th Bde. 26th Div. at Sherrington, Wiltshire. Nov. 1914 billets in Worcester. April 1915 Salisbury Plain. (Longbridge Deveril). 21.9.15 landed at Boulogne. 11 to 24 Nov. 1915 to Salonika. 30.9.18 78th Bde. 26th Div. Bulgaria; east of Strumica.
12th and 13th (Reserve) Battalions.
  Formed at Plymouth Nov. 1914 as service bns. of K4 in 98th Bde. of original 33rd Div. Dec. 1914 Millbrook, Plymouth (12) and Looe (13). Jan. 1915 12th at Fowey. 10.4.15 became 2nd reserve bns. and 98th Bde. became 10th Reserve Bde. May 1915 Wareham. Oct. 1915 13th at Blandford. July 1916 12th Swanage and 13th Wareham. 1.9.16 13th Bn. became 46th Training Reserve Bn. and 12th Bn. was absorbed in 10th Reserve Bde.
14th (Service) Battalion. (Severn Valley Pioneers).
  Raised at Worcester on 10.9.15 by Lt. Col. H. Webb, M.P. Mar. 1916 taken over by War Office and moved to Salisbury Plain—Larkhill & Codford. 21.6.16 landed at Havre and joined 63rd Bde. 11.11.18 Pioneer Bn. 63rd Div. Belgium; Bougnies, south of Mons.
15th (Transport Workers) Battalion.
  Formed at Swindon Dec. 1916. 1917 at Swindon. 1918 Southampton.
16th (Transport Workers) Battalion.
  Formed at Bristol Mar. 1917. Jan. 1918 at Southampton and then to Swindon.
17th (Service) Battalion.
  Formed near Hazebrouck on 28.6.18 from 17th (Garrison) Bn. (former 1st Garrison Guard) and absorbed cadre of 12th Yorkshire Regt. and cadre of 10th Bn. Now Pioneer Bn. 40th Div. 11.11.18 Pioneer Bn. 40th Div. France; Lannoy, south of Roubaix.
1st (Reserve) Garrison Battalion.
  Formed Jan. 1916 formed at Portsmouth. 1917 Ryde. By Jan. 1918 back at Portsmouth and by June, 1918 at Dublin.

THE EAST LANCASHIRE REGIMENT

1st Battalion.
  4.8.14 Colchester: 11th Bde. 4th Div. 18 Aug. Harrow. 22.8.14 landed at Havre. 1.2.18 to 103rd Bde. 34th Div. at Boisleux. 26.5.18 to 183rd Bde. 61st Div. 11.11.18 183rd Bde. 61st Div. France; Bermerain, south of Valenciennes.
2nd Battalion.
  4.8.14 Wynberg, South Africa. 1.10.14 sailed from Cape Town 30.10.14 landed at Southampton and to Hursley Park in 24th Bde. 8th Div. 6.11.14 landed at Havre. 18.10.15 24th Bde. to 23rd Div. 15.7.16 24th Bde. returned to 8th Div. 3.2.18 to 25th Bde. 8th Div. 11.11.18 25th Bde. 8th Div. France; Pommeroeul, west of Mons.
3rd (Reserve) Battalion.
  4.8.14 Preston. 8 Aug. to Plymouth. 1.6.17 to Saltburn and Marske for summer of 1917 (Tees Garrison) At Saltburn to end.
1/4th Battalion T.F.
  4.8.14 Blackburn: East Lancashire Bde. East Lancashire

Div. Aug. to Chesham Fold Camp, Bury. 10.9.14 sailed from Southampton for Egypt, arriving Alexandria 25.9.14 26.5.15 formation became 126th Bde. 42nd Div. 10.5.15 landed on Gallipoli. 29.12.15 to Mudros. 17.1.16 arrived Alexandria. Mar. 1917 to France. 14.2.18 to 198th Bde. 66th Div. absorbing 2/4th Bn. and becoming 4TH BATTALION. 7.4.18 reduced to training cadre. 16.8.18 to 118th Bde. 39th Div. on L. of C. 11.11.18 118th Bde. 39th Div. France; Havre.

1/5th Battalion T.F.
4.8.14 Burnley: East Lancashire Bde. East Lancashire Div. Subsequent record same as 1/4th Bn. to Feb. 1918 when it remained with 126th Bde. 42nd Div. 11.11.18 126th Bde. 42nd Div. France; Hautmont, S.W. of Maubeuge.

2/4th Battalion T.F.
Formed at Blackburn Sept. 1914. Nov. 1914 to Southport in 198th Bde. 66th Div. May 1915 to Burgess Hill, Sussex. June 1915 to Peas Pottage, south of Crawley. Oct. 1915 Crowborough. Mar. 1916 Colchester. 2.3.17 landed at Havre. 19.2.18 absorbed by 1/4th Bn.

2/5th Battalion T.F.
Formed at Burnley Sept. 1914. Subsequent record same as 2/4th Bn. until Feb. 1918 when it remained in 198th Bde. 66th Div. April 1918 reduced to training cadre. 31.7.18 disbanded in France.

3/4th and 3/5th Battalions T.F.
Formed at Blackburn and Burnley Mar. 1915. By early 1916 at Witley, Surrey. 8.4.16 became 4th and 5th (Reserve) Bns. 1.9.16 4th (Reserve) Bn. absorbed 5th (Reserve) Bn. at Witley in East Lancs. Reserve Bde. T.F. Oct. 1916 to Southport. Jan. 1917 to Ripon. July 1917 to Whitby and by April 1918 at Scarborough where it remained.

6th (Service) Battalion.
Formed at Preston Aug. 1914—K1—to 38th Bde. 13th Div. at Lucknow Barracks, Tidworth. Jan. 1915 to Winchester in billets. Feb. 1915 Alma Barracks, Blackdown. 16.6.15 sailed from Avonmouth. 26.6.15 Alexandria. 2.7.15 Mudros. 7.7.15 landed at Gallipoli. 18.12.15 left Gallipoli for Mudros. Jan. 1916 to Egypt landing at Port Said 23.1.16. Feb. 1916 to Mesopotamia leaving Suez 14.2.16 and landing at Basra 6.3.16. 31.10.18 38th Bde. 13th Div. Mesopotamia; Abu Saida, N.E. of Baghdad.

7th (Service) Battalion.
Formed at Preston Sept. 1914—K2—to 56th Bde. 19th Div. at Tidworth. Dec. 1914 to Andover in billets. Feb. 1915 Clevedon in billets. End Mar. 1915 Perham Down, Salisbury Plain. 18.7.15 landed at Boulogne. 22.2.18 disbanded in France.

8th (Service) Battalion.
Formed at Preston Sept. 1914—K3—to 74th Bde. 25th Div. at Codford. Nov. 1914 to Bournemouth in billets and became Army Troops 25th Div. Mar. 1915 to 112th Bde. 37th Div. at Ludgershall. End July 1915 landed at Boulogne. 21.2.18 disbanded in France; 20 officers and 400 men to 11th Bn.

9th (Service) Battalion.
Formed at Preston Sept. 1914—K3—to 65th Bde. 22nd Div. at Lewes. Nov. 1914 Seaford. Dec. 1914 Eastbourne in billets. April 1915 Seaford. June 1915 Aldershot, Tweseldown and then Talavera Barracks. 5.9.15 landed at Boulogne. 28.10.15 sailed from Marseilles for Salonika arriving 5.11.15. 30.9.18 65th Bde. 22nd Div. Macedonia; N.W. of Lake Doiran.

10th (Reserve) Battalion.
Formed at Plymouth Oct. 1914 as a service bn. of K4 in 99th Bde. of original 33rd Div. Dec. 1914 Teignmouth. 10.4.15 became a second reserve bn. May 1915 Swanage. Aug. 1915 Wareham in 10th Reserve Bde. 1.9.16 became 47th Training Reserve Bn. in 10th Reserve Bde. at Wareham.

11th (Service) Battalion. (Accrington).
Raised 2.9.14 by the Mayor and town of Accrington. Feb. 1915 to Caernarvon in billets. May 1915 to Penkridge Bank, Cannock Chase in 94th Bde. 31st Div. July 1915 Ripon. 5.8.15 taken over by the War Office. Sept. 1915 to Salisbury Plain. Dec. 1915 to Egypt, leaving Plymouth 19.12.15 arriving Alexandria 1.1.16. Mar. 1916 to France arriving Marseilles 8.3.16. 11.2.18 to 92nd Bde. 31st Div. 11.11.18 92nd Bde. 31st Div. Belgium: Boschstraet, east of Renaix.

12th (Reserve) Battalion.
Formed about May 1915 at Chadderton Camp, Oldham from depot coys. of 11th Bn. as a local reserve bn. Autumn 1915 Prees Heath in 17th Reserve Bde. 1.9.16 became 75th Training Reserve Bn. in 17th Reserve Bde. at Prees Heath.

13th (Service) Battalion.
On 11.6.18 the 8th Garrison Guard Bn. in France became the 13th (Garrison) Bn. in 119th Bde. 40th Div. near St. Omer. 13.7.18 word 'Garrison' omitted from title and became a Service Bn. 11.11.18 119th Bde. 40th Div. Belgium; south of Roubaix.

THE EAST SURREY REGIMENT

1st Battalion.
4.8.14 Dublin: 14th Bde. 5th Div. 15.8.14 landed at Havre. 12.1.16 14th Bde. became 95th Bde. in 5th Div. Dec. 1917 to Italy. April 1918 returned to France arriving Frevent 6 April. 11.11.18 95th Bde. 5th Div. France; Le Quesnoy.

2nd Battalion.
4.8.14 Chaubattia, India. Nov. 1914 to England, landing at Devonport 23 Dec. To Winchester and 85th Bde. 28th Div. 19.1.15 landed at Havre. Oct. 1915 to Egypt arriving Alexandria 30 Oct. 26.11.15 left Alexandria and arrived Salonika 1 Dec. 30.9.18 85th Bde. 28th Div. Macedonia; Dzuma Obasi, north of Lake Doiran.

3rd (Reserve) Battalion.
4.8.14 Kingston-on-Thames. Aug. 1914 to Dover where it remained throughout the war. (Dover Garrison).

4th (Extra Reserve) Battalion.
4.8.14 Kingston-on-Thames. Aug. 1914 to Plymouth. June 1915 to Saltash. Sept. 1917 to Felixstowe where it remained. (Harwich Garrison).

1/5th Battalion T.F.
4.8.14 17 St. George's Road, Wimbledon: Surrey Bde. Home Counties Div. To Chatham, Maidstone and Canterbury. 29.10.14 embarked at Southampton for India arriving Bombay 2.12.14 and Home Counties Div. was then broken up. Dec. 1917 to Mesopotamia, leaving Bombay 21 Dec. landing at Basra on 27 Dec. 10.2.18 to 55th Bde. 18th Indian Div. 31.10.18 55th Bde. 18th Indian Div. Mesopotamia; on Lesser Zab River, north of Tikrit.

1/6th Battalion T.F.
4.8.14 Drill Hall, Orchard Road, Kingston-on-Thames: Surrey Bde. Home Counties Div. Aug. Maidstone and by end of month at Canterbury. 29.10.14 embarked at Southampton for India arriving Bombay 2.12.14 and Home Counties Div. was then broken up. 1.2.17 embarked at Karachi for Aden arriving 7 Feb. Jan. 1918 returned to India arriving Bombay 14 Jan. Remained in India.

2/5th Battalion T.F.
Formed at Wimbledon Sept. 1914. Nov. 1914 to Windsor

in 200th Bde. 67th Div. May 1915 Tunbridge Wells. Nov. 1915 to Reigate in billets. June 1916 at Sevenoaks and July to Gore Street, Thanet. Winter 1916–17 at Westgate. April 1917 Gore Street. Nov. 1917 disbanded.

2/6th Battalion T.F.
Formed at Kingston-on-Thames Sept. 1914. Nov. 1914 Windsor in 200th Bde. 67th Div. June 1915 Tunbridge Wells. Oct. 1915 to Redhill in billets. July 1916 Gore Street, Thanet. Oct. 1916 to Margate. April 1917 Gore Street. Nov. 1917 disbanded.

3/5th and 3/6th Battalions T.F.
Formed at Wimbledon and Kingston-on-Thames July 1915 and by Jan. 1916 at Cambridge. April 1916 to Crowborough and on 8.4.16 became 5th and 6th (Reserve) Bns. 1.9.16 5TH (RESERVE) BN. absorbed 6th Bn. in Home Counties Reserve Bde. T.F. Oct. 1916 Tonbridge and Sept. 1918 to Tunbridge Wells to end of the war.

7th (Service) Battalion.
Formed at Kingston-on-Thames Aug. 1914—K1—to Purfleet in 37th Bde. 12th Div. Nov. 1914 Sandgate in billets. Feb. 1915 Albuhera Barracks, Aldershot. 2.6.15 landed at Boulogne. 5.2.18 disbanded in France.

8th (Service) Battalion.
Formed at Kingston-on-Thames Sept. 1914—K2—to Purfleet in 55th Bde. 18th Div. April 1915 Colchester. May 1915 to Salisbury Plain. 28.7.15 landed at Boulogne. 11.11.18 55th Bde. 18th Div. France; Pommereuil, east of Le Cateau.

9th (Service) Battalion.
Formed at Kingston-on-Thames Sept. 1914—K3—to Shoreham in 72nd Bde. 24th Div. About Nov. 1914 to Worthing in billets. April 1915 Shoreham. June 1915 Blackdown. 1.9.15 landed at Boulogne. 11.11.18 72nd Bde. 24th Div. France; moving to Bavai.

10th (Reserve) Battalion.
Formed at Dover 26.10.14 as a service bn. of K4 in 95th Bde. of original 32nd Div. 10.4.15 became a second reserve bn. and 95th Bde. became 7th Reserve Bde. May 1915 Purfleet. Sept. 1915 Shoreham. May 1916 Dover. 1.9.16 became 30th Training Reserve Bn. in 7th Reserve Bde. at Dover.

11th (Reserve) Battalion.
Formed at Devonport 1.11.14 as a service bn. of K4 in 100th Bde. of original 33rd Div. Dec. 1914 to Dartmouth. 10.4.15 became a second reserve bn. Summer 1915 Colchester Sept. 1915 in 5th Reserve Bde. 1.9.16 became 21st Training Reserve Bn. in 5th Reserve Bde. at Shoreham.

12th (Service) Battalion. (Bermondsey).
Raised on 14.5.15 by the Mayor and Borough of Bermondsey. Oct. 1915 to Witley and 122nd Bde. 41st Div. Feb. 1916 Marlborough Lines, Aldershot. 2.5.16 landed at Havre. Nov. 1917 to Italy, arriving Mantua 17 Nov. Mar. 1918 returned to France, arriving Mondicourt 5 Mar. 11.11.18 122nd Bde. 41st Div. Belgium; Etichove, south of Audenarde.

13th (Service) Battalion. (Wandsworth).
Raised 16.6.15 by the Mayor and Borough of Wandsworth. 28.8.15 taken over by the War Office. Sept. 1915 to Witley and 41st Div. Oct. 1915 to 118th Bde. 39th Div. in Barrosa Barracks, Aldershot. Nov. 1915 Witley. 23.2.16 to 120th Bde. 40th Div. at Blackdown. 4.6.16 landed at Havre. 16.2.18 to 119th Bde. 40th Div. 5.5.18 reduced to training cadre. 3.6.18 to 34th Div. 17.6.18 to 39th Div. 30.6.18 to 7th Bde. 25th Div. at Boulogne and crossed to England and Aldershot. 16.7.18 to Lowestoft and reconstituted with newly formed 15th Bn. 3.11.18 disbanded.

14th (Reserve) Battalion.
Formed at Wandsworth summer 1915 as a local reserve bn. from depot coys. of 12th and 13th Bns. Nov. 1915 to Gravesend. June 1916 absorbed in other bns. of 26th Reserve Bde.

A 15th Battalion was formed at Lowestoft on 1.6.18 and absorbed in 13th Battalion in July.

THE DUKE OF CORNWALL'S LIGHT INFANTRY

1st Battalion.
4.8.18 Curragh: 14th Bde. 5th Div. 15.8.14 landed at Havre. 12.1.16 14th Bde. became 95th Bde. in 5th Div. Dec. 1917 to Italy, April 1918 returned to France arriving Frevent 7 April. 11.11.18 95th Bde. 5th Div. France; Le Quesnoy.

2nd Battalion.
4.8.14 Hong Kong. Arrived in England early Nov. 1914 and to 82nd Bde. 27th Div. at Winchester. 21.12.14 landed at Havre. 27.11.14 embarked at Marseilles for Salonika, arriving 5 Dec. 30.9.18 82nd Bde. 27th Div. Macedonia; Dedeli, N.W. of Lake Doiran.

3rd (Reserve) Battalion.
4.8.14 Bodmin. Aug. 1914 to Falmouth. May 1915 to Freshwater, Isle of Wight and remained here (in Portsmouth Garrison) until the end of the war.

1/4th Battalion T.F.
4.8.14 Truro: Devon & Cornwall Bde. Wessex Div. Aug. 1914 to Falmouth and end Aug. Perham Down, Salisbury Plain. 9.10.14 sailed from Southampton with Wessex Div. for India arriving Bombay 10 Nov. Wessex Div. was broken up. 22 Jan. 1916 sailed from Bombay for Aden arriving 28 Jan. Feb. 1917 to Egypt arriving Suez 13 Feb. To L. of C. 14.4.17 to 232nd Bde. 4.6.17 to 233rd Bde. 25.6.17 to 234th Bde. 75th Div. 31.10.18 234th Bde. 75th Div. Palestine; Kerkus, south of Haifa.

1/5th Battalion T.F.
4.8.14 Bodmin: Devon & Cornwall Bde. Wessex Div. Aug. 1914 to Falmouth and end Aug. Salisbury Plain. The volunteers for foreign service were posted to the 1/4th Bn. to bring it up to establishment and as the Bn. was now under strength it was replaced in the Wessex Div. by 1/6th Devons. To Newquay. 1915 at Falmouth. April 1916 to Perham Down then Tidworth as Pioneer Bn. 61st Div. 22.5.16 landed at Havre. 11.11.18 Pioneer Bn. 61st Div. France; Parquiaux, N.W. of Le Quesnoy.

2/4th Battalion T.F.
Formed at Truro Sept. 1914. 2/Devon & Cornwall Bde. 2/Wessex Div. On Salisbury Plain. 12.12.14 embarked at Southampton with 2/Wessex Div. for India arriving Karachi 9.1.15 and division broken up. Remained in India throughout the war.

2/5th Battalion T.F.
Formed at Bodmin May 1915. To Tavistock. Spring 1916 Hursley Park, near Winchester. 8.4.16 became 5th (Reserve) Bn. 1.9.16 absorbed by 4th (Reserve) Bn.

A 3/5th Bn. was not formed but the 2/5th was employed in the same way as a third line unit.

3/4th Battalion T.F.
Formed at Bodmin Mar. 1915. Oct. 1915 Bournemouth. Spring 1916 Hursley Park. 8.4.16 became 4TH (RESERVE) BN. 1.9.16 absorbed 2/5th Bn. in Wessex Reserve Bde. at Hursley Park, Winchester. Oct. 1916 to Bournemouth. Mar. 1917 Sutton Veny. Oct. 1917 Larkhill. April 1918 to Ireland in 15th and, later 27th, Bde. at Buncrana.

6th (Service) Battalion.
Formed at Bodmin Aug. 1914—K1—to Aldershot in 43rd

Bde. 14th Div. Nov. 1914 Witley. Feb. 1915 Aldershot. 22.5.15 landed at Boulogne. 20.2.18 disbanded in France.

7th (Service) Battalion.
Formed at Bodmin Sept. 1914—K2—to Aldershot and Woking in 61st Bde. 20th Div. Nov. Pirbright. Feb. 1915 Witley. Mar. 1915 Amesbury. 25.7.15 landed at Boulogne. 11.11.18 61st Bde. 20th Div. France; St. Waast La Vallee, east of Cambrai.

8th (Service) Battalion.
Formed at Bodmin Sept. 1914—K3—to Codford in 79th Bde. 26th Div. Nov. 1914 to Bath in billets. May 1915 Sutton Veny. 22.9.15 landed at Boulogne. 13.11.15 sailed from Marseilles for Salonika arriving 23 Nov. 30.9.18 79th Bde. 26th Div. Macedonia; near Hamzali, N.W. of Lake Doiran.

9th (Reserve) Battalion.
Formed at Falmouth 29.10.14 as a service bn. of K4 in 103rd Bde. of original 34th Div. 10.4.15 became a second reserve bn. May 1915 Wareham in 10th Reserve Bde. 1.9.16 absorbed in Training Reserve Bns. of 10th Reserve Bde. at Wareham.

10th (Service) Battalion. (Cornwall Pioneers).
Raised at Truro 29.3.15 by the Mayor and City. June 1915 Penzance. Oct. 1915 Hayle. 24.8.15 taken over by the War Office. 20.6.16 landed at Havre and to 2nd Div. as Pioneer Bn. 16.7.17 to 7.11.17 attached to 66th Div. 11.11.18 Pioneer Bn. 2nd Div. France; Ruesnes, N.W. of Le Quesnoy.

11th (Reserve) Battalion.
Formed from depot coys. of 10th Bn. at Launceston in Nov. 1915 as a local reserve bn. Mar. 1916 Chiseldon. 1.9.16 became 95th Training Reserve Bn. in 22nd Reserve Bde. at Chiseldon.

12th (Labour) Battalion.
Formed at Plymouth April 1916 and went to France to be Army Troops Fourth Army. April 1917 became 156th and 157th Labour Coys. Labour Corps.

A 13th Bn. was formed at Aldeburgh on 1.6.18 and was absorbed in the 6th Bn. Somerset Light Infantry at Cromer on 20.6.18.

THE DUKE OF WELLINGTON'S (WEST RIDING REGIMENT)

1st Battalion.
4.8.14 Lahore. Remained in India throughout the war.

2nd Battalion.
4.8.14 Dublin: 13th Bde. 5th Div. 16.8.14 landed at Havre. 14.1.16 to 12th Bde. 4th Div. 10.2.18 to 10th Bde. 4th Div. 11.11.18 10th Bde. 4th Div. France; Preseau, S.E. of Valenciennes.

3rd (Reserve) Battalion.
4.8.14 Halifax. Aug. 1914 to Earsdon, near North Shields. May 1915 to North Shields where it remained (in Tyne Garrison).

1/4th Battalion T.F.
4.8.14 Halifax: 2nd West Riding Bde. West Riding Div. Aug. 1914 to coast defences near Hull and Grimsby. 5.11.14 to Doncaster in billets. 14.4.15 landed at Boulogne. 12.5.15 formation became 147th Bde. 49th Div. 11.11.18 147th Bde. 49th Div. France; Auby, north of Douai.

1/5th Battalion T.F.
4.8.14 Huddersfield: 2nd West Riding Bde. West Riding Div. Subsequent record similar to 1/4th Bn. until Jan. 1918. 30.1.18 to 186th Bde. 62nd Div. absorbing 2/5th Bn. becoming 5TH BATTALION. 11.11.18 186th Bde. 62nd Div. France; east of Maubeuge.

1/6th Battalion T.F.
4.8.14 Skipton-in-Craven: 2nd West Riding Bde. West Riding Div. Subsequent record similar to 1/4th Bn.

1/7th Battalion T.F.
4.8.14 Milnsbridge: 2nd West Riding Bde. West Riding Div. Subsequent record similar to 1/4th Bn.

2/4th Battalion T.F.
Formed at Halifax Sept. 1914. Mar. 1915 to Derbyshire in 186th Bde. 62nd Div. May 1915 to Thoresby Park, near Ollerton. Oct. 1915 Retford area. Nov. 1915 Newcastle. Jan. 1916 Salisbury Plain. June 1916 Halesworth, Suffolk. Oct. 1916 Bedford. Jan. 1917 to France. 11.11.18 186th Bde. 62nd Div. France; east of Maubeuge.

2/5th Battalion T.F.
Formed at Huddersfield Oct. 1914. Subsequent record same as 2/4th Bn. until Jan. 1918. 30.1.18 absorbed by 1/5th Bn.

2/6th Battalion T.F.
Formed at Skipton Sept. 1914. Subsequent record same as 2/4th Bn. until Jan. 1918. 31.1.18 disbanded in France.

2/7th Battalion T.F.
Formed at Milnsbridge Oct. 1914. Subsequent record same as 2/4th Bn. to June 1918. 18.6.18 reduced to training cadre and returned to England joining 14th Div. at Aldershot where the cadre was absorbed by the newly formed 29th Bn. Durham L.I.

3/4th, 3/5th, 3/6th & 3/7th Battalions T.F.
Formed Mar. 1915 and on 8.4.16 became 4th, 5th, 6th and 7th (Reserve) Bns. at Clipstone. 1.9.16 4th and 6th Bns. absorbed 5th and 7th at Clipstone in West Riding Reserve Bde. Oct. 1917 to Rugeley, Cannock Chase. July 1918 to Bromeswell, near Woodbridge. Oct. 1918 to Southend.

8th (Service) Battalion.
Formed at Halifax Aug. 1914—K1—to Belton Park, Grantham in 34th Bde. 11th Div. 18.1.15 to 32nd Bde. 11th Div. April 1915 Witley. July 1915 sailed from Liverpool for Mediterranean arriving at Mudros. 6.8.15 landed at Suvla Bay. Dec. 1915 to Mudros. 7.2.16 arrived in Egypt. July 1916 to France. 13.2.18 disbanded in France.

9th (Service) Battalion.
Formed at Halifax Sept. 1914—K2—to Wareham area in 52nd Bde. 17th Div. Oct. 1914 Bovington. Nov. 1914 Wimborne. June 1915 Hursley. About 15 July 1915 landed at Boulogne. 11.11.18 52nd Bde. 17th Div. France; south of Maubeuge.

10th (Service) Battalion.
Formed at Halifax Sept. 1914—K3—to Frensham in 69th Bde. 23rd Div. Dec. 1914 Aldershot. Feb. 1915 Folkestone. May 1915 Bramshott. End of Aug. 1915 landed at Havre. Nov. 1917 to Italy. 4.11.18 69th Bde. 23rd Div. Italy; west of Pordenone.

11th (Reserve) Battalion.
Formed at Halifax Nov. 1914 as a service bn. of K4 in 89th Bde. of original 30th Div. 10.4.15 became a second reserve bn. July 1915 Lichfield. Nov. 1915 Brocton, Cannock Chase in 3rd Reserve Bde. 1.9.16 absorbed in Training Reserve Bns. of 3rd Reserve Bde. at Brocton.

12th (Labour) Battalion.
Formed Mar. 1916 at Marton Hall, near Middlesbrough and went to France. To Third Army Troops. April 1917 became 24th and 25th Coys. of Labour Corps.

13th (Service) Battalion.
On 25.5.18 the 3rd Garrison Guard Bn., recently formed in France, became 13th (Garrison) Bn. in 177th Bde. 59th Div. 16.6.18 to 178th Bde. 59th Div. 16.7.18 designation 'Garrison' ceased. 11.11.18 178th Bde. 59th Div. Belgium; north of Tournai.

14th (Service) Battalion.
Formed on 7.7.18 at Clacton from training cadre of 8th Bn. Leicestershire Regt. 3.11.18 disbanded.

THE BORDER REGIMENT

1st Battalion.
4.8.14 Maymyo, Burma. 9.12.14 sailed from Bombay and arrived Avonmouth 10.1.15. To Rugby and 87th Bde. 29th Div. 17.3.15 sailed from Avonmouth and arrived Alexandria 28.3.15 To Mudros 12 April. 25.4.15 landed at Gallipoli. 9.1.16 Mudros and to Alexandria by 16 Jan. Mar. 1916 to France. 11.11.18 87th Bde. 29th Div. Belgium; near Celles, S.W. of Renaix.

2nd Battalion.
4.8.14 Pembroke Dock. 5.9.14 to Lyndhurst and 20th Bde. 7th Div. 6.10.14 landed at Zeebrugge. Nov. 1917 to Italy arriving 23 Nov. 4.11.18 20th Bde. 7th Div. Italy; Pozzo, on River Tagliamento, east of Pordenone.

3rd (Reserve) Battalion.
4.8.14 Carlisle. 8 Aug. Shoeburyness. Jan. 1916 Conway. Nov. 1916 Barrow. Mar. 1917 Great Crosby, near Liverpool (in Mersey Garrison) to end of war.

1/4th (Cumberland and Westmorland) Battalion T.F.
4.8.14 Drill Hall, Strand Road, Carlisle: Army Troops attached East Lancs. Div. Aug. Barrow. Sept. 1914 Sittingbourne in Middlesex Bde. Home Counties Div. 29.10.14 sailed from Southampton with Home Counties Div. for India and arrived Rangoon early in Dec. Division was broken up. Remained in India throughout the war.

1/5th (Cumberland) Battalion T.F.
4.8.14 Workington: Army Troops attached East Lancs. Div. Aug. Barrow. 26.10.14 landed at Havre, to L. of C. 5.5.15 149th Bde. 50th Div. 20.12.15 151st Bde. 50th Div. 12.2.18 Pioneer Bn. 66th Div. 7.5.18 97th Bde. 32nd Div. and absorbed personnel of 11th Bn. 31.7.18 absorbed cadre of 11th Bn. 11.11.18 97th Bde. 32nd Div. France; near Avesnes.

2/4th (Cumberland and Westmorland) Battalion T.F.
Formed at Kendal Oct. 1914. 7.12.14 to Blackpool, in billets 4.3.15 sailed from Avonmouth for India arriving Bombay 31 Mar. Remained in India throughout the war.

2/5th (Cumberland) Battalion T.F.
Formed at Kendal Oct. 1914. In Nov. 1915 at Falkirk and with 2/4th and 2/5th Bns. Royal Scots Fusiliers formed No. 13 Bn. in 194th Bde. 65th Div. and in Jan. 1916 absorbed by 2/4th Bn. Royal Scots Fusiliers.

3/4th and 3/5th Battalions T.F.
Formed about Mar. 1915. Dec. 1915 3/4th Bn. to Ramsey, Isle of Man. 8.4.16 became 4th and 5th (Reserve) Bns. 1.9.16 4TH (RESERVE) BN. absorbed 5th Bn. in East Lancs. Reserve Bde. T.F. at Witley. Jan. 1917 to Ripon. May 1917 to Hunmanby, near Scarborough. Nov. 1917 to Filey where it remained.

6th (Service) Battalion.
Formed at Carlisle Aug. 1914—K1—to Belton Park, Grantham and 33rd Bde. 11th Div. April 1915 Frensham. 1.7.15 sailed from Liverpool and arrived Mudros 18 July. 20 to 31 July at Helles and back to Mudros. 7.8.15 landed at Suvla Bay. 18.12.15 Imbros. 1.2.16 Alexandria. 30.6.16 left Alexandria for France arriving Marseilles 6 July. 9.2.18 disbanded in France at Mazingarbe.

7th (Service) Battalion.
Formed at Carlisle 7.9.14—K2—to Wool in 51st Bde. 17th Div. Dec. 1914 Andover. Jan. 1915 Bovington. June 1915 Winchester area. 15.7.15 landed at Boulogne. 22.9.17 absorbed Westmorland & Cumberland Yeomanry (21 officers and 239 men) now dismounted after serving as XI Corps Cavalry Regiment. Became 7th (Westmorland & Cumberland Yeo.) Bn. 11.11.18 51st Bde. 17th Div. France; Aulnoye.

8th (Service) Battalion.
Formed at Carlisle Sept. 1914—K3—to Codford in 75th Bde. 25th Div. Nov. 1914 to Boscombe in billets. May 1915 Romsey. June 1915 Aldershot. 27.9.15 landed at Boulogne. 22.6.18 to Composite Bde. in 50th Div. 7.7.18 disbanded in France.

9th (Service) Battalion. (Pioneers).
Formed at Carlisle Sept. 1914—K3—to Lewes and Seaford in 66th Bde. 22nd Div. Nov. 1914 Eastbourne in billets. Feb. 1915 became Pioneer Bn. 22nd Div. Mar. 1915 Seaford. Mat 1915 Aldershot. 4.9.15 landed at Havre. 29.10.15 sailed from Marseilles for Salonika arriving 7 Nov. 30.9.18 Pioneer Bn. 22nd Div. Macedonia; N.W. of Lake Doiran.

10th (Reserve) Battalion.
Formed Oct. 1914 at Southend as a service bn. of K4. 10.4.15 became a second reserve bn. May 1915 Billericay. Sept. 1915 to Seaford in 4th Reserve Bde. 1.9.16 absorbed in Training Reserve Bns. of 4th Reserve Bde. at Seaford.

11th (Service) Battalion. (Lonsdale).
Raised 17.9.14 by the Earl of Lonsdale and an Executive Committee in Carlisle, Kendal and Workington with H.Q. at Penrith. Oct. 1914 to Blackhall Racecourse, Carlisle. May, 1915 to Prees Heath in 97th Bde. 32nd Div. June 1915 to Wensley. Aug. 1915 to Fovant, Salisbury Plain. 27.8.15 taken over by the War Office. 23.11.15 landed at Boulogne. 10.5.18 reduced to training cadre, surplus personnel to 1/5th Bn. 13.5.18 to 66th Div. 31.7.18 cadre absorbed by 1/5th Bn.

12th (Reserve) Battalion.
Formed at Prees Heath as a local reserve bn. from depot coys. of 11th Bn. In 17th Reserve Bde. 1.9.16 absorbed in 75th Training Reserve Bn. (former 12th East Lancs. Regt.) of 17th Reserve Bde. at Prees Heath.

A 13th Bn. was formed at Lowestoft on 1.6.18 and absorbed in 11th Hampshire Regt. on 18.6.18.

THE ROYAL SUSSEX REGIMENT

1st Battalion.
4.8.14 Peshawar. Remained in India throughout the war.

2nd Battalion.
4.8.14 Woking: 2nd Bde. 1st Div. Aug. 1914 landed in France. 11.11.18 2nd Bde. 1st Div. France; S.W. of Bohain.

3rd (Reserve) Battalion.
4.8.14 Chichester. Aug. 1914 Dover. May 1915 to Newhaven (in Newhaven Garrison) where it remained.

1/4th Battalion T.F.
4.8.14 Horsham: Army Troops attached Home Counties Div. 24.4.15 to 160th Bde. 53rd Div. at Cambridge. May 1915 to Bedford. July 1915 to Mediterranean—Mudros. 9.8.15 landed at Suvla Bay. Dec. 1915 to Egypt. May 1918 left 53rd Div. and went to France. Alexandria 17 June and Taranto 22 June. 30.6.18 to 101st Bde. 34th Div. at Proven. 14.8.18 absorbed cadre of 13th Bn. 11.11.18 101st Bde. 34th Div. Belgium; west of Courtrai.

1/5th (Cinque Ports) Battalion T.F.
4.8.14 Drill Hall, Middle Street, Hastings: Army Troops attached Home Counties Div. Early 1915 to France. 21.2.15 to 2nd Bde. 1st Div. 20.8.15 to 48th Div. as Pioneer Bn. Nov. 1917 to Italy. 4.11.18 Pioneer Bn. 48th Div. Austria; east of Trent.

1/6th (Cyclist) Battalion T.F.
4.8.14 18, Montpelier Place, Brighton: Aug. 1914 to end of 1915 in Norfolk attached to 1st Mounted Div. July 1916 at St. Leonards in General Reserve and Mar. 1917 at Folkestone. July 1917 at Wingham, Kent attached to 1st Mounted Div. Early 1918 to Ireland at Tralee attached 6th Cyclist Bde. and in Aug. 1918 at Limerick.

2/4th and 2/5th (Cinque Ports) Battalion T.F.
Formed at Horsham and Hastings Jan. 1915 and Nov. 1914. Sept. 1915 absorbed by 3rd Line Bns. which then became 2/4th and 2/5th. 8.4.16 became 4th and 5th (Reserve) Bns. at ? Cambridge. 1.9.16 4TH (RESERVE) BATTALION absorbed 5th (Reserve) and 3/6th (Cyclist) Bns. at Tunbridge Wells in Home Counties Reserve Bde. No further change.

2/6th (Cyclist) Battalion T.F.
Formed at Brighton Nov. 1914. Aug. and Sept. 1915 attached to 68th Div. at Bedford. Nov. 1915 to Chiseldon and converted to infantry. Feb. 1916 to India. (see 1/9th Hant. page 79).

3/4th and 3/5th Battalions T.F.
Formed at Horsham and Hastings in Mar. and June 1915. Sept. 1915 became 2/4th and 2/5th Bns. (see above).

3/6th (Cyclist) Battalion T.F.
Formed at Purfleet in 1916. 1.9.16 absorbed in 4th (Reserve) Bn.

7th (Service) Battalion.
Formed at Chichester 12.8.14—K1—to Sobraon Barracks, Colchester in 36th Bde. 12th Div. Oct. 1914 to Shorncliffe. Dec. 1914 to Folkestone in billets. Mar. 1915 to Ramillies Barracks, Aldershot. 1.6.15 landed at Boulogne. 11.11.18 36th Bde. 12th Div. France; Landas, east of Orchies.

8th (Service) Battalion. (Pioneers).
Formed at Chichester Sept. 1914—K2—to Colchester in 54th Bde. 18th Div. 4.2.15 became Pioneer Bn. 18th Div. May 1915 to Salisbury Plain. End July 1915 landed at Boulogne. 11.11.18 Pioneer Bn. 18th Div. France; near Le Cateau.

9th (Service) Battalion.
Formed at Chichester Sept. 1914—K3—to South Downs in 73rd Bde. 24th Div. Dec. 1914 to Portslade in billets. April 1915 Shoreham. June 1915 Woking. 1.9.15 landed at Boulogne. 11.11.18 73rd Bde. 24th Div. France; near Bavai.

10th (Reserve) Battalion.
Formed at Dover Oct. 1914 as a sevice bn. of K4 in 97th Bde. of original 32nd Div. 10.4.15 became a second reserve bn. May 1915 to Colchester. Sept. 1915 to Shoreham in 5th Reserve Bde. 1.9.16 became 23rd Training Reserve Bn. in 5th Reserve Bde. at Shoreham.

11th (Service) Battalion. (1st South Down).
Raised at Bexhill 7.9.14 by C. Lieut. Col. Lowther, M.P. and committee July 1915 to Maidstone. 1.7.15 taken over by the War Office. Sept. 1915 Aldershot. Oct. 1915 to Witley and 116th Bde. 39th Div. Mar. 1916 landed at Havre. 23.5.18 reduced to training cadre. 30.6.18 to 25th Div. at Boulogne and to England. At Aldershot and then to Deal where the bn. was reconstituted absorbing 13th Royal West Kents. End Aug. back to Aldershot in 75th Bde. 25th Div. 9.9.18 75th Bde. became 236th and left 25th Div. 17.10.18 sailed from Dundee for North Russia.

12th (Service) Battalion. (2nd South Down).
Raised at Bexhill 3.11.14 by Lieut. Col. C. Lowther, M.P. and committee. Subsequent record same as 11th Bn. to Feb. 1918, then 8.2.18 disbanded in France.

13th (Service) Battalion. (3rd South Down).
Raised at Bexhill 20.11.14 by Lieut. Col. C. Lowther, M.P. and committee. Subsequent record same as 11th Bn. to May 1918, then 23.5.18 reduced to training cadre. 17.6.18 to 118th Bde. 39th Div. 14.8.18 disbanded and personnel to 1/4th Bn.

14th (Reserve) Battalion.
Formed at Bexhill Aug. 1915 as a local reserve bn. from depot coys. of 11th, 12th and 13th Bns. Oct. 1915 to Colchester in 23rd Reserve Bde. May 1916 Aldershot. 1.9.16 absorbed in Training Reserve Bns. of 23rd Reserve Bde. at Aldershot.

15th Battalion T.F.
On 1.1.17 70th Provisional Bn. at Burnham, Somerset in 215th Bde. 72nd Div. became 15th Bn. The 70th Bn. was formed in 1915 from home service personnel of the T.F. Bns. and joined 72nd Div. in Nov. 1916 on formation. Jan. 1917 Bedford. May 1917 Ipswich. Early 1918 72nd Div. broken up, went to Cambridge and was disbanded about Mar. 1918.

16th (Sussex Yeomanry) Battalion T.F.
Formed 3.1.17 at Mersa Matruh, Egypt from dismounted Sussex Yeomanry in 230th Bde. 74th Div. May 1918 to France, leaving Alexandria 1 May arriving Marseilles 7 May. 11.11.18 230th Bde. 74th Div. Belgium; Tournai.

17th (Service) Battalion.
On 26.5.18 the 5th Garrison Guard Bn., recently formed in France, and in 176th Bde. 59th Div. became 17th (Garrison) Bn. On 16.7.18 the title 'Garrison' was dropped. 11.11.18 176th Bde. 59th Div. Belgium; N.E. of Tournai.

51st (Graduated) Battalion.
On 27.10.17 253rd (G) Bn. (formerly 99th Training Reserve Bn. from 12th R. West Kent) in 213th Bde. 71st Div. at Colchester became 51st Bn. 26.2.18 to 191st Bde. 64th Div. at Cromer .71st Div. was broken up. April 1918 to Thetford where it remained.

52nd (Graduated) Battalion.
On 27.10.17 256th (G) Bn. (formerly 100th Training Reserve Bn. from 24th Middlesex) in 214th Bde. 71st Div. at Colchester became 52nd Bn. Early Nov. 1917 to 212st Bde. 71st Div. 18.2.18 to 191st Bde. 64th Div. at Cromer. 71st Div. was broken up. April 1918 to Thetford where it remained.

53rd (Young Soldier) Battalion.
On 27.10.17 97th (Y.S.) Bn. (formed Aug. 1917) in 23rd Reserve Bde. at Aldershot became 53rd Bn. No further change.

THE HAMPSHIRE REGIMENT

1st Battalion.
4.8.14 Colchester: 11th Bde. 4th Div. 18 Aug. Harrow. 23.8.14 landed at Havre. 11.11.18 11th Bde. 4th Div. France; Haspres, N.W. of Solesmes.

2nd Battalion.
4.8.14 Mhow. 16.11.14 embarked at Bombay arriving Plymouth 22 Dec. to Romsey. 13.2.15 to Stratford-on-Avon and 88th Bde. 29th Div. Mar. Warwick. 29.3.15 sailed from Avonmouth and arrived Alexandria 2 April. 13.4.15 Lemnos. 25.4.15 landed on Gallipoli. 8.1.16 left Gallipoli and to Alexandra on 13 Jan. Mar. 1916 to France—Marseilles on 21st. 11.11.18 88th Bde. 29th Div. Belgium; near Lessines.

3rd (Reserve) Battalion.
4.8.14 Winchester. Aug. Parkhurst, Isle of Wight. Jan. 1915 to Gosport where it remained (Portsmouth Garrison.)

1/4th Battalion T.F.
4.8.14 Winchester: Hampshire Bde. Wessex Div. To Bulford. 9.10.14 embarked at Southampton for India

arriving 11 Nov. division broken up. Mar. 1915 to Mesopotamia landing at Basra 18.3.15 in 33rd Indian Bde. April 1915 30th Indian Bde. 12th Indian Div. 7.12.15 H.Q. and one coy. besieged in Kut al Amara until 29.4.16 when they were captured after the surrender. The remainder of the Bn. formed a composite Bn. with 1/5th Buffs. in 35th Indian Bde. May 1916 reconstituted and with 35th Bde. to 14th Indian Div. July 1916 Corps Troops, Tigris Corps. Nov. 1916 to 36th Indian Bde. 14th Indian Div. 31.10.18 36th Indian Bde. 14th Indian Div. North Persia; Zenjan, S.W. of Resht, near Caspian Sea.

1/5th Battalion T.F.
4.8.14 Carlton Place, Southampton: Hampshire Bde. Wessex Div. Subsequent record same as 1/4th Bn. to Nov. 1914 and then remained in India throughout the war.

1/6th (Duke of Connaught's Own) Battalion T.F.
4.8.14 Connaught Road, Portsmouth: Hampshire Bde. Wessex Div. Subsequent record same as 1/4th Bn. to Nov. 1914. In India until Sept. 1917 and then to Mesopotamia arriving Basra on 16th. To 52nd Bde. 17th Indian Div. 31.10.18 52nd Bde. 17th Indian Div. Mesopotamia; Fatha, on Tigris north of Tikrit.

1/7th Battalion T.F.
4.8.14 177, Holdenhurst Road, Bournemouth: Hampshire Bde. Wessex Div. Subsequent record same as 1/4th Bn. to Nov. 1914. In India until Jan. 1918 and then to Aden where it remained.

1/8th (Isle of Wight Rifles, 'Princess Beatrice's') Battalion T.F.
4.8.14 Newport: unallotted. Isle of Wight till April 1915 then to 163rd Bde. 54th Div. at Bury St. Edmunds. May 1915 Watford. 30.7.15 sailed from Liverpool. 6.8.15 Mudros. 9.8.15 landed at Suvla Bay. 3.12.15 left Gallipoli and went to Egypt arriving Alexandria 19 Dec. 31.10.18 163rd Bde. 54th Div. Palestine; near Beirut.

1/9th (Cyclist) Battalion T.F.
4.8.14 Hamilton House, Commercial Road, Southampton. Unallotted. 8.8.14 to Louth, Lincs. Oct. 1914 Chichester. April 1915 St. Leonards. Nov. 1915 to Chiseldon joining three other cyclist bns. (2/6th Royal Sussex, 1/25 London and 1/1st Kent) for conversion to infantry. They formed a brigade originally intended for East Africa. 4.2.16 sailed from Devonport for India. Oct. 1918 to Siberia. Vladivostock 28.11.18. In Russia and Siberia until Nov. 1919 and then returned to England via Canada. Southampton 5.12.19.

2/4th Battalion T.F.
Formed on Salisbury Plain Sept. 1914. Oct. 1914 Winchester. 2/1st Hampshire Bde. 2/Wessex Div. 13.12.14 embarked at Southampton. 11.1.15 arrived Karachi; Div. broken up. 29.4.17 embarked Karachi for Egypt—Suez 15.5.17 to 233rd Bde. 75th Div. May 1918 left 75th. Div. for France. Alexandria 26.5.18, Marseilles 1st June 5.6.18 to 186th Bde. 62nd Div. 11.11.18 186th Bde. 62nd Div. France; east of Maubeuge.

2/5th Battalion T.F.
Formed on Salisbury Plain Sept. 1914. Oct. 1914 Lyndhurst. 2/1st Hampshire Bde. 2/Wessex Div. Nov. 1914 Southampton. 13.12.14 embarked Southampton and arrived Bombay 4 Jan. 1915. Mar. 1917 to Egypt arriving Ismailia 5.4.17. To 232nd Bde. 75th Div. Aug. 1918 disbanded in Palestine. 5 officers and 300 men to 1/4th Wiltshire Regt.

2/6th (Duke of Connaught's Own) Battalion T.F.
Formed at Portsmouth Sept. 1914. At Petersfield, Bournemouth and Hursley Park, 1.9.16 absorbed by 5th 5th Reserve Bn.

3/6th Bn. not formed.

2/7th Battalion T.F.
Formed at Bournemouth Sept. 1914. Subsequent record same as 2/5th Bn. to Jan. 1915. Sept. 1917 to Mesopotamia arriving Basra 11th Sept. Until Sept. 1918 L. of C. then attached to 38th Bde. 13th Div. 31.10.18 attd. 38th Bde. 13th Div. Mesopotamia; near Delli Abbas, N.E. of Baghdad.

2/8th (Isle of Wight Rifles, 'Princess Beatrice's') Battalion T.F.
Formed at Newport Dec. 1914. At Hursley Park and Bournemouth. May have become 3/8th Bn. 1.9.16 absorbed by 4th Reserve Bn.

2/9th (Cyclist) Battalion T.F.
Formed at Louth Sept. 1914. Oct. 1914 to Oct. 1917 at Chichester and Bognor. Oct. 1917 to Sandown. April 1918 Herringfleet, near Lowestoft attached 225th Bde. Oct. 1918 to Lowestoft in billets.

3/4th Battalion T.F.
Formed March 1915 at Winchester. Autumn 1915 Bournemouth. 8.4.16 became 4TH RESERVE Bn. now at Romsey. 1.9.16 absorbed 2/8th Bn. in Wessex Reserve Bde. at Romsey. Feb. 1917 to Sutton Veny. About June 1917 absorbed 5th Reserve Bn. Oct. 1917 to Larkhill. April 1918 to Ireland, Belfast in 15th Reserve Bde.

3/5th Battalion T.F.
Formed at Southampton March 1915. Autumn 1915 Bournemouth. 8.4.16 became 5TH RESERVE BN. now at Romsey. 1.9.16 absorbed 2/6th, 7th (Reserve) and 3/9th Bns. in Wessex Reserve Bde. at Romsey. Feb. 1917 to Sutton Veny. About June 1917 absorbed by 4th Reserve Bn.

3/7th Battalion T.F.
Formed at Bournemouth March 1915. 8.4.16 became 7th Reserve Bn. at Romsey. 1.9.16 absorbed by 5th Reserve Bn. at Romsey.

3/9th (Cyclist) Battalion T.F.
Formed April 1916 at Fort Southwick, Portsmouth. 1.9.16 absorbed by 5th Reserve Bn. at Romsey.

10th (Service) Battalion.
Formed at Winchester Aug. 1914—K1—to Dublin, Army Troops attached 10th Div. Sept. 1914 Mullingar. March 1915 The Curragh, now 29th Bde. 10th Div. May 1915 Basingstoke. 7.7.15 sailed from Liverpool. 26.7.15 arrived Mudros. 6.8.15 landed at Gallipoli. 30.9.15 Mudros. 6.10.15 arrived Salonica. 2.11.16 to 82nd Bde. 27th Div. 30.9.18 82nd Bde. 27th Div. Macedonia; Dedeli, N.W. of Lake Doiran.

11th (Service) Battalion. (Pioneers).
Formed at Winchester Sept. 1914—K2—to Dublin, Army Troops attached 16th Div. Sept. 1914 Mullingar. Dec. 1914 Pioneer Bn. 16th Div. Mar. 1915 Kilworth. Sept. 1915 to Aldershot. 18.12.15 landed at Havre. 2.5.18 reduced to cadre. 18.6.18 Folkestone to Boulogne with 16th Div. To Lowestoft and reconstituted with 13th Border Regt. 3.7.18 to Aldershot 1.8.18 landed at Boulogne. 11.11.18 Pioneer Bn. 16th Div. Belgium; Antoing, south of Tournai.

12th (Service) Battalion.
Formed at Winchester Oct. 1914—K3—to Codford in 79th Bde. 26th Div. Nov. 1914 to Basingstoke in billets. Mar. 1915 Bath. May 1915 Sutton Veny. Sept. 1915 to France. 15.11.15 sailed from Marseilles and arrived Salonika 25 Nov. 30.9.18 79th Bde. 26th Div. Macedonia; N.W. of Lake Doiran.

13th (Reserve) Battalion.
Formed at Parkhurst Oct. 1914 as a service bn. of K4 in 96th Bde. of original 32nd Div. 10.4.15 became a 2nd Reserve bn. May 1915 Wareham. Sept. 1915 Bovington

in 8th Reserve Bde. 1.9.16 became 34th Training Reserve Bn. in 8th Reserve Bde. at Wool.

14th (Service) Battalion. (1st Portsmouth).
Raised at Portsmouth on 3.9.14 by the Mayor and local committee. 30.5.15 taken over by the War Office. Gosport. Oct. 1915 to Witley and 116th Bde. 39th Div. 6.3.16 landed at Havre. 22.3.18 disbanded at Haut Allaines, France.

15th (Service) Battalion. (2nd Portsmouth).
Raised at Portsmouth on 5.4.15 by the Mayor and local committee. 30.5.15 taken over by the War Office. Oct. 1915 to Aldershot in 122nd Bde. 41st Div. Feb. 1916 Marlborough Lines. Early May 1916 to France. 27.9.17 amalgamated with 1/1st Hampshire Yeomanry (12 officers & 307 men) at Caestre and became 15TH (HAMPSHIRE YEOMANRY) BATTALION. The yeomanry had been serving as IX Corps Cav. Regt. before being dismounted. 12.11.17 Italy arriving Mantua 17 Nov. 1–5 Mar. 1918 returned to France. 11.11.18 122nd Bde. 41st Div. Belgium; Neukerke, south of Audenarde.

16th (Reserve) Battalion. (Portsmouth)
Formed at Portsmouth Sept. 1915 from depot coys. of 14th and 15th Bns. as a Local Reserve Bn. Jan. 1916 Chiseldon in 22nd Reserve Bde. 1.9.16 became 96th Training Reserve Bn. in 22nd Reserve Bde. at Chiseldon.

17th Battalion T.F.
On 1.1.17 84th Provisional Bn. in 227th Bde. at Herne Bay became 17th Bn. The 84th Provisional Bn. had been formed in 1915 from Home Service personnel of the T.F. Bns. Oct. 1917 to Whitstable. Feb. 1918 to Southwold where it remained.

18th (Home Service) Battalion.
Formed at Alton Dec. 1916 and to 213th Bde. 71st Div. at Aldershot. Mar. 1917 to Colchester. Dec. 1917 disbanded.

1st Garrison Battalion.
Formed at Portland April 1916 and went to France in 1916. 31.7.18 became 19TH GARRISON BATTALION.

51st (Graduated) Battalion.
On 27.10.17 280th Graduated Bn. T.R. (formerly new 33rd Bn.) in 201st Bde. 67th Div. at Canterbury became 51st Bn. Mar. 1918 to Foxhall Heath, Ipswich where it remained in 67th Div.

52nd (Graduated) Battalion.
On 27.10.17 281st Graduated Bn. T.R. (formerly new 93rd Bn.) in 201st Bde. 67th Div. at Canterbury became 52nd Bn. Mar. 1918 to Foxhall Heath, Ipswich where it remained in 67th Div.

53rd (Young Soldier) Battalion.
On 27.10.17 the new 37th Young Soldier Bn. T.R. at Sutton Veny in 8th Reserve Bde. became 53rd Bn. Jan. 1918 to Rolleston where it remained.

THE SOUTH STAFFORDSHIRE REGIMENT

1st Battalion.
4.8.14 Pietermaritzburg. 27.8.14 sailed from Capetown. 19.9.14 landed at Southampton and joined 22nd Bde. 7th Div. at Lyndhurst. 7.10.14 landed at Zeebrugge. 20.12.15 to 91st Bde. 7th Div. 18–25 Nov. 1917 to Italy. 14.11.18 91st Bde. 7th Div. Italy; west of Udine.

2nd Battalion.
4.8.14 Aldershot: 6th Bde. 2nd Div. 13.8.14 landed at Havre. 11.11.18 6th Bde. 2nd Div. France; Amfroipret, north of Foret de Mormal.

3rd (Reserve) Battalion.
4.8.14 Lichfield. Aug. 1914 Plymouth. May 1915 Sunderland. Nov. 1916 Forest Hall, Newcastle where it remained. (Tyne Garrison).

4th (Extra Reserve) Battalion.
4.8.14 Lichfield. Aug. 1914 Jersey. Sept. 1916 Marske then Redcar. About June 1917 to Canterbury in 67th Div. 10.10.17 landed at Havre and to 7th Bde. 25th Div. 22.6.18 with 25th Composite Bde. to 50th Div. 11.7.18 reduced to training cadre and joined 116th Bde. 39th Div. at Etaples on 16.8.18. 6.11.18 disbanded.

1/5th Battalion T.F.
4.8.14 Drill Hall, Walsall; Staffordshire Bde. North Midland Div. To Luton area. Nov. 1914 Bishops Stortford area. 3.3.15 landed at Havre. May 1915 formation became 137th Bde. 46th Div. Jan. 1916 to Egypt. Feb. 1916 returned to France. 11.11.18. 137th Bde. 46th Div. France; Sains du Nord, S.E. of Avesnes.

1/6th Battalion T.F.
4.8.14 Drill Hall, Wolverhampton: Staffordshire Bde. North Midland Div. Subsequent record same as 1/5th Bn.

2/5th Battalion T.F.
Formed at Walsall Sept. 1914. Jan. 1915 176th Bde. 59th Div. in Luton area. July 1915 to St. Albans area. April 1916 to Ireland, Dublin and the Curragh. Jan. 1917 to Fovant area, Salisbury Plain. 25.2.17 landed at Havre. 30.1.18 disbanded.

2/6th Battalion T.F.
Formed at Wolverhampton Sept. 1914. Subsequent record same as 2/5th Bn. till 1918. 9.5.18 reduced to Training Cadre and to 66th Div. 31.7.18 disbanded, personnel to 1/6th Bn.

3/5th and 3/6th Battalions T.F.
Formed in 1915. April 1916 at Catterick became 5th and 6th Reserve Bns. 1.9.16 amalgamated to form 5th Reserve Bn. at Catterick. Mar. 1917 at Lincoln. July to Dec. Mablethorpe. 1918 Lincoln and Sutton-on-Sea. Nov. 1918 Mablethorpe. In North Midland Res. Bde. T.F.

7th (Service) Battalion.
Formed at Lichfield Aug. 1914—K1—to Grantham in 33rd Bde. 11th Div. April 1915 to Frensham area. July 1915 embarked at Liverpool. 7.8.15 landed at Gallipoli. Dec. 1915 to Imbros. Feb. 1916 in Egypt. July 1916 to France. 11.11.18 33rd Bde. 11th Div. Belgium; south of Mons.

8th (Service) Battalion.
Formed at Lichfield Sept. 1914—K2—to Wareham in 51st Bde. 17th Div. then West Lulworth and Wool. June 1915 to Winchester area. 14.7.15 landed at Boulogne. 23.2.18 disbanded; personnel to 2/6th & 7th Bns. and 7th Entrenching Bn.

9th (Service) Battalion. (Pioneers).
Formed at Lichfield Sept. 1914—K3—Army Troops, attached 23rd Div. at Bourley Bottom, Aldershot. Dec. 1914 to Talavera Barracks, Aldershot and became Pioneer Bn. 23rd Div. Mar. 1915 to Shorncliffe area. May 1915 to Oxney Park, Bordon. 24.8.15 landed at Boulogne. Nov. 1917 to Italy. 4.11.18 Pioneer Bn. 23rd Div. Italy; Rorai Grande, west of Pordenone.

10th (Reserve) Battalion.
Formed at Plymouth in Oct. 1914 as a service bn. of K3 but in Nov. to K4 in 99th Bde. of original 33rd Div. Dec. 1914 Tavistock. 10.4.15 became a 2nd reserve bn. May 1915 Harrogate. Nov. 1915 Rugeley, Cannock Chase in 2nd Reserve Bde. 1.9.16 absorbed in Training Reserve Bns. of 2nd Reserve Bde. at Rugeley.

11th (Reserve) Battalion.
Formed in Jersey in Oct. 1914 as a service bn. of K4 and not alloted to a formation. 10.4.15 became a 2nd reserve bn. May 1915 Harrogate. Oct. 1915 Rugeley, Cannock Chase in 2nd Reserve Bde. 1.9.16 became 9th Training Reserve Bn. at Rugeley in 2nd Reserve Bde.

12th (Labour) Battalion.
Formed probably at Brocklesby in June 1916 and went to France. July 1916 to April 1917 Fifth Army Troops. April 1917 transferred to Labour Corps becoming 26th and 27th Labour Coys.
1st Garrison Battalion.
Formed at Lichfield Jan. 1917 and went to India.

THE DORSETSHIRE REGIMENT

1st Battalion.
4.8.14 Belfast: 15th Bde. 5th Div. 16.8.14 landed at Havre. 31.12.15 to 95th Bde. 32nd Div. 7.1.16 brigade became 14th Bde. 11.11.18 14th Bde. 32nd Div. France; Flaumont, east of Avesnes.
2nd Battalion.
4.8.14 Poona: 16th Bde. Poona Div. 6.11.14 landed at Fao, Persian Gulf. 29.4.16 captured at Kut al Amara. While the battalion was besieged in Kut a composite English Bn. was formed on 4.2.16 at El Orah on the Tigris composed of drafts and recovered wounded from 2nd Norfolk and 2nd Dorsets. It had two coys. from each regiment and was nicknamed the Norsets. The Bn. was in 21st Bde. 7th Indian Div. On 21.7.16 the composite bn. was broken up and the 2nd Bn. reconstituted and became Corps Troops, Tigris Corps. Sept. 1916 to Tigris Defences. Jan. 1917 to 9th Bde. 3rd Indian Div. April 1918 to Egypt landing at Suez on 23 April. 31.10.18 9th Bde. 3rd Indian Div. Palestine; Zawata, S.W.(?) of Nazareth.
3rd (Reserve) Battalion.
4.8.14 Dorchester. Aug. 1914 to Weymouth. June 1915 to Wyke Regis where it remained. (Portland Garrison).
1/4th Battalion T.F.
4.8.14 Dorchester: South Western Bde. Wessex Div. Aug. to Salisbury Plain. 9.10.14 sailed from Southampton for India landing at Bombay on 10 Nov. Div. broken up. 18.2.16 sailed from Karachi and landed Basra 23 Feb. in 42nd Bde. May 1916 42nd Bde. to 15th Indian Div. 31.10.18 42nd Bde. 15th Indian Div. Mesopotamia: Dhibban, near Khan Baghdadi, on Euphrates N.W. of Baghdad.
2/4th Battalion T.F.
Formed Sept. 1914 and to Salisbury Plain in 2/South Western Bde. 2/Wessex Div. Oct. 1914 to Dorchester in billets. 12.12.14 embarked at Southampton for India arrving Bombay early Jan. Div. broken up. 15.8.17 embarked Bombay for Egypt arriving Suez 29 Aug. To 234th Bde. 75th Div. 2.5.18 to 233rd Bde. 75th Div. Aug. 1918 disbanded in Palestine.
3/4th Battalion T.F.
Formed in 1915 at Bath and to Cheddar. Autumn 1915 at Bournemouth. Spring 1916 Romsey and on 8.4.16 became 4TH RESERVE BN. 1.9.16 in Wessex Reserve Bde. at Romsey. Oct. 1916 Bournemouth. Feb. 1917 Sutton Veny. Oct. 1917 Larkhill April 1918 to Ireland and Londonderry where it remained.
5th (Service) Battalion.
Formed at Dorchester Aug. 1914—K1—to Belton Park, Grantham as Army Troops attached 11th Div. 18.1.15 to 34th Bde. 11th Div. 3.7.15 sailed from Liverpool. 10.7.15 Mudros 23.7.15 Imbros. 6.8.15 landed at Suvla Bay. 16.12.15 Mudros then Imbros. 1.2.16 Alexandria. 3.7.16 sailed from Alexandria and arrived Marseilles 9 July. 11.11.18 34th Bde. 11th Div. Belgium; Les Trieux, west of Aulnois.
6th (Service) Battalion.
Formed at Dorchester 6.9.14—K2—to Wareham as Army Troops attached 17th Div. Mar. 1915 50th Bde. 17th Div. May 1915 Romsey. 14.7.15 landed at Boulogne. 11.11.18 50th Bde. 17th Div. France; Eclaibes, north of Avesnes.
7th (Reserve) Battalion.
Formed at Weymouth Nov. 1914 as a service bn. of K4 in 102nd Bde. of original 34th Div. 10.4.15 became a 2nd Reserve bn. May 1915 Wool. July 1915 Wareham. Oct. 1915 Wool in 8th Reserve Bde. 1.9.16 became 35th Training Reserve Bn. in 8th Reserve Bde. at Wool.
8th (Home Service) Battalion.
Formed at Wool on 1.9.16 as 2nd (Home Service) Garrison Bn. Sept. 1916 Portland. 1.11.16 became 8th (Home Service) Bn. 7.11.16 to 219th Bde. 73rd Div. at Blackpool. Jan. 1917 to Danbury, Essex. Dec. 1917 disbanded.
1st (Home Service) Garrison Battalion.
Formed at Wyke Regis in June 1916. Aug. 1916 Weymouth. Nov. 1916 Portland. Jan. 1917 disbanded.

A 9th Battalion was formed at Aldeburgh on 1.6.18 and absorbed in the 6th Wiltshire Regt. on 18.6.18.

THE PRINCE OF WALES'S VOLUNTEERS (SOUTH LANCASHIRE REGIMENT)

1st Battalion.
4.8.14 Quetta. Remained in India throughout the war.
2nd Battalion.
4.8.14 Tidworth: 7th Bde. 3rd Div. 14.8.14 landed at Havre. 18.10.15 7th Bde. to 25th Div. 26.10.15 to 75th Bde. 25th Div. 21.6.18 to 64th Bde. 21st Div. 30.6.18 to 89th Bde. 30th Div. 11.11.18 89th Bde. 30th Div. Belgium; Ellezelles, east of Renaix.
3rd (Reserve) Battalion.
4.8.14 Warrington. Aug. 1914 to Crosby, near Liverpool. Mar. 1917 to Barrow-in-Furness where it remained (Barrow Garrison).
1/4th Battalion T.F.
4.8.14 Drill Hall, Warrington: South Lancs. Bde. West Lancs. Div. 13.8.14 Dunfermline. Oct. 1914 Tunbridge Wells. Feb. 1915 left West Lancs. Div. and landed at Havre 13.2.15. To 7th Bde. 3rd Div. 12.10.15 Pioneer Bn. 3rd Div. 9.1.16 Pioneer Bn. 55th Div. 11.11.18 Pioneer Bn. 55th Div. Belgium; Erchonwelz, west of Ath.
1/5th Battalion T.F.
4.8.14 Drill Hall, St. Helens: South Lancs. Bde. West Lancs. Div. Aug. 1914 to Edinburgh. Oct. 1914 Tunbridge Wells. Feb. 1915 left West Lancs. Div. and landed at Havre 13.2.15. To 12th Bde. 4th Div. 4.11.15 12th Bde. attached to 36th Div. 6.1.16 to 166th Bde. 55th Div. 11.11.18 166th Bde. 55th Div. Belgium; Moulbaix, S.W. of Ath.
2/4th Battalion T.F.
Formed Sept. 1914 at Warrington. Feb. 1915 Ashford in 172nd Bde. 57th Div. June 1916 Mytchett, Aldershot. Oct. 1916 Blackdown. 16.2.17 landed at Boulogne. 11.11.18 172nd Bde. 57th Div. France; Lille.
2/5th Battalion T.F.
Formed Sept. 1914 at St. Helens. Feb. 1915 Ashford in 172nd Bde. 57th Div. June 1916 Mytchett, Aldershot. Oct. 1916 Blackdown. 20.2.17 landed at Boulogne. 25.2.18 disbanded in France at Steenwerck.
3/4th and 3/5th Battalions T.F.
Formed April 1915. Autumn 1915 Blackpool. Early 1916 Oswestry. 8.4.16 became 4th and 5th Reserve Bns. 1.9.16 4TH RESERVE BN. absorbed 5th Reserve Bn. in West Lancs. Reserve Bde. at Oswestry. April 1918 to Ireland and stationed at Dublin.
6th (Service) Battalion.
Formed at Warrington Aug. 1914—K1—to Tidworth in 38th Bde. 13th Div. Jan. 1915 to Winchester in billets.

Feb. 1915 Blackdown. June 1915 sailed from Avonmouth for Mediterranean. 38th Bde. to Helles from 7 to 31 July 1915 then Mudros. 4.8.15 landed at Anzac. 20.12.15 left Gallipoli to Mudros. Jan. 1916 Egypt. Feb. 1916 to Mesopotamia. 31.10.18 38th Bde. 13th Div. Mesopotamia; near Delli Abbas, N.E. of Baghdad.

7th (Service) Battalion.
Formed at Warrington Sept. 1914—K2—to Tidworth in 56th Bde. 19th Div. Dec. 1914 Andover in billets, Feb. 1915 Clevedon in billets. Mar. 1915 Tidworth. 18.7.15 landed at Boulogne. 22.2.18 disbanded in France.

8th (Service) Battalion.
Formed at Warrington Sept. 1914—K3—to Codford in 75th Bde. 25th Div. Nov. 1914 Bournemouth in billets. May 1915 Wokingham. June 1915 Aldershot. Sept. 1915 to France. 16.2.18 disbanded in France.

9th (Service) Battalion.
Formed at Warrington Sept. 1914—K3—to Seaford in 66th Bde. 22nd Div. Dec. 1914 Eastbourne in billets. Mar. 1915 Seaford. May 1915 Bourley, Aldershot. 7.9.15 landed at Boulogne. 29.10.15 sailed from Marseilles and arrived Salonika 5.11.15. 30.9.18 66th Bde. 22nd Div. Macedonia; north of Lake Doiran.

10th (Reserve) Battalion.
Formed at Crosby Oct. 1914 as a service bn. of K4 in 105th Bde. of original 35th Div. By Dec. 1914 at Heswall. 10.4.15 became a 2nd Reserve Bn. July 1915 Kimnel. Aug. 1915 Prees Heath in 11th Reserve Bde. 1.9.16 became 51st Training Reserve Bn. in 11th Reserve Bde. at Prees Heath.

11th (Service) Battalion. (St. Helens Pioneers).
Raised at St. Helens 1.9.14 by Lord Derby. Feb. 1915 Bangor. By 15.5.15 had joined 30th Div. at Grantham as Pioneer Bn. 15.8.15 taken over by the War Office. Sept. 1915 to Larkhill. 7.11.15 landed at Havre. 15.5.18 reduced to Training Cadre. 19.6.18 to 66th Div. 30.6.18 joined 25th Div. at Boulogne and crossed to England. 3.7.18 absorbed 18th Bn. and reconstituted. To Aldershot. 8.10.18 to France. 13.10.18 joined 25th Div. at Premont as Pioneer Bn. 11.11.18 Pioneer Bn. 25th Div. France; Maroilles, east of Landrecies.

12th (Service) Battalion.
Formed at Warrington June 1915 as a Bantam bn. Jan. 1916 to Blackdown in 120th Bde. 40th Div. 2.3.16 absorbed by 11th Bn. King's Own.

13th (Reserve) Battalion.
Formed at Oswestry Sept. 1915 from depot coys. of 11th Bn. as a Local Reserve Bn. Nov. 1915 Prescot in 16th Reserve Bde. By April 1916 Altcar. 1.9.16 absorbed in Training Reserve Bns. of 16th Reserve Bde. at Altcar.

14th Battalion T.F.
On 1.1.17 49th Provisional Bn. at Hemsby, Norfolk in 224th Bde. became 14th Bn. It had been formed in 1915 from Home Service personnel of T.F. Bns. End 1917 to Palling on Norfolk coast east of Stalham and remained in this area.

15th (Transport Workers) Battalion.
Formed at Bebington in Dec. 1916 for work in Birkenhead Docks.

16th (Transport Workers) Battalion.
Formed at Prescot April 1917 for work in docks on the Mersey.

17th (Transport Workers) Battalion.
Formed at Bidston, Cheshire in April 1918 by transfer of men from existing Transport Workers Bns. who were employed on canal work. The unit worked on canals linking the ports with industrial areas.

An 18th Bn. was formed at North Walsham on 1.6.18 and absorbed by the 11th Bn. on 3.7.18.

THE WELSH REGIMENT

1st Battalion.
4.8.14 Chakrata. 20.11.14 sailed from Karachi and arrived Plymouth 22 Dec. To Hursley Park in 84th Bde. 28th Div. 18.1.15 landed at Havre. 24.11.15 embarked at Marseilles for Salonika, via Egypt, and arrived 25 Nov. 30.9.18 84th Bde. 28th Div. Macedonia; north of Lake Doiran.

2nd Battalion.
4.8.14 Bordon: 3rd Bde. 1st Div. 13.8.14 landed at Havre. 11.11.18 3rd Bde. 1st Div. France; Fresnoy le Grand, S.W. of Bohain.

3rd (Reserve) Battalion.
4.8.14 Cardiff. June 1916 to Barry. Oct. 1916 Kinmel. May 1917 to Redcar (Tees Garrison) where it remained.

1/4th Battalion T.F.
4.8.14 Carmarthen: South Wales Bde. Army Troops. Nov. 1914 Tunbridge Wells. Feb. 1915 to Scotland on Forth and Tay Defences. 17.4.15 to 159th Bde. 53rd Div. at Bedford. 19.7.15 sailed from Devonport for Mudros, arrived 5 Aug. 9.8.15 landed at Suvla Bay. 8.10.15 amalgamated with 1/5th Bn. to form 4th Welsh Composite Bn. 11.12.15 left Gallipoli for Egypt. 10.2.16 resumed identity. 30.7.18 1/4th and 1/5th Bns. formed 4/5th Bn. 31.10.18 159th Bde. 53rd Div. Palestine: 53rd Div. was moving back from Palestine to Egypt.

1/5th Battalion T.F.
4.8.14 Pontypridd: South Wales Brigade. Army Troops. Subsequent record same as 1/4th Bn.

1/6th (Glamorgan) Battalion T.F.
4.8.14 Swansea: South Wales Bde. Army Troops. 29.10.14 landed at Havre; to L of C. 5.7.15 to 84th Bde. 28th Div. 23.10.15 to 3rd Bde. 1st Div. 15.5.16 became Pioneer Bn. 1st Div. 11.11.18 Pioneer Bn. 1st Div. France; La Vallee Mulatre, N.E. of Bohain.

1/7th (Cyclist) Battalion, T.F.
4.8.14 1 Newport Road, Cardiff: unallotted. 1914 to Scotland at Berwick and Montrose. 1915 to Saltburn. Early 1917 Seaton Carew. Summer 1917 to Middlesbrough where it remained. (Tees Garrison).

2/4th Battalion T.F.
Formed at Carmarthen Oct. 1914. Nov. 1915 absorbed by 2/4th K.S.L.I. at Bedford.

2/5th Battalion T.F.
Formed at Pontypridd Nov. 1914. Nov. 1915 absorbed by 2/6th Cheshire Regt. at Bedford.

2/6th (Glamorgan) Battalion T.F.
Formed at Swansea Dec. 1914. Nov. 1915 absorbed by 2/5th Royal Welsh Fusiliers at Bedford.

2/7th (Cyclist) Battalion T.F.
Formed at Cardiff autumn 1914. By July 1916 at Holt, Norfolk. Early 1917 at Fakenham, attached 223rd Bde. Summer 1917 Holt and 1918 Hunstanton. Summer 1918 Melton Constable where it remained still attached to 223rd Bde.

3/4th, 3/5th and 3/6th Battalions T.F.
Formed at Carmarthen, Pontypridd and Swansea about Mar. 1915. To Milford Haven. 8.4.16 became Reserve Bns. 1.9.16 4TH (RESERVE) BN. absorbed 5th and 6th Reserve Bns. at Milford Haven where it remained (Milford Haven Garrison).

3/7th (Cyclist) Battalion T.F.
Formed at Cardiff in spring 1915. To Milford Haven(?). About Mar. 1916 disbanded.

8th (Service) Battalion. (Pioneers).
Formed at Cardiff Aug. 1914—K1—to Parkhouse, Salisbury Plain in 40th Bde. 13th Div. About Oct. to Chiseldon. Dec. 1914 Bournemouth in billets. Jan. 1915

Pioneer Bn. 13th Div. Feb. 1915 Aldershot. 15.6.15 sailed from Avonmouth for Mudros. 5.8.15 landed at Anzac, Gallipoli. Dec. 1915 left Gallipoli and Egypt in Jan. 1916. Feb. 1916 to Mesopotamia. 31.10.18 Pioneer Bn. 13th Div. Mesopotamia; Delli Abbas area, N.E. of Baghdad.

9th (Service) Battalion.
Formed at Cardiff Sept. 1914—K2—to Salisbury Plain in 58th Bde. 19th Div. Nov. 1914 to Basingstoke in billets. Jan. 1915 Weston-super-Mare. May 1915 Perham Down. July 1915 landed at Havre. 11.11.18 58th Bde. 19th Div. France; Wargnies; north of Le Quesnoy.

10th (Service) Battalion. (1st Rhondda).
Raised in the Rhondda Valley by D. Watts Morgan, M.P. in Sept. 1914. To Codford St. Mary in 76th Bde. 25th Div. It was formed as a battalion of K3 but on 30.9.14 went to join the other locally raised units in 129th Bde. 43rd Div. at Rhyl. 29.4.15 formation became 114th Bde. 38th Div. Aug. 1915 to Winchester. Dec. 1915 landed at Havre. 6.2.18 disbanded in France.

11th (Service) Battalion.
Formed at Cardiff Sept. 1914—K3—to South Downs in 67th Bde. 22nd Div. Dec. 1914 Hastings. April 1915 Seaford. May 1915 Aldershot. 6.9.15 landed at Boulogne. 30.10.15 sailed from Marseilles for Salonika arriving 8 Nov. 30.9.18 67th Bde. 22nd Div. Macedonia; N.W. of Lake Doiran.

12th (Reserve) Battalion.
Raised at Cardiff 23.10.14 as a service bn. of K4 in 104th Bde. of original 35th Div. 10.4.15 became a 2nd Reserve Bn. To Kinmel in 13th Reserve Bde. 1.9.16 became 58th Training Reserve Bn. in 13th Reserve Bde. at Kinmel.

13th (Service) Battalion. (2nd Rhondda).
Raised at Cardiff 23.10.14 and to Rhyl in 129th Bde. 43rd Div. 29.4.15 formation became 114th Bde. 38th Div. Aug. 1915 to Winchester. Dec. 1915 landed at Havre. 11.11.18 114th Bde. 38th Div. France; Ecuelin, east of Aulnoye.

14th (Service) Battalion. (Swansea).
Raised at Swansea by the Mayor and Corporation with the Swansea Football and Cricket Club. Subsequent record same as 13th Bn.

15th (Service) Battalion. (Carmarthenshire).
Raised by the Carmarthenshire County Committee about Oct. 1914. Subsequent record same as 13th Bn.

16th (Service) Battalion. (Cardiff City).
Raised at Cardiff in Nov. 1914 by the Lord Mayor and Corporation. Dec. 1914 to Colwyn Bay in 130th Bde. 43rd Div. The bn. had been formed at Porthcawl in Nov. 29.4.15 formation became 115th Bde. 38th Div. Aug. 1915 to Winchester. Dec. 1915 landed at Havre. 7.2.18 disbanded in France.

17th (Service) Battalion. (1st Glamorgan).
Raised Dec. 1914 as a Bantam Bn. and went to Rhyl attached to 43rd Div. Feb. 1915 Rhos. July 1915 to Prees Heath in 119th Bde. 40th Div. Sept. 1915 Aldershot. June 1916 landed in France. 9.2.18 disbanded in France.

18th (Service) Battalion. (2nd Glamorgan).
Raised Jan. 1915 as a Bantam Bn. and went to Porthcawl attached to 43rd Div. July 1915 to Prees Heath in 119th Bde. 40th Div. Sept. 1915 Aldershot. June 1916 landed in France. 5.5.18 reduced to training cadre. 18.6.18 to 47th Bde. 16th Div. at Boulogne and crossed to England. Went to North Walsham and on 20.6.18 was reconstituted by absorbing 25th Bn. 7.7.18 joined 47th Bde. 16th Div. at Aldershot. 29.7.18 landed in France. 11.11.18 47th Bde. 16th Div. Belgium; south of Tournai.

19th (Service) Battalion. (Glamorgan Pioneers).
Formed at Colwyn Bay Feb. 1915 as Pioneer Bn. 43rd Div. 29.4.15 formation became 38th Div. Aug. 1915 Winchester. Dec. 1915 landed at Havre. 11.11.18 Pioneer Bn. 38th Div. France; near Aulnoye.

20th (Reserve) Battalion. (3rd Rhondda).
Formed at (?) St. Asaph in July 1915 as a local reserve bn. from depot coys. of 10th and 13th Bns. Sept. 1915 Kinmel in 13th Reserve Bde. 1.9.16 became 60th Training Reserve Bn. at Kinmel in 13th Reserve Bde.

21st (Reserve) Battalion.
Formed at Colwyn Bay in July 1915 as a local reserve bn. from depot coys. of 14th, 15th, 16th and 19th Bns. Sept. 1915 Kinmel. 1.9.16 became 61st Training Reserve Bn. at Kinmel in 13th Reserve Bde.

22nd (Reserve) Battalion.
Formed at Prees Heath in Sept. 1915 as a local reserve bn. from depot coys. of 17th and 18th Bns. Oct. 1915 Conway Mar. 1916 Kinmel in 14th Reserve Bde. 1.9.16 became 66th Training Reserve Bn. at Kinmel in 14th Reserve Bde.

23rd (Service) Battalion. (Welsh Pioneers).
Formed at Porthcawl Sept. 1915. Mar. 1916 Aldershot. 13.5.16 to 22.6.16 attached to 69th Div. at Thetford. 13.7.16 embarked at Devonport for Salonika arriving 24.8.16. To 28th Div. as Pioneer Bn. 30.9.18 Pioneer Bn. 28th Div. Macedonia; north of Lake Doiran.

NOTE ON LOCALLY RAISED BATTALIONS

The eight locally raised battalions (13th, 14th, 15th, 16th, 17th, 18th, 19th and 23rd) were formed under the authority of the Welsh National Executive Committee in the same way as these battalions of the other two Welsh regiments (see note on page 67 under Royal Welsh Fusiliers). But in most cases the first steps towards the formation of these units came from individuals and local organizations. The battalions were taken over by the War Office in 1915.

24th (Pembroke and Glamorgan Yeomanry) Battalion T.F.
Formed in Egypt 2.2.17 from two dismounted yeomanry regiments—Pembroke and Glamorgan—previously in 4th Dismounted Bde. To 231st Bde. 74th Div. May 1918 to France, landing at Marseilles 7 May. 11.11.18 231st Bde. 74th Div. Belgium; Ath.

A 25th Battalion was formed at North Walsham on 1.6.18 and absorbed by 18th Bn. on 20.6.18.

51st (Graduated) Battalion.
On 27.10.17 the 226th Graduated Bn. (formerly 63rd Training Reserve Bn. from 18th and 20th R.W.F.) at Halesworth in 203rd Bde. 68th Div. became 51st Bn. To Yarmouth for the winter and by May 1918 at Herringfleet where it remained.

52nd (Graduated) Battalion.
On 27.10.17 the 234th Graduated Bn. (formerly 65th Training Reserve Bn. from 14th S.W.B.) at Herringfleet in 205th Bde. 68th Div. became 52nd Bn. To Lowestoft for the winter and by May 1918 at Saxmundham then to Henham Park, east of Halesworth where it remained.

53rd (Young Soldier) Battalion.
On 27.10.17 the 64th Young Soldier Bn. Training Reserve (formerly 21st R.W.F.) at Kinmel in 14th Reserve Bde. became 53rd Bn. No further change.

THE BLACK WATCH (ROYAL HIGHLANDERS)

1st Battalion.
4.8.14 Oudenarde Barracks, Aldershot: 1st Bde. 1st Div. 14.8.14 landed at Havre. 11.11.18 1st Bde. 1st Div. France; Fresnoy-le-Grand, S.W. of Bohain.

2nd Battalion.
4.8.14 Bareilly: Bareilly Bde., Meerut Div. 21.9.14 sailed from Karachi for France, landing Marseilles 12.10.14. Dec. 1915 to Mesopotamia, embarking Marseilles 5.12.15 and arrived Basra 31.12.15. Formation by now was 21st Indian Bde. 7th Indian Div. 4.2.16 owing to heavy casualties formed the Highland Bn. with 1st Seaforth Highlanders in 19th Bde. 7th Ind. Div. 12.7.16 resumed identity in 21st Ind. Bde. 7th Ind. Div. Jan. 1918 to Palestine, sailing from Koweit 1.1.18 and arriving Suez 13 Jan. 31.10.18 21st Indian Bde. 7th Indian Div. Palestine; Ras El Rados, N.E. of Tripoli.

3rd (Reserve) Battalion.
4.8.14 Perth, 8.8.14 to Nigg, Ross-shire. Nov. 1917 to Aghada, Queenstown, Ireland. 24.3.18 to the Curragh where it remained.

1/4th (City of Dundee). Battalion T.F.
4.8.14 Drill Hall, Dundee: Black Watch Bde., Army Troops. Sept. 1914 Buddon, near Carnoustie. 26.2.15 landed at Havre. 4.3.15 to Bareilly Bde. Meerut Div. 26.9.15 amalgamated with 2nd Bn. Nov. 1915 resumed identity and 6.11.15 to 139th Bde. 46th Div. 14.11.15 to 44th Bde. 15th Div. 7.1.16 to 154th Bde. 51st Div. at Rainneville. 29.2.16 to 118th Bde. 39th Div. 15.3.16 amalgamated with 1/5th Bn. at La Belle Hotesse to form 4/5th Bn. in 118th Bde. 39th Div. 4/5th Bn. 14.5.18 to 46th Bde. 15th Div. and absorbed surplus from 9th Bn. 5.6.18 to 44th Bde. 15th Div. 11.11.18 44th Bde. 15th Div. Belgium; Huissignies, south of Ath.

1/5th (Angus and Dundee) Battalion T.F.
4.8.14 Arbroath: Black Watch Bde., Army Troops. Aug. Tay Defences, Broughty Ferry. 2.11.14 landed at Havre. 13.11.14 to 24th Bde. 8th Div. 18.10.15 became Pioneer Bn. 8th Div. 6.1.16 to 154th Bde. 51st Div. 29.2.16 to 118th Bde. 39th Div. 15.3.16 amalgamated with 1/4th Bn. to form 4/5th Bn. (see above).

1/6th (Perthshire) Battalion T.F.
4.8.14 Tay St., Perth: Black Watch Bde., Army Troops. 6.8.14 Queensferry, Forth Defences. Nov. 1914 Tay Defences. 16.4.15 to 2nd Highland Bde. Highland Div. at Bedford. 2.5.15 landed at Boulogne. 12.5.14 formation became 153rd Bde. 51st Div. 11.11.18 153rd Bde. 51st Div. France; Iwuy, N.E. Cambrai.

1/7th (Fife) Battalion T.F.
4.8.14 St. Andrews: Black Watch Bde., Army Troops. 7.8.14 Kinghorn, Forth Defences. 16.4.15 to 2nd Highland Bde. Highland Div. at Bedford. Subsequent record same as 1/6th Bn.

2/4th (City of Dundee) Battalion T.F.
Formed Sept. 1914 at Dundee. To Broughty Ferry, Tay Defences. Jan. 1915 Hawick, Roxburgh in 2/1st Black Watch Bde. About June 1915 Bridge of Earn, Perthshire. Oct. 1915 to 191st Bde. 64th Div. Auchterarder. Nov. 1915 absorbed 2/5th Bn. Mar. 1916 to Norwich and in summer to Kelling Heath, near Holt. To Cromer for winter and back to Kelling for summer. Dec. 19 1917 disbanded.

2/5th (Angus and Dundee) Battalion T.F.
Formed at Forfar in Sept. 1914. Jan. 1915 Hawick, Roxburgh in 2/1st Black Watch Bde. Spring 1915 Clyde Defences. About June 1915 Bridge of Earn, Perthshire. Oct. 1915 to 191st Bde. 64th Div. Nov. 1915 absorbed by 2/4th Bn.

2/6th (Perthshire) Battalion T.F.
Formed at Perth Sept. 1914. Jan. 1915 Hawick, Roxburgh in 2/1st Black Watch Bde. April 1915 North Queensferry. May 1915 Bridge of Earn. About Nov. 1915 to 192nd Bde. 64th Div. at Blairgowrie. Mar. 1916 to Norwich and Taverham for the summer. Autumn to Norwich. Summer 1917 Witton Hall, North Walsham. Sept. 1917 disbanded.

2/7th (Fife) Battalion T.F.
Formed at St. Andrews Sept. 1914. Jan. 1915 Hawick in 2/1st Black Watch Bde. April 1915 to Kinghorn. June 1915 Bridge of Earn. Oct. 1915 to 192nd Bde. 64th Div. and to Grangemouth. Jan. 1916 at Milnathort. Mar. 1916 to Norwich and Taverham for the summer. Autumn to Norwich. Summer 1917 to Westwick, near North Walsham. Disbanded April 1918.

3/4th, 3/5th, 3/6th and 3/7th Battalions T.F.
Formed at Dundee and Forfar in Mar. 1915 (4 & 5) and at Perth and St. Andrews in April 1915 (6 & 7). Summer 1915 all at Bridge of Earn. Later in the year to Ripon. 8.4.16 all units became Reserve Bns. 1.9.16 all units amalgamated in 4TH (RESERVE) BATTALION at Ripon in Highland Reserve Bde. T.F. About May 1918 to Edinburgh: no further change.

8th (Service) Battalion.
Formed at Perth 21 Aug. 1914—K1—to 26th Bde. 9th Div. at Albuhera Barracks, Aldershot. Sept. to Maida Barracks. Jan. 1915 to billets at Alton. Mar. 1915 St. Lucia Barracks, Bordon. 10.5.15 landed at Boulogne. 11.11.18 26th Bde. 9th Div. Belgium; Harlebeke, north of Courtrai.

9th (Service) Battalion.
Formed at Perth 13.9.14—K2—to 44th Bde. 15th Div. at Albuhera Barracks, Aldershot. Nov. 1914 to billets at Liss. Feb. 1915 Chiseldon. May 1915 Park House Camp, Tidworth. 8.7.15 landed at Boulogne. 7.2.18 to 46th Bde. 15th Div. 19.5.18 reduced to cadre, surplus to 4/5th Bn. 21.5.18 to 118th Bde. 39th Div. 17.6.18 joined 16th Div. at Boulogne and crossed to England. 19.6.18 reconstituted at Deal, absorbing the newly formed 15th Bn. 2.7.18 to 47th Bde. 16th Div. at Aldershot. 28.7.18 landed at Boulogne. 11.11.18 47th Bde. 16th Div. Belgium; near Rumes, S.W. of Tournai.

10th (Service) Battalion.
Formed at Perth 13.9.14—K3—to 77th Bde. 26th Div. at Codford St. Mary, Salisbury Plain. Nov. 1914 to billets at Bristol. Mar. 1915 Sutton Veny. 20.9.15 landed at Boulogne. Nov. 1915 to Salonika, arriving 24 Nov. July 1918 left 26th Div. and returned to France landed at Taranto on 7 July. 21.7.18 to 197th Bde. 66th Div. at Serqueux. 20.9.18 197th Bde. to L. of C. 15.10.18 disbanded at Haudricourt, personnel to 1st, 6th and 14th Bns.

11th (Reserve) Battalion.
Formed Oct. 1914 as a service bn. of K4 in 101st Bde. of original 34th Div. at Nigg, Ross-shire. 10.4.15 became a second reserve bn. May 1915 at Tain in 9th Reserve Bde. Oct. 1915 Catterick. May 1916 to Lochend Camp, Dunfermline 1.9.16 became 38th Training Reserve Bn. in 9th Reserve Bde. at Dunfermline.

12th (Labour) Battalion.
Formed at Blairgowrie in May 1916. End June 1916 to France: Army Troops Third and Fourth Armies. May 1917 became 5th and 6th Labour Coys., Labour Corps.

13th(Scottish Horse Yeomanry) Battalion T.F.
Formed at Abbassia on 1.10.16 from 1st and 2nd Scottish Horse, and details from 3rd Scottish Horse, three dismounted yeomanry regiments. To Salonika, arriving 21.10.16 and to 81st Bde. 27th Div. June 1918 to France via Taranto arriving Forges les Eaux on 24.6.18. 15.7.18 to 149th Bde. 50th Div. at Martin Eglise. 11.11.18 149th Bde. 50th Div. France; Semousies, north of Avesnes.

14th (Fife and Forfar Yeomanry) Battalion T.F.
Formed at Moascar, Egypt on 21.12.16 from the dismounted yeomanry regiment. To 229th Bde. 74th Div.

May 1918 to France arriving Marseilles 7.5.18. 11.11.18 229th Bde. 74th Div. Belgium; east of Tournai.

A 15th Battalion was formed at Deal on 1.6.18 and absorbed in 9th Bn. on 19.6.18.

THE OXFORDSHIRE AND BUCKINGHAMSHIRE LIGHT INFANTRY

1st Battalion.
4.8.14 Ahmednagar: 17th Bde. 6th (Poona) Div. 27.11.14 arrived in Mesopotamia. 29.4.16 captured at Kut al Amara. Jan. 1916 Provisional Bn. formed from reinforcements at Wadi to 28th Bde. 7th Indian Div. June 1916 to L. of C. 6.7.16 Provisional Bn. became 1st Bn. 19.10.17 to 50th Bde. 15th Indian Div. 31.10.18 50th Bde. 15th Indian Div. Mesopotamia; Hit, N.W. of Baghdad.

2nd Battalion.
4.8.14 Aldershot: 5th Bde. 2nd Div. 14 Aug. landed at Boulogne. 11.11.18 5th Bde. 2nd Div. France; Villers Pol.

3rd (Reserve) Battalion.
4.8.14 Oxford. Aug. to Portsmouth. Oct. 1917 to Dover till end of war. (Dover Garrison).

1/4th Battalion T.F.
4.8.14 Oxford: S. Midland Bde. S. Midland Div. Aug. to Writtle near Chelmsford. 30.3.15 landed at Boulogne. May 1915 formation became 145th Bde. 48th Div. Nov. 1917 to Italy. 4.11.18 145th Bde. 48th Div. Austria; near Trent.

1/1st Buckinghamshire Battalion T.F.
4.8.14 Aylesbury: S. Midland Bde. S. Midland Div. Subsequent record same as 1/4th Bn.

2/4th Battalion T.F.
Formed at Oxford in Sept. 1914. Jan. 1915 to Northampton in 184th Bde. 61st Div. Mar. 1915 to Chelmsford. Mar. 1916 to Salisbury Plain. 26.5.16 landed at Havre. 11.11.18 184th Bde. 61st Div. France; Maresches, S.E. of Valenciennes.

2/1st Buckinghamshire Battalion T.F.
Formed at Aylesbury in Sept. 1914. Subsequent record same as 2/4th Bn. but disbanded at Germaine on 22.2.18 and personnel to 25th Entrenching Bn.

3/4th and 3/1st Buckinghamshire Battalions T.F.
Formed at Oxford and Aylesbury in May and April 1915. To Weston-super-Mare and on 8.4.16 became 4th (Reserve) and 1st Reserve Bucks Bns. 1.9.16 4th Bn. absorbed 1st Reserve Bucks Bn. at Ludgershall in South Midland Reserve Bde. T.F. In autumn to Cheltenham and by March 1917 at Catterick. July 1917 to Seaton Delaval, Northumberland where it remained until the end of the War (Tyne Garrison).

5th (Service) Battalion.
Formed at Oxford Aug. 1914—K1—to 42nd Bde. 14th Div. at Aldershot. Nov. to billets at Cranleigh, near Guildford. Feb. 1915 to Salamanca Barracks, Aldershot. 21.5.15 landed at Boulogne. 27.4.18 reduced to cadre at Isbergues, near Aire. 16.6.18 cadre to 16th Div. and to England. 20.6.18 absorbed by 18th Gloucesters at Clacton.

6th (Service) Battalion.
Formed at Oxford Sept. 1914—K2—to 60th Bde. 20th Div. at Aldershot. Mar. 1915 to Larkhill, Salisbury Plain. 22.7.15 landed at Boulogne. 15.2.18 disbanded at La Clytte; personnel to 2/4th and 5th Bns. and 14th Entrenching Bn.

7th (Service) Battalion.
Formed at Oxford Sept. 1914—K3—to 78th Bde. 26th Div. at Codford St. Mary. Nov. 1914 to April 1915 in billets at Oxford and then to Fovant and Longbridge Deverill. 21.9.15 landed at Boulogne. 13–26 Nov. 1915 Marseilles to Salonika. 30.9.18 78th Bde. 26th Div. Macedonia; east of Strumica.

8th (Service) Battalion. (Pioneers).
Formed at Oxford Oct. 1914—K3—to Codford as Army Troops attached to 26th Div. Nov. 1914 to billets in Oxford. 25.1.15 became a Pioneer Bn. for 26th Div. Mar. 1915 to Sutton Veny. 19.9.15 landed at Havre. 17 to 24 Nov. 1915 Marseilles to Salonika. 30.9.18 Pioneer Bn. 26th Div. Macedonia; near Strumica.

9th (Reserve) Battalion.
Formed at Portsmouth Oct. 1914 as a service bn. of K4 in 96th Bde. of original 32nd Div. 10.4.15 became a 2nd reserve bn. and 96th Bde. became 8th Reserve Bde. at Wareham. 1.9.16 became 36th Training Reserve Bn. at Wareham in 8th Reserve Bde.

10th Battalion T.F.
On 1.1.17 the 83rd Provisional Bn. at West Mersea in 216th Bde. 72nd Div. became the 10th Bn. The battalion had been formed about June 1915 from Home Service personnel of the T.F. Bns. Jan. 1917 to Bedford. May 1917 to Ipswich. By July 1917 had left 72nd Div. and was disbanded at Ipswich on 21.11.17.

11th (Garrison) Battalion.
On 31.7.18 the 2nd Garrison Bn. in France became the 11th Bn. (see below).

1st Garrison Battalion.
Formed Sept. 1915 at Portland and went to India in Feb. 1916.

2nd (Garrison) Battalion.
Formed July 1916 at Portland and went to France in July 1916. Became 11th (Garrison) Battalion on 13.7.18 (see above).

THE ESSEX REGIMENT

1st Battalion.
4.8.14 Mauritius. Arrived in England by Dec. 1914 and went to Harwich. 18.1.15 to Banbury joining 88th Bde. 29th Div. 5.3.15 Warwick. 21.3.15 embarked at Avonmouth and arrived Alexandria 3.4.15. 14.4.15 to Mudros. 25.4.15 landed at Gallipoli. 8.1.16 left Gallipoli and went to Egypt. 16.3.16 sailed from Alexandria for Marseilles. 4.2.18 to 112th Bde. 37th Div. at Wardrecques. 11.11.18 112th Bde. 37th Div. France; Bethencourt, N.W. of Le Cateau.

2nd Battalion.
4.8.14 Chatham: 12th Bde. 4th Div. To Cromer, Norwich and Harrow. 24.8.14 landed at Havre. 12th Bde. to 36th Div. from 5.11.15 to 3.2.16 and Bn. was attached to 109th Bde. 11.11.18 12th Bde. 4th Div. France; Artres, south of Valenciennes.

3rd (Reserve) Battalion.
4.8.14 Warley. Aug. 1914 Harwich. Mar. 1916 to Felixstowe where it remained. (Harwich Garrison).

1/4th Battalion T.F.
4.8.14 Brentwood: Essex Bde. East Anglian Div. End Aug. 1914 Norwich. April 1915 Colchester. May 1915 formation became 161st Bde. 54th Div. May 1915 St. Albans. 21.7.15 sailed from Devonport for Mediterranean: Lemnos. 12.8.15 landed at Suvla Bay. 4.12.15 to Mudros. 17.12.15 Alexandria. 31.10.18 161st Bde. 54th Div. Palestine; near Beirut.

1/5th Battalion T.F.
4.8.14 Association Buildings, Market Road, Chelmsford: Essex Bde. East Anglian Div. Subsequent record similar to 1/4th Bn.

1/6th Battalion T.F.
4.8.14 West Ham: Essex Bde. East Anglian Div. Subsequent record similar to 1/4th Bn.

1/7th Battalion T.F.
4.8.14 Walthamstow Lodge, Church Hill, Walthamstow: Essex Bde. East Anglian Div. Subsequent record similar to 1/4th Bn.

1/8th (Cyclist) Battalion T.F.
4.8.14 Colchester: unallotted. Aug. 1914 Essex coast with H.Q. at Wivenhoe till 1916. Jan. to Oct. 1917 at Southminster attached to 73rd Div. Oct. 1917 Margate. Feb. 1918 to Ireland to Enniskillen. Mar. 1918 Curragh, then Tulla, Co. Clare. Oct. 1918 Naas, Co. Kildare.

2/4th Battalion T.F.
Formed at Brentwood Oct. 1914. Dec. 1914 Stamford in 206th Bde. 69th Div. Jan. 1915 Yarmouth. Early summer Thetford. Dec. 1915 disbanded.

2/5th Battalion T.F.
Formed at Chelmsford Oct. 1914. Dec. 1914 Peterborough in 206th Bde. 69th Div. Early summer 1915 Thetford. July 1916 Harrogate. April 1917 to Welbeck. Winter 1917 to Middlesbrough. Mar. 1918 disbanded.

2/6th Battalion T.F.
Formed at West Ham Nov. 1914. Dec. 1914 to Peterborough in 206th Bde. 69th Div. Early summer 1915 at Thetford. July 1916 at Harrogate, April 1917 to Welbeck. Winter 1917 to Stockton. Jan. 1918 disbanded.

2/7th Battalion T.F.
Formed at Walthamstow Nov. 1914. Dec. 1914 to Peterborough in 206th Bde. 69th Div. Early summer 1915 at Thetford. July 1916 at Harrogate. April 1917 to Welbeck. 10.10.17 to 201st Bde. 67th Div. at Ramsgate. Mar. 1918 disbanded.

2/8th (Cyclist) Battalion T.F.
Formed at Colchester Sept. 1914. Mar. 1915 Great Clacton. Early 1915 Mistley and Manningtree. Aug. 1916 Foxhall Heath, Ipswich. Nov. 1916 Faversham. April 1917 Little Clacton. Oct. 1917 Hollesley Bay, Suffolk. April 1918 Bawdsey where it remained attached to 67th Div.

3/4th, 3/5th, 3/6th and 3/7th Battalions T.F.
Formed May 1915 at Brentwood, Chelmsford, West Ham and Walthamstow. Aug. 1915 Windsor Great Park. Oct. 1915 Halton Park. 8.4.16 became Reserve Bns. 1.9.16 4TH RESERVE BN. absorbed 5th, 6th and 7th Reserve Bns. at Halton Park in East Anglian Reserve Bde. By Aug. 1917 at Crowborough. About Aug. 1918 to Hastings.

3/8th (Cyclist) Battalion T.F.
Formed at Colchester April 1915 and disbanded about April 1916.

9th (Service) Battalion.
Formed at Warley Aug. 1914—K1—to Shorncliffe in 35th Bde. 12th Div. Mar. 1915 to Blenheim Barracks, Aldershot. 31.5.15 landed at Boulogne. 11.11.18 35th Bde. 12th Div. France; Hergnies, east of Orchies.

10th (Service) Battalion.
Formed at Warley Sept. 1914—K2—to Shorncliffe then Colchester in 53rd Bde. 18th Div. May 1915 to Codford St. Mary, Salisbury Plain. 26.7.15 landed at Boulogne. 11.11.18 53rd Bde. 18th Div. France; Le Cateau.

11th (Service) Battalion.
Formed at Warley Sept. 1914—K3—to Shoreham in 71st Bde. 24th Div. Jan. 1915 Brighton in billets. Mar. 1915 Shoreham. June 1915 to Blackdown. 30.8.15 landed at Boulogne. 11.10.15 71st Bde. to 6th Div. 27.10.15 to 18th Bde. 6th Div. 11.11.18 18th Bde. 6th Div. France; Becquigny, north of Bohain.

12th (Reserve) Battalion.
Formed at Harwich 26.10.14 as a service bn. of K4 in 106th Bde. of original 35th Div. Jan. 1915 to White City, London. 10.4.15 became a 2nd Reserve Bn. May 1915 to Colchester. Mar. 1916 to Harwich in 6th Reserve Bde. 1.9.16 absorbed in Training Reserve Bns. of 6th Reserve Bde. at Harwich.

13th (Service) Battalion. (West Ham).
Raised at West Ham 27.12.14 by the Mayor and Borough. May 1915 to Brentwood. 1.7.15 taken over by the War Office. Aug. 1915 to Clipstone and 100th Bde. 33rd Div. then to Perham Down, Salisbury Plain. 17.11.15 landed at Boulogne. 22.12.15 to 6th Bde. 2nd Div. at Bethune. 10.2.18 disbanded in France.

14th (Reserve) Battalion.
Formed at Brentwood Sept. 1915 from Depot Coys. of 13th Bn. as a Local Reserve Bn. July 1915 Cambridge. Oct. 1915 to Colchester in 23rd Reserve Bde. Jan. 1916 Northampton. May 1916 to Tweseldown, Aldershot. 1.9.16 became 98th Training Reserve Bn. in 23rd Reserve Bde. at Aldershot.

15th Battalion T.F.
On 1.1.17 65th Provisional Bn. at Yarmouth in 225th Bde. became 15th Bn. It had been formed in 1915 from Home Service personnel of T.F. Bns. 27.4.18 became a Garrison Guard Bn. May 1918 to France and on 12 May to 177th Bde. 59th Div. By 16.7.18 title Garrison Guard discontinued. 11.11.18 177th Bde. 59th Div. Belgium; Grand Rejet, north of Tournai.

16th Battalion T.F.
On 1.1.17 66th Provisional Bn. at Fleet in 213th Bde. 71st Div. became 16th Bn. It had been formed in 1915 from Home Service personnel of T.F. Bns. Mar. 1917 to Colchester. Dec. 1917 disbanded.

17th Battalion T.F.
On 1.1.17 67th Provisional Bn. at Sheringham in 223rd Bde. became 17th Bn. It had been formed in 1915 from Home Service personnel of T.F. Bns. By July 1917 at Weybourne in 223rd Bde. where it remained.

18th (Home Service) Battalion.
Formed at Yarmouth 27.4.18 to replace 15th Bn. in 225th Bde. and no further change.

1st Garrison Battalion.
Formed at Denham, Bucks. on 21.7.15 and embarked at Devonport 24.8.15 for Mudros arriving 3.9.15. Served on Gallipoli. Feb. 1916 to Egypt. Remained in Egypt and Palestine until the end of the war.

2nd Garrison Battalion.
Formed Jan. 1916 at Halton Park. In 1916 to India where it remained.

THE SHERWOOD FORESTERS (NOTTINGHAMSHIRE AND DERBYSHIRE REGIMENT)

1st Battalion.
4.8.14 Bombay. Sailed from India 3.9.14 and landed at Plymouth 2 Oct. and joined 24th Bde. 8th Div. at Hursley Park, near Winchester. 5.11.14 landed at Havre. 18.10.15 with 24th Bde. to 23rd Div. 15.7.16 24th Bde. returned to 8th Div. 11.11.18 24th Bde. 8th Div. Belgium; Bermissart, west of Mons.

2nd Battalion.
4.8.14 Sheffield: 18th Bde. 6th Div. Aug. Cambridge. 11.9.14 landed at St. Nazaire. 27.10.15 to 71st Bde. 6th Div. 11.11.18 71st Bde. 6th Div. France; Bohain.

3rd (Reserve) and 4th (Extra Reserve) Battalions.
4.8.14 Derby. Aug. 1914 3rd Bn. to Plymouth and 4th to Sunderland. May 1915 3rd Bn. to Sunderland. The two bns. were on East Coast defences, based on Sunderland, until the end of the war. (Tyne Garrison).

1/5th Battalion T.F.
4.8.14 Drill Hall, Derby: Notts. & Derby Bde. North Midland Div. Aug. 1914 Harpenden. Nov. 1914 Braintree

area. 25.2.15 landed in France. 12.5.15 formation became 139th Bde. 46th Div. 11.11.18 139th Bde. 46th Div. France; Cartignies, S.W. of Avesnes.

1/6th Battalion T.F.
4.8.14 Corporation Street, Chesterfield: Notts. & Derby Bde. North Midland Div. Subsequent record similar to 1/5th Bn.

1/7th (Robin Hood) Battalion T.F.
4.8.14 The Drill Hall, Derby Road, Nottingham: Notts. & Derby Bde. North Midland Div. Aug. 1914 Harpenden. Nov. 1914 Braintree area. 25.2.15 landed in France. 12.5.15 formation became 139th Bde. 46th Div. 31.1.18 to 178th Bde. 59th Div. absorbing 2/7th Bn. and became 7th Bn. 7.5.18 reduced to cadre. 29.5.18 to 30th Div. 19.6.18 to 66th Div. 15.8.18 to 116th Bde. 39th Div. and remained near Etaples until the end of the war.

1/8th Battalion T.F.
4.8.14 Newark: Notts. & Derby Bde. North Midland Div. Subsequent record similar to 1/5th Bn.

2/5th Battalion T.F.
Formed at Derby 16.10.14. Jan. 1915 to Luton in 178th Bde. 59th Div. Aug. 1915 to Watford. April 1916 to Ireland; Dublin and in July 1916 at the Curragh. Jan. 1917 returned to England at Fovant, Salisbury Plain. 26.2.17 landed in France. 7.5.18 reduced to cadre. 2.6.18 to 16th Div. 17.6.18 to 34th Div. 28.6.18 to 117th Bde. 39th Div. 3.8.18 disbanded in France.

2/6th Battalion T.F.
Formed at Chesterfield 14.9.14. 2 Nov. to Buxton in Empire Hotel. 3.2.15 to Luton and 178th Bde. 59th Div. June 1915 to Dunstable. 9.8.15 to Watford. 26.4.16 to Ireland at Dublin. July 1916 at the Curragh. 12.1.17 to Fovant, Salisbury Plain. 25.2.17 landed at Boulogne. 7.5.18 reduced to cadre; to L. of C. and disbanded on 31.7.18.

2/7th (Robin Hood) Battalion T.F.
Formed at Nottingham 19.9.14. Subsequent record same as 2/5th Bn. until 6.2.18 when it was absorbed by 1/7th Bn.

2/8th Battalion T.F.
Formed at Newark 11.9.14. Subsequent record same as 2/5th Bn. until 6.2.18 when it was disbanded in France.

3/5th and 3/6th Battalions T.F.
Formed at Derby and Chesterfield on 29.3.15 and 1.3.15. Oct. 1915 to Grantham. 8.4.16 became 5th and 6th Reserve Bns. at Grantham. 1.9.16 5th Bn. absorbed 6th Bn. at Grainthorpe. Mar. 1917 at Louth and by Nov. 1917 at Saltfleet until the end of the war. In North Midland Res. Bde. T.F.

3/7th and 3/8th Battalions T.F.
Formed at Nottingham and Newark 1.3.15 and 26.2.15. Oct. 1915 to Grantham. 8.4.16 became 7th and 8th Reserve Bns. at Saltfleet. 1.9.16 7th Bn. absorbed 8th Bn. in North Midland Res. Bde. T.F. 1917 at Saltfleet and for most of 1918 at Louth.

9th (Service) Battalion.
Formed at Derby 24.8.14—K1—to Grantham in 33rd Bde. 11th Div. April 1915 to Frensham area. July 1915 embarked at Liverpool for Mudros. 20 to 31 July at Helles. 7.8.15 landed at Suvla. Dec. 1915 to Imbros. Feb. 1916 in Egypt. July 1916 to France. 11.11.18 33rd Bde. 11th Div. Belgium, south of Mons.

10th (Service) Battalion.
Formed at Derby 13.9.14—K2—to 51st Bde. 17th Div. at Wool. Oct. 1914 West Lulworth. Dec. Wool. Mar. 1915 West Lulworth. June 1915 to Winchester. 14.7.15 landed in France. 11.11.18 51st Bde. 17th Div. France; near Aulnoye.

11th (Service) Battalion.
Formed at Derby 3.10.14—K3—to 70th Bde. 23rd Div. at Frensham. Dec. 1914 Stanhope Lines, Aldershot. Feb. 1915 to Shorncliffe area. May 1915 Bordon. 27.8.15 landed in France. 70th Bde. to 8th Div. from 18.10.15 to 17.7.16. Nov. 1917 to Italy. 13.9.18 left 23rd Div. in Italy and joined 74th Bde. 25th Div. on 18.9.18 at St. Riquier, France. 11.11.18 74th Bde. 25th Div. France; near Landrecies.

12th (Service) Battalion. (Pioneers).
Formed at Derby 1.10.14—K3—Army Troops attached 24th Div. in Shoreham area. April 1915 became Pioneer Bn. 24th Div. 29 Aug. 1915 landed in France. 11.11.18 Pioneer Bn. 24th Div. France; Le Louvion, east of Bavai.

13th (Reserve) Battalion.
Formed at Plymouth in Oct. 1914 as a service bn. of K4 in 98th Bde. of original 33rd Div. Dec. 1914 Lostwithiel. 10.4.15 became a 2nd reserve bn. June 1915 Lichfield. Nov. 1915 Rugeley. Feb. 1916 Brocton in 3rd Reserve Bde. 1.9.16 became 12th Training Reserve Bn. at Brocton in 3rd Reserve Bde.

14th (Reserve) Battalion.
Formed at Lichfield in Oct. 1914 as a service bn. of K4 in 91st Bde. of original 30th Div. 10.4.15 became a 2nd reserve bn. and Bde. became 3rd Reserve Bde. Mar. 1916 Brocton. 1.9.16 became 13th Training Reserve Bn. at Brocton in 3rd Reserve Bde.

15th (Service) Battalion. (Nottingham).
Raised at Nottingham in Feb. 1915 by the Mayor and a committee as a bantam bn. At Nottingham. June 1915 to Masham, Yorks. and 105th Bde. 35th Div. 27.8.15 taken over by the War Office. Aug. 1915 to Salisbury Plain. 1.2.16 landed in France. 11.11.18 105th Bde. 35th Div. Belgium; N.E. of Renaix.

16th (Service) Battalion. (Chatsworth Rifles).
Raised at Derby by the Duke of Devonshire and the Derbyshire T.F. Association on 16.4.15. 4.5.15 Buxton. 8.6.15 Redmires, near Sheffield. 2.9.15 to Hursley, Winchester and 117th Bde. 39th Div. 30.9.15 to Oudenarde Barracks, Aldershot. 8.11.15 to Witley. 6.3.16 landed at Havre. 16.5.18 reduced to training cadre. 16.8.18 to 66th Div. 20.9.18 with 197th Bde. to L. of C. south of Aumale until the end of the war.

17th (Service) Battalion. (Welbeck Rangers).
Raised at Nottingham by the Mayor and Recruiting Committee on 1.6.15 At Nottingham. Oct. 1915 to Aldershot and 117th Bde. 39th Div. Nov. 1915 to Witley. 10.12.15 taken over by the War Office. 6.3.16 landed in France. 12.2.18 disbanded in France.

18th (Service) Battalion.
Formed at Derby 28.7.15 as a bantam bn. Autumn 1915 to 121st Bde. 40th Div. at Aldershot. 2.4.16 absorbed by 13th Yorks. Regt. at Woking.

19th (Reserve) Battalion.
Formed at Brocklesby Aug. 1915 as a local reserve bn. from depot coys. of 15th, 16th and 17th Bns. Nov. 1915 Ripon in 19th Reserve Bde. Jan. 1916 Harrogate. July 1916 Durham. 1.9.16 absorbed in Training Reserve Bns. of 19th Reserve Bde. at Newcastle.

20th (Labour) Battalion.
Formed at Derby May 1916 and went to Frnace. June 1916 to April 1917 Fifth Army Troops. April 1917 transferred to Labour Corps as 28th and 29th Labour Coys.

21st Battalion T.F.
On 1.1.17 the 29th Provisional Bn. at Walton-on-the-Naze in 226th Bde. became the 21st Bn. The Bn. had been formed about June 1915 from Home Service personnel of the T.F. Bns. July 1917 at Frinton and by Nov. at Clacton. 12.1.18 disbanded.

1st Garrison Battalion.
Formed at Lichfield July 1915. Oct. 1915 to Malta and then to Egypt where it remained.

51st (Graduated) Battalion.
On 27.10.17 the 246th Graduated Bn. (formerly new 15th Training Reserve Bn.) at Thoresby in 208th Bde. 69th Div. became the 51st Bn. Jan. to April 1918 at Doncaster and then to Welbeck where it remained.

52nd (Graduated) Battalion.
On 27.10.17 the 278th Graduated Bn. (formerly 14th Training Reserve Bn. from 14th Manchesters) at Canterbury in 200th Bde. 67th Div. became the 52nd Bn. Jan. 1918 Willsborough, near Ashford. Feb. 1918 to 207th Bde. 69th Div. at Clipstone. April 1918 to 208th Bde. 69th Div. May 1918 to Welbeck where it remained.

53rd (Young Soldier) Battalion.
On 27.10.17 the 13th Young Soldier Bn. (formerly 14th Sherwood Foresters) at Rugeley, Cannock Chase became the 53rd Bn. In 1st Reserve Bde. About Oct. 1918 to Clipstone.

THE LOYAL NORTH LANCASHIRE REGIMENT

1st Battalion.
4.8.14 Tournay Barracks, Aldershot: 2nd Bde. 1st Div. 13.8.14 landed at Havre. 7.2.18 to 1st Bde. 1st Div. 11.11.18 1st Bde. 1st Div. France; Fresnoy-le-Grand, S.W. of Bohain.

2nd Battalion.
4.8.14 Bangalore. 16.10.14 sailed from India in 27th Indian Bde. 3.11.14 landed at Tanga, German East Africa. 5 Nov. re-embarked and landed at Mombasa on 7 Nov. 10.5.16 to 20.8.16 in South Africa for recovery from ill health. Dec. 1916 to Egypt, landing Suez 18 Jan. To L. of C. 14.4.17 to 75th Div. 9.8.17 to Sidi Bishr Dec. 1917 to L. of C. and (?) XXI Corps Troops. 18.5.18 sailed from Suez for France, arriving Marseilles 27 May. 4.6.18 to 94th Bde. 31st Div. 28.6.18 to 101st Bde. 34th Div. 11.11.18 101st Bde. 34th Div. Belgium; Wevelghem, east of Menin.

3rd (Reserve) Battalion.
4.8.14 Preston. 9.8.14 to Felixstowe where it remained throughout the war. (Harwich Garrison).

1/4th Battalion T.F.
4.8.14 9 Avenham Lane, Preston: North Lancs. Bde. West Lancs. Div. 22.8.14 to Swindon. Nov. 1914 Sevenoaks. April 1915 North Lancs. Bde. to Highland Div. at Bedford. 4.5.15 landed at Boulogne. 12.5.15 formation became 154th Bde. 51st Div. 7.1.16 to 164th Bde. 55th Div. 11.11.18 164th Bde. 55th Div. Belgium; Villers St. Amand, west of Ath.

1/5th Battalion T.F.
4.8.14 Bolton: North Lancs. Bde. West Lancs. Div. Aug. 1914 to Chipping Sodbury and later to Sevenoaks. Feb. 1915 left division and landed Havre 13.2.15. To 16th Bde. 6th Div. 11.6.15 to 151st Bde. 50th Div. 21.12.15 to 26th Bde. 9th Div. 8.1.16 to 166th Bde. 55th Div. 4.2.18 to 170th Bde. 57th Div. and absorbed 4/5th Bn. 11.11.18 170th Bde. 57th Div. France; Hellemmes, east of Lille.

2/4th Battalion T.F.
Formed at Preston Oct. 1914. Spring 1915 to Ashford area in 170th Bde. 57th Div. July 1916 Aldershot. Oct. 1916 Blackdown. 8.2.17 landed at Havre. 11.11.18 170th Bde. 57th Div. France; Hellemmes, east of Lille.

2/5th Battalion T.F.
Formed at Bolton Oct. 1914. Spring 1915 to Ashford area in 170th Bde. 57th Div. July 1916 Aldershot. Oct. 1916 Blackdown. 9.2.17 landed at Havre. 5.2.18 became Pioneer Bn. 57th Div. 11.11.18 Pioneer Bn. 57th Div. Belgium; Tournai.

3/4th and 3/5th Battalions T.F.
Formed at Preston and Bolton in May and April 1915. June 1915 Kirkham, Lancashire. Oct. 1915 Blackpool. Spring 1916 to Oswestry. 8.4.16 became Reserve Bns. 1.9.16 4TH (RESERVE) BN. absorbed 5th Reserve Bn. in West Lancs. Reserve Bde. T.F. at Oswestry. April 1918 to Ireland and stationed at Dublin.

4/5th Battalion T.F.
Formed in 1915 and to Ashford area in 170th Bde. 57th Div. July 1916 Aldershot. Oct. 1916 Blackdown. 12.2.17 landed at Havre. 4.2.18 absorbed by 1/5th Bn.

6th (Service) Battalion.
Formed at Preston Aug. 1914—K1—to Tidworth in 38th Bde. 13th Div. Feb. 1915 Blackdown. 17.6.15 sailed from Avonmouth for Mediterranean—Mudros. 6 to 31 July with 38th Bde. to Helles. 4.8.15 landed at Anzac, Gallipoli. 20.12.15 to Mudros. Jan. 1916 to Egypt. Feb. 1916 to Mesopotamia, leaving Port Said 14 Feb. arriving Basra 5 Mar. 31.10.18 38th Bde. 13th Div. Mesopotamia; Abu Saida on right bank of River Diyala, N.E. Baghdad.

7th (Service) Battalion.
Formed at Preston Sept. 1914—K2—to Tidworth in 56th Bde. 19th Div. Dec. 1914 Whitchurch. Mar. 1915 Tidworth. 17.7.15 landed at Boulogne. 10.2.18 disbanded in France.

8th (Service) Battalion.
Formed at Preston Sept. 1914—K3—to Salisbury Plain in 74th Bde. 25th Div. Dec. 1914 Boscombe in billets. Jan. 1915 Bournemouth. Mar. 1915 Boscombe. May 1915 Romsey. June 1915 Aldershot. 16.9.15 landed at Boulogne. 26.10.15 to 7th Bde. 25th Div. 16.2.18 disbanded in France at Courcelles.

9th (Service) Battalion.
Formed at Preston Sept. 1914—K3—to Salisbury Plain in 74th Bde. 25th Div. Dec. 1914 Christchurch. Jan. 1915 Southbourne. May 1915 Romsey. June 1915 Blenheim Barracks, Aldershot. 26.9.15 landed at Boulogne. 21.6.18 with 8th Border Regt. formed No. 2 Bn. in Composite Bde. 22.6.18 Bde. to 50th Div. and left on 7 July. 12.8.18 disbanded in France.

10th (Service) Battalion.
Formed at Preston Oct. 1914—K3—to South Downs and Eastbourne as Army Troops attached to 22nd Div. April 1915 to 112th Bde. 37th Div. at Ludgershall. 1.8.15 landed at Boulogne. 4.2.18 disbanded in France.

11th (Reserve) Battalion.
Formed at Felixstowe Oct. 1914 as a service bn. of K4 in 94th Bde. of original 31st Div. Mar. 1915 Chichester. 10.4.15, became a 2nd Reserve Bn. May 1915 Billericay. Sept. 1915 Seaford in 4th Reserve Bde. 1.9.16 became 17th Training Reserve Bn. at Seaford in 4th Reserve Bde.

1/12th Battalion T.F. (Pioneers).
Formed at Lytham Aug. 1915. 13.5.16 to 1.6.16 attached 69th Div. at Thetford. 1.6.16 to 60th Div. as Pioneer Bn. at Sutton Veny. 22.6.16 landed at Havre. 16.11.16 to 32nd Div. as Pioneer Bn. Jan. 1917 left 32nd Div. and embarked at Marseilles for Salonika arriving 23 Jan. and rejoined 60th Div. June 1917 to Egypt. 10.4.18 to 74th Div. at Sarafand. May 1918 to France, leaving Alexandria 1 May and Marseilles 7 May. 11.11.18 Pioneer Bn. 74th Div. Belgium; Frasnes, west of Ath.

2/12th Battalion T.F.
Formed at Lytham Mar. 1916 8.4.16 became a Reserve Bn. To Oswestry. 1.9.16 absorbed by 4th (Reserve) Bn.

13th (Home Service) Battalion.
Formed at Blackpool 4.12.16 in 219th Bde. 73rd Div. Jan.

1917 to Danbury, Essex. Oct. 1917 to Southend. Disbanded on 29.3.18.
14th Battalion T.F.
On 1.1.17 42nd Provisional Bn. at Blackpool in 218th Bde. 73rd Div. became 14th Bn. The Bn. had been formed in 1915 from Home Service personnel of T.F. Bns. Jan. 1917 to Witham, Essex. Dec. 1917 disbanded.
15th (Service) Battalion.
Formed at Cromer 1.6.18. 19.6.18 absorbed 11th Bn. The King's (Liverpool Regt.) and went to Brookwood as Pioneer Bn. 14th Div. 5.7.18 landed at Boulogne. 11.11.18 Pioneer Bn. 14th Div. Belgium; Estampuis, east of Roubaix.

THE NORTHAMPTONSHIRE REGIMENT

1st Battalion.
4.8.14 Blackdown, Aldershot: 2nd Bde. 1st Div. 13.8.14 landed at Havre. 11.11.18 2nd Bde. 1st Div. France; Fresnoy-le-Grand, S.W. of Bohain.
2nd Battalion.
4.8.14 Alexandria. Oct. 1914 arrived in England and joined 24th Bde. 8th Div. at Hursley Park, Winchester. 5.11.14 landed at Havre. 24th Bde. was with 23rd Div. from 18.10.15 to 15.7.16. 11.11.18 24th Bde. 8th Div. Belgium; Bermissart, west of Mons.
3rd (Reserve) Battalion.
4.8.14 Northampton. Aug. 1914 Portland. May 1915 Gillingham, Kent. Oct. 1915. Strood. Mar. 1916. Gillingham. May 1918 Scrapsgate, Sheppey where it remained. (Thames and Medway Garrison).
1/4th Battalion T.F.
4.8.14 Clare Street, Northampton: East Midlands Bde. East Anglian Div. Aug. 1914 to Bury St. Edmunds. May 1915 formation became 162nd Bde. 54th Div. and moved to St. Albans area. July 1915 sailed for Lemnos. 15.8.15 landed at Suvla Bay. Dec. 1915 to Egypt. 31.10.18 162nd Bde. 54th Div. Palestine; Beirut.
2/4th Battalion T.F.
Formed at Northampton 27.11.14. Early in 1915 to 207th Bde. 69th Div. around Thetford. June 1916 to Harrogate. Oct. 1916 to Stockton. May 1917 Carburton Camp, Notts. By Nov. 1917 Clipstone. 14.3.18 disbanded: personnel to 4th (Reserve) Bn.
3/4th Battalion T.F.
Formed at Northampton 12.5.15. Aug. 1915 Windsor Great Park. Oct. 1915 Halton Park, Tring. 8.4.16 became 4th (Reserve) Bn. 1.9.16 in East Anglian Reserve Bde. T.F. at Halton Park. About Aug. 1917 Crowborough. Sept. 1918 St. Leonards.
5th (Service) Battalion. (Pioneers).
Formed at Northampton Aug. 1914—K1—Army Troops attached to 12th Div. at Shorncliffe. Nov. 1914 Hythe. Jan. 1915 became Pioneer Bn. 12th Div. Feb. 1915 to Aldershot. 30.5.15 landed in France. 11.11.18 Pioneer Bn. 12th Div. France; east of Orchies.
6th (Service) Battalion.
Formed at Northampton Sept. 1914—K2—Army Troops attached to 18th Div. at Colchester. Nov. 1914 to 54th Bde. 18th Div. May 1915 to Salisbury Plain. 26.7.15 landed in France. 11.11.18 54th Bde. 18th Div. France; near Le Cateau.
7th (Service) Battalion.
Formed at Northampton Sept. 1914—K3—73rd Bde. 24th Div. South Downs. In billets at Southwick Nov. 1914 to April 1915. June 1915 to Inkerman Barracks, Woking. 2.9.15 landed at Boulogne. 11.11.18 53rd Bde. 18th Div. France; Louvignies, near Bavai.

8th (Reserve) Battalion.
Formed at Weymouth Oct. 1914 as a service bn. of K4 in 103rd Bde. of original 34th Div. Jan. 1915 Penzance. 10.4.15 became a 2nd reserve bn. May 1915 Colchester. Mar. 1916 Sittingbourne. 1.9.16 became 28th Training Reserve Bn. at ? Maidstone in 6th Reserve Bde.
9th Battalion T.F.
On 1.1.17 the 62nd Provisional Bn. in 223rd Bde. at Cley, Norfolk became the 9th Bn. The Bn. had been formed about June 1915 from Home Service personnel of 2/4th Bn. Remained at Cley in 223rd Bde. until the summer of 1918 and then to Sheringham until the end of the war.
1st Garrison Battalion.
Formed at Warlingham Sept. 1915. Oct. 1915 to Egypt and later to Palestine. Oct. 1918 to Salonika.
2nd (Home Service) Garrison Battalion.
Formed at Isle of Grain, near Sheerness, in June 1916. Aug. 1917 became 13th Bn. Royal Defence Corps.

PRINCESS CHARLOTTE OF WALES'S (ROYAL BERKSHIRE REGIMENT)

1st Battalion.
4.8.14 Mandora Barracks, Aldershot: 6th Bde. 2nd Div. 13.8.14 landed at Rouen. 13.12.15 to 99th Bde. 2nd Div. 11.11.18 99th Bde. 2nd Div. France; Escarmain, north of Solesmes.
2nd Battalion.
4.8.14 Jhansi. 20.8.14 sailed from India. 22.10.14 landed in England and to 25th Bde. 8th Div. at Winchester. 5.11.14 landed at Havre. 11.11.18 25th Bde. 8th Div. Belgium; Pommeroeul, west of Mons.
3rd (Reserve) Battalion.
4.8.14 Reading. Aug. 1914 to Portsmouth until Nov. 1917. Nov. 1917 to Ireland and at Dublin until the end of the war.
1/4th Battalion T.F.
4.8.14 St. Mary's Butts, Reading: South Midland Bde. South Midland Div. Aug. 1914 to Chelmsford area. 31.3.15 landed at Boulogne. 13.5.15 formation became 145th Bde. 48th Div. Nov. 1917 to Italy. 4.11.18 145th Bde. 48th Div. Austria; Vigalzano, east of Trent.
2/4th Battalion T.F.
Formed at Reading 6.11.14. To Maidenhead. Feb. 1915 to Northampton in 184th Bde. 61st Div. April 1915 to Chelmsford. Mar. 1915 to Salisbury Plain. 27.5.16 landed at Havre. 11.11.18 184th Bde. 61st Div. France; Sepmeries, S.E. of Valenciennes.
3/4th Battalion T.F.
Formed at Chelmsford 25.3.15. To Weston-super-Mare for the winter. 8.4.16 became 4th (Reserve) Bn. 1.9.16 South Midland Reserve Bde. at Ludgershall. By Oct. 1916 at Cheltenham. Mar. 1917 at Catterick. July 1917 to Cambois, north of Blyth, where it remained (Tyne Garrision).
5th (Service) Battalion.
Formed at Reading on 25.8.14—K1—to 35th Bde. 12th Div. at Shorncliffe. Jan. 1915 to billets in Folkestone. 1.3.15 to Malplaquet Barracks, Aldershot. 31.5.15 landed at Boulogne. 6.2.18 to 36th Bde. 12th Div. 11.11.18 36th Bde. 12th Div. France; Vieux Conde.
6th (Service) Battalion.
Formed at Reading Sept. 1914—K2—Oct. 1914 to 53rd Bde. 18th Div. at Colchester. May 1915 to Salisbury Plain. 26.7.15 landed at Boulogne. 12.2.18 disbanded in France; personnel to 1st, 2nd and 5th Bns.
7th (Service) Battalion.
Formed at Reading Sept. 1914—K3—to 78th Bde. 26th Div. at Codford St. Mary. Nov. 1914 to billets in Reading.

May 1915 to Fovant. July Longbridge Deverill. 20.9.15 landed at Havre. 11–24 Nov. 1915 to Salonika. 30.9.18 78th Bde. 26th Div. Macedonia; Hamazill Pass, near Strumica.

8th (Service) Battalion.
Formed at Reading Sept. 1914—K3—Army Troops attached 26th Div. Salisbury Plain. Nov. 1914 to billets in Reading. May 1915 to Sutton Veny. 8.8.15 landed at Havre and to 1st Bde. 1st Div. 2.2.18 to 53rd Bde. 18th Div. 11.11.18 53rd Bde. 18th Div. France; Le Cateau.

9th (Reserve) Battalion.
Formed at Portsmouth in Oct. 1914 as a service bn. of K4 in 96th Bde. of original 32nd Div. 10.4.15 became a 2nd Reserve Bn. Bde. became 8th Reserve Bde. May 1915 Wool. 1.9.16 became 37th Training Reserve Bn. at Wool in 8th Reserve Bde.

10th (Labour) Battalion.
Formed at Portsmouth May 1916. 20.6.16 to France. April 1917 transferred to Labour Corps as 158th and 159th Labour Coys.

11th (Labour) Battalion.
Formed at Parkhurst June 1916. 24.7.16 to France. April 1917 transferred to Labour Corps as 160th and 161st Labour Coys.

12th (Labour) Battalion.
Formed at Freshwater June 1916 and to France in Aug. April 1917 transferred to Labour Corps as 162nd and 163rd Labour Coys.

13th (Labour) Battalion.
Formed at Cosham July 1916. 21.9.16 to France. April 1917 transferred to Labour Corps as 164th and 165th Labour Coys.

1st (Home Service) Garrison Battalion.
Formed at Portsmouth Aug. 1916. Aug. 1917 became 14th Bn. Royal Defence Corps.

THE QUEEN'S OWN (ROYAL WEST KENT REGIMENT)

1st Battalion.
4.8.14 Dublin; 13th Bde. 5th Div. 15.8.14 landed at Havre. Dec. 1917 to Italy arriving Fontivilla 17 Dec. April 1918 returned to France, detraining in Doullens area 6 April. 11.11.18 13th Bde. 5th Div. France; Pont sur Sambre, S.W. of Maubeuge.

2nd Battalion.
4.8.14 Multan. 30.1.15 left Bombay, arrived Basra 6.2.15 in 12th Indian Bde. Nov. 1915 two coys. attached to 30th Bde. 6th Indian Div. and besieged in Kut al Amara Dec. 1915 to April 1916: captured 29 April. Remainder of Bn. in Jan. 1916 to 34th Bde. May 1916 34th Bde. to 15th Indian Div. Aug. 1917 34th Bde. to 17th Indian Div. 31.10.18 34th Bde. 17th Indian Div. Mesopotamia; Fattah Gorge on Tigris north of Tikrit.

3rd (Reserve) Battalion.
4.8.14 Maidstone. Aug. 1914 to Chatham where it remained until summer of 1918 and then to Leysdown on Isle of Sheppey. (Thames and Medway Garrison).

1/4th Battalion T.F.
4.8.14 Drill Hall, Tonbridge: Kent Bde. Home Counties Div. To Dover, Canterbury and by mid Sept. in Sandwich area. 30.10.14 sailed from Southampton for India arriving early Dec. Div. broken up. Remained in India throughout the war.

1/5th Battalion T.F.
4.8.14 Drill Hall, East Street, Bromley: Kent Bde. Home Counties Div. To Dover, Canterbury and by mid Sept. in Sandwich area. 30.10.14 sailed from Southampton for India, arriving early Dec. Div. broken up. Dec. 1917 to Mesopotamia, landing at Basra 11 Dec. in 54th Bde. 18th Indian Div. 31.10.18 54th Bde. 18th Indian Div. Mesopotamia; near Sharqat on Tigris north of Tikrit.

2/4th Battalion T.F.
Formed Sept. 1914 at Tonbridge. Nov. 1914 to Ascot in 202nd Bde. 67th Div. In April 1915 the 202nd (2/Kent) Bde. formed The Kent Composite Bn. (H.Q. and one coy. from 2/4th R.W.K. and one coy. each from 2/4th and 2/5th East Kent and 2/5th R.W.K.). 24.4.15 Composite Bn. to 160th Bde. 53rd Div. at Cambridge. May 1915 to Bedford. 14.6.15 Composite Bn. became 2/4th R.W.K. 20.7.15 sailed from Southampton to Alexandria and Mudros. 10.8.15 landed at Suvla Bay. 13.12.15 left Gallipoli for Egypt. 25.8.18 left 53rd Div. and was disbanded on 13.9.18.

2/5th Battalion T.F.
Formed Sept. 1914 at Bromley. Nov. 1914 to Ascot in 202nd Bde. 67th Div. May 1915 to Kent. Nov. 1915 Tonbridge. July 1916 at Canterbury. Mar. 1917 Ashford. By July 1917 Barham Downs, Canterbury. Nov. 1917 disbanded at Canterbury.

3/4th Battalion T.F.
When Kent Composite Bn. became 2/4th Bn. on 14.6.15 the remaining portion of 2/4th at Ascot in 202nd Bde. 67th Div. became 3/4th Bn. May 1915 to Kent. July 1916 at Canterbury. Mar. 1917 at Ashford. May 1917 left 67th Div. and landed at Havre on 1.6.17. Attached to 9th Div. and 34th Div. 22.6.17 to 51st Bde. 17th Div. 12.7.17 to 2.8.17 acted as Pioneers 17th Div. 3.8.17 to 52nd Bde. 17th Div. 20.2.18 disbanded in France.

3/5th Battalion T.F.
Formed at Bromley July 1915. To Cambridge. 8.4.16 at Crowborough became 5th Reserve Bn. 1.9.16 absorbed by by 4th (Reserve) Bn.

4/4th Battalion T.F.
Formed July 1915. To Cambridge. 8.4.16 became 4TH (RESERVE) BN. at Crowborough. 1.9.16 absorbed 5th (Reserve) Bn. at Crowborough in Home Counties Reserve Bde. By Oct. 1916 at Tunbridge Wells where it remained.

6th (Service) Battalion.
Formed at Maidstone 14.8.14—K1—to Colchester in 37th Bde. 12th Div. and in Sept. to Purfleet. Dec. 1914 to Hythe in billets. Feb. 1915 to Aldershot. 1.6.15 landed at Boulogne. 11.11.18 37th Bde. 12th Div. France; Lecelles, N.W. of St. Amand.

7th (Service) Battalion.
Formed at Maidstone 5.9.14—K2—to Purfleet in 55th Bde. 18th Div. April 1915 Colchester. May 1915 Codford, Salisbury Plain. 27.7.15 landed at Havre. 9.2.18 to 53rd Bde. 18th Div. 11.11.18 53rd Bde. 18th Div. France; Le Cateau.

8th (Service) Battalion.
Formed at Maidstone 12.9.14—K3—to Shoreham in 72nd Bde. 24th Div. Dec. 1914 Worthing in billets. April 1915 Shoreham. July 1915 Blackdown. 30.8.15 landed at Boulogne. 11.11.18 72nd Bde. 24th Div. France; La Rolies, east of Bavai.

9th (Reserve) Battalion.
Formed at Chatham 24.10.14 as a service bn. of K4 in 93rd Bde. of original 31st Div. 10.4.15 became a 2nd Reserve bn. and 93rd Bde. became 5th Reserve Bde. June 1915 Canterbury. July 1915 Colchester. Sept. 1915 Shoreham. 1.9.16 absorbed in Training Reserve Bns. of 5th Reserve Bde. at Shoreham.

10th (Service) Battalion. (Kent County).
Raised at Maidstone 3.5.15 by Lord Harris, Vice Lieutenant of Kent at the request of the Army Council.

July 1915 in 118th Bde. 39th Div. Oct. 1915 to 123rd Bde. 41st Div. Nov. (?) taken over by the War Office. Jan. 1916 to Aldershot—Wellington Lines. 4.5.16 landed in France. Nov. 1917 to Italy. Mar. 1918 returned to France, arriving Doullens 7 Mar. 11.11.18 123rd Bde. 41st Div. Belgium, Rooverst, west of Nederbrakel.

11th (Service) Battalion. (Lewisham).
Raised at Lewisham on 5.5.15 by the Mayor and local committee and trained at Catford. July 1915 to 118th Bde. 39th Div. Oct. 1915 to 122nd Bde. 41st Div. 11.11.15 taken over by the War Office. Jan. 1916 to Aldershot in Tournay Barracks. 3.5.16 landed in France. Nov. 1917 to Itlay. Mar. 1918 returned to France, arriving Doullens 7 Mar. 16.3.18 disbanded in France.

12th (Reserve) Battalion.
Formed in Feb. 1916 from depot coys. of 10th and 11th Bns. as a Local Reserve Bn. To Northampton in 23rd Reserve Bde. May 1916 to Aldershot. 1.9.16 became 99th Training Reserve Bn. at Aldershot in 23rd Reserve Bde.

A 13th Battalion was formed at Cromer on 1.6.18 and absorbed by 11th Royal Sussex Regt. about July 1918.

1st (Home Service) Garrison Battalion.
Formed at Rochester Mar. 1916 and remained there until it became 15th Bn. Royal Defence Corps in Aug. 1917.

THE KING'S OWN (YORKSHIRE LIGHT INFANTRY)

1st Battalion.
4.8.14 Singapore. 27.9.14 sailed from Singapore and arrived Southampton 9 Nov. To Hursley Park. 18 Nov. Harwich. 17.12.14 to Hursley Park 83rd Bde. 28th Div. 16.1.15 landed at Havre. 26.10.15 sailed from Marseilles for Salonika via Alexandria arriving Salonika 7.12.15. 20.6.18 left 28th Div. for France. Taranto 2 July. 16.7.18 to 151st Bde. 50th Div. at Dieppe. 11.11.18 151st Bde. 50th Div. France; Monceau, N.W. of Avesnes.

2nd Battalion.
4.8.14 Dublin: 13th Bde. 5th Div. 16.8.14 landed at Havre. 28.12.15 to 97th Bde. 32nd Div. 11.11.18 97th Bde. 32nd Div. France; Haut Lieu, S.W. of Avesnes.

3rd (Reserve) Battalion.
4.8.14 Pontefract. Oct. 1914 Hull. April 1916 Withernsea. Oct. 1916 Hedon. June 1918 at Pocklington. Aug. 1918 Patrington. (Humber Garrison).

1/4th Battalion T.F.
4.8.14 Wakefield: 3rd West Riding Bde. West Riding Div. Aug. 1914 Doncaster. Nov. 1914 Gainsborough. Feb. 1915 York. 12.4.15 landed in France. 12.5.15 formation became 148th Bde. 49th Div. 11.11.18 148th Bde. 49th Div. France; Leforest, north of Douai.

1/5th Battalion T.F.
4.8.14 Drill Hall, French Gate, Doncaster. 3rd West Riding Bde. West Riding Div. Subsequent record similar to 1/4th Bn. until 2.2.18 and then to 187th Bde. 62nd Div. absorbing 2/5th Bn. and becoming 5th Bn. 11.11.18 187th Bde. 62nd Div. France; Sous le Bois, near Maubeuge.

2/4th Battalion T.F.
Formed at Wakefield 30.9.14. Mar. 1915 to Bulwell near Nottingham in 187th Bde. 62nd Div. April 1915 Strensall. May 1915 Beverley. Nov. 1915 Gateshead. Jan. 1916 Larkhill, Salisbury Plain. June 1916 Flixton Park, near Bungay. Oct. 1916 Wellingborough. 15.1.17 landed at Havre. 11.11.18 187th Bde. 62nd Div. France; Sous le Bois, near Maubeuge.

2/5th Battalion T.F.
Formed at Doncaster 10.9.14. Subsequent record similar to 2/4th Bn. until 2.2.18 and then absorbed by 1/5th Bn.

3/4th and 3/5th Battalions T.F.
Formed Mar. 1915. To Clipstone. 8.4.16 became Reserve Bns. 1.9.16 4th (Reserve) Bn. absorbed 5th Bn. at Clipstone in West Riding Reserve Bde. Oct. 1917 Rugeley, Cannock Chase. July 1918 Bromeswell, near Woodbridge. Oct. 1918 to Southend.

6th (Service) Battalion.
Formed at Pontefract 12.8.14—K1—to Inkerman Barracks, Woking in 43rd Bde. 14th Div. Nov. 1914 Witley. Feb. 1915 Aldershot. 21.5.15 landed at Boulogne. 19.2.18 disbanded in France.

7th (Service) Battalion.
Formed at Pontefract 12.9.14—K2—to Woking in 61st Bde. 20th Div. Feb. 1915 Witley. May 1915 Salisbury Plain. 24.7.15 landed at Boulogne. 20.2.18 disbanded in France.

8th (Service) Battalion.
Formed at Pontefract Sept. 1914—K3—to Frensham in 70th Bde. 23rd Div. Dec. 1914 Aldershot. Feb. 1915 Hythe. May 1915 Bordon. Aug. 1915 landed in France. 70th Bde. with 8th Div. from 18.10.15 to 17.7.16. Nov. 1917 to Italy. 4.11.18 70th Bde. 23rd Div. Italy; Rorai Piccolo, west of Pordenone.

9th (Service) Battalion.
Formed at Pontefract Sept. 1914—K3—to Berkhamsted in 64th Bde. 21st Div. Oct. 1914 to Halton Park, Tring. Nov. 1914 to Maidenhead in billets. April 1915 Halton Park. Aug. 1915 Witley. Sept. 1915 landed in France. 11.11.18 64th Bde. 21st Div. France; moving to Limont Fontaine, N.E. of Aulnoye.

10th (Service) Battalion.
Formed at Pontefract Sept. 1914—K3—subsequent record same as 9th Bn. until 13.2.18 when it was disbanded in France.

11th (Reserve) Battalion.
Formed at Hull Oct. 1914 as a service bn. of K4 in 90th Bde. of original 30th Div. Nov. 1914 Harrogate. 10.4.15 became a 2nd reserve bn. and 90th Bde. became 2nd Reserve Bde. Nov. 1915 Rugeley, Cannock Chase. 1.9.16 became 8th Training Reserve Bn. at Rugeley in 2nd Reserve Bde.

12th (Service) (Miners) (Pioneers).
Raised at Leeds by the West Yorkshire Coalowners Association on 5.9.14 and went to Farnley Park, Otley. May 1915 to Burton Leonard, near Ripon as Pioneer Bn. 31st Div. 15.8.15 taken over by the War Office. Oct. 1915 to Fovant, Salisbury Plain. 6.12.15 embarked at Liverpool for Egypt, arriving 22 Dec. 2.3.16 left Egypt, arriving Marseilles 9 Mar. From 1.7.17 to 30.11.17 attached to Fifth Army Troops for work on Light Railways. 11.11.18 Pioneer Bn. 31st Div. Belgium, Renaix.

13th (Reserve) Battalion. (Pioneers).
Formed at Ripon Oct. 1915 from Depot Coys. of 12th Bn. as a Local Reserve Bn. in 19th Reserve Bde. Jan. 1916 Harrogate. May 1916 Gosforth. 1.9.16 absorbed in Training Reserve Bns. of 19th Reserve Bde. at Newcastle.

14th (Home Service) Battalion.
Formed about Nov. 1916 (could have been 3rd (Home Service) Garrison Bn. for a short time) and to 216th Bde. 72nd Div. Jan. 1917 Bedford. May 1917 Ipswich. Early 1918 72nd Div. broken up and the battalion was disbanded at Bury St. Edmunds on 1.4.18.

15th (Service) Battalion.
On 11.6.18 the 10th Garrison Guard Bn. (recently formed in France) became the 15th (Garrison) Bn. in 120th Bde. 40th Div. at Buysscheure, near St. Omer, 13.7.18 title 'Garrison' discontinued. 11.11.18 120th Bde. 40th Div. Belgium; Herinnes, east of Roubaix.

1st (Reserve) Garrison Battalion.
Formed at Newcastle in Feb. 1916. May 1916 Killingholme. Sept. 1916 Middlesbrough. Mar. 1917 Seaton Carew. About May 1918 to Ireland and at Berehaven, Co. Cork.

2nd Garrison Battalion.
Formed at South Dalton in June 1916. July 1916 to France and was in Fourth Army Troops until July 1918 then to L. of C. 31.7.18 became 16TH (GARRISON) BN.
For 3rd (Home Service) Garrison Bn. see 14th Bn.

51st (Graduated) Battalion.
On 27.10.17 the 264th Graduated Bn. (formerly 90th Training Reserve Bn. from 12th East Yorks.) at Ipswich in 217th Bde. 72nd Div. became 51st Bn. Jan. 1918 72nd Div. broken up and Bn. went to 208th Bde. 69th Div. at Doncaster. By May 1918 at Welbeck and to 207th Bde. 69th Div. About Aug. 1918 to Clipstone where it remained.

52nd (Graduated) Battalion.
On 27.10.17 the 270th Graduated Bn. (formerly 91st Training Reserve Bn. from 15th York & Lancs) at Danbury in 219th Bde. 73rd Div. became 52nd Bn. Jan. 1918 to 208th Bde. 69th Div. at Doncaster. By May 1918 at Welbeck and to 207th Bde. 69th Div. About Aug. 1918 to Clipstone where it remained.

53rd (Young Soldier) Battalion.
On 27.10.17 the 8th Young Soldier Bn. (formerly 11th K.O.Y.L.I.) at Cannock Chase in 2nd Reserve Bde. became 53rd Bn. By Nov. 1918 at Clipstone in 2nd Reserve Bde.

THE KING'S (SHROPSHIRE LIGHT INFANTRY)

1st Battalion.
4.8.14 Tipperary: 16th Bde. 6th Div. 20 Aug. Cambridge. 10.9.14 landed at St. Nazaire. 11.11.18 16th Bde. 6th Div. France; Bohain.

2nd Battalion.
4.8.14 Secunderabad. Sailed from Bombay 13 Oct. Nov. 1914 landed at Plymouth and to Winchester joining 80th Bde. 27th Div. 21.12.14 landed at Havre. To Salonika, landing on 4.12.15. 30.9.18 80th Bde. 27th Div. Macedonia; north of Doiran.

3rd (Reserve) Battalion.
4.8.14 Shrewsbury. Aug. Pembroke Dock. Nov. 1914 to Mar. 1915 Edinburgh, then back to Pembroke Dock. Dec. 1917 to Crosshaven, Queenstown Harbour, Cork. Early in 1918 to Fermoy, until the end of the war.

1/4th Battalion T.F.
4.8.14 Shrewsbury: Army Troops attached Welsh Div. Aug. to Cardiff. 4.9.14 Sittingbourne. 29.10.14 embarked at Southampton for India joining Middlesex Bde. Home Counties Div. 1.12.14 arrived Bombay. 10.2.15 arrived Singapore with detachment at Andaman Isles. April 1915 two coys. to Hong Kong. 13.4.17 concentrated at Singapore. 19.4.17 arrived Colombo. 30.5.17 arrived Cape Town. 29.6.17 sailed from Cape Town and landed at Plymouth 27.7.17 re-embarked at Southampton and landed at Havre 29.7.17. 18.8.17 to 190th Bde. 63rd Div. 4.2.18 to 56th Bde. 19th Div. 11.11.18 56th Bde. 19th Div. France; Bry west of Bavai.

2/4th Battalion T.F.
Formed at Shrewsbury Oct. 1914. Shrewsbury and Cardiff. July to Nov. 1915 Ramsay, Isle of Man. 26.11.15 to 204th Bde. 68th Div. at Bedford. In 1916 Lowestoft and Yarmouth. In summer of 1917 at Aldeburgh and by Dec. 1917 appears to have been absorbed in the other battalions of 204th Bde.

3/4th Battalion T.F.
Formed May 1915 at Shrewsbury. Stationed at Oswestry and Tenby. April 1916 became 4th (Reserve) Bn. 1917 at Swansea and 1918 at Pembroke Dock. (Milford Haven Garrison).

5th (Service) Battalion.
Formed at Shrewsbury Aug. 1914—K1—to 42nd Bde. 14th Div. at Aldershot. Nov. 1914 to Mar. 1915 in billets at Chiddingfold then back to Aldershot. 20.5.15 landed at Boulogne. 4.2.18 disbanded at Jussy. Personnel to 1st, 1/4th, 6th and 7th Bns.

6th (Service) Battalion.
Formed at Shrewsbury Sept. 1914—K2—to 60th Bde. 20th Div. at Aldershot. April 1915 to Larkhill, Salisbury Plain. 22.7.15 landed at Boulogne. 11.11.18 60th Bde. 20th Div. France; N.W. of Maubeuge.

7th (Service) Battalion.
Formed at Shrewsbury Sept. 1914—K3—to 76th Bde. 25th Div. at Codford, Salisbury Plain. Nov. 1914 to May 1915 in billets at Bournemouth. May at Romsey. June to Aldershot. 28.9.15 landed at Boulogne. 15.10.15 76th Bde. to 3rd Div. 19.10.15 to 8th Bde. 3rd Div. 11.11.18 8th Bde. 3rd Div. France; Romeries, near Solesmes.

8th (Service) Battalion.
Formed at Shrewsbury in Sept. 1914—K3—to 66th Bde., 22nd Div. at Seaford. Dec. 1914 to billets in Eastbourne. Mar. 1915 Seaford. May 1915 Aldershot. 5.9.15 landed in France. 28.10.15 sailed from Marseilles and landed at Salonika on 6 Nov. 30.9.18 66th Bde. 22nd Div. Macedonia; near Lake Doiran.

9th (Reserve) Battalion.
Formed at Pembroke Dock in Oct. 1914 as a service bn. of K4 in 104th Bde. of original 35th Div. 10.4.15 became a 2nd reserve bn. June Kinmel. Aug. 1915 Prees Heath in 11th Reserve Bde. 1.9.16 became 48th Training Reserve Bn. at Prees Heath in 11th Reserve Bde.

10th (Shropshire and Cheshire Yeomanry) Battalion T.F.
Formed at Cairo on 2.3.17 from the two dismounted yeomanry regiments in 231st Bde. 74th Div. May 1918 to France with 74th Div. arriving Marseilles on 7th May. 11.11.18 231st Bde. 74th Div. Belgium: near Ath.

THE DUKE OF CAMBRIDGE'S OWN (MIDDLESEX REGIMENT)

1st Battalion.
4.8.14 Woolwich. 11.8.14 landed at Havre as L. of C. Troops. 22.8.14 to 19th Bde. forming at Valenciennes. 12.10.14 19th Bde. to 6th Div. 31.5.15 19th Bde. to 27th Div. 19.8.15 19th Bde. to 2nd Div. 25.11.15 19th Bde. to 33rd Div. Bn. to 98th Bde. 33rd Div. 11.11.18 98th Bde. 33rd Div. France; Sassegnies, S.W. of Aulnoye.

2nd Battalion.
4.8.14 Malta. Sept. 1914 to England and Hursley Park in 23rd Bde. 8th Div. 7.11.14 landed at Havre. 11.11.18 23rd Bde. 8th Div. Belgium; Douvrain. N.W. of Mons.

3rd Battalion.
4.8.14 Cawnpore. Dec. 1914 arrived in England to Winchester and 85th Bde. 28th Div. 19.1.15 landed at Havre. 25.10.15 embarked at Marseilles for Salonika (via Alexandria) arriving 2.12.15. 30.9.18 85th Bde. 28th Div. Macedonia; Dzuma Obasi, north of Lake Doiran.

4th Battalion.
4.8.14 Devonport: 8th Bde. 3rd Div. 14.8.14 landed at Boulogne. 14.11.15 to 63rd Bde. 21st Div. 8.7.16 63rd Bde. to 37th Div. 11.11.18 63rd Bde. 37th Div. France; moving to Caudry, S.W. of Solesmes.

5th and 6th (Reserve) Battalions.
4.8.14 Mill Hill. Aug. 1914 to Rochester (5th) and Gillingham (6th). Nov. 1915 6th to Chatham. Mar. 1916 5th to Chatham. During 1917 and 1918 the 5th Bn. was

at Gillingham and the 6th at Chatham. (Thames and Medway Garrison).

1/7th Battalion T.F.
4.8.14 Priory Road, Hornsea: Middlesex Bde. Home Counties Div. 5/9th Aug. Isle of Grain. Then Sittingbourne. 4.9.14 embarked for Gibraltar. Feb. 1915 returned to England, arriving Avonmouth 13 Feb. To Barnet. 13.3.15 landed at Havre. 15.3.15 to 23rd Bde. 8th Div. 23 June to 2 Aug. amalgamated with 1/8th Bn. 8.2.16 to 167th Bde. 56th Div. 11.11.18 167th Bde. 56th Div. France; Le Dessous, Blaregnies, N.E. of Bavai. (The battalion left the Home Counties Div. when it went to Gibraltar in Sept. 1914).

1/8th Battalion T.F.
4.8.14 202A Hanworth Road, Hounslow: Middlesex Bde. Home Counties Div. To Sheerness for a few days then to Sittingbourne. Sept. 1914 left Home Counties Div. and went to Gibraltar, arriving 17 Sept. Feb. 1915 returned to England. 9.3.15 landed at Havre. 11.3.15 to 85th Bde. 28th Div. 21.6.15 to 8th Div. and amalgamated with 1/7th Bn. from 23 June to 2 Aug. 27.8.15 to 25th Bde. 8th Div. 23.10.15 to 70th Bde. 8th Div. 9.2.16 to 167th Bde. 56th Div. at Airaines. 11.11.18 167th Bde. 56th Div. France; Blaregnies, N.E. of Bavai.

1/9th Battalion T.F.
4.8.14 The Drill Hall, Pound Lane, Willesden Green, N.W.: Middlesex Bde. Home Counties Div. To Minster, near Sheerness for a few days then to Sittingbourne. 30.10.14 sailed from Southampton for India, arriving Bombay 2 Dec. Div. broken up. 19.11.17 left Karachi and landed Basra 24 Nov. To 53rd Bde. 18th Indian Div. 31.10.18 53rd Bde. 18th Indian Div. Mesopotamia; north of Lesser Zab River, north of Tikrit.

1/10th Battalion T.F.
4.8.14 Stamford Brook Lodge, Ravenscourt Park, W.: Middlesex Brigade, Home Counties Div. To Sheerness for a few days then to Sittingbourne. 30.10.14 sailed from Southampton for India, arriving Bombay 2 Dec. Div. broken up. Remained in India till the end of the war.

2/7th Battalion T.F.
Formed at Hornsey Sept. 1914. 24.9.14 Barnet. Nov. 1914 to Egham in 201st Bde. 67th Div. Feb. 1915 left 67th Div. and sailed from Southampton 2 Feb. for Gibraltar, arriving 7 Feb. Aug. 1915 to Egypt, arriving Alexandria 31 Aug. Served in the Western Frontier Force from Nov. 1915. 9.5.16 sailed from Alexandria for France, arriving Marseilles 15 June. To quarantine camp for typhus. 10.6.16 to Rouen and disbanded on 15.6.16. The 3/7th Bn. in England now became the 2/7th Bn.

2/8th Battalion T.F.
Formed at Hampton Court(?) Sept. 1914. Nov. 1914 to Staines in 201st Bde. 67th Div. Subsequent record same as 2/7th Bn. Also disbanded on 15.6.16 and 3/8th Bn. in England now became 2/8th.

2/9th Battalion T.F.
Formed at Willesden Sept. 1914. Nov. 1914 Staines in 201st Bde. 67th Div. By Nov. 1915 Sevenoaks. July 1916 at Barham, near Canterbury. Summer 1917 Patrixbourne. Nov. 1917 disbanded.

2/10th Battalion T.F.
Formed at Stamford Brook Sept. 1914. Nov. 1914 Staines in 201st Bde. 67th Div. 24.4.15 to Welsh Border Bde. Welsh Div. at Cambridge. May 1915 to Bedford. 13.5.15 formation became 160th Bde. 53rd Div. 18.7.15 sailed from Devonport to Imbros arriving—via Egypt—8 Aug. 9.8.15 landed at Suvla Bay. Dec. 1915 to Egypt. 19.8.18 left 53rd Div. and disbanded at El Kantara.

3/7th Battalion T.F.
Formed at Hornsey Feb. 1915. To Staines in 201st Bde. 67th Div. About May 1915 to Kent. When 2/7th Bn. was disbanded in France became 2/7TH BN. at Barham, near Canterbury. Summer 1917 at Scotland Hill, near Canterbury. Nov. 1917 disbanded.

3/8th Battalion T.F.
Formed at Hounslow Feb. 1915. May 1915 Staines in 201st Bde. 67th Div. To Kent in 1915. When 2/8th Bn. was disbanded in France became 2/8TH BN. at Bourne Park, near Canterbury. Summer 1917 at Scotland Hill, near Canterbury. Oct. 1917 disbanded.

3/9th Battalion T.F.
Formed at Willesden Mar. 1915. To Cambridge. 8.4.16 became 9th (Reserve) Bn. 1.9.16 absorbed in 7th (Reserve) Bn. at Purfleet.

3/10th Battalion T.F.
Formed May 1915. To Kent in 201st Bde. 67th Div. July 1916 at Bourne Park, near Canterbury. 1.6.17 landed at Havre having left 67th Div. To South African Bde. 9th Div. to 23.6.17. On 2.8.17 to 10th Bde. 4th Div. 20.2.18 disbanded in France.

4/7th Battalion T.F.
Formed May 1915. To Cambridge later Purfleet. 8.4.16 became 7th (Reserve) Bn. 1.9.16 absorbed 8th, 9th and 10th (Reserve) Bns. at Purfleet in Home Counties Reserve Bde. About Sept. 1916 to Tunbridge Wells where it remained.

4/8th and 4/10th Battalions T.F.
Formed about May 1915. To Cambridge and Purfleet. 8.4.16 became Reserve Bns. 1.9.16 absorbed by 7th (Reserve) Bn.

11th (Service) Battalion.
Formed at Mill Hill Aug. 1914—K1—to Colchester in 36th Bde. 12th Div. Nov. 1914 Shorncliffe. Feb. 1915 Ramillies Barracks, Aldershot. June 1915 landed at Boulogne. 7.2.18 disbanded in France.

12th (Service) Battalion.
Formed at Mill Hill Aug. 1914—K2—to Colchester in 54th Bde. 18th Div. May 1915 Codford, Salisbury Plain. 26.7.15 landed at Havre. 13.2.18 disbanded in France.

13th (Service) Battalion.
Formed at Mill Hill Sept. 1914—K3—to South Downs in 73rd Bde. 24th Div. Dec. 1914 Hove. May 1915 Shoreham. June 1915 Pirbright. 2.9.15 landed at Boulogne. 11.11.18 73rd Bde. 24th Div. France; moving to Le Louvion, east of Bavai.

14th (Reserve) Battalion.
Formed at Gravesend Oct. 1914 as a service bn. of K4 in 93rd Bde. of original 31st Div. Jan. 1915 to Halling, near Maidstone 10.4.15 became a 2nd reserve bn. and 93rd Bde. became 5th Reserve Bde. May 1915 Colchester. Oct. 1915 Shoreham. 1.9.16 became 24th Training Reserve Bn. at Shoreham in 5th Reserve Bde.

15th (Reserve) Battalion.
Formed at (?) Gillingham in Oct. 1914 as a service bn. of K4 in 93rd Bde. of original 31st Div. Dec. 1914 Snodland near Maidstone. 10.4.15 became a 2nd reserve bn. and 93rd Bde. became 5th Reserve Bde. May 1915 to Colchester. Oct. 1915 Shoreham. 1.9.16 absorbed in T.R. Bns. of 5th Reserve Bde.

16th (Service) Battalion. (Public Schools).
Raised in London 1.9.14 by Lieut. Col. J. J. Mackay with a recruiting office at 24 St. James' Street. To Kempton Park. Dec. 1914 Warlingham. July 1915 to Clipstone and 100th Bde. 33rd Div. Aug. 1915 Perham Down. 10.8.15 taken over by the War Office. 17.11.15 landed at Boulogne. 25.2.16 to GHQ Troops. 25.4.16 to 86th Bde. 29th Div. 11.2.18 disbanded near Poperinghe.

17th (Service) Battalion. (1st Football).
Raised in London 12.12.14 by Rt. Hon. W. Joynson

Hicks M.P. To White City. April 1915 Cranleigh. July 1915 to Clipstone and 100th Bde. 33rd Div. Aug. 1915 Perham Down. 1.9.15 taken over by the War Office. 18.11.15 landed at Boulogne. 8.12.15 to 6th Bde. 2nd Div. 10.2.18 disbanded in France.

18th (Service) Battalion. (1st Public Works Pioneers).
Raised in London 19.1.15 by Lieut. Col. John Ward M.P. Feb. 1915 Alexandra Palace. May 1915 Rayleigh. July 1915 to Clipstone and Pioneers 33rd Div. 1.7.15 taken over by the War Office. Aug. 1915 Salisbury Plain. 15.11.15 landed at Havre. 11.11.18 Pioneer Bn. 33rd Div. France; Berlaimont, west of Aulnoye.

19th (Service) Battalion. (2nd Public Works Pioneers).
Raised in London April 1915 by Lieut. Col. John Ward M.P. at Hornsey. 1.7.15 taken over by the War Office. Oct. 1915 to Aldershot as Pioneer Bn. 41st Div. 2.5.16 landed at Havre. Nov. 1917 to Italy, arriving Vigasio on 21 Nov. Mar. 1918 returned to France, arriving Mondicourt on 8 Mar. 11.11.18 Pioneer Bn. 41st Div. Belgium; Berchem on Scheldt, N.W. of Renaix.

20th (Service) Battalion. (Shoreditch).
Raised in Shoreditch by the Mayor and Borough on 18.5.15. July 1915 to 118th Bde. 39th Div. 15.8.15 taken over by the War Office. Oct. 1915 to Aldershot. Feb. 1916 to Witley and 121st Bde. 40th Div. June 1916 landed in France. 6.5.18 reduced to training cadre. 31.5.18 to 16th Div. 16.6.18 to 43rd Bde. 14th Div. at Boulogne and crossed to Folkestone next day: to Brookwood. 20.6.18 reconstituted and absorbed 34th Bn. 5.7.18 landed at Boulogne. 11.11.18 43rd Bde. 14th Div. Belgium; Warcoing on Scheldt, east of Roubaix.

21st (Service) Battalion. (Islington).
Raised in Islington by the Mayor and Borough on 18.5.15. July 1915 to 118th Bde. 39th Div. Taken over by the War Office in Aug. Oct. 1915 to Aldershot. Feb. 1916 to Witley and 121st Bde. 40th Div. June 1916 landed in France. 5.2.18 to 119th Bde. 40th Div. 5.5.18 reduced to training cadre. 3.6.18 to 34th Div. 17.6.18 39th Div. 30.6.18 to 74th Bde. 25th Div. at Boulogne and crossed to Folkestone. At Aldershot left 25th Div. and went to Cromer. May have returned to Aldershot later.

22nd (Service) Battalion.
Formed at Mill Hill in June 1915 as a bantam bn. Oct. 1915 to Aldershot in 121st Bde. 40th Div. Feb. 1916 to Witley. 2.4.16 disbanded.

23rd (Service) Battalion. (2nd Football).
Raised in London 29.6.15 by Rt. Hon. W. Joynson Hicks M.P. July 1915 Cranleigh. Nov. 1915 Aldershot in 123rd Bde. 41st Div. May 1916 landed in France. Nov. 1917 to Italy, arriving Vigasio 21 Nov. Mar. 1918 returned to France, arriving Mondicourt 8 Mar. 11.11.18 123rd Bde. 41st Div. Belgium; near Nederbrakel.

24th (Reserve) Battalion.
Formed from depot coys. of 16th Bn. as a Local Reserve Bn. at Tring in Oct. 1915. Dec. 1915 at Northampton in 23rd Reserve Bde. May 1916 Aldershot. 1.9.16 became 100th Training Reserve Bn. at Aldershot in 23rd Reserve Bde.

25th (Reserve) Battalion.
Formed from depot coys. of 18th, 19th and 26th Bns. as a Local Reserve bn. at Tring in Oct. 1915. Dec. 1915 at Northampton in 23rd Reserve Bde. May 1916 Aldershot. 1.9.16 became 25th (Garrison) Bn. (see below).

25th (Garrison) Battalion.
Formed from 25th (Reserve) Bn. at Aldershot on 1.9.16. On 3.11.16 to 213th Bde. 71st Div. Some accounts say that the title "Garrison" was discontinued on 1.11.16 but other sources, including the Army List, retain the "Garrison" until the end of the war. 22.12.16 left 71st Div. and embarked at Devonport for Far East. 1.4.17 arrived Hong Kong, having left two coys. at Singapore. Aug. 1918 the complete bn. went to Siberia, landing at Vladivostock on 3 Aug. Remained in Siberia until Sept. 1919 and then returned to England.

26th (Service) Battalion. (3rd Public Works Pioneers).
Raised in London 9.8.15 by Lieut. Col. John Ward M.P. At Alexandra Park. Taken over by the War Office. Nov. 1915 Hornchurch. Dec. 1915 Witley. June 1916 attached 69th Div. in Norfolk. July–Aug. 1916 attached 62nd Div. at Flixton Park, near Bungay. Left 62nd Div. for Devonport and embarked for Salonika, arriving 24 Aug. To 27th Div. as Pioneer Bn. 30.9.18 Pioneer Bn. 27th Div. Macedonia; Izlis, west of Kosturino, N.W. of Lake Doiran.

27th and 28th (Reserve) Battalions.
Formed in 1915 as Local Reserve Bns. from depot coys. of 17th and 23rd Bns. and 20th and 21st Bns. Dec. 1915 Northampton in 23rd Reserve Bde. May 1916. 1.9.16 became 101st and 102nd Training Reserve Bns. at Aldershot in 23rd Reserve Bde.

29th (Works) Battalion.
Formed at Mill Hill July 1916. By Mar. 1917 at Thetford. April 1917 transferred to Labour Corps as 5th Labour Bn.

30th and 31st (Works) Battalions.
Formed at Crawley July 1916 and Mill Hill Sept. 1916. 30th to Reading where it remained. 31st Bn. to Sevenoaks in 1917 and at Reigate, Harpenden and Croydon in 1918.

32nd Battalion T.F.
On 1.1.17 the 63rd Provisional Bn. at Gorleston in 225th Bde. became the 32nd Bn. The 63rd Provisional Bn. had been formed in 1915 from Home Service personnel of T.F. Bns. Remained at Gorleston in 225th Bde.

33rd (Works) Battalion.
Formed at Mill Hill in Jan. 1917 and transferred to Labour Corps in April 1917 as 6th Labour Bn.

A 34th Battalion was formed on 1.6.18 at St. Olaves near Lowestoft and absorbed by the 20th Bn. at Brookwood on 20.6.18.

1st (Home Service) Garrison Battalion.
Formed at Mill Hill in May 1916. Aug. 1917 at Chattenden, near Rochester became 16th Bn. Royal Defence Corps.

51st (Graduated) Battalion.
On 27.10.17 the 209th (Graduated) Bn. (formerly 97th Training Reserve Bn. from 12th Royal West Surrey) at Taverham in 193rd Bde. 64th Div. became 51st Bn. To Norwich for the winter, Mar. 1918 Sheringham then Taverham. By Nov. 1918 back at Norwich.

52nd (Graduated) Battalion.
On 27.10.17 the 250th Graduated Bn. (formerly 101st Training Reserve Bn. from 27th Middlesex) at Colchester in 212th Bde. 71st Div. became 52nd Bn. 71st Div. broken up in Feb. 1918 and went to 193rd Bde. 64th Div. at Norwich. May 1918 Taverham and Nov. 1918 back at Norwich.

53rd (Young Soldier) Battalion.
On 27.10.17 the 102nd Young Soldier Bn. (formerly 28th Middlesex) at Aldershot in 23rd Reserve Bde. became the 53rd Bn. No further change.

THE KING'S ROYAL RIFLE CORPS

1st Battalion.
4.8.14 Salamanca Barracks, Aldershot: 6th Bde. 2nd Div. 13.8.14 landed at Rouen. 13.12.15 to 99th Bde. 2nd Div. 11.11.18 99th Bde. 2nd Div. France; Capelle, N.E. of Solesmes.

2nd Battalion.
   4.8.14 Blackdown: 2nd Bde. 1st Div. 13.8.14 landed at Havre. 11.11.18 2nd Bde. 1st Div. France; Fresnoy le Grand, S.W. of Bohain.
3rd Battalion.
   4.8.14 Meerut. 16.10.14 sailed from Bombay and arrived at Plymouth. To Winchester and 80th Bde. 27th Div. 21.12.14 landed at Havre. Nov. 1915 to Salonika, embarking Marseilles 18 Nov. and arriving Salonika 5 Dec. 30.9.18 80th Bde. 27th Div. Macedonia; Rabrovo, south of Kosturino and N.W. of Lake Doiran.
4th Battalion.
   4.8.14 Gharial. 16.10.14 sailed from Bombay and arrived at Plymouth 18 Nov. with 3rd Bn. To Winchester and 80th Bde. 27th Div. Dec. 1914 landed at Havre. Nov. 1915 to Salonika, sailing from Marseilles 19 Nov. and arriving Salonika on 25 Nov. June 1918 left 27th Div. and returned to France via Itea and Taranto, arriving Serqueux early July. 16.7.18 to 151st Bde. 50th Div. at Martin Eglise. 11.11.18 151st Bde. 50th Div. France; St. Remy-Chaussee, N.W. of Avesnes.
5th and 6th (Reserve) Battalions.
   4.8.14 Winchester. 9.8.14 to Sheerness and remained in this area until the end of the war. In 1917 and 1918 the 5th Bn. was at Sheerness and the 6th Bn. at Queenborough. (Thames and Medway Garrison).
7th (Service) Battalion.
   Formed at Winchester 19.8.14—K1—to Marlborough Lines, Aldershot in 41st Bde. 14th Div. Nov. 1914 to Grayshott, near Hindhead in billets. Feb. 1915 Bordon. Mar. 1915 Aldershot. 19.5.15 landed at Boulogne. 2.2.18 to 43rd Bde. 14th Div. 25.4.18 reduced to cadre. 16.6.18 to 16th Div. at Boulogne and returned to England. Cadre absorbed by 34th Bn. London Regt. at Clacton.
8th (Service) Battalion.
   Formed at Winchester 21.8.14—K1—to Aldershot in 41st Bde. 14th Div. Nov. 1914 Hindhead in billets. Feb. 1915 Bordon. Mar. 1915 Aldershot. May 1915 landed at Boulogne. 27.4.18 reduced to cadre. 16.6.18 to 34th Div. 27.6.18 to 39th Div. 3.8.18 disbanded at Desvres.
9th (Service) Battalion.
   Formed at Winchester Aug. 1914—K1—to Aldershot in 42nd Bde. 14th Div. Nov. 1914 Petworth in billets. Feb. 1915 Aldershot. 20.5.15 landed at Boulogne. 27.4.18 reduced to cadre. 16.6.18 to 34th Div. 27.6.18 to 39th Div. 3.8.18 disbanded at Desvres.
10th (Service) Battalion.
   Formed at Winchester 14.9.14—K2—to Blackdown in 59th Bde. 20th Div. Feb. 1915 Witley. April 1915 Hamilton Camp, near Stonehenge. 21.7.15 landed at Boulogne. 5.2.18 disbanded at Dickebusch, south of Ypres.
11th (Service) Battalion.
   Formed at Winchester Sept. 1914—K2—to Blackdown in 59th Bde. 20th Div. Feb. 1915 Witley. April 1915 Larkhill, Salisbury Plain. 21.7.15 landed at Boulogne. 11.11.18 59th Bde. 20th Div. France; Jenlain, north of Le Quesnoy.
12th (Service) Battalion.
   Formed at Winchester 21.9.14—K2—to Cowshot, Bisley. Nov. 1914 Blackdown. 17.2.15 to Hindhead in billets. 10.4.15 to Larkhill, Salisbury Plain. 22.7.15 landed at Boulogne. 11.11.18 60th Bde. 20th Div. France; Maubeuge.
13th (Service) Battalion.
   Formed at Winchester 7.10.14—K3—to Halton Park, Wendover as Army Troops attached 21st Div. Nov. 1914 to Amersham and Great Missenden in billets. April 1915 Windmill Hill, Salisbury Plain and to 111th Bde. 37th Div. 31.7.15 landed at Boulogne. 11.11.18 111th Bde. 37th Div. France; Caudry.

14th and 15th (Reserve) Battalions.
   Formed at Sheerness in Oct. 1914 as service bns. of K4 in 92nd Bde. of original 31st Div. Nov. 1914 to Westcliff-on-Sea in billets. 10.4.15 became 2nd reserve bns. and 92nd Bde. became 4th Reserve Bde. May 1915 to Belhus Park, Aveling, near Purfleet. Sept. 1915 to Seaford. 1.9.16 14th Bn. absorbed in Training Reserve Bns. of 4th Reserve Bde. and 15th Bn. became 18th Training Reserve Bn. in same brigade.
16th (Service) Battalion. (Church Lads Brigade).
   Raised at Denham, Bucks by Field Marshal Lord Grenfell (Comdt.) on 19.9.14 from past and present members of the Church Lads Brigade. Mar. 1915 Rayleigh, Essex. May 1915 Denham. June 1915 to Clipstone and 100th Bde. 33rd Div. 1.7.15 taken over by the War Office. Aug. 1915 Perham Down, Salisbury Plain. 17.11.15 landed at Havre. 11.11.18 100th Bde. 33rd Div. France; Petit Maubeuge.
17th (Service) Battalion. (British Empire League).
   Raised in London by the British Empire League on 16.4.15. H.Q. at Norfolk House, Laurence Pountney Hill E.C. and parades held in Green Park and then to Paddockhurst, S.E. of Worth, Sussex. July 1915 to 117th Bde. 39th Div. 1.8.15 taken over by the War Office. Sept. 1915 Hursley Park. Nov. 1915 Witley. Jan. 1916 Aldershot and Witley again. 8.3.16 landed at Havre. 16.5.18 reduced to training cadre. 16.8.18 to 66th Div. 20.9.18 with 197th Bde. to L. of C. at Durcat. Remained here.
18th (Service) Battalion. (Arts and Crafts).
   Raised at Gidea Park, Essex by Major Sir Herbert Raphael on 4.6.15. 4.9.15 taken over by the War Office. Oct. 1915 to Witley in 122nd Bde. 41st Div. Nov. 1915 Ramillies Barracks, Aldershot. Witley in Feb. and back to Aldershot. 3.5.16 landed at Havre. Nov. 1917 to Italy. Mar. 1918 returned to France. 11.11.18 122nd Bde. 41st Div. Belgium; Nukerke, south of Audenarde.
19th (Reserve) Battalion.
   Formed at Bexhill in Oct. 1915 as a local reserve bn. from depot coys. of 16th and 17th Bns. Nov. 1915 to Andover in 24th Reserve Bde. Feb. 1916 Banbury in 26th Reserve Bde. May 1916 Wimbledon. 1.9.16 became 109th Training Reserve Bn. at Wimbledon in 26th Reserve Bde.
20th (Service) Battalion. (British Empire League Pioneers).
   Raised in London 20.8.15 by the British Empire League: parades in Green Park. Feb. 1916 Wellingborough attached to 23rd Reserve Bde. 30.3.16 landed at Havre. 19.5.16 to 3rd Div. as Pioneer Bn. 11.11.18 Pioneer Bn. 3rd Div. France; Ruesnes; N.W. of Le Quesnoy.
21st (Service) Battalion. (Yeoman Rifles).
   Raised in Northern Command about Sept. 1915 from farmers. Two coys. from Yorkshire, one from Northumberland and Durham and one coy. from Lincoln, Leicestershire and Norfolk. At Duncombe Park, Helmsley, Yorkshire. Jan. 1916 to Aldershot and 124th Bde. 41st Div. 4.5.16 landed in France. Nov. 1917 to Italy. Mar. 1918 returned to France, Sombrin 8 Mar. 16.3.18 disbanded in France.
22nd (Reserve) Battalion.
   Formed about Sept. 1915 as a local reserve bn. from depot coys. of 20th Bn. Oct. 1915 Andover area in 24th Reserve Bde. By Feb. 1916 Banbury in 26th Reserve Bde. June 1916 Wimbledon. 1.9.16 became 110th Training Reserve Bn. at Wimbledon in 26th Reserve Bde.
23rd (Reserve) Battalion.
   Formed in autumn of 1915 as a local reserve bn. from depot coys. of 18th Bn. Jan. 1916 Banbury in 26th Reserve Bde. April 1916 Wimbledon. 1.9.16 became 111th Training Reserve Bn. at Wimbledon in 26th Reserve Bde.

24th (Reserve) Battalion.
Formed at Skipton in April 1916 as a local reserve bn. from depot coys. of 21st Bn. May 1916 to Blyth in 21st Reserve Bde. 19.5.16 Cambois. 1.9.16 absorbed in Training Reserve Bns. of 21st Reserve Bde.

25th (Service) Battalion. (Pioneers).
On 13.5.18 the 2nd Provisional Garrison Guard Bn. (recently formed in France) joined 59th Div. and became 25th (Garrison) Bn. 16.6.18 became Pioneer Bn. 59th Div. 16.7.18 title "Garrison" discontinued. 11.11.18 Pioneer Bn. 59th Div. Belgium; north of Tournai.

51st (Graduated) Battalion.
On 27.10.17 the 284th Graduated Bn. (formerly 17th Training Reserve Bn. from 11th Loyal N. Lancs) at Canterbury in 202nd Bde. 67th Div. became the 51st Bn. Jan. 1918 at Margate. About Mar. 1918 to Colchester where it remained.

52nd (Graduated) Battalion.
On 27.10.17 the 285th Graduated Bn. (formerly 22nd Training Reserve Bn. from 16th Royal Fusiliers) at Canterbury in 202nd Bde. 67th Div. became the 52nd Bn. About Mar. 1918 to Colchester where it remained.

53rd (Young Soldier) Battalion.
On 27.10.17 the 20th Young Soldier Bn. (formerly 15th Rifle Brigade) at Northampton in 4th Reserve Bde. became the 53rd Bn. No further change.

THE DUKE OF EDINBURGH'S (WILTSHIRE REGIMENT)

1st Battalion.
4.8.14 Tidworth: 7th Bde. 3rd Div. 14.8.14 landed at Rouen. 18.10.15 7th Bde. to 25th Div. 21.6.18 to 110th Bde. 21st Div. 11.11.18 110th Bde. 21st Div. France; Berlaimont, N.W. of Avesnes.

2nd Battalion.
4.8.14 Gibraltar. 31.8.14 sailed for England arriving Southampton 3 Sept. To Lyndhurst and 21st Bde. 7th Div. 7.10.14 landed at Zeebrugge. 19.12.15 21st Bde. to 30th Div. 13.5.18 to 58th Bde. 19th Div. 11.11.18 58th Bde. 19th Div. France; Eth, N.W. of Bavai.

3rd (Reserve) Battalion.
4.8.14 Devizes. Aug. to Weymouth. April 1915 Dorchester. July 1915 Weymouth (Portland Garrison). About Sept. 1917 to Sittingbourne, Kent in Sittingbourne S.R. Bde. No further change. (Thames and Medway Garrison).

1/4th Battalion T.F.
4.8.14 Fore Street, Trowbridge: South Western Bde. Wessex Div. Aug. to Salisbury Plain. 9.10.14 sailed from Southampton for India arriving Bombay about 9 Nov. Div. now broken up. Sept. 1917 to Egypt, arriving Suez 25.9.17 to 233rd Bde. 75th Div. 3.5.18 to 232nd Bde. 75th Div. 31.10.18 232nd Bde. 75th Div. Palestine, near Haifa.

2/4th Battalion T.F.
Formed at Trowbridge in Oct. 1914. In 2/South Western Bde. 2/Wessex Div. 12.12.14 embarked at Southampton for India, arriving Bombay early in Jan. 1915 and the div. was broken up. Remained in India throughout the war.

3/4th Battalion T.F.
Formed Mar. 1915 and by the autumn at Bournemouth. 8.4.16 became 4TH (RESERVE) BN. 1.9.16 Wessex Reserve Bde. at Hursley Park, near Winchester. Oct. 1916 Bournemouth. Feb. 1917 Sutton Veny, Salisbury Plain. Oct. 1917 Larkhill. May 1918 to Ireland and stationed at Dublin.

5th (Service) Battalion.
Formed at Devizes in Aug. 1914—K1—to Assaye Barracks, Tidworth as Army Troops, 13th Div. Oct. 1914 Chiseldon. Dec. 1914 Cirencester in billets and to 40th Bde. 13th Div. replacing 8th Welsh Regt. which became Pioneer Bn. Feb. 1915 Woking. May 1915 Bisley. 1.7.15 sailed from Avonmouth for Mediterranean and Mudros. 16 to 30 July at Helles. 4.8.15 landed at Anzac. Jan. 1916 to Egypt. Feb. 1916 to Mesopotamia. 31.10.18 40th Bde. 13th Div. Mesopotamia; Altun Kupri, north of Kirkuk.

6th (Service) Battalion.
Formed at Devizes in Sept. 1914—K2—to Salisbury Plain as Army Troops, 19th Div. Dec. 1914 to Basingstoke in billets and to 58th Bde. 19th Div. replacing 5th S.W.B. which became Pioneer Bn. Mar. 1915 Perham Down. July 1915 landed in France. 20.9.17 amalgamated with Wiltshire Yeo. (14 officers and 232 men) and became 6th (Royal Wiltshire Yeomanry) Bn. The yeomanry regt.[1] had been serving as XV Corps Cavalry Regt. 13.5.18 reduced to training cadre, surplus to 2nd Bn., and to 30th Div. 16.6.18 joined 42nd Bde. 14th Div. at Boulogne and crossed to England. 18.6.18 at Brookwood reconstituted with newly-formed 9th Dorsets. 4.7.18 landed at Boulogne. 11.11.18 42nd Bde. 14th Div. Belgium; Dottignies, N.E. of Roubaix.

7th (Service) Battalion.
Formed at Devizes in Sept. 1914—K3—to Codford, Salisbury Plain in 79th Bde. 26th Div. Nov. 1914 Marlborough in billets April 1915 Sutton Veny. Sept. 1915 landed in France. Nov. 1915 to Salonika. June 1918 left 26th Div. and returned to France, arriving Serqueux 1 July. 16.7.18 to 150th Bde. 50th Div. at Martin Eglise. 11.11.18 150th Bde. 50th Div. France; near Dourlers, north of Avesnes.

8th (Reserve) Battalion.
Formed at Weymouth Nov. 1914 as a service bn. of K4 in 102nd Bde. of original 34th Div. Feb. 1915 Trowbridge. 10.4.15 became a 2nd Reserve Bn. May 1915 Wareham in 8th Reserve Bde. 1.9.16 absorbed in Training Reserve Bns. of 8th Reserve Bde. at Wareham.

THE MANCHESTER REGIMENT

1st Battalion.
4.8.14 Jullundur: Jullundur Bde. 3rd (Lahore) Div. 29.8.14 sailed from Karachi for Europe arriving Marseilles 26 Sept. 10.12.15 embarked at Marseilles and landed at Basra 8.1.16. Mar. 1918 to Egypt. 31.10.18 8th Indian Bde. 3rd Indian Div. Palestine; Jaljulye, N.E. of Jaffa.

2nd Battalion.
4.8.14 Curragh: 14th Bde. 5th Div. 17.8.14 landed at Havre. 30.12.15 14th Bde. to 32nd Div. 6.2.18 to 96th Bde. 32nd Div. 11.11.18 96th Bde. 32nd Div. France; Sambreton, south of Landrecies.

3rd (Reserve) and 4th (Extra Reserve) Battalions.
4.8.14 Ashton-under-Lyne. Aug. 1914 to Humber Defences. Oct. 1914 to Cleethorpes (3rd) and Riby (4th). The two bns. remained on the Lincolnshire coast in Humber Garrison until the end of the war. 3rd Bn. at Cleethorpes and 4th at Riby, Tetney and Grimsby. (Humber Garrison).

1/5th Battalion T.F.
4.8.14 Bank Chambers, Wigan: Manchester Bde. East Lancs Div. End Aug. camp near Rochdale. 10.9.14 sailed from Southampton for Egypt arriving Alexandria 25 Sept. 6.5.15 landed at Gallipoli. 26.5.15 formation became 127th Bde. 42nd Div. Jan. 1916 to Egypt. Mar.

[1] Now dismounted.

1917 to France. 11.11.18 127th Bde. 42nd Div. France; Hautmont area, S.W. of Maubeuge.

1/6th Battalion T.F.
4.8.14 3 Stretford Road, Hulme, Manchester: Manchester Bde. East Lancs Div. Subsequent record similar to 1/5th Bn.

1/7th Battalion T.F.
4.8.14 Burlington Street, Manchester: Manchester Bde. East Lancs Div. Subsequent record similar to 1/5th Bn.

1/8th (Ardwick) Battalion T.F.
4.8.14 Ardwick, near Manchester: Manchester Bde. East Lancs Div. Subsequent record similar to 1/5th Bn. to Feb. 1918 and then 19.2.18 to 126th Bde. 42nd Div. 11.11.18 126th Bde. 42nd Div. France; Hautmont, S.W. of Maubeuge.

1/9th Battalion T.F.
4.8.14 Ashton-under-Lyne: East Lancs Bde. East Lancs Div. End Aug. camp near Bury. 10.9.14 sailed from Southampton for Egypt arriving Alexandria 25 Sept. About 10.5.15 landed at Gallipoli. 26.5.15 formation became 126th Bde. 42nd Div. End Dec. 1915 to Mudros. Jan. 1916 to Egypt. Mar. 1917 to France. 19.2.18 to 198th Bde. 66th Div. absorbing 2/9th Bn. and becoming 9TH BN. April 1918 reduced to training cadre. 22.7.18 to 199th Bde. 13.8.18 reconstituted by absorbing 13th Bn. (from 22nd Div. at Salonika). 11.11.18 199th Bde. 66th Div. France; Solre-le-Chateau, east of Avesnes.

1/10th Battalion T.F.
4.8.14. Oldham: East Lancs Bde. East Lancs Div. Subsequent record similar to 1/9th Bn. till Feb. 1918 when the Bn. remained in 42nd Div. 11.11.18 126th Bde. 42nd Div. France; Hautmont, S.W. of Maubeuge.

2/5th Battalion T.F.
Formed at Wigan Aug. 1914. Nov. 1914 in 199th Bde. 66th Div. Remained in Lancashire until about May 1915 and then to Crowborough area. Mar. 1916 Colchester. Feb. 1917 landed in France. April 1918 reduced to training cadre. 31.7.18 disbanded in France.

2/6th Battalion T.F.
Formed at Manchester Aug. 1914. Subsequent record same as 2/5th Bn.

2/7th Battalion T.F.
Formed at Manchester Aug. 1914. Subsequent record same as 2/5th Bn.

2/8th (Ardwick) Battalion T.F.
Formed at Ardwick Aug. 1914. Subsequent record same as 2/5th Bn. till Feb. 1918. Then it was disbanded in France on 13.2.18.

2/9th Battalion T.F.
Formed at Ashton-under-Lyne in Aug. 1914. Nov. 1914 to 198th Bde. 66th Div. Remained in Lancashire until about May 1915 and then to Crowborough area. Mar. 1916 Colchester. Feb. 1917 landed in France. 19.2.18 absorbed by 1/9th Bn.

2/10th Battalion T.F.
Formed at Oldham in Aug. 1914. Subsequent record same as 2/9th Bn. until Feb. 1918 when it was disbanded on 15.2.18.

3/5th, 3/6th and 3/7th Battalions T.F.
Formed at Wigan (5th) May 1915 and Manchester (6th & 7th) Mar. 1915. Early in 1916 to Witley, Surrey. 8.4.16 became Reserve Bns. 1.9.16 5TH (RESERVE) BN. absorbed 6th and 7th Bns. at Witley in East Lancs Reserve Bde. Oct. 1916 Southport. Jan. 1917 Ripon. July 1917 Scarborough where it remained.

3/8th, 3/9th and 3/10th Battalions T.F.
Formed Mar. 1915 at Ardwick, Ashton-under-Lyne and Oldham. Early in 1916 to Witley, Surrey. 8.4.16 became Reserve Bns. 1.9.16 8TH (RESERVE) BN. absorbed 9th and 10th Bns. at Witley in East Lancs Reserve Bde. Oct. 1916 Southport. Jan. 1917 Ripon. By July 1917 Hunmanby. April 1918 Filey where it remained.

11th (Service) Battalion.
Formed at Ashton-under-Lyne Aug. 1914—K1—to Grantham in 34th Bde. 11th Div. April 1915 Witley. 30.6.15 embarked at Liverpool for Mudros, then Imbros. 6.8.15 landed at Suvla Bay. Dec. 1915 to Imbros. Jan. 1916 Egypt. July 1916 to France. 11.11.18 34th Bde. 11th Div. France; le Camp Perdu, N.E. of Bavai.

12th (Service) Battalion.
Formed at Ashton-under-Lyne Sept. 1914—K2—to Wool in 52nd Bde. 17th Div. Jan. 1915 Wimborne. Feb. 1915 Wool area. May 1915 Hursley Park. About 15.7.15 landed at Boulogne. 24.9.17 absorbed R.H.Q. and two sqdns. Duke of Lancaster's Yeo. (7 officers and 125 men). Now dismounted after serving as III Corps Cavalry Regt. Became 12th (Duke of Lancaster's Own Yeomanry) Bn. 11.11.18 52nd Bde. 17th Div. France; near Beaufort, south of Maubeuge.

13th (Service) Battalion.
Formed at Ashton-under-Lyne in Sept. 1914—K3—to Seaford, originally as Army Troops 25th Div. but soon to 66th Bde. 22nd Div. in place of 14th Bn. Nov. 1914 to Eastbourne in billets. Mar. 1915 Seaford. May 1915 Aldershot. Early Sept. 1915 landed in France. Oct./Nov. 1915 to Salonika. 22.6.18 left 22nd Div. for France arriving Abancourt 11 July. 21.7.18 to 66th Div. 13.8.18 absorbed by 9th Bn.

14th (Reserve) Battalion.
Formed at Lichfield about Oct. 1914 originally intended for 66th Bde. 22nd Div. as a bn. of K3 but soon replaced by 13th Bn. Now went to K4 and 91st Bde. of original 30th Div. 10.4.15 became a 2nd reserve bn. in 3rd Reserve Bde. remaining at Lichfield. Jan. 1916 to Brocton, Cannock Chase. 1.9.16 became 14th Training Reserve Bn. at Brocton in 3rd Reserve Bde.

15th Battalion was not formed.

16th (Service) Battalion. (1st City).
Raised at Manchester 28.8.14 by the Lord Mayor and City. At Heaton Park. April 1915 to Belton Park, Grantham in 90th Bde. 30th Div. 29.8.15 taken over by the War Office. Sept. 1915 Larkhill. 6.11.15 landed at Boulogne. 13.5.18 reduced to training cadre. 18.6.18 to 42nd Bde. 14th Div. at Boulogne and crossed to England. To Cowshot and reconstituted with newly-formed 29th Bn. 4.7.18 landed at Boulogne. 11.11.18 42nd Bde. 14th Div. France; Petit Audenarde, on Belgian frontier N.E. of Roubaix.

17th (Service) Battalion. (2nd City).
Raised at Manchester 28.8.14 by the Lord Mayor and City. Subsequent record same as 16th Bn. to Feb. 1918; then 11.2.18 to 21st Bde. 30th Div. 15.5.18 reduced to training cadre. 19.6.18 to 66th Div. 30.7.18 absorbed by 13th Bn. at Haudricourt.

18th (Service) Battalion. (3rd City).
Raised at Manchester 28.8.14 by the Lord Mayor and City. Subsequent record same as 16th Bn. to Feb. 1918; then disbanded on 20.2.18 at Haut Allaines.

19th (Service) Battalion. (4th City).
Raised at Manchester 28.8.14 by the Lord Mayor and City. Subsequent record same as 16th Bn. to Dec. 1915; then on 21.12.15 to 21st Bde. 30th Div. 6.2.18 disbanded in France.

20th (Service) Battalion. (5th City).
Raised at Manchester 8.11.14 by the Lord Mayor and City. To Morecambe. April 1915 to Grantham and 91st Bde. 30th Div. 10.8.15 taken over by the War Office. Sept. 1915 Larkhill. Early Nov. 1915 landed at Boulogne.

20.12.15 91st Bde. to 7th Div. and Bn. to 22nd Bde. 7th Div. Nov. 1917 to Italy. 13.9.18 left 7th Div. and returned to France joining 7th Bde. 25th Div. at Canchy on 16 Sept. 11.11.18 7th Bde. 25th Div. France; Landrecies area.

21st (Service) Battalion. (6th City).
Raised at Manchester 13.11.14 by the Lord Mayor and City. Jan. 1915 Morecambe. April 1915 Grantham in 91st Bde. 30th Div. 10.8.15 taken over by the War Office. Sept. 1915 Larkhill. Early Nov. 1915 landed at Boulogne. 20.12.15 91st Bde. to 7th Div. Nov. 1917 to Italy. 13.9.18 left 7th Div. and returned to France joining 7th Bde. 25th Div. at Canchy on 16 Sept. 11.11.18 7th Bde. 25th Div. France; Landrecies area.

22nd (Service) Battalion. (7th City).
Raised at Manchester 21.11.14 by the Lord Mayor and City. Dec. 1914 to Morecambe. Subsequent record same as 21st Bn. until Sept. 1918 when it remained in Italy with the 7th Div. 4.11.18 91st Bde. 7th Div. Italy; west of Udine.

23rd (Service) Battalion. (8th City).
Raised at Manchester 21.11.14 by the Lord Mayor and City as a bantam bn. Dec. 1914 to Morecambe. June 1915 to Masham, Yorkshire and 104th Bde. 35th Div. Aug. 1915 taken over by the War Office and to Salisbury Plain. Jan. 1916 landed at Boulogne. Early in 1917 ceased to be a bantam bn. 16.2.18 disbanded in France.

24th (Service) Battalion. (Oldham) (Pioneers).
Raised at Oldham 24.10.14 by the Mayor and Town. Mar. 1915 Llanfairfechan. April 1915 Grantham and 91st Bde. 30th Div. 10.8.15 taken over by the War Office. Sept. 1915 Larkhill. Early Nov. 1915 landed at Boulogne. 20.12.15 91st Bde. to 7th Div. and to 22nd Bde. 7th Div. 22.5.16 became Pioneer Bn. 7th Div. Nov. 1917 to Italy. 4.11.18 Pioneer Bn. 7th Div. Italy; near Udine.

25th (Reserve) Battalion.
Formed about Sept. 1915 as a local reserve bn. from depot coys. of 16th, 17th and 18th Bns. Nov. 1915 Prees Heath in 16th Reserve Bde. Dec. 1915 Southport. May 1916 Altcar. 1.9.16 became 69th Training Reserve Bn. at Altcar in 16th Reserve Bde.

26th (Reserve) Battalion.
Formed about Sept. 1915 as a local reserve bn. from depot coys. of 19th, 20th and 21st Bns. Subsequent record same as 25th Bn. and became 70th Training Reserve Bn. on 1.9.16.

27th (Reserve) Battalion.
Formed about Sept. 1915 as a local reserve bn. from depot coys. of 22nd, 23rd and 24th Bns. Subsequent record same as 25th Bn. and became 71st Training Reserve Bn. on 1.9.16.

28th Battalion T.F.
On 1.1.17 the 45th Provisional Bn. at Blackpool in 219th Bde. 73rd Div. became the 28th Bn. The bn. had been formed in 1915 from Home Service personnel of T.F. Bns. Jan. 1917 to Maldon. Summer 1917 to Woodham Mortimer, near Maldon. Oct. 1917 to Southend. Early in 1918 the 73rd Div. was broken up and the bn. was disbanded at Southend in Mar. 1918.

A 29th Battalion was formed at Walsham in 1.6.18 and absorbed by 16th Bn. at Aldershot in June.

1st Garrison Battalion.
Formed at Knowsley Park Sept. 1915. Feb. 1916 to India.

2nd (Home Service) Garrison Battalion.
Formed at Knowsley Park Feb. 1916 and disbanded about July 1917.

51st (Graduated) Battalion.
On 27.10.17 the 225th Graduated Bn. (formerly 50th Training Reserve Bn. from 14th Cheshire) at Halesworth in 203rd Bde. 68th Div. became the 51st Bn. To Yarmouth for the winter and by May 1918 at Herringfleet where it remained.

52nd (Graduated) Battalion.
On 27.10.17 the 229th Graduated Bn. (formerly 51st Training Reserve Bn. from 10th South Lancs) at Southwold in 203rd Bde. 68th Div. became the 52nd Bn. To Yarmouth for the winter and by May 1918 at Herringfleet where it remained.

53rd (Young Soldier) Battalion.
On 27.10.17 the 74th Training Reserve Bn. (formerly 17th Cheshire) and now a Young Soldier Bn. became the 53rd Bn. At Prees Heath in 14th Reserve Bde. and soon to Kinmel where it remained.

THE PRINCE OF WALES'S (NORTH STAFFORDSHIRE REGIMENT)

1st Battalion.
4.8.14 Buttevant: 17th Bde. 6th Div. 17 Aug. Cambridge. 31 Aug. Newmarket. 12.9.14 landed at St. Nazaire. 18.10.15 to 72nd Bde. 24th Div. 11.11.18 72nd Bde. 24th Div. France; Feignies, west of Maubeuge.

2nd Battalion.
4.8.14 Rawal Pindi. Remained in India throughout the war.

3rd (Reserve) Battalion.
4.8.14 Lichfield. Aug. 1914 to Plymouth. May 1915 Seaham. Sept. 1915 Forest Hall. Oct. 1916 Wallsend where it remained. (Tyne Garrison).

4th (Extra Reserve) Battalion.
4.8.14 Lichfield. Aug. 1914 to Guernsey. Sept. 1916 Marske. By Mar. 1917 at Saltburn. About June 1917 to 200th Bde. 67th Div. at Westbere, near Canterbury. 7.10.17 left 67th Div. and landed at Havre: attached to 167th Bde. 56th Div. until 9 Nov. 15.11.17 to 106th Bde. 35th Div. at Brielen, near Ypres. 3.2.18 to 105th Bde. 35th Div. 11.11.18 105th Bde. 35th Div. Belgium; Audenhove, N.E. of Renaix.

1/5th Battalion T.F.
4.8.14 Drill Hall, Hanley: Staffordshire Bde. North Midland Div. Nov. 1914 Bishops Stortford area. 4.3.15 landed in France. 12.5.15 formation became 137th Bde. 46th Div. Jan. 1916 to Egypt. Feb. 1916 returned to France. 30.1.18 to 176th Bde. 59th Div. and absorbed 2/5th Bn. 9.5.18 reduced to training cadre and to 16th Div. 17.6.18 to 34th Div. 27.6.18 to 117th Bde. 39th Div. 12.8.18 to 116th Bde. 39th Div. 6.11.18 demobilized near Etaples.

1/6th Battalion T.F.
4.8.14 Burton-on-Trent: Staffordshire Bde. North Midland Div. To Luton area. Nov. 1914 Bishops Stortford area. 4.3.15 landed in France. 12.5.15 formation became 137th Bde. 46th Div. Jan. 1916 to Egypt. Feb. 1916 returned to France. 11.11.18 137th Bde. 46th Div. France; Sains du Nord, S.E. of Avesnes.

2/5th Battalion T.F.
Formed at Hanley 1.11.14. Jan. 1915 176th Bde. 59th Div. in Luton area. July 1915 to St. Albans area. April 1916 to Ireland, Dublin and the Curragh. Jan. 1917 to Fovant area, Salisbury Plain. 25.2.17 landed in France. 6.2.18 absorbed by 1/5th Bn.

2/6th Battalion T.F.
Formed at Burton 11.11.14. Jan. 1915 176th Bde. 59th Div. in Luton area. July 1915 to St. Albans area. April 1916 to Ireland, Dublin and the Curragh. Jan. 1917 to Fovant area, Salisbury Plain. 25.2.17 landed in France.

9.5.18 reduced to training cadre and to 66th Div. 31.7.18 absorbed by 1/6th Bn.

3/5th and 3/6th Battalions T.F.
Formed at Hanley and Burton in May 1915. Oct. 1915 Grantham. 8.4.16 became 5th and 6th (Reserve) Bns. 1.9.16 5th Bn. absorbed 6th Bn. at Catterick in North Midland Reserve Bde. T.F. By Mar. 1917 at Lincoln. July 1917 Mablethorpe, where it remained.

7th (Service) Battalion.
Formed at Lichfield 29.8.14—K1—to 39th Bde. 13th Div. on Salisbury Plain, Tidworth. Jan. 1915 Basingstoke. Feb. 1915 Blackdown, Aldershot. June 1915 sailed from Avonmouth. July 1915 landed at Gallipoli. 26.1.16 arrived in Egypt. 29.2.16 landed in Mesopotamia. July 1918 with 39th Bde. to North Persia Force. Aug. 1918 Baku. 31.10.18 39th Bde. North Persia; Enzeli.

8th (Service) Battalion.
Formed at Lichfield 18.9.14—K2—to 57th Bde. 19th Div. on Salisbury Plain. Dec. 1914 billets in Bristol. Feb. 1915 Weston-super-Mare. April 1915 Tidworth. 18.7.15 landed in France. 7.2.18 to 56th Bde. 19th Div. 11.11.18 56th Bde. 19th Div. France; Bry, west of Bavai.

9th (Service) Battalion (Pioneers).
Formed at Lichfield 20.9.14—K3—Army Troops attached 22nd Div. on South Downs. Dec. 1914 billets in Hastings. 20.4.15 to 37th Div. as Pioneer Bn. at Windmill Hill, Salisbury Plain. 29.7.15 landed at Havre. 11.11.18 Pioneer Bn. 37th Div. France; south of Le Quesnoy.

10th (Reserve) Battalion.
Formed at Plymouth Oct. 1914 as a service bn. of K3 but soon to K4 in 99th Bde. of original 33rd Div. Dec. 1914 Okehampton. 10.4.15 became a 2nd reserve bn. June 1915 to Darlington Nov. 1915 to Rugeley, Cannock Chase in 1st Reserve Bde. 1.9.16 became 3rd Training Reserve Bn. at Rugeley in 1st Reserve Bde.

11th (Reserve) Battalion.
Formed in Guernsey Oct. 1914 as a service bn. of K4. Feb. 1915 Alderney. 10.4.15 became a 2nd reserve bn. July 1915 to Darlington. Sept. 1915 Rugeley, Cannock Chase in 1st Reserve Bde. 1.9.16 became 4th Training Reserve Bn. at Rugeley in 1st Reserve Bde.

12th (Service) Battalion.
On 11.6.18 the 11th Garrison Guard Bn. in France became the 12th (Garrison) Bn. North Staffords and on 15.6.18 it joined 119th Bde. 40th Div. near St. Omer. 13.7.18 "Garrison" in title replaced by "Service". 11.11.18 119th Bde. 40th Div. France; south of Roubaix.

13th (Garrison) Battalion.
On 31.7.18 the 1st Garrison (see below) in France became the 13th (Garrison) Bn.

1st (Garrison) Battalion.
Formed at South Dalton in April 1916 and went to France in May 1916. 31.7.18 became 13th (Garrison) Bn. North Staffords (see above).

2nd (Home Service) Garrison Battalion.
Formed in Guernsey Nov. 1916. Remained in Guernsey and in August 1917 became 17th Bn. Royal Defence Corps.

THE YORK AND LANCASTER REGIMENT

1st Battalion.
4.8.14 Jubbulpore. 22.11.14 sailed from Bombay for England arriving Southampton 23 Dec. To Hursley Park and 83rd Bde. 28th Div. 17.1.15 landed at Havre. Oct. 1915 to Egypt and then to Salonika in early Dec. 30.9.18 83rd Bde. 28th Div. Macedonia; Tronovo, near Bulgarian frontier north of Lake Doiran.

2nd Battalion.
4.8.14 Limerick: 16th Bde. 6th Div. Aug. 1914 Cambridge. 9.9.14 landed at St. Nazaire. 11.11.18 16th Bde. 6th Div. France; Bohain.

3rd (Reserve) Battalion.
4.8.14 Pontefract. Aug. 1914 Cleadon, Durham. Jan. 1915 Sunderland. Aug. 1915 Durham. Feb. 1916 Sunderland where it remained. (Tyne Garrison).

1/4th (Hallamshire) Battalion T.F.
4.8.14 Sheffield: 3rd West Riding Bde. West Riding Div. Aug. 1914 Doncaster. Nov. 1914 Gainsborough. Feb. 1915 York (?). 14.4.15 landed at Boulogne. 12.5.15 formation became 148th Bde. 49th Div. 11.11.18 148th Bde. 49th Div. France; Leforest, north of Douai.

1/5th Battalion T.F.
4.8.14 Drill Hall, Rotherham: 3rd West Riding Bde. West Riding Div. Subsequent record same as 1/4th Bn.

2/4th (Hallamshire) Battalion T.F.
Formed at Sheffield 21.9.14. Mar. 1915 to Bulwell, near Nottingham in 187th Bde. 62nd Div. April 1915 Strensall, May 1915 Beverley. Nov. 1915 Gateshead. Jan. 1916 Larkhill. June 1916 Flixton Park, near Bungay. Oct. 1916 Wellingborough. Jan. 1917 landed at Havre. 11.11.18 187th Bde. 62nd Div. France; Sous-le-Bois, near Maubeuge.

2/5th Battalion T.F.
Formed at Rotherham 3.10.14. Subsequent record same as 2/4th Bn. until Feb. 1918 and then disbanded in France on 3.2.18.

3/4th and 3/5th Battalions T.F.
Formed Mar. 1915. To Clipstone. 8.4.16 became Reserve Bns. 1.9.16 4TH (RESERVE) BN. absorbed 5th Reserve Bn. at Clipstone in West Riding Reserve Bde. Oct. 1917 to Rugeley, Cannock Chase. 23.7.18 to Woodbridge. 19.10.18 to Southend.

6th (Service) Battalion.
Formed at Pontefract Aug. 1914—K1—to Belton Park, Grantham in 32nd Bde. 11th Div. April 1915 Witley. 3.7.15 sailed from Liverpool arriving Mudros 10 July. 6.8.15 landed at Suvla Bay. Dec. 1915 Mudros. Feb. 1916 Egypt. July 1916 to France. 11.11.18 32nd Bde. 11th Div. Belgium; Havay, north of Maubeuge.

7th (Service) Battalion. (Pioneers).
Formed at Pontefract Aug. 1914—K2—to Wareham in 50th Bde. 17th Div. Mar. 1915 became Pioneer Bn. 17th Div. May 1915 Hursley Park. 14.7.15 landed at Boulogne. 11.11.18 Pioneer Bn. 17th Div. France; Limont-Fontaine, south of Maubeuge.

8th (Service) Battalion.
Formed at Pontefract Sept. 1914—K3—to Frensham in 70th Bde. 23rd Div. Nov. 1914 Aldershot Feb. 1915 Hythe. May 1915 Bordon. 27.8.15 landed at Boulogne. 70th Bde. with 8th Div. 18.10.15 to 17.7.16. Nov. 1917 to Italy. 11.11.18 70th Bde. 23rd Div. Italy; Porcia area, west of Pordenone.

9th (Service) Battalion.
Formed at Pontefract Sept. 1914—K3—to Frensham in 70th Bde. 23rd Div. Nov. 1914 Aldershot. Feb. 1915 to Lyminge, Kent. May 1915 Bordon. Subsequent record same as 8th Bn.

10th (Service) Battalion.
Formed at Pontefract Sept. 1914—K3—to Halton Park in 63rd Bde. 21st Div. Dec. 1914 Leighton Buzzard in billets. May 1915 Tring. Aug. 1915 Witley. 11.9.15 landed at Boulogne. 8.7.16 63rd Bde. to 37th Div. 4.2.18 disbanded in France.

11th (Reserve) Battalion.
Formed about Sept. 1914 as a service bn. of K3 for 63rd Bde. 21st Div. but soon replaced by 12th West Yorks and

became a bn. of K4 in 90th Bde. of original 30th Div. at Harrogate. 10.4.15 became a 2nd reserve bn. and 90th Bde. became 2nd Reserve Bde. May 1915 Otley. Nov. 1915 Rugeley, Cannock Chase. 1.9.16 absorbed in Training Reserve Bns. of 2nd Reserve Bde. at Rugeley.

12th (Service) Battalion. (Sheffield).
Raised at Sheffield 5.9.14 by the Lord Mayor and City. At Sheffield. May 1915 to Penkridge, Cannock Chase in 94th Bde. 31st Div. July 1915 Ripon. 15.8.15 taken over by the War Office. Oct. 1915 Salisbury Plain. Dec. 1915 to Egypt. Mar. 1916 to France. 17.2.18 disbanded in France.

13th (Service) Battalion. (1st Barnsley).
Raised at Barnsley 17.9.14 by the Mayor and Town. Dec. 1914 Silkstone. May 1915 Penkridge, Cannock Chase in 94th Bde. 31st Div. July 1915 Ripon. 15.8.15 taken over by the War Office. Oct. 1915 Salisbury Plain. Dec. 1915 to Egypt. Mar. 1916 to France. 11.11.18 94th Bde. 31st Div. Belgium; Renaix.

14th (Service) Battalion. (2nd Barnsley).
Raised at Barnsley 30.11.14 by the Mayor and Town. May 1915 to Penkridge, Cannock Chase in 94th Bde. 31st Div. Subsequent record same as 12th Bn. and disbanded on 16.2.18.

15th (Reserve) Battalion.
Formed at Silkstone July 1915 as a local reserve bn. from depot coys. of 12th, 13th and 14th Bns. Nov. 1915 Brocton, Cannock Chase. Dec. 1915 Colsterdale. July 1916 Newsham, near Blyth. 1.9.16 became 91st T.R. Bn. in 21st Reserve Bde. at Blyth.

16th (Transport Workers) Battalion.
Formed Mar. 1916 at Colsterdale. Dec. 1916 Durham. July 1917 Durham. Nov. 1917 Catterick where it remained.

17th (Labour) Battalion.
Formed at Brocklesby July 1916 and went to France on L. of C. April 1917 transferred to Labour Corps as 30th & 31st Labour Coys.

18th (Service) Battalion.
Formed at Margate 11.6.18. To Pirbright and absorbed 2/7th West Yorks. cadre and to 41st Bde. 14th Div. 3.7.18 landed at Boulogne. 11.11.18 41st Bde. 14th Div. Belgium; Watrelos, near Roubaix.

THE DURHAM LIGHT INFANTRY

1st Battalion.
4.8.14 Nowshera. Remained in India throughout the war.

2nd Battalion.
4.8.14 Lichfield: 18th Bde. 6th Div. 8 Aug. Dunfermline. 13 Aug. Cambridge. 10.9.14 landed at St. Nazaire. 11.11.18 18th Bde. 6th Div. France; Busigny.

3rd (Reserve) Battalion.
4.8.14 Newcastle-on-Tyne. Aug. 1914 to South Shields where it remained (Tyne Garrison).

4th (Extra Reserve) Battalion.
4.8.14 Barnard Castle. Aug. to Tyne Defences. Dec. 1914 Killingworth. Jan. 1915 Forest Hall, Newcastle till Sept. 1915 then Seaham Harbour where it remained (Tyne Garrison).

1/5th Battalion T.F.
4.8.14 Drill Hall, Stockton-on-Tees: York & Durham Bde. Northumbrian Div. 10 Aug. coast defence at Hartlepools. 5.9.14 brigade camp at Ravensworth Park, near Gateshead. Oct. Newcastle. 18.4.15 landed at Boulogne. 14.5.15 formation became 150th Bde. 50th Div. 12.2.18 to 151st Bde. 50th Div. 15.7.18 reduced to training cadre on L. of C. 16.8.18 to 117th Bde. 39th Div. at Rouen. 9.11.18 disbanded.

1/6th Battalion T.F.
4.8.14 Drill Hall, Bishop Auckland: D.L.I. Bde. Northumbrian Div. Aug. 1914 Bolden Colliery. Sept. Ravensworth Park. Oct. 1914 Newcastle. About 17 April 1915 landed at Boulogne. 14.5.15 formation became 151st Bde. 50th Div. 3.6.15 owing to heavy casualties at Ypres the 1/6th and 1/8th Bns. amalgamated as 6/8th Bn. and resumed identities on 11.8.15. 15.7.18 reduced to training cadre on L. of C. 16.8.18 to 117th Bde. 39th Div. at Rouen. 6.11.18 disbanded.

1/7th Battalion T.F.
4.8.14 Livingstone Road, Sunderland: D.L.I. Bde. Northumbrian Div. Aug. coast defence. Sept. Ravensworth Park. Oct. 1914 Newcastle. About 17.4.15 landed at Boulogne. 14.5.15 formation became 151st Bde. 50th Div. 16.11.15 became Pioneer Bn. 50th Div. 20.6.18 Pioneer Bn. 8th Div. 11.11.18 Pioneer Bn. 8th Div. Belgium; Harchies, N.E. of Conde. Absorbed 22nd Bn. 3.7.18.

1/8th Battalion T.F.
4.8.14 Gilesgate, Durham: D.L.I. Bde. Northumbrian Div. Subsequent record similar to 1/6th Bn.

1/9th Battalion T.F.
4.8.14 Burt Terrace, Gateshead: D.L.I. Bde. Northumbrian Div. Subsequent record similar to 1/6th Bn. until 12.2.18 and then went to 62nd Div. as Pioneer Bn. 11.11.18 Pioneer Bn. 62nd Div. France; Sous-le-Bois, suburb of Maubeuge.

2/5th Battalion T.F.
Formed at Stockton in Sept. 1914. Mar. 1915 Long Benton, near Newcastle in 189th Bde. 63rd Div. July 1915 Cramlington. Nov. 1915 Retford. July 1916 63rd Div. broken up and 189th Bde. to Catterick. 31.10.16 left bde. and went to Salonika as a Garrison Bn. via Havre (1 Nov.) and Marseilles arriving 15.11.16. To XVI Corps Troops. 1.3.17 to 228th Bde. attached to 28th Div. 30.9.18 228th Bde. under command Greek Crete Div. Macedonia; near Doiran.

2/6th Battalion T.F.
Formed at Ravensworth Park, near Gateshead Sept. 1914. Early 1915 to Leam Camp, Heworth, near Gateshead in 190th Bde. 63rd Div. Nov. 1915 Doncaster. July 1916 63rd Div. broken up and 190th Bde. to Catterick. 29.11.16 to 214th Bde. 71st Div. at Andover. Mar. 1917 Colchester. About Sept. 1917 to Frinton and 226th Bde. 1.5.18 became a Garrison Guard Bn. and landed at Calais on 6 May. To 177th Bde. 59th Div. at Hestrus. By 16.7.18 title 'Garrison Guard', ceased. 11.11.18 177th Bde. 59th Div. Belgium; Lessines.

2/7th Battalion T.F.
Formed at Sunderland 16.9.14. Early 1915 to Leam Camp, Heworth, near Gateshead in 190th Bde. 63rd Div. Nov. 1915 Doncaster. July 1916 63rd Div. broken up and 190th Bde. to Catterick. 29.11.16 to 214th Bde. 71st Div. at Andover. March 1917 Colchester. 12.2.18 214th Bde. to 67th Div. at Colchester. Sept. 1918 left 67th Div. and became a Garrison Bn. 7.10.18 embarked for North Russia and went to Archangel.

2/8th Battalion T.F.
Formed at Durham in Oct. 1914. Subsequent record same as 2/7th Bn. until Nov. 1916 then on 29.11.16 went to 214th Bde. 71st Div. at Basingstoke. Mar. 1917 to Colchester. Had left 67th Div. by 9.7.17 and was disbanded in Dec. 1917.

2/9th Battalion T.F.
Formed at Ravensworth Park on 11.9.14. Subsequent record same as 2/7th Bn. until Nov. 1916 then embarked at Southampton on 4.11.16 for Salonika via Havre and Marseilles arriving on 15.11.16. Became Army Troops and

remained in the neighbourhood of Salonika until the end of the war.

3/5th, 3/6th, 3/7th, 3/8th and 3/9th Battalions T.F.
Formed at home stations about June 1915. 8.4.16 became Reserve Bns. at (?) Catterick. 1.9.16 5TH (RESERVE) BN. absorbed the other four bns. at (?) Newcastle in Northumbrian Reserve Bde. By Oct. 1916 Redcar and Catterick by Dec. 1916. Summer 1917 Hornsea. Spring 1918 Sutton-on-Hull where it remained. (Humber Garrison).

10th (Service) Battalion.
Formed at Newcastle 22.8.14—K1—to Woking in 43rd Bde. 14th Div. Sept. 1914 Aldershot. Nov. 1914 Witley. Feb. 1915 Corunna Barracks, Aldershot. 21.5.15 landed at Boulogne. 12.2.18 disbanded in France.

11th (Service) Battalion. (Pioneers).
Formed at Newcastle Sept. 1914—K2—to Woking in 61st Bde. 20th Div. Nov. 1914 Pirbright. 6.1.15 became Pioneer Bn. 20th Div. Feb. 1915 Witley. Mar. 1915 Larkhill. 20.7.15 landed at Havre. 11.11.18 Pioneer Bn. 20th Div. France; Feignies, N.W. Maubeuge.

12th (Service) Battalion.
Formed at Newcastle Sept. 1914—K3—to Bullswater, near Pirbright in 68th Bde. 23rd Div. Nov. 1914 Malplaquet Barracks, Aldershot. Feb. 1915 Willesborough, near Ashford. May 1915 Bramshott. 26.8.15 landed at Boulogne Nov. 1917 to Italy. 4.11.18 68th Bde. 23rd Div. Italy; Talponedo, N.W. of Pordenone.

13th (Service) Battalion.
Formed at Newcastle Sept. 1914—K3—to Bullswater, near Pirbright in 68th Bde. 23rd Div. Nov. 1914 Malplaquet Barracks, Aldershot. Feb. 1915 Ashford, Kent. May 1915 Bramshott. 26.8.15 landed at Boulogne. Nov. 1917 to Italy. 14.9.18 left 23rd Div. and returned to France joining 74th Bde. 25th Div. at St. Riquier on 19.9.18. 11.11.18 74th Bde. 25th Div. France; Bousies, north of Le Cateau.

14th (Service) Battalion.
Formed at Newcastle Sept. 1914—K3—to Aylesbury in 64th Bde. 21st Div. Oct. 1914 Halton Park. Nov. 1914 High Wycombe, in billets. April 1915 Halton Park. July 1915 Witley. 11.9.15 landed at Boulogne. 28.11.15 to 18th Bde. 6th Div. 1.2.18 disbanded in France.

15th (Service) Battalion.
Formed at Newcastle Sept. 1914—K3—to Halton Park in 64th Bde. 21st Div. Dec. 1914 to Maidenhead in billets. April 1915 Halton Park. July 1915 Witley. 11.9.15 landed at Boulogne. 11.11.18 64th Bde. 21st Div. France; Berlaimont.

16th (Reserve) Battalion.
Formed at Durham Oct. 1914 as a service bn. of K4 in 89th Bde. of original 30th Div. 10.4.15 became a 2nd reserve bn. and 89th Bde. became 1st Reserve Bde. July 1915 Darlington. Nov. 1915 Rugeley, Cannock Chase. 1.9.16 became 1st Training Reserve Bn. at Rugeley in 1st Reserve Bde.

17th (Reserve) Battalion.
Formed at Barnard Castle as a service bn. of K4 in 89th Bde. of original 30th Div. 10.4.15 became a 2nd reserve bn. and 89th Bde. became 1st Reserve Bde. July 1915 Darlington. Nov. 1915 Rugeley, Cannock Chase. 1.9.16 became 2nd Training Reserve Bn. at Rugeley in 1st Reserve Bde.

18th (Service) Battalion. (1st County).
Raised in County of Durham 10.9.14 by Col. R. Burdon and a committee (President, the Earl of Durham) at Cocken Hall, NNE of Durham. Dec. 1914 Fencehouses, near Houghton le Spring. Feb. 1915 Cocken Hall. Mar. 1915 Fencehouses. May 1915 Cramlington then Ripon to 93rd Bde. 31st Div. 15.8.15 taken over by the War Office. Sept. 1915 Fovant. 6.12.15 embarked at Liverpool for Egypt—Port Said 21 Dec. 6.3.16 sailed from Port Said for France, arriving Marseilles 11 Mar. 11.11.18 93rd Bde. 31st Div. Belgium; moving to Quesnau, east of Renaix.

19th (Service) Battalion. (2nd County).
Raised in Durham as a bantam bn. on 13.1.15 by the Durham Parliamentary Recruiting Committee at West Hartlepool. May 1915 Cocken Hall. June 1915 to Masham and 106th Bde. 35th Div. July 1915 Perham Down. 15.8.15 taken over by the War Office. 1.2.16 landed at Havre. Jan. 1917 ceased to be a bantam bn. 8.2.18 to 104th Bde. 35th Div. 11.11.18 104th Bde. 35th Div. Belgium; Everbecq, west of Grammont.

20th (Service) Battalion. (Wearside).
Raised in Sunderland 10.7.15 by the Mayor and Committee. Aug. 1915 Wensley Dale. Oct. 1915 Barnard Castle. Jan. 1916 taken over by the War Office and to Aldershot and 123rd Bde. 41st Div. 5.5.16 landed at Havre. Nov. 1917 to Italy—Locon Plage 14 Nov. Mantua area 19 Nov. Mar. 1918 returned to France, Doullens 7 Mar. 17.3.18 to 124th Bde. 41st Div. 11.11.18 124th Bde. 41st Div. Belgium; west of Nederbrakel.

21st (Reserve) Battalion.
Formed at Cocken Hall July 1915 as a local reserve bn. from depot coys. of 18th and 20th Bns. Nov. 1915 Catterick in 20th Reserve Bde. April 1916 Hornsea. 1.9.16 became 87th Training Reserve Bn. at Hornsea in 20th Reserve Bde.

22nd (Service) Battalion. (3rd County Pioneers).
Raised in the county on 1.10.15 by the Durham Recruiting Committee. At West Hartlepool. 9.3.16 taken over by the War Office and to Catterick. 17.6.16 landed at Havre, attached to 19th Div. until 2.7.16 and then Pioneer Bn. 8th Div. 3.7.18 absorbed by 1/7th Bn.

23rd (Reserve) Battalion.
Formed at Catterick Oct. 1915 as a local reserve bn. from depot coys. of 19th Bn. April 1916 to Atwick, near Hornsea in 20th Reserve Bde. 1.9.16 absorbed in Training Reserve Bns. of 20th Reserve Bde. at Hornsea.

24th Battalion was not formed.

25th (Works) Battalion.
Formed at Pocklington May 1916. Aug. 1916 at Skipton. April 1917 transfrred to Labour Corps becoming 7th Labour Bn.

26th Battalion T.F.
On 1.1.17 the 23rd Provisional Bn. at Clacton in 222nd Bde. became the 26th Bn. (23rd Provisional Bn. had been formed in 1915 from Home Service personnel of T.F. Bns.) April 1917 to Westgate where it remained in 222nd Bde.

27th Battalion T.F.
On 1.1.17 the 25th Provisional Bn. at St. Osyth in 222nd Bde. became the 27th Bn. (25th Provisional Bn. had been formed in 1915 from Home Service personnel of T.F. Bns.) April 1917 to the Isle of Thanet until the end of the war.

28th (Home Service) Battalion.
Formed at Frinton on 27.4.18 to replace 2/6th Bn. in 226th Bde. No change.

29th (Service) Battalion.
Formed at Margate on 1.6.18 and went to Brookwood, Aldershot absorbing cadre of 2/7th Duke of Wellington's in 41st Bde. 14th Div. 3.7.18 landed at Boulogne. 11.11.18 41st Bde. 14th Div. Belgium; Herseaux, east of Tourcoing.

1st (Home Service) Garrison Battalion.
Formed June 1916 at Blyth. To Ireland at Cork. 1.4.17 became 1st (Home Service) Garrison Bn. Royal Munster Fusiliers.

51st (Graduated) Battalion.
On 27.10.17 the 258th Graduated Bn. (formerly 4th T.R. Bn. from 11th North Staffords) at Ipswich in 215th Bde. 72nd Div. became 51st Bn. 15.1.18 to 206th Bde. 69th Div. at Durham. Mar. 1918 Guisborough and autumn 1918 Catterick.

52nd (Graduated) Battalion.
On 27.10.17 the 273rd Graduated Bn. (formerly 86th T.R. Bn. from 31st Northd. Fus.) at Arbour Lane, Chelmsford in 220th Bde. 73rd Div. became 52nd Bn. 15.1.18 to 206th Bde. 69th Div. at Stockton. Mar. 1918 Guisborough. Autumn 1918 Catterick.

53rd (Young Soldier) Battalion.
On 27.10.17 the 2nd T.R. (Y.S.) Bn. (formerly 17th D.L.I.) at Rugeley, Cannock Chase became 53rd Bn. in 1st Reserve Bde. By Nov. 1918 at Clipstone.

THE HIGHLAND LIGHT INFANTRY

1st Battalion.
4.8.14 Ambala: Sirhind Bde. 3rd (Lahore) Div. Sept. 1914 to Egypt on way to France and Sirhind Bde. remained while the rest of the division went on to France. 1.12.14 landed at Marseilles and rejoined Lahore Div. on 9 Dec. Dec. 1915 to Mesopotamia arriving in Jan. 1916. Jan. 1917 left Lahore Div. and to Tigris Defences. Sept. 1917 to 51st Bde. 17th Indian Div. 31.10.18 51st Bde. 17th Indian Div. Mesopotamia; Huwaish, on Tigris north of Sharqat.

2nd Battalion.
4.8.14 Maida Barracks, Aldershot: 5th Bde. 2nd Div. 14.8.14 landed at Boulogne. 11.11.18 5th Bde. 2nd Div. France; Villers Pol.

3rd (Reserve) Battalion.
4.8.14 Hamilton. Aug. 1914 to Portsmouth. May 1915 returned to Scotland to Malleny, S.W. of Currie. Remained in Edinburgh area in Edinburgh S.R. Bde. until July 1918 and then to Haddington. (Forth Garrison).

4th (Extra Reserve) Battalion.
4.8.14 Hamilton. Aug. 1914 to Plymouth. May 1915 returned to Scotland to Haddington in Edinburgh S.R. Bde. until early 1917 and then to Hawick. End 1917 to Wormit and Sept. 1918 to Arbroath. (Tay Garrison).

1/5th (City of Glasgow) Battalion T.F.
4.8.14 24 Hill Street, Garnethill, Glasgow: H.L.I. Bde. Lowland Div. To Dunfermline. 11.5.15 formation became 157th Bde. 52nd Div. 26.5.15 sailed from Devonport and arrived Alexandria 5 June 28.6.15 sailed from Alexandria arrived Mudros 1 July. 3.7.15 landed at Gallipoli. 8.1.16 left Gallipoli for Mudros. Feb. 1916 to Egypt. 11–17.4.18 Alexandria to Marseilles. 11.11.18 157th Bde. 52nd Div. Belgium; near Jurbise, N.W. of Mons.

1/6th (City of Glasgow) Battalion T.F.
4.8.14 173 Yorkhill Street, Glasgow: H.L.I. Bde. Lowland Div. Subsequent record similar to 1/5th Bn.

1/7th (Blythswood) Battalion T.F.
4.8.14 69 Main Street, Bridgeton, Glasgow: H.L.I. Bde. Lowland Div. Subsequent record similar to 1/5th Bn.

8th (Lanark) Battalion T.F.
4.8.14 Lanark: attached Lothian Inf. Bde. Scottish Coast Defences. There is little information available about this unit. One source states that as there were insufficient volunteers for service overseas it was disbanded in May 1916 and the personnel posted to the 8th Provisional Bn., which had been formed from the 8th H.L.I. in 1915. But it is possible that the volunteers for service overseas had been drafted to the other four Territorial battalions of the regiment. 2nd and 3rd Line battalions were not formed.

1/9th (Glasgow Highland) Battalion T.F.
4.8.14 81 Greendyke Street, Glasgow: H.L.I. Bde. Lowland Div. To Dunfermline. Nov. 1914 left Lowland Div. and landed in France 5 Nov. 23.11.14 to 5th Bde. 2nd Div. 30.1.16 to G.H.Q. Troops. 29.5.16 to 100th Bde. 33rd Div. 11.11.18 100th Bde. 33rd Div. France; Petit Maubeuge.

2/5th (City of Glasgow) Battalion T.F.
Formed Sept. 1914. Jan. 1915 196th Bde. 65th Div. By Aug. 1915 at Dunfermline. Nov. 1915 to Jan. 1916 became No. 21 Bn. Mar. 1916 to Danbury, Essex. Jan. 1917 to Ireland, at the Curragh. Aug. 1917 Dublin. Nov. 1917 the Curragh. Mar. 1918 65th Div. broken up and the Bn. was disbanded by May 1918.

2/6th (City of Glasgow) Battalion T.F.
Formed Sept. 1914. Subsequent record similar to 2/5th Bn. but was No. 22 Bn. from Nov. 1915 to Jan. 1916 and went to Maldon in Mar. 1916.

2/7th (Blythswood) Battalion T.F.
Formed Sept. 1914. Jan. 1915 196th Bde. 65th Div. Aug. 1915 at Dunfermline. Nov. 1915 to Jan. 1916 became No. 23 Bn. Mar. 1916 Danbury. Jan. 1917 to Ireland at Galway and Naas. Aug. 1917 Dublin and disbanded by the end of the year.

2/9th (Glasgow Highland) Battalion T.F.
Formed Sept. 1914. Jan. 1915 196th Bde. 65th Div. Aug. 1915 to Dunfermline. Nov. 1915 to Jan. 1916 became No. 24 Bn. Mar. 1916 Maldon. Jan. 1917 to Ireland and the Curragh. Aug. 1917 Dublin. Mar. 1918 65th Div. broken up and the Bn. was disbanded by May 1918.

3/5th and 3/7th Battalions T.F.
Formed Mar. 1915 8.4.16 at Ripon, became Reserve Bns. 1.9.16 5TH (RESREVE) BN. at Catterick absorbed 7th (Res.) Bn. in Lowland Reserve Bde. July 1917 absorbed 6th (Reserve) Bn. Sept. 1917 Edinburgh. Dec. 1917 Bridge of Allan, Stirling where it remained. (Forth Garrison).

3/6th and 3/9th Battalions T.F.
Formed Mar. 1915. 8.4.16 at Ripon became Reserve Bns. 1.9.16 6TH (RESERVE) BN. at Catterick absorbed 9th (Res.) Bn. in Lowland Reserve Bde. July 1917 absorbed by 5th (Res.) Bn.

10th (Service) Battalion.
Formed at Hamilton Aug. 1914—K1—to Bordon in 28th Bde. 9th Div. Mar. 1915 Bramshott. May 1915 landed at Boulogne. 6–14.5.16 attached S.A. Bde. 9th Div. 14.5.16 to 46th Bde. 15th Div. and amalgamated with 11th Bn. to form 10th/11th Bn. 1.2.18 to 119th Bde. 40th Div. 16.2.18 to 120th Bde. 40th Div. 6.5.18 reduced to training cadre. 3.6.18 to 34th Div. 16.6.18 to 14th Div. at Boulogne and crossed to England going to Brookwood, Aldershot in 43rd Bde. 14th Div. 21.6.18 absorbed newly formed 22nd Bn. and became 10th Bn. 5.7.18 landed at Boulogne. 11.11.18 43rd Bde. 14th Div. Belgium; N.W. of Helchin, east of Tourcoing.

11th (Service) Battalion.
Formed at Hamilton Aug. 1914—K1—to Bordon in 28th Bde. 9th Div. Mar. 1915 Bramshott. May 1915 landed at Boulogne 6–14.5.16 attached S.A. Bde. 9th Div. 14.5.16 to 46th Bde. 15th Div. and amalgamated with 10th Bn. to form 10th/11th Bn.

12th (Service) Battalion.
Formed at Hamilton Sept. 1914—K2—to Bordon in 46th Bde. 15th Div. Mar. 1915 Romsey. April 1915 Chisledon. July 1915 landed in France. 3.2.18 to 106th Bde. 35th Div. 11.11.18 106th Bde. 35th Div. Belgium; near Ten Berg, west of Grammont.

13th (Reserve) Battalion.
Formed at Gosport Nov. 1914 as a service bn. of K4 in 97th Bde. of original 32nd Div. 10.4.15 became a 2nd Reserve

bn. May 1915 Stobs, Roxburgh. Oct. 1915 Catterick in 12th Reserve Bde. April 1916 Leven, Fife. 1.9.16 became 52nd Training Reserve Bn. at Leven in 12th Reserve Bde.

14th (Service) Battalion.
Formed at (?) Hamilton about July 1915 as a bantam bn. To Troon, Ayrshire. Sept. 1915 to Blackdown and 120th Bde. 40th Div. 2.3.16 absorbed 13th Scottish Rifles. June 1916 landed in France. 6.5.18 reduced to training cadre. 3.6.18 to 34th Div. 17.6.18 to 39th Div. 16.8.18 to 66th Div. 20.9.18 to L. of C. in 197th Bde. near Aumale where it remained. Ceased to be a bantam bn. early in 1917.

15th (Service) Battalion. (1st Glasgow).
Raised in Glasgow 2.9.14 by the Lord Provost and City with many recruits from the Glasgow Tramways. To Gailes, Ayrshire. May 1915 to Prees Heath in 97th Bde. 32nd Div. June 1915 to Wensleydale. 1.7.15 taken over by the War Office. Aug. 1915 Salisbury Plain. Nov. 1915 landed at Boulogne. 3.1.16 to 14th Bde. 32nd Div. 11.11.18 14th Bde. 32nd Div. France; east of Avesnes.

16th (Service) Battalion. (2nd Glasgow).
Raised in Glasgow 2.9.14 by the Lord Provost and City with many recruits from the Glasgow Boys' Brigade. To Gailes. May 1915 to Prees Heath in 97th Bde. 32nd Div. June 1915 to Wensleydale. 1.7.15 taken over by the War Office. Aug. 1915 to Codford. 23.11.15 landed at Boulogne. 22.2.18 became Pioneer Bn. 32nd Div. 11.11.18 Pioneer Bn. 32nd Div. France; Avesnelles, east of Avesnes.

17th (Service) Battalion. (3rd Glasgow).
Raised in Glasgow 10.9.14 by the Chamber of Commerce. To Troon. Subsequent record similar to 16th Bn. until Feb. 1918 when it was disbanded on 11.2.18.

18th (Service) Battalion. (4th Glasgow).
Raised in Glasgow 26.2.15 by the Lord Provost and City as a bantam bn. and to Girvan, Ayrshire. May 1915 Gailes. June 1915 Masham, Yorks. in 106th Bde. 35th Div. July 1915 taken over by the War Office. Aug. 1915 Salisbury Plain. 1.2.16 landed at Havre. Early in 1917 ceased to be a bantam bn. 23.9.17 Glasgow Yeomanry (RHQ A and B Sqdns, 4 officers and 146 men) formerly V Corps Cav. Regt., now dismounted, amalgamated with the bn. at Aizecourt le Bas. Became 18th (R. Glasgow Yeo) Bn. 11.11.18 106th Bde. 35th Div. Belgium; west of Grammont.

19th (Reserve) Battalion.
Formed at Gailes July 1915 as a local reserve bn. from depot coys. of 15th, 16th and 17th Bns. Oct. 1915 Ripon in 18th Reserve Bde. Mar. 1916 Montrose. 1.9.16 became 78th Training Reserve Bn. at Montrose in 18th Reserve Bde.

20th (Reserve) Battalion.
Formed at Ripon Oct. 1915 as a local reserve bn. from depot coys. of 18th Bn. In 18th Reserve Bde. 1.9.16 became 79th Training Reserve Bn. at Montrose in 18th Reserve Bde.

21st Battalion T.F.
On 1.1.17 the 9th Provisional Bn. at Deal in 221st Bde. became the 21st Bn. (The 9th Provisional Bn. had been formed from Home Service personnel of the T.F. Bns. in 1915). Later in 1917 at Sandwich. By Jan. 1918 at Deal. May 1918 at Ramsgate where it remained in 221st Bde.

A 22nd Bn. was formed at Deal on 1.6.18 and absorbed by the 10th Bn. at Aldershot on 21.6.18.

1st (Reserve) Garrison Battalion.
Formed at Fort George about May 1916. Remained at Fort George until Jan. 1918 and then to Maryhill, Glasgow.

51st (Graduated) Battalion.
On 27.10.17 the 201st Graduated Bn. (formerly 54th T.R. Bn. from 14th Royal Scots) became the 51st Bn; at Cromer in 191st Bde. 64th Div. Nov. 1917 Holt. April 1918 Thetford. Oct. 1918 Fakenham.

52nd (Graduated) Battalion.
On 27.10.17 the 205th Graduated Bn. (formerly 56th T.R. Bn. from 12th Cameron Highlanders) became the 52nd Bn; at Witton Hall, Norwich in 192nd Bde. 64th Div. April 1918 Kelling. Oct. 1918 Sheringham.

53rd (Young Soldier) Battalion.
On 27.10.17 the 53rd Young Soldier Bn. (formerly 9th K.O.S.B.) at Kirkcaldy, Fife in Lowland Reserve Bde. T.F. became the 53rd Bn. No further change. (Forth Garrison).

SEAFORTH HIGHLANDERS
(ROSS-SHIRE BUFFS, THE DUKE OF ALBANY'S)

1st Battalion.
4.8.14 Agra: Dehra Dun Bde. 7th (Meerut) Div. Mid Sept. 1914 sailed for France, arriving Marseilles about 12 Oct. Dec. 1915 to Mesopotamia: formation now 19th Indian Bde. 7th (Meerut) Div. 4.2.16 owing to heavy casualties the Bn. was amalgamated with 2nd Black Watch to form the Highland Bn. in 19th Indian Bde. 7th (Meerut) Div. 12.7.16 resumed identity in same formation End Dec. 1917 to Egypt and Palestine, landing at Suez early Jan. 1918. 31.10.18 19th Indian Bde. 7th (Meerut) Div. Palestine; Khan Abdi, N.E. of Tripoli.

2nd Battalion.
4.8.14 Shorncliffe: 10th Bde. 4th Div. To Harrow. About 22 Aug. 1914 landed in France. 11.11.18 10th Bde. 4th Div. France; S.E. of Valenciennes.

3rd (Reserve) Battalion.
4.8.14 Fort George. Aug. 1914 to Cromarty where it remained until the end of the war. (Cromarty Garrison).

1/4th (Ross Highland) Battalion T.F.
4.8.14 Dingwall; Seaforth & Cameron Bde. Highland Div. 15.8.14 to Bedford. Nov. 1914 left Highland Div. and landed at Havre 7.11.14. 12.12.14 to Dehra Dun Bde. 7th (Meerut) Div. 6.11.15 to 137th Bde. 46th Div. 13.11.15 to 46th Bde. 15th Div. 7.1.16 to 154th Bde. 51st Div. 11.11.18 154th Bde. 51st Div. France; Escaudoeuvres N.E. of Cambrai.

1/5th (The Sutherland and Caithness Highland) Battalion T.F.
4.8.14 Golspie: Seaforth & Cameron Bde. Highland Div. 15.8.14 to Bedford. About 2.5.15 landed in France. 12.5.15 formation became 152nd Bde. 51st Div. 11.11.18 152nd Bde. 51st Div. France; Iwuy, N.E. of Cambrai.

1/6th (Morayshire) Battalion T.F.
4.8.14 Elgin: Seaforth & Cameron Bde. Highland Div. Subsequent record same as 1/5th Bn.

2/4th (Ross Highland) Battalion T.F.
Formed at Dingwall Sept. 1914. Jan. 1915 191st Bde. 64th Div. April 1915 Fort George. July 1915 Blair Atholl. Oct. 1915 Pitlochry in billets. Nov. 1915 to Jan. 1916 title was No. 1 Bn. Mar. 1916 Norwich. June 1916 Blickling Park. July 1916 Kelling, near Holt. Oct. 1916 to Cromer in billets. May 1917 Kelling. End 1917 Cromer and disbanded in June 1918.

2/5th (The Sutherland and Caithness Highland) Battalion T.F.
Formed at Golspie Sept. 1914. Jan. 1915 191st Bde. 64th Div. April 1915 Fort George. July 1915 Blair Atholl. Oct. 1915 absorbed by 2/6th Bn.

2/6th (Morayshire) Battalion T.F.
Formed at Elgin Sept. 1914. Jan. 1915 191st Bde. 64th Div. April 1915 Fort George. July 1915 Blair Atholl. Oct. 1915 to (?) Crieff in billets and absorbed 2/5th Bn. Nov. 1915 to Jan. 1916 title was No. 2 Bn. Mar. 1916 Norwich. June 1916 Blickling Park. July 1916 Kelling, near Holt. Oct. 1916 Cromer in billets. May 1917 Kelling. Sept. 1917 disbanded.

3/4th, 3/5th and 3/6th Battalions T.F.
Formed in Mar. 1915. May 1915 to Ardersier, near Nairn. Nov. 1915 Ripon. 8.4.16 became Reserve Bns. 1.9.16 4TH (RESERVE) BN. absorbed 5th and 6th Reserve Bns. at Ripon in Highland Reserve Bde. T.F. May 1918 to Glencorse, near Edinburgh where it remained. (Forth Garrison).

7th (Service) Battalion.
Formed at Fort George Aug. 1914—K1—to Aldershot in 26th Bde. 9th Div. Jan. 1915 Alton in billets. Mar. 1915 Bordon. May 1915 landed at Boulogne. 11.11.18 26th Bde. 9th Div. Belgium; Harlebeke, north of Courtrai.

8th (Service) Battalion.
Formed at Fort George Sept. 1914—K2—to Aldershot in 44th Bde. 15th Div. Nov. 1914 Petersfield. Feb. 1915 Chiseldon. May 1915 Tidworth. July 1915 landed at Boulogne. 11.11.18 44th Bde. 15th Div. Belgium; near Huissignies, south of Ath.

9th (Service) Battalion. (Pioneers).
Formed at Fort George Oct. 1914. Nov. 1914 to Aldershot and on 3 Dec. attached to 9th Div. Early in 1915 became Pioneer Bn. 9th Div. Feb. 1915 Rowledge, near Farnham. 10.5.15 landed in France. 11.11.18 Pioneer Bn. 9th Div. Belgium; near Harlebeke, north of Courtrai.

10th (Reserve) Battalion.
Formed at Cromarty 28.10.14 as a service bn. of K4 in 101st Bde. of original 34th Div. 10.4.15 became a 2nd reserve bn. in 9th Reserve Bde. May 1915 Tain. Oct. 1915 Catterick. April 1916 Dunfermline. 1.9.16 became 39th Training Reserve Bn. at Dunfermline in 9th Training Reserve Bde.

1st Garrison Battalion.
Formed at Tillicoultry in July 1916. Aug. 1916 to Salonika. 1.3.17 to 228th Bde. attached 28th Div. 30.9.18 228th Bde. (which was under the command of the Greek Crete Div.) Macedonia; near Doiran.

THE GORDON HIGHLANDERS

1st Battalion.
4.8.14 Plymouth: 8th Bde. 3rd Div. 14.8.14 landed at Boulogne. 12.9.14 to Army Troops after heavy losses at Le Cateau. 30.9.14 returned to 8th Bde. 3rd Div. 19.10.15 to 76th Bde. 3rd Div. 11.11.18 76th Bde. 3rd Div. France; La Longueville, east of Bavai.

2nd Battalion.
4.8.14 Cairo. 13.9.14 sailed from Alexandria for U.K. arriving Southampton 1 Oct. To Lyndhurst, New Forest and 20th Bde. 7th Div. 7.10.14 landed at Zeebrugge. Nov. 1917 to Italy. 4.11.18 20th Bde. 7th Div. Italy; east of River Tagliamento near Bonzieco.

3rd (Reserve) Battalion.
4.8.14 Aberdeen. Remained at Aberdeen throughout the war providing drafts of over 800 officers and 20,000 men (Aberdeen Garrison).

1/4th Battalion T.F.
4.8.14 Aberdeen: Gordon Bde. Highland Div. Aug. 1914 Bedford. Feb. 1915 left Highland Div. and landed at Havre on 20 Feb. 27.2.15 to 8th Bde. 3rd Div. at La Clytte. 10.10.15 to 76th Bde. 3rd Div. 23.2.16 to 154th Bde. 51st Div. 11.11.18 154th Bde. 51st Div. France; Cambrai.

1/5th (Buchan and Formartin) Battalion T.F.
4.8.14 Peterhead: Gordon Bde. Highland Div. Aug. 1914 Bedford. April (?) 1915 Bde. bedame 2nd Highland Bde. 3.5.15 landed at Boulogne. 12.5.15 formation became 153rd Bde. 51st Div. 2.2.18 to 183rd Bde. 61st Div. 1.6.18 to 44th Bde. 15th Div. and on 8 June absorbed surplus personnel of 8th/10th Bn. when it was reduced to cadre. 11.11.18 44th Bde. 15th Div. Belgium; Chievres, south of Ath.

1/6th (Banff and Donside) Battalion T.F.
4.8.14 Keith: Gordon Bde. Highland Div. Aug. 1914 Bedford. Nov. 1914 left Highland Div. and landed at Havre on 10 Nov. 5.12.14 to 20th Bde. 7th Div. 5.1.16 to L. of C. Troops. 1.6.16 to 152nd Bde. 51st Div. 6.10.18 amalgamated with 1/7th Bn. to form 6th/7th BN. 11.11.18 152nd Bde. 51st Div. France; Thun l'Eveque, north of Cambrai.

1/7th (Deeside Highland) Battalion T.F.
4.8.14 Banchory: Gordon Bde. Highland Div. Aug. 1914 to Bedford. April (?) 1915 Bde. became 2nd Highland Bde. 3.5.15 landed at Boulogne. 12.5.15 formation became 153rd Bde. 51st Div. 5.10.18 to 153rd Bde. and amalgamated with 1/6th Bn.

The Shetland Companies T.F.
4.8.14 Lerwick: Army Troops, attached Gordon Bde. Highland Div. Very little information is available about these two companies. For the first part of the war they were employed on guarding wireless and cable installations in the Shetlands. In June 1915 they joined the 51st Div. in France, probably attached to a battalion of the Gordon Highlanders in 153rd Bde. At the end of 1916, after heavy losses in the Battles of the Somme, they were absorbed in the Gordon Highlanders (?) 4th Bn.

2/4th Battalion T.F.
Formed at Aberdeen Sept. 1914 Jan. 1915 192nd Bde. 64th Div. 1915 Perthshire. Nov. 1915 absorbed by 2/5th Bn.

2/5th (Buchan and Formartin) Battalion T.F.
Formed at Peterhead in Oct. 1914. Jan. 1915 192nd Bde. 64th Div. 1915 in Perthshire. Nov. 1915 absorbed 2/4th Bn. and became No. 5 Bn. until Jan. 1916. Mar. 1916 Norwich. Jan. 1917 Witton Hall, North Walsham. Early in 1918 left 64th Div. and was later disbanded on 31.7.18.

2/6th (Banff and Donside) Battalion T.F.
Formed at Keith in Oct. 1914. Jan. 1915 192nd Bde. 64th Div. 1915 in Perthshire. Nov. 1915 absorbed by 2/7th Bn.

2/7th (Deeside Highland) Battalion T.F.
Formed at Banchory in Oct. 1914. Jan. 1915 192nd Bde. 64th Div. 1915 in Perthshire. Nov. 1915 absorbed 2/6th Bn. and became No. 6 Bn. until Jan. 1916. Mar. 1916 Norwich. Jan. 1917 Witton Hall, North Walsham. July 1917 left 64th Div. and was later disbanded on 30.9.17.

3/4th, 3/5th, 3/6th and 3/7th Battalions T.F.
Formed in Feb. 1915 (3/4th) and other Bns. in May 1915. Nov. 1915 Ripon. 8.4.16 became Reserve Bns. 1.9.16 4TH RESERVE BN. absorbed 5th, 6th and 7th Reserve Bn. at Ripon in Highland Reserve Bde. T.F. Feb. 1918 Edinburgh. Sept. 1918 Dreghorn near Kilmarnock where it remained. (Forth Garrison).

8th (Service) Battalion.
Formed at Aberdeen Aug. 1914—K1—to Aldershot in 26th Bde. 9th Div. Feb. 1915 Bordon. 10.5.15 landed at Boulogne. 7.5.16 to 44th Bde. 15th Div. near Bethune and on 11 May amalgamated with 10th Bn. to form 8th/10th Bn. 6.6.18 reduced to training cadre—surplus personnel absorbed by 1/5th Bn.—cadre to 118th Bde. 39th Div. 17.8.18 cadre disbanded.

9th (Service) Battalion. (Pioneers).
Formed at Aberdeen Sept. 1914—K2—to Aldershot in

British Regiments 1914–1918 105

44th Bde. 15th Div. Nov. 1914 Haslemere. 12.1.15 became Pioneer Bn. 15th Div. Feb. 1915 Perham Down. May 1915 Andover. July 1915 landed in France. 11.11.8 Pioneer Bn. 15th Div. Belgium; south of Ath.

10th (Service) Batatlion.
Formed at Aberdeen Sept. 1914—K2—to Aldershot in 44th Bde. 15th Div. Nov. 1914 Midhurst. Mar. 1915 Chisledon. May 1915 Tidworth. July 1915 landed in France. 11.5.16 amalgamated with 8th Bn. to form 8th/10th Bn.

11th (Reserve) Battalion.
Formed at Aberdeen in Oct. 1914 as a service bn. of K4. Not allotted to a formation. 10.4.15 became a 2nd Reserve Bn. May 1915 Dornoch. Oct. 1915 Catterick in 9th Reserve Bde. June 1916 Bridge of Allan. 1.9.16 became 42nd Training Reserve Bn. at Bridge of Allan(?) in 9th Training Reserve Bde.

1st Garrison Battalion.
Formed in 1916—was known as 12th Bn. for a short time. In Oct. 1916 at Blairgowrie. Jan. 1917 to India.

51st (Graduated) Battalion.
On 27.10.17 the 202nd Graduated Bn. (formerly 38th Training Reserve Bn. from 11th Black Watch) at Cromer in 191st Bde. 64th Div. became the 51st Bn. April 1918 to Thetford where it remained.

52nd (Graduated) Battalion.
On 27.10.17 the 286th Graduated Bn. (formerly 40th Training Reserve Bn. from 8th Cameron Highlanders(at Canterbury in 202nd Bde. 67th Div. became the 52nd Bn. About Mar. 1918 to Colchester where it remained.

53rd (Young Soldier) Battalion.
On 27.10.17 the 42nd Training Reserve Bn. (formerly 11th Gordon Highlanders) at Tillicoultry, Clackmannanshire became the 53rd Bn. About Nov. 1917 to Lowland Reserve Bde. T.F. and remained at Tillicoultry.

THE QUEEN'S OWN CAMERON HIGHLANDERS

1st Battalion.
4.8.14 Edinburgh. 14.8.14 landed at Havre; Army Troops. 5.9.14 to 1st Bde. 1st Div. 19.3.16 absorbed 1/4th Bn. 11.11.18 1st Bde. 1st Div. France; Fresnoy-le-Grand, S.W. of Bohain.

2nd Battalion.
4.8.14 Poona. 16.10.14 sailed from Bombay for U.K., arriving Devonport 16 Nov. To Winchester and joined 81st Bde. 27th Div. 20.12.14 landed at Havre. 29.11.15 sailed from Marseilles for Salonika, arriving 5 Dec. 30.9.18 81st Bde. 27th Div. Macedonia; Izlis, N.W. of Doiran.

3rd (Reserve) Battalion.
4.8.14 Inverness. Aug. 1914 to Cromarty and then Invergordon. Nov. 1917 to Ireland and at Birr. Mar. 1918 Ballyvonare, Co. Cork. April 1918 Limerick and later back to Ballyvonare (near Buttevant).

1/4th Battalion T.F.
4.8.14 Inverness: Seaforth & Cameron Bde. Highland Div. Aug. 1914 Bedford. Feb. 1915 left Highland Div. and landed at Havre 20 Feb. 23.2.15 to 24th Bde. 8th Div. 8.4.15 to 21st Bde. 7th Div. 20.12.15 to 91st Bde. 7th Div. 7.1.16 to 154th Bde. 51st Div. 28.2.16 left 51st Div. and went to base. 19.3.16 absorbed in 1st Bn.

2/4th Battalion T.F.
Formed at Inverness Sept. 1914. Jan. 1915 191st Bde. 64th Div. April 1915 Fort George. July 1915 Blair Atholl. Oct. 1915 Aberfeldy and from Nov. 1915 to Jan. 1916 was No. 3 Bn. Mar. 1916 Norwich. June 1916 Blickling. July 1916 Kelling. Oct. 1916 Cromer. April 1917 Kelling. Oct. 1917 Cromer. Feb. 1918 left 64th Div. and was disbanded.

3/4th Battalion T.F.
Formed at Inverness April 1915. Nov. 1915 Ripon. 8.4.16 became 4th Reserve Bn. July 1916 disbanded.

5th (Service) Battalion.
Formed at Inverness Aug. 1914—K1—to Aldershot in 26th Bde. 9th Div. Feb. 1915 to Bordon in Guadaloupe Barracks. 10.5.15 landed at Boulogne. 11.11.18 26th Bde. 9th Div. Belgium; Harlebeke, north of Courtrai.

6th (Service) Battalion.
Formed at Inverness in Sept. 1914—K2—to Maida Barracks, Aldershot in 45th Bde. 15th Div. Nov. 1914 Bramshott. Feb. 1915 Basingstoke. April 1915 Chisledon. 10.7.15 landed at Boulogne. 11.11.18 45th Bde. 15th Div. Belgium; moving from Baugnies to Ellignies Ste. Anne, south of Leuze.

7th (Service) Battalion.
Formed at Inverness 28.9.14. At Inverness until Nov. and then to Salamanca Barracks, Aldershot. 13.1.15 to 44th Bde. 15th Div. in place of 9th Gordon Highlanders which became Pioneer Bn. Jan. 1915 Liphook in billets. Feb. 1915 Cirencester in billets. April 1915 Chisledon. May 1915 Parkhouse, Tidworth. 9.7.15 landed at Boulogne. 10.6.18 reduced to training cadre (21 officers and 383 men to 6th Bn.) and to 118th Bde. 39th Div. 14.8.18 disbanded at Listergaux, S.W. of Audruicq.

8th (Reserve) Battalion.
Formed at Invergordon in Nov. 1914 as a service bn. of K4 in 101st Bde. of original 34th Div. Feb. 1915 Inverness. 10.4.15 became a 2nd Reserve bn. June 1915 Tain. Oct. 1915 Catterick in 9th Reserve Bde. Mar. 1916 Stirling. 1.9.16 became 40th Training Reserve Bn. at Stirling in 9th Training Reserve Bde.

9th (Labour) Battalion.
Formed at Blairgowrie in Aug. 1916. 6.9.16 landed at Havre. To L. of C. April 1917 transferred to Labour Corps as 7th and 8th Labour Coys.

10th (Lovat's Scouts) Battalion T.F.
Formed at Cairo 27.9.16 from two dismounted Yeomanry Regiments—1/1st and 1/2nd Lovat's Scouts. 20.10.16 landed at Salonika and to 82nd Bde. 27th Div. on 1 Nov. June 1918 left 27th Div. and went to France. 6.7.18 to L. of C. Troops.

11th (Service) Battalion.
On 10.6.18 the 6th Garrison Gaurd Bn. (recently formed in France) joined 120th Bde. 40th Div. in the Lederzeele area north of St. Omer, and became the 11th Garrison Bn. On 13.7.18 the title 'Garrison' was omitted from the title. 11.11.18 120th Bde. 40th Div. Belgium; Warcoing, on River Scheldt, east of Roubaix.

1st (Home Service) Garrison Battalion.
Formed at Invergordon in Feb. 1917. Aug. 1917 became 18th Bn. Royal Defence Corps.

THE ROYAL IRISH RIFLES

1st Battalion.
4.8.14 Aden. 27.9.14 embarked for U.K. arriving Liverpool on 22 Oct. then to Hursley Park, Winchester joining 25th Bde. 8th Div. 6.11.14 landed at Havre. 3.2.18 to 107th Bde. 36th Div. 11.11.18 107th Bde. 36th Div. Belgium; Mouscron, N.E. of Tourcoing.

2nd Battalion.
4.8.14 Tidworth: 7th Bde. 3rd Div. 14.8.14 landed at Rouen. 18.10.15 7th Bde. to 25th Div. 26.10.15 to 74th Bde. 25th Div. 13.11.17 to 108th Bde. 36th Div. and absorbed 7th Bn. at Ypres. 8.2.18 to 107th Bde. 36th Div.

11.11.18 107th Bde. 36th Div. Belgium; Mouscron, N.E. of Tourcoing.

3rd (Reserve) Battalion.
4.8.14 Belfast. 8 Aug. to Dublin until May 1916 and then returned to Belfast. April 1918 to England at Larkhill in Irish Reserve Bde. May 1918 absorbed 17th, 18th, 19th and 20th (Reserve) Bns. No further change.

4th (Extra Reserve) Battalion.
4.8.14 Newtownards. 6 Aug. Holywood and detachments on coast defences April 1915 Carrickfergus. Nov. 1917 Newry. April 1918 to England at Larkhill in Irish Reserve Bde. No further change.

5th (Extra Reserve) Battalion.
4.8.14 Downpatrick. Sept. 1914 Belfast. May 1915 Holywood. Mar. 1918 Ballykinlar. April 1918 to England at Larkhill in Irish Reserve Bde. No further change.

6th (Service) Battalion.
Formed at Dublin Aug. 1914—K1—Sept. to Fermoy in 29th Bde. 10th Div. Oct. 1914 Dublin. Feb. 1915 The Curragh. May 1915 to England at Hackwood Park, Basingstoke. 7.7.15 sailed from Liverpool for Mudros, via Alexandria, arriving 26 July. 5.8.15 landed at Anzac Cove. 29.9.15 to Mudros. 4/5 Oct. 1915 to Salonika. Sept. 1917 to Egypt and Palestine arriving Alexandria 19 Sept. 15.5.18 disbanded at Deir en Nidham, E.N.E. of Ludd.

7th (Service) Battalion.
Formed at Belfast in Sept. 1914—K2—to Mallow in 48th Bde. 16th Div. (originally allotted to 47th Bde.) Jan. 1915 Ballyvonare, near Buttevant. 5.3.15 absorbed a company of Royal Jerset Militia (6 officers and 224 men). June 1915 Ballyhooly, near Fermoy. Sept. 1915 to England at Aldershot. 20.12.15 landed at Havre. 23.8.17 to 49th Bde. 16th Div. 14.10.17 to 108th Bde. 36th Div. 14.11.17 absorbed by 2nd Bn.

The following locally raised battalions were formed from the Ulster Volunteer Force. A fuller account is given at the note at the foot of page 71 under The Royal Inniskilling Fusiliers.

8th (Service) Battalion. (East Belfast).
Raised in Belfast Sept. 1914 from the Belfast Volunteers. To Ballykinlar in 107th Bde. 36th Div. July 1915 to Seaford. Oct. 1915 landed at Boulogne. 107th Bde. with 4th Div. from 5.11.15 to 3.2.16. 29.8.17 amalgamated with 9th Bn. to form 8TH/9TH BN. 7.2.18 disbanded in France.

9th (Service) Battalion. (West Belfast).
Raised in Belfast Sept. 1914 from the Belfast Volunteers. To Ballykinlar in 107th Bde. 36th Div. Subsequent record same as 8th Bn.

10th (Service) Battalion. (South Belfast).
Raised in Belfast Sept. 1914 from the Belfast Volunteers. To Newcastle in 107th Bde. 36th Div. Jan. 1915 to Ballykinlar. July 1915 Seaford. Oct. 1915 landed at Boulogne. 107th Bde. with 4th Div. from 5.11.15 to 3.2.16 20.2.18 disbanded in France.

11th (Service) Battalion. (South Antrim).
Raised in Co. Antrim Sept. 1914 from the Antrim Volunteers. To 108th Bde. 36th Div. Dec. 1914 Clandeboye. July 1915 Seaford. Oct. 1915 landed at Boulogne. 13.11.17 amalgamated with 13th Bn. to form 11TH/13TH BN. 18.2.18 disbanded in France.

12th (Service) Battalion. (Central Antrim).
Raised in Co. Antrim Sept. 1914 from the Antrim Volunteers. Nov. 1914 Newtownards in 108th Bde. 36th Div. July 1915 Seaford. Oct. 1915 landed at Boulogne. 11.11.18 108th Bde. 36th Div. Belgium; Mouscron, N.E. of Tourcoing.

13th (Service) Battalion. (1st Co. Down).
Raised in Co. Down Sept. 1914 from the Co. Down Volunteers. To Clandeboye in 108th Bde. 36th Div. Subsequent record same as 11th Bn.

14th (Service) Battalion. (Young Citizens).
Raised in Belfast Sept. 1914 from the Belfast Volunteers. To 109th Bde. 36th Div. Dec. 1914 Bundoran, Co. Donegal. Jan. 1915 Randalstown. July 1915 Seaford. Oct. 1915 landed at Boulogne. 18.2.18 disbanded in France.

15th (Service) Battalion. (North Belfast).
Raised in Belfast Sept. 1914 from the Belfast Volunteers. To Ballykinlar in 107th Bde. 36th Div. July 1915 Seaford. Oct. 1915 landed at Boulogne. 107th Bde. with 4th Div. from 5.11.15 to 3.2.16. 11.11.18 107th Bde. 36th Div. Belgium, Mouscron, N.E. of Tourcoing.

16th (Service) Battalion. (2nd Co. Down) (Pioneers).
Raised in Co. Down Sept. 1914 from the Co. Down Volunteers at Lurgan. Jan. 1915 became Pioneer Bn. 36th Div. July 1915 Seaford. Oct. 1915 landed at Boulogne. 11.11.18 Pioneer Bn. 36th Div. Belgium; Mouscron, N.E. of Tourcoing.

17th (Reserve) Battalion.
Formed at Newcastle Mar. 1915 as a local reserve bn. from depot coys of 8th, 9th and 10th Bns. Oct. 1915 Ballykinlar in 15th (Ulster) Reserve Bde. Aug. 1917 Dundalk. April 1918 to England and absorbed in 3rd Bn. at Larkhill in May 1918.

18th (Reserve) Battalion.
Formed at Holywood April 1915 as a local reserve bn. from depot coys. of 11th and 12th Bns. July 1915 Clandeboye in 15th (Ulster) Reserve Bde. April 1918 to England and absorbed in 3rd Bn. at Larkhill in May 1918.

19th (Reserve) Battalion.
Formed at Newcastle about Oct. 1915 as a local reserve bn. from depot coys. of 14th and 15th Bns. End 1915 Newtownards and early 1916 back to Newcastle: in 15th (Ulster) Reserve Bde. April 1918 to England and absorbed in 3rd Bn. at Larkhill in May 1918.

20th (Reserve) Battalion.
Formed at Holywood about Nov. 1915 as a local reserve bn. from depot coys. of 13th and 16th Bns. To Dublin(?) in Dec. and by Feb. 1916 at Newtownards in 15th (Ulster) Reserve Bde. April 1918 to England and absorbed in 3rd Bn. at Larkhill in May 1918.

1st Garrison Battalion.
Formed in Dublin Nov. 1915 and went to India in Feb. 1916.

NOTE

The locally raised Service battalions of the Royal Irish Rifles were included in the Ulster Division when it was formed in September 1914. The infantry brigades were numbered 1st, 2nd and 3rd.

On 28 October 1914 the Ulster Division became the 36th (Ulster) Division and the infantry brigades were numbered 107th, 108th and 109th on 2 November 1914.

PRINCESS VICTORIA'S (ROYAL IRISH FUSILIERS)

1st Battalion.
4.8.14 Shorncliffe: 10th Bde. 4th Div. To York. 18 Aug. Harrow. 23.8.14 landed at Boulogne. 3.8.17 to 36th Div. and on 24 Aug. to 107th Bde. 8.2.18 to 108th Bde. 36th Div. 11.11.18 108th Bde. 36th Div. Belgium; Mouscron, N.E. of Tourcoing.

2nd Battalion.
4.8.14 Quetta. Oct. 1914 to U.K. arriving Winchester 20 Nov. and joining 82nd Bde. 27th Div. 19.12.14 landed

in France. Nov. 1915 to Salonika. 2.11.16 to 31st Bde. 10th Div. Sept. 1917 to Egypt and Palestine. 31.10.18 31st Bde. 10th Div. Palestine; Masudiye, N.W. of Nablus.

3rd (Reserve) Battalion.
4.8.14 Armagh. Aug. 1914 Lough Swilly and then Londonderry. April 1915 Buncrana. Nov. 1916 Clonmany, Co. Donegal. April 1918 to England at Rugeley, Cannock Chase and absorbed 4th Bn. July 1918 Bawdsey, Suffolk in West Riding Reserve Bde. T.F. Oct. 1918 Southend.

4th (Extra Reserve) Battalion.
4.8.14 Cavan. Aug. 1914 Belfast and Carrickfergus. Mar. 1915 Buncrana. April 1915 Belfast. April 1916 Dublin. Nov. 1917 Ballincollig, Cork in 25th Reserve Bde. April 1918 to England at Rugeley and absorbed by 3rd Bn.

5th (Service) Battalion.
Formed at Armagh Aug. 1914—K1—to Dublin in 31st Bde. 10th Div. April 1915 Basingstoke. July 1915 sailed from Liverpool for Gallipoli. 7.8.15 landed at Suvla Bay. Oct. 1915 to Salonika. 2.11.16 absorbed 6th Bn. Sept. 1917 to Egypt and Palestine. 30.4.18 left 10th Div. and embarked at Port Said on 18 May for France arriving Marseilles 27 May. 23.7.18 to 66th Div. 24.8.18 to 48th Bde. 16th Div. and absorbed 11th Bn. 11.11.18 48th Bde. 16th Div. Belgium; Antoing, south of Tournai.

6th (Service) Battalion.
Formed at Armagh Aug. 1914—K1—to Dublin in 31st Bde. 10th Div. Subsequent record same as 5th Bn. until 2.11.16 when it was absorbed by 5th Bn.

7th (Service) Battalion.
Formed at Armagh Sept. 1914—K2—to Tipperary in 49th Bde. 16th Div. Sept. 1915 to Pirbright. Feb. 1916 landed in France 15.10.16 amalgamated with 8th Bn. to form 7th/8th Bn. 10.2.18 disbanded in France.

8th (Service) Battalion.
Formed at Armagh Sept. 1914—K2—to Tipperary in 49th Bde. 16th Div. July 1915 Newry. Subsequent record same as 7th Bn.

9th (Service) Battalion. (Co. Armagh).
Raised in Sept. 1914 from the Armagh, Monaghan and Cavan Volunteers. To 2nd Bde. Ulster Div. 28.10.14 Ulster Div. became 36th (Ulster) Div. and on 2.11.14 2nd Bde. became 108th. Nov. 1914 Belfast. Feb. 1915 Newtownards. July 1915 Seaford. Oct. 1915 landed at Boulogne. 25.9.17 absorbed B and C Sqdns. 2nd North. Irish Horse (304 men), previously X Corps Cav. Regt and now dismounted. Became 9th (North Irish Horse) Bn. 11.11.18. 108th Bde. 36th Div. Belgium; Mouscron, N.E. of Tourcoing.
For details of formation of 36th (Ulster) Div. see note at the foot of page 71 under The Royal Inniskilling Fusiliers.

10th (Reserve) Battalion.
Formed at Lurgan Sept. 1915 as a local reserve bn. from depot coys. of 9th Bn. Jan. 1916 Newtownards in 15th (Ulster) Reserve Bde. Aug. 1917 at Armagh. April 1918 to England at Rugeley and absorbed by 3rd Bn. in May 1918.

11th (Service) Battalion.
Formed at Greatham, near West Hartlepool, on 1.6.18. Perhaps partly from 3rd (Reserve) Garrison Bn. 18.6.18 absorbed cadre of 7th Bn. Royal Dublin Fusiliers. 28.6.18 to 48th Bde. 16th Div. at Aldershot. End July 1918 to France. 29.8.18 absorbed by 5th Bn.

1st Garrison Battalion.
Formed at Dublin Sept. 1915. Feb. 1916 to India. May 1917 Burma.

2nd Garrison Battalion.
Formed at Dublin April 1916. May 1916 Templemore, Co. Tipperary. Aug. 1916 to Salonika. From 1.3.17 to 6.8.17 in 228th Bde. attached 28th Div. 30.9.18 Macedonia; L. of C.

3rd (Reserve) Garrison Battalion.
Formed Dec. 1916 (?) Dublin. April 1917 Bere Island, Bantry Bay. May 1918 Seaton Carew. June 1918 Greatham. May have helped to form 11th Bn. Oct. 1918 Castle Eden, near West Hartlepool. (Tees Garrison).

THE CONNAUGHT RANGERS

1st Battalion.
4.8.14 Ferozepore: Ferozepore Bde. 3rd (Lahore) Div. 28.8.14 embarked at Karachi for Europe and arrived Marseilles 26 Sept. (in Egypt 14 to 19 Sept.). 5.12.14 1st and 2nd Bns. amalgamated at Le Touret, N.E. of Bethune. 11.12.15 sailed from Marseilles for Mesopotamia, arriving Basra 10.1.16. Temporarily to 9th Indian Bde. 3rd Indian Div. and Feb. 1916 returned to 7th Indian Bde. 3.4.18 sailed from Kuwait for Egypt. 15.4.18 landed at Suez. 31.10.18 7th Indian Bde. 3rd Indian Div. Palestine; Nazareth.

2nd Battalion.
4.8.14 Barrosa Barracks, Aldershot: 5th Bde. 2nd Div. 14.8.14 landed at Boulogne. 26.11.14 to Ferozepore Bde. 3rd (Lahore) Div. and on 5 Dec. amalgamated with 1st Bn. at Le Touret.

3rd (Reserve) Battalion.
4.8.14 Galway. 8 Aug. Crosshaven, Cork Harbour. Sept. 1914 Kinsale. Nov. 1917 to England at Newcastle-on-Tyne. About May 1918 to Dover and absorbed 4th Bn. No further change. (Dover Garrison).

4th (Extra Reserve) Battalion.
4.8.14 Boyle. Aug. Queenstown. Mar. 1915 Bere Island. Feb. 1916 Fermoy. May 1916 Crosshaven. Nov. 1917 to Scotland at Nigg, Perthshire. Early 1918 Fort George. May 1918 absorbed by 3rd Bn. at Dover.

5th (Service) Battalion.
Formed in Dublin Aug. 1914—K1—Sept. to Kilworth in 29th Bde. 10th Div. Oct. 1914 Dublin. Jan. 1915 the Curragh. May 1915 to England at Hackwood Park, Basingstoke. 9.7.15 embarked at Devonport and arrived Mudros about 25 July. 5.8.15 landed at Anzac (29th Bde. was attached to Australian & N.Z. Corps). 30.9.15 Mudros. 5.10.15 embarked for Salonika. Sept. 1917 to Egypt. April 1918 left 10th Div. and went to France, arriving Marseilles 1 June. 7 to 28 June 14th Div. 22.7.18 to 197th Bde. 66th Div. at Serqueux. 25.8.18 to 199th Bde. 66th Div. 11.11.18 199th Bde. 66th Div. France; near Sivry, east of Avesnes.

6th (Service) Battalion.
Formed at Kilworth Sept. 1914—K2—to Fermoy in 47th Bde. 16th Div. Sept. 1915 to England at Blackdown. 18.12.15 landed at Havre. 13.4.18 reduced to training cadre. 5 officers and 281 men to 2nd Bn. Leinster Regt. 17.6.18 cadre to 34th Div. 27.6.18 to 117th Bde. 39th Div. 3.8.18 cadre disbanded.

PRINCESS LOUISE'S
(ARGYLL AND SUTHERLAND HIGHLANDERS)

1st Battalion.
4.8.14 Dinapore. 19.10.14 embarked at Bombay for U.K. landing at Plymouth 19 Nov. and to Winchester joining 81st Bde. 27th Div. 20.12.14 landed at Havre. 27.11.15 embarked at Marseilles. 12.12.15 landed at Salonika. 30.9.18 81st Bde. 27th Div. Macedonia; Izlis, N.W. of Doiran.

2nd Battalion.
4.8.14 Fort George. 14.8.14 landed at Boulogne as L. of C. Troops. 22.8.14 joined 19th Bde. forming at Valenciennes. 12.10.14 19th Bde. attached to 6th Div. 31.5.15 19th Bde. attached to 27th Div. 19.8.15 19th Bde. to 2nd Div. in place of 4th Guards Bde. 25.11.15 19th Bde. to 33rd Div. and Bn. to 98th Bde. 33rd Div. on 27.11.15. 11.11.18 98th Bde. 33rd Div. France; Sassegnies, S.W. of Aulnoye.

3rd (Reserve) Battalion.
4.8.14 Stirling. Aug. 1914 Woolwich. May 1915 Edinburgh. Mar. 1917 Dreghorn. Nov. 1917 to Ireland at Kinsale in 25th Reserve Bde. No further change.

4th (Extra Reserve) Battalion.
4.8.14 Paisley. Aug. 1914 to Devonport. Nov. 1914 Sunderland. Feb. 1915 Plymouth. May 1915 Edinburgh. July 1918 Dunbar. (Forth Garrison).

1/5th (Renfrewshire) Battalion T.F.
4.8.14 Drill Hall, Finnart Street, Greenock: attached Black Watch Bde., Army Troops. Scottish Coast Defences. 24.4.15 to H.L.I. Bde. Lowland Div. at Dunfermline. 11.5.15 formation became 157th Bde. 52nd Div. 1.6.15 embarked at Devonport. 12 June Alexandria and 1.7.15 arrived Mudros. 3.7.15 landed at Cape Helles. 8.1.16 to Mudros. Feb. 1916 to Egypt. 11.4.18 sailed from Alexandria and arrived Marseilles 17 April. 28.6.18 left 52nd Div. and to 103rd Bde. 34th Div. at Bambecque. 11.11.18 103rd Bde. 34th Div. France; Halluin.

1/6th (Renfrewshire) Battalion T.F.
4.8.14 66 High Street, Paisley: A. & S.H. Bde. Highland Div. Aug. 1914 to Bedford. 15.4.15 to 1st Highland Bde. May 1915 to France. 12.5.15 formation became 152nd Bde. 51st Div. 12.6.16 to 5th Div. as Pioneer Bn. Dec. 1917 to Italy. April 1918 returned to France. 5.10.18 to 153rd Bde. 51st Div. 11.11.18 153rd Bde. 51st Div. France; near Houdain, north of Cambrai.

1/7th Battalion T.F.
4.8.14 Stirling: A. & S.H. Bde. Highland Div. Aug. 1914 Bedford. Dec. 1914 left Highland Div. and landed in France on 16 Dec. 6.1.15 to 10th Bde. 4th Div. 27.5.15 amalgamated with 1/9th Bn. from 27th Div. 20.7.15 resumed identity. 1.3.16 to 154th Bde. 51st Div. 11.11.18 154th Div. 51st Div. France; north of Cambrai.

1/8th (The Argyllshire) Battalion T.F.
4.8.14 Dunoon: A. & S.H. Bde. Highland Div. Aug. 1914 Bedford. 15.4.15 to 1st Highland Bde. May 1915 to France. 12.5.15 formation became 152nd Bde. 51st Div. 7.2.18 to 183rd Bde. 61st Div. 1.6.18 to 45th Bde. 15th Div. and absorbed surplus personnel of 11th Bn. which had been reduced to cadre. 11.11.18 45th Bde. 15th Div. Belgium; south of Leuze.

1/9th (The Dumbartonshire) Battalion T.F.
4.8.14 Hartfield, Dumbarton: A. & S.H. Bde. Highland Div. Aug. 1914 Bedford. Early in 1915 left Highland Div. and went to France. 23.2.15 to 81st Bde. 27th Div. 21.5.15 to 10th Bde. 4th Div. and on 27 May amalgamated with 1/7th Bn. 20.7.15 resumed identity and to VI Corps Troops. 27.2.16 to Base and used to supply drafts.

2/5th (Renfrewshire) Battalion T.F.
Formed at Greenock Sept. 1914. 30.11.15 absorbed by 2/8th Bn.—temporarily No. 9 Bn.—in 193rd Bde. 64th Div.

2/6th (Renfrewshire) Battalion T.F.
Formed at Paisley Sept. 1914 and by Aug. 1915 at Falkirk in 193rd Bde. 64th Div. Autumn 1915 to Forfarshire (Angus) for the winter. From 8.11.15 to 11.1.16 became No. 10 Bn. Mar. 1916 Norwich. April 1917 Taverham. Oct. 1917 Norwich. By Mar. 1918 had left 64th Div. and was disbanded on 13.3.18.

2/7th Battalion T.F.
Formed at Stirling Sept. 1914 and by Aug. 1915 at Falkirk in 193rd Bde. 64th Div. Autumn 1915 to Forfarshire (Angus) for the winter. From 8.11.15 to 11.1.16 became No. 11 Bn. Mar. 1916 to Norwich. April 1917 Taverham. Disbanded in the autumn of 1917.

2/8th (The Argyllshire) Battalion T.F.
Formed at Dunoon Sept. 1914 and by Aug. 1915 at Falkirk in 193rd Bde. 64th Div. Autumn 1915 to Forfarshire (Angus) for the winter. From 8.11.15 to 11.1.16 became No. 9 Bn. and on 30.11.15 absorbed 2/5th Bn. Mar. 1916 to Norwich and later to Sheringham. April 1917 Taverham. Oct. 1917 Norwich. Early 1918 left 64th Div. and was disbanded on 19.7.18.

2/9th (The Dumbartonshire) Battalion T.F.
Formed at Dumbarton Sept. 1914 and by Aug. 1915 at Falkirk in 193rd Bde. 64th Div. Autumn 1915 to Forfarshire (Angus) for the winter. From 8.11.15 to 11.1.16 became No. 12 Bn. Mar. 1916 to Norwich. April 1917 Taverham and disbanded in Oct. 1917.

3/5th, 3/6th, 3/7th, 3/8th and 3/9th Battalions T.F.
Formed at home stations about April 1915. Summer 1915 may have been at Bridge of Earn, Perthshire. Autumn 1915 Ripon. 8.4.16 became Reserve Bns. 1.9.16 5th (Reserve) Bn. absorbed 6th, 7th, 8th and 9th (Reserve) Bns. at Ripon in Highland Reserve Bde. T.F. May 1918 Galashiels where it remained. (Forth Garrison).

10th (Service) Battalion.
Formed at Stirling Aug. 1914—K1—to Bordon in 27th Bde. 9th Div. Nov. 1914 New Alresford in billets. Feb. 1915 Bramshott. 11.5.15 landed in France. 6.5.16 to 26th Bde. 9th Div. 17.2.18 to 97th Bde. 32nd Div. 11.11.18 97th Bde. 32nd Div. France; near Avesnes.

11th (Service) Battalion.
Formed at Stirling Sept. 1914—K2—to Aldershot in 45th Bde. 15th Div. Nov. 1914 Bramshott. Feb. 1915 Basingstoke. April 1915 Chiseldon. 9.7.15 landed at Boulogne. 9.6.18 reduced to training cadre, surplus personnel to 1/8th Bn. Cadre to 118th Bde. 39th Div. 30.7.18 X Corps Reinforcement. 26.8.18 disbanded.

12th (Service) Battalion.
Formed at Stirling Sept. 1914—K3—to Codford St. Mary in 77th Bde. 26th Div. Oct. 1914 Bristol in billets. Feb. 1915 Sutton Veny. Sept. 1915 landed at Boulogne. Nov. 1915 to Salonika. 30.9.18 77th Bde. 26th Div. Macedonia; near Strumica, north-west of Lake Doiran.

13th (Reserve) Battalion.
Formed at Blackheath in Nov. 1914 as a service bn. of K4 in 106th Bde. of original 35th Div. Jan. 1915 White City, London. 10.4.15 became a 2nd reserve bn. and to Dorking. June 1915 Tain. Oct. 1915 Richmond in 9th Reserve Bde. About June 1916 to Dunfermline. 1.9.16 became 41st Training Reserve Bn. at Dunfermline in 9th Training Reserve Bde.

14th (Service) Battalion.
Formed early in 1915 and by June at Plymouth. Sept. 1915 to 118th Bde. 39th Div. at Witley. 23.2.16 to 120th Bde. 40th Div. at Blackdown. June 1916 landed at Havre. 7.4.18 to 90th Bde. 30th Div. after posting 24 officers and 496 men as drafts and reduced to cadre. 15.6.18 to 14th Div. at Boulogne and crossed to England. To Cowshot, near Pirbright and on 18 June reconstituted by absorbing 17th Bn. and to 42nd Bde. 14th Div. 4.7.18 landed at Boulogne. 11.11.18 42nd Bde. 14th Div. Belgium; Evregnies, east of Roubaix.

15th (Reserve) Battalion.
Formed at Gailes in Nov. 1915. May have been a service bn. for a short period. Mar. 1916 Montrose. June 1916

Lanark. 1.9.16 absorbed in Training Reserve Bns. of 9th Training Reserve Bde. at Dunfermline.
16th Battalion T.F.
On 1.1.17 the 3rd Provisional Bn. at Sandwich in 221st Bde. became the 16th Bn. The 3rd Provisional Bn. had been formed about May 1915 from Home Service personnel of T.F. Bns. Remained at Sandwich in 221st Bde.

A 17th Bn. was formed at Deal on 1.6.18 and absorbed in the 14th Bn. at Cowshot on 18.6.18.

THE PRINCE OF WALES'S LEINSTER REGIMENT (ROYAL CANADIANS)

1st Battalion.
4.8.14 Fyzabad. 16.10.14 sailed from Bombay for U.K. landing at Plymouth on 16 Nov. To Morne Hill, Winchester in 82nd Bde. 27th Div. 20.12.14 landed at Havre. 26.11.15 embarked at Marseilles and landed at Salonika on 11 Dec. 2.11.16 to 29th Bde. 10th Div. 14.9.17 sailed from Salonika and landed at Alexandria 18 Sept. 31.10.18 29th Bde. 10th Div. Palestine; near Nablus.
2nd Battalion.
4.8.14 Cork: 17th Bde. 6th Div. 18 Aug. Cambridge then to Newmarket. 12.9.14 landed at St. Nazaire. 14.10.15 17th Bde. to 24th Div. at Reninghelst and to 73rd Bde. 24th Div. on 19 Oct. 1.2.18 to 47th Bde. 16th Div. at Tincourt and absorbed personnel from disbanded 7th Bn. 13.4.18 absorbed 5 officers and 281 men from 6th Connaught Rangers (reduced to cadre). 23.4.18 to 88th Bde. 29th Div. at Hondeghem. 11.11.18 88th Bde. 29th Div. Belgium; west of Lessines.
3rd (Reserve) Battalion.
4.8.14 Birr. 8 Aug. Cork. Nov. 1917 to England and Portsmouth. May 1918 absorbed 4th and 5th Bns. No further change. (Portsmouth Garrison).
4th (Extra Reserve) Battalion.
4.8.14 Maryborough. 7 Aug. Crosshaven, Cork Harbour. Nov. 1914 Passage West. May 1915 to England and Devonport. Sept. 1915 returned to Ireland and the Curragh. April 1916 Limerick. Aug. 1917 Tralee. Nov. 1917 to England and Dover. May 1918 absorbed by 3rd Bn. at Portsmouth.
5th (Extra Reserve) Battalion.
4.8.14 Drogheda. 7 Aug. Queenstown. Oct. 1914 Passage West. May 1915 to England at Plymouth. Sept. 1915 returned to Ireland and Mullingar in 25th Reserve Bde. April 1916 The Curragh. June 1917 Laytown near Drogheda. Aug. 1917 Boyle. Sept. 1917 Birr. Nov. 1917 to Scotland at Glencorse, near Edinburgh. May 1918 absorbed by 3rd Bn. at Portsmouth.
6th (Service) Battalion.
Formed at Dublin Aug. 1914—K1—Sept. to Fermoy in 29th Bde. 10th Div. then to the Curragh. Oct. 1914 Birr. Feb. 1915 The Curragh. May 1915 to England at Basingstoke. 9.7.15 sailed from Liverpool arriving Mudros 26 July. 5.8.15 landed at Anzac (attached to Australian & N.Z. Corps). 29.9.15 to Mudros 4/5.10.15 to Salonika. 14.9.17 embarked at Salonika for Egypt arriving Alexandria 19 Sept. May 1918 left 10th Div. for France from Port Said 23 May arriving Marseilles 1 June. 7 to 19 June 14th Div. 19–28 June 34th Div. 20.7.18 to 198th Bde. 66th Div. 12.9.18 disbanded at Abancourt.
7th (Service) Battalion.
Formed at Fermoy Oct. 1914—K2—in 47th Bde. 16th Div. Jan. 1915 Kilworth. Sept. 1915 to England at Blackdown. 18.12.15 landed at Havre. 14.2.18 disbanded at Tincourt; personnel to 2nd Bn. and 19th Entrenching Bn.

THE ROYAL MUNSTER FUSILIERS

1st Battalion.
4.8.14 Rangoon. Sailed for the U.K. Dec. 1914, arriving Avonmouth 10.1.15. To Coventry joining 86th Bde. 29th Div. 16.3.15 sailed from Avonmouth for Alexandria and then about 10 April to Mudros. 25.4.15 landed at Helles.* Early Jan. 1916 left Gallipoli for Egypt. 16.3.16 sailed from Port Said and arrived Marseilles 22.3.16. 25.4.16 to L. of C. 28.5.16 to 48th Bde. 16th Div. and on 30 May absorbed 3 officers and 146 men from the disbanded 9th Bn. 22.11.16 to 47th Bde. 16th Div. and absorbed 21 officers and 446 men from the disbanded 8th Bn. 19.4.18 absorbed surplus of 2nd Bn. which was reduced to cadre. 20.4.18 to 172nd Bde. 57th Div. 11.11.18 172nd Bde. 57th Div. France; Lille.
2nd Battalion.
4.8.14 Malplaquet Barracks, Aldershot: 1st (Guards) Bde. 1st Div. 14.8.14 landed at Havre. 14.9.14 to Army Troops. 9.11.14 to 3rd Bde. 1st Div. 30.5.16 absorbed 7 officers and 140 men from the disbanded 9th Bn. 3.2.18 to 48th Bde. 16th Div. 19.4.18 reduced to training cadre and surplus personnel to 1st Bn. 31.5.18 to 94th Bde. 31st Div. 6.6.18 reconstituted with drafts from the disbanded 6th Bn. 16.6.18 to L. of C. 15.7.18 to 150th Bde. 50th Div. at Martin Eglise. 11.11.18 150th Bde. 50th Div. France; Sars Poteries, N.E. of Avesnes.
3rd (Reserve) Battalion.
4.8.14 Tralee. Aug. to Berehaven, Bantry Bay. Oct. 1914 Cork. May 1915 Aghada, Cork Harbour. Oct. 1917 Ballingcollig. Nov. 1917 to England at Devonport. April 1918 Plymouth. About May 1918 absorbed 4th and 5th Bns. Remained at Plymouth (Plymouth Garrison).
4th (Extra Reserve) Battalion.
4.8.14 Kinsale. Aug. to Queenstown. Nov. 1914 Aghada, Cork Harbour. May 1915 South Shields. Sept. 1915 Fermoy. Feb. 1916 Bere Island. April 1917 the Curragh. Aug. 1917 Castlebar, Co. Mayo. About Nov. 1917 to Scotland at Dreghorn. April 1918 Portobello. About May 1918 absorbed by 3rd Bn. at Plymouth.
5th (Extra Reserve) Battalion.
4.8.14 Limerick. Aug. to Queenstown. Oct. 1914 Bere Island. Mar. 1915 Crosshaven, Cork Harbour. May 1915 North Shields. Sept. 1915 the Curragh. Aug. 1917 Galway. Nov. 1917 to Scotland at Invergordon. April 1918 Fort George. About May 1918 absorbed by 3rd Bn. at Plymouth.
6th (Service) Battalion.
Formed at Tralee Aug. 1914—K1—to the Curragh in 30th Bde. 10th Div. May 1915 to England at Basingstoke. 9.7.15 sailed from Liverpool and arrived Mudros end of July. 7.8.15 landed at Suvla Bay. 2.10.15 to Mudros, then to Salonika. 3.11.16 absorbed 7th Bn. Sept. 1917 to Egypt. 30.4.18 left 10th Div. and went to France arriving Marseilles 1 June. 5.6.18 absorbed by 2nd Bn. Cadre to 117th Bde. 39th Div. on 27.6.18 and disbanded on 3.8.18.
7th (Service) Battalion.
Formed at Tralee Aug. 1914—K1—to the Curragh in 30th Bde. 10th Div. Subsequent record same as 6th Bn. which absorbed the 7th Bn. on 3.11.16.
8th (Service) Battalion.
Formed in Sept. or Oct. 1914—K2—to Fermoy in 47th Bde. 16th Div. Nov. 1914 Mitchelstown, Co. Cork. Feb. 1915 Templemore. May 1915 Fermoy. Sept. 1915 to

* On 30.4.15, after heavy casualties, the 1st Royal Munster Fusiliers and 1st Royal Dublin Fusiliers were amalgamated for a short time into a composite bn. known as the "Dubsters". 19.5.15 resumed identity.

England at Blackdown, Aldershot. About 18.12.15 landed at Havre. 30.5.16 absorbed 12 officers and 200 men from the disbanded 9th Bn. 23.11.16 disbanded in France: 21 officers and 446 men to 1st Bn.

9th (Service) Battalion.
Formed in Sept. or Oct. 1914—K2—to Kilworth in 48th Bde. 16th Div. Jan. 1915 Ballyvonare, near Buttevant. June 1915 Ballyhooly, near Fermoy. Sept. 1915 to England at Blackdown, near Aldershot. About 20.12.15 landed at Havre. 30.5.16 disbanded in France: personnel to 1st, 2nd and 8th Bns.

1st (Garrison) Battalion.
Formed on 1.4.17 at Cork as a Home Service Garrison Bn. from 1st (Home Service) Garrison Bn. Durham Light Infantry. Nov. 1917 to England at Prees Heath. 11.11.17 H.Q. and three coys. formed 1st Garrison Bn. which went to Italy where it remained on the L. of C. until the end of the war.

2nd (Home Service) Garrison Battalion.
Formed at Prees Heath in Nov. 1917 from one coy. of the 1st Garrison Bn. April 1918 to Cosham, Portsmouth where it remained (Portsmouth Garrison).

THE ROYAL DUBLIN FUSILIERS

1st Battalion.
4.8.14 Madras. 19.11.14 sailed from Bombay for U.K. arriving Plymouth 21 Dec. to Torquay in billets. Jan. 1915 to Nuneaton joining 86th Bde. 29th Div. 16.3.15 sailed from Avonmouth arriving Alexandria 30 Mar. 9.4.15 to Mudros. 25.4.15 landed at Helles. 30.4.15 after heavy casualties amalgamated with 1st Royal Munster Fusiliers to form a composite bn. known as the "Dubsters" in 87th Bde. 19.5.15 resumed identity. 1.1.16 left Gallipoli for Mudros and on 8 Jan. to Egypt. 13.3.16 sailed from Alexandria for France, arriving Marseilles 19 Mar. 19.10.17 to 48th Bde. 16th Div. 10.2.18 absorbed 10 officers and 200 men from 8th/9th Bn. 14.4.18 1st and 2nd Bns. amalgamated at Clety, south of St. Omer. 19.4.18 1st Bn. reconstituted with personnel from 2nd Bn. which was reduced to cadre. 26.4.18 to 86th Bde. 29th Div. from 16th Div. 11.11.18 86th Bde. 29th Div. Belgium; St. Genois, S.E. of Courtrai.

2nd Battalion.
4.8.14 Gravesend: 10th Bde. 4th Div. To Harrow. 22.8.14 landed at Boulogne. 15.11.16 to 48th Bde. 16th Div. 10.2.18 absorbed 10 officers and 200 men from the disbanded 8th/9th Bn. 19.4.18 amalgamated with 1st Bn. 19.4.18 reduced to cadre surplus personnel to 1st Bn. 1.6.18 to 94th Bde. 31st Div. 6.6.18 reconstituted and absorbed surplus of 7th Bn. which was reduced to cadre. 16.6.18 to L. of C. 15.7.18 to 149th Bde. 50th Div. at Martin Eglise. 11.11.18 149th Bde. 50th Div. France; near Dourlers, north of Avesnes.

3rd (Reserve) Battalion.
4.8.14 Naas. Aug. 1914 Queenstown. Remained at Cork until Nov. 1917 and then to Pembroke. Dec. 1917 Gateshead. About May 1918 absorbed 4th, 5th and 11th Bns. May 1918 Grimsby and remained in Grimsby area—Weelsby and Waltham—until the end of the war. (Humber Garrison).

4th (Extra Reserve) Battalion.
4.8.14 Dublin. Aug. 1914 Queenstown. Oct. 1914 to England at Sittingbourne and returned to Ireland at the end of 1915 at Templemore. April 1916 Mullingar. Nov. 1917 to England at Brocklesby, near Grimsby. About May 1918 absorbed in 3rd Bn.

5th (Extra Reserve) Battalion.
4.8.14 Dublin. Aug. 1914 Queenstown. Oct. 1914 to England at Sittingbourne and returned to Ireland Sept. 1915 at the Curragh in 25th Reserve Bde. Aug. 1917 Longford. Nov. 1917 to Scotland at Glencorse near Edinburgh. About May 1918 absorbed in 3rd Bn.

6th (Service) Battalion.
Formed at Naas Aug. 1914—K1—to the Curragh in 30th Bde. 10th Div. May 1915 to England at Basingstoke. 11.7.15 sailed from (?)Devonport to Mitylene. 7.8.15 landed at Suvla Bay. Oct. 1915 to Salonika. Sept. 1917 to Egypt and Palestine. 27.5.18 left 10th Div. for France, sailing from Alexandria 3.7.18 and arriving Taranto 8 July. 21.7.18 to 197th Bde. 66th Div. 10.9.18 to 198th Bde. 66th Div. 11.11.18 198th Bde. 66th Div. France; near Avesnes.

7th (Service) Battalion.
Formed at Naas Aug. 1914—K1—to the Curragh in 30th Bde. 10th Div. Feb. 1915 Dublin. May 1915 to England at Basingstoke. Subsequent record same as 6th Bn. until April 1918. Then left 10th Div. and went to France embarking at Alexandria on 23 May and arriving Marseilles 1 June. 6.6.18 reduced to cadre and surplus personnel to 2nd Bn. 10.6.18 cadre to 16th Div. at Samer, returned to England and on 18.6.18 was absorbed by the newly formed 11th Bn. Royal Irish Fusiliers at Greatham, Durham.

8th (Service) Battalion.
Formed Sept. 1914—K2—to Buttevant in 48th Bde. 16th Div. June 1915 Ballyhooly, near Fermoy. Sept. 1915 to England at Blackdown. Dec. 1915 landed at Havre. 24.10.17 amalgamated with 9th Bn. to form 8th/9th Bn. in 48th Bde. 10.2.18 disbanded in France, personnel to 1st and 2nd Bns.

9th (Service) Battalion.
Formed Sept. 1914—K2—to Buttevant in 48th Bde. 16th Div. June 1915 Ballyhooly, near Fermoy. Sept. 1915 to England at Blackdown. Dec. 1915 landed at Havre. 24.10.17 amalgamated with 8th Bn. to form 8th/9th Bn.

10th (Service) Battalion.
Formed at Dublin at the end of 1915. Aug. 1916 to England at Pirbright and 19.8.16 landed at Havre. To 190th Bde. 63rd Div. 23.6.17 to 48th Bde. 16th Div. 24.10.17 absorbed surplus personnel from amalgamation of 8th and 9th Bns. 15.2.18 disbanded in France.

11th (Reserve) Battalion.
Formed at Dublin July 1916. By Jan. 1918 at Aldershot and about May 1918 absorbed in 3rd Bn. at Plymouth.

THE RIFLE BRIGADE
(THE PRINCE CONSORT'S OWN)

1st Battalion.
4.8.14 Colchester: 11th Bde. 4th Div. 18.8.14 Harrow School. 23.8.14 landed at Havre. 11.11.18 11th Bde. 4th Div. France; Haspres, N.W. of Solesmes.

2nd Battalion.
4.8.14 Kuldana. 20.9.14 sailed from Bombay for U.K. arriving Liverpool 22 Oct. To Hursley Park, Winchester joining 25th Bde. 8th Div. 6.11.14 landed at Havre. 11.11.18 25th Bde. 8th Div. Belgium; Pommeroeul, west of Mons.

3rd Battalion.
4.8.14 Cork: 17th Bde. 6th Div. 18.8.14 Cambridge then Newmarket. 12.9.14 landed at St. Nazaire. 14.10.15 17th Bde. to 24th Div. 11.11.18 17th Bde. 24th Div. France; Bavai.

4th Battalion.
4.8.14 Dagshai. Mid Oct. sailed from Bombay for U.K.

arriving Devonport about 18 Nov. To Magdalen Hill Camp, Winchester joining 80th Bde. 27th Div. 21.12.14 landed at Havre. Nov. 1915 to Salonika. 30.9.18 80th Bde. 27th Div. Macedonia; Rabrovo, N.W. of Lake Doiran.

5th (Reserve) Battalion.
4.8.14 Winchester. Aug. 1914 to Minster, Isle of Sheppey where it remained throughout the war. (Thames & Medway Garrison).

6th (Reserve) Battalion.
4.8.14 Winchester. Aug. 1914 to Sheerness, Isle of Sheppey. Mar. 1916 Eastchurch where it remained (Thames & Medway Garrison).

7th (Service) Battalion.
Formed at Winchester 21 Aug. 1914—K1—to Malplaquet Barracks, Aldershot in 41st Bde. 14th Div. Nov. 1914 Elstead, near Farnham in billets. Mar. 1915 Aldershot. May 1915 to France. 27.4.18 reduced to cadre. 17.6.18 to England with 14th Div. at Pirbright and cadre absorbed by newly formed 33rd Bn. London Regt.

8th (Service) Battalion.
Formed at Winchester 21 Aug. 1914—K1—to Malplaquet Barracks, Aldershot in 41st Bde. 14th Div. Nov. 1914 Grayshott, near Hindhead in billets. Mar. 1915 Aldershot. May 1915 to France. 27.4.18 reduced to cadre. 16.6.18 left 14th Div. and on 19 June to 34th Div. 26.6.18 the Official History says that 18 officers and 857 men left the unit to reconstitute the 7th/8th Bn. Royal Inniskilling Fusiliers (but from only a cadre?). However, the regimental history says that in May and June the 8th Rifle Brigade was administering a composite battalion of men from Irish regiments and they may have provided the men for the 7th/8th Inniskillings. 27.6.18 to 117th Bde. 39th Div. 3.8.18 disbanded in Desvres area.

9th (Service) Battalion.
Formed at Winchester 21 Aug. 1914—K1—to Aldershot in 42nd Bde. 14th Div. Nov. 1914 Petworth in billets. Feb. 1915 Aldershot. May 1915 to France. 27.4.18 reduced to cadre. 16.6.18 left 14th Div. 27.6.18 to 117th Bde. 39th Div. 3.8.18 disbanded in Desvres area.

10th (Service) Battalion.
Formed at Winchester Sept. 1914—K2—to Blackdown in 59th Bde. 20th Div. Feb. 1915 Witley. April 1915 Hamilton Camp, near Stonehenge. 21.7.15 landed at Boulogne. 5.2.18 disbanded near La Clytte. Personnel to 3rd, 11th, 12th and 13th Bns.

11th (Service) Battalion.
Formed at Winchester Sept. 1914—K2—to Blackdown in 59th Bde. 20th Div. Feb. 1915 Witley. April 1915 Hamilton Camp, near Stonehenge. 21.7.15 landed at Boulogne. 11.11.18 59th Bde. 20th Div. France; Jenlain, west of Bavai.

12th (Service) Battalion.
Formed at Winchester Sept. 1914—K2—to Blackdown in 60th Bde. 20th Div. Feb. 1915 Witley. April 1915 Larkhill. 22.7.15 landed at Boulogne. 11.11.18 60th Bde. 20th Div. France; Bettignies, north of Maubeuge.

13th (Service) Battalion.
Formed at Winchester Oct. 1914—K3—Army Troops attached to 21st Div. Nov. 1914 High Wycombe in billets. April 1915 to Andover and 111th Bde. 37th Div. About 31.7.15 landed at Boulogne. 11.11.18 111th Bde. 37th Div. France; moving to Caudry, S.E. of Cambrai.

14th and 15th (Reserve) Battalions.
Formed at Southend Oct. 1914 as service bns. of K4 in 92nd Bde. of original 31st Div. 10.4.15 became 2nd reserve bns. and 92nd Bde. became 4th Reserve Bde. May 1915 Purfleet. June 1915 Belhus Park, Aveley, Essex. Sept. 1915 Seaford. 1.9.16 became 19th and 20th Training Reserve Bns. at Seaford in 4th Training Reserve Bde.

16th (Service) Battalion. (St. Pancras).
Raised in the borough of St. Pancras 2.4.15 by Parliamentary Recruiting Committee. 19.7.15 taken over by the War Office. Aug. 1915 to Hursley Park, Winchester in 117th Bde. 39th Div. Sept. 1915 Marlborough Lines, Aldershot. Nov. 1915 Witley. About 8.3.16 landed at Havre. 16.5.18 reduced to cadre. 16.8.18 to 66th Div. at Abancourt. 20.9.18 to L. of C. in 197th Bde. at Haudricourt, S.W. of Aumale.

17th (Reserve) Battalion.
Formed in Oct. 1915 from depot coys. of 16th Bn. as a local reserve bn. at ? Charrington Hall. In 26th Reserve Bde. Jan. 1916 Banbury. April 1916 Wimbledon. 1.9.16 became 112th Training Reserve Bn. at Wimbledon in 26th Reserve Bde.

18th (London), 19th (Western), 20th (Northern), 21st (Midland), 22nd (Wessex & Welsh), 23rd (North Western) and 24th (Home Counties) Battalions T.F.
The seven battalions were formed as Territorial units by A.C.I. 28 of November 1915 from Supernumerary Territorial Force Companies. These companies had been formed under Army Order 187 of May 1915 from National Reservists who were employed on guarding vulnerable points. The battalions were used for garrison duty abroad and they all went overseas in 1916.

18th, 23rd and 24th Battalions went to India. 19th and 20th Battalions went to Egypt and Palestine. 21st Battalion went to Egypt and in Sept. 1918 to India. 22nd Battalion went to Egypt and in November 1916 to Salonika. Here it joined 228th Bde. attached to 28th Div. 30.9.18 228th Bde. (under command of Greek Crete Div.). Macedonia; near Doiran.

25th (Reserve) Garrison Battalion T.F.
Formed in Aug. 1916 and was at Falmouth until the end of the war. (Falmouth Garrison).

51st (Graduated) Battalion.
On 27.10.17 the 237th Graduated Bn. (formerly 19th Training Reserve Bn. from 14th Rifle Bde.) at Welbeck in 206th Bde. 69th Div. became the 51st Bn. Jan. 1918 ?Aldershot. Feb. 1918 to 201st Bde. 67th Div. at Ipswich. June 1918 Foxhall Heath, near Ipswich where it remained.

52nd (Graduated) Battalion.
On 27.10.17 the 241st Graduated Bn. (formerly 21st Training Reserve Bn. from 11th East Surrey) at Clipstone in 207th Bde. 69th Div. became 52nd Bn. Feb. 1918 to 202nd Bde. 67th Div. at Colchester where it remained.

53rd (Young Soldier) Battalion.
On 27.10.17 the 18th Young Soldier Bn. of the Training Reserve (formerly 15th K.R.R.C.) at Northampton in 4th Reserve Bde. became the 53rd Bn. No further change.

Infantry Territorial Force

HONOURABLE ARTILLERY COMPANY INFANTRY

1/1st Battalion.
4.8.14 Armoury House, Finsbury, London E.C. Army Troops, attached 1st London Div. 12.9.14 Belhus Park, Aveley, Essex. 20.9.14 landed at St. Nazaire and to L. of C. 10.11.14 to 8th Bde. 3rd Div. 9.12.14 to 7th Bde. 3rd Div. 14.10.15 to G.H.Q. Troops. 9.7.16 to 190th Bde. 63rd Div. 29.6.17 to G.H.Q. Troops. 26.9.18 to 4th Guards Bde. which was in Cavalry Corps. 25.10.18 to G.H.Q. Troops. 11.11.18 France; Ecuires, south of Montreuil.

2/1st Battalion.
Formed at Finsbury 2.9.14. To Belhus Park, Aveley, Essex. Nov. 1914 Blackheath. Feb. 1915 Tower of London. Aug. 1915 Richmond Park. Nov. 1915 Wimbledon in billets. Jan. 1916 Orpington. July 1916 Tadworth, Surrey. Sept. 1916 Tower of London. 3.10.16 landed at Havre and to 22nd Bde. 7th Div. at Steenwerck. 20.11.17 entrained for Italy and arrived Legnago on 25 Nov. 4.11.18 22nd Bde. 7th Div. Italy, west of Udine.

3/1st Battalion.
Formed at Walton-on-Thames Dec. 1914. May 1915 Richmond Park. Nov. 1915 Richmond in billets. Mar. 1916 Blackheath. 8.4.16 became 1st Reserve Bn. May 1916 Richmond Park. 1.9.16 in 1st London Reserve Bde. T.F. Oct. 1916 Tower of London under London District where it remained.

THE MONMOUTHSHIRE REGIMENT

1/1st Battalion.
4.8.14 Stow Hill, Newport: Welsh Border Bde. Welsh Div. To Pembroke Dock. 10.8.14 Oswestry. End Aug. Northampton. Dec. 1914 Bury St. Edmunds. Jan. 1915 Cambridge. Feb. 1915 left Welsh Div. and landed in France on 13 Feb. To 84th Bde. 28th Div. 27.5.15 amalgamated with 1/2nd and 1/3rd Bns. in 84th Bde. 11.8.15 resumed identity. 3.9.15 to 46th Div. as Pioneer Bn. 11.11.18 Pioneer Bn. 46th Div. France, S.W. of Avesnes.

1/2nd Battalion.
4.8.14 Osborne Road, Pontypool: Welsh Border Bde. Welsh Div. To Pembroke Dock. 10.8.14 Osestry. End Aug. Northampton. Nov. 1914 left Welsh Div. and landed at Havre 7.11.14. 20 Nov. to 12th Bde. 4th Div. at Le Bizet. 27.5.15 amalgamated with 1/1st and 1/3rd Bns. at Vlamertinghe in 84th Bde. 28th Div. 24.7.15 resumed identity and rejoined 12th Bde. 4th Div. 30.1.16 to L. of C. 1.5.16 to 29th Div. as Pioneer Bn. 11.11.18 Pioneer Bn. 29th Div. Belgium; Celles, west of Renaix.

1/3rd Battalion.
4.8.14 Abergavenny: Welsh Border Bde. Welsh Div. To Pembroke Dock. 10.8.14 Oswestry. End Aug. Northampton. Dec. 1914 Bury St. Edmunds. Jan. 1915 Cambridge. Feb. 1915 left Welsh Div. and landed in France 14 Feb. 3.3.15 to 83rd Bde. 28th Div. 27.5.15 amalgamated with 1/1st and 1/2nd Bns. at Vlamertinghe in 84th Bde. 28th Div. 11.8.15 resumed identity and rejoined 83rd Bde. 2.9.15 to 49th Div. and became Pioneer Bn. on 18.9.15. 9.8.16 to G.H.Q. Troops. 31.8.16 broken up and personnel posted to 1/1st and 1/2nd Bns.

2/1st Battalion.
Formed at Newport Sept. 1914. 20.2.15 to Welsh Border Bde. Welsh Div. at Cambridge. 19.4.15 to 205th Bde. 68th Div. at Northampton. July 1915 Bedford. Nov. 1916 Lowestoft. Spring 1917 Herringfleet. Autumn 1917 Lowestoft. Early 1918 left 68th Div. and was disbanded on 31.3.18.

2/2nd Battalion.
Formed at Pontypool Sept. 1914. Nov. 1914 to Northampton in Welsh Border Bde. Welsh Div. Dec. 1914 Cambridge. April 1915 to 205th Bde. 68th Div. at Northampton. Subsequent record same as 2/1st Bn. Disbanded on 20.4.18.

2/3rd Battalion.
Formed at Abergavenny Sept. 1914. Feb. 1915 to Welsh Border Bde. Welsh Div. at Cambridge. April 1915 to 205th Bde. 68th Div. at Northampton. July 1915 Bedford. Nov. 1916 Lowestoft. Spring 1917 Herringfleet. Aug. 1917 disbanded and absorbed in 2/1st and 2/2nd Bns.

3/1st, 3/2nd and 3/3rd Battalions.
Formed at home stations Feb. 1915. All to Abergavenny. Sept. 1915 Oswestry. 8.4.16 became Reserve Bns. 1.9.16 1st Bn. absorbed 2nd and 3rd in Welsh Reserve Bde. T.F. Summer 1917 Gobowen. 10.7.17 absorbed 1st Reserve Brecknock Bn. Mar. 1918 Kinmel. July 1918 Herne Bay and remained here.

4th Battalion.
On 1.1.17 the 48th Provisional Bn. at Cromer in 224th Bde. became 4th Bn. The 48th Provisional Bn. had been formed in June 1915 from Home Service personnel of Monmouth and Hereford Bns. Summer 1917 Mundesley. May 1918 Happisburgh, Norfolk where it remained in 224th Bde.

THE CAMBRIDGESHIRE REGIMENT

1/1st Battalion.
4.8.14 14 Corn Exchange Street, Cambridge: East Midland Bde. East Anglian Div. To Romford then Long Melford to Bury St. Edmunds. Sept. 1914 Stowlangtoft, near Bury. Nov. 1914 Bury St. Edmunds. Feb. 1915 left East Anglian Div. and went to France, landing at Havre 15 Feb. To 82nd Bde. 27th Div. 15.11.15 to VII Corps Troops and then Training Bn. for 3rd Army School at Flixecourt. 29.2.16 to 118th Bde. 39th Div. 9.5.18 to 35th Bde. 12th Div. and adsorbed 11 officers and 408 men from 7th Suffolk which was reduced to cadre. 11.11.18 35th Bde. 12th Div. France; Hergnies, N.E. of St. Amand.

2/1st Battalion.
Formed at Cambridge Sept. 1914. Dec. 1914 to Peterborough in 207th Bde. 69th Div. Feb. 1915 to Bury St. Edmunds taking place of 1/1st Bn. in East Midland Bde. East Anglian Div. April 1915 rejoined 207th Bde. at Peterborough. June 1915 Newmarket. Nov. 1915 formed 4/1st Bn. which went to 208th Bde. 69th Div. June 1916 Harrogate. Oct. 1916 Marton Hall, nr. Middlesbrough. May 1917 Carburton, near Ollerton. 8.10.17 to 200th Bde. 67th Div. at Canterbury. Disbanded in Mar. 1918.

3/1st Battalion.

Formed at Cambridge Feb. 1915. Aug. 1915 Windsor. Oct. 1915 Halton Park, Tring. 8.4.16 became 1st (Reserve) Bn. 1.9.16 in East Anglian Reserve Bde. T.F. at Halton Park. 23.7.17 combined with 4th (Reserve) Bn. Suffolk Regt. to form Cambridge and Suffolk Reserve Bn. Aug. 1917 Crowborough. About Aug. 1918 to Hastings.

4/1st Battalion.
Formed at Newmarket Nov. 1915 by 2/1st Bn. and went to 208th Bde. 69th Div. at Bury St. Edmunds. June 1916 Harrogate. Oct. 1916 Doncaster. May 1917 Thoresby, near Ollerton. Oct. 1917 disbanded.

THE LONDON REGIMENT

1/1st (City of London) Battalion (Royal Fusiliers). 4.8.14 Handel Street, Bloomsbury, W.C.: 1st London Bde. 1st London Div. 4 Aug. to war station guarding railway from London to Newhaven. 4.9.14 sailed from Southampton with 1st London Bde. for Malta arriving on 14 Sept. 11.2.15 left Malta for U.K. arriving Avonmouth 21 Feb. 11.3.15 landed at Havre and to 25th Bde. 8th Div. 8.2.16 to 167th Bde. 56th Div., forming in Hallencourt area. 6.2.18 absorbed disbanded 2/1st Bn. and became 1st Bn. 11.11.18 167th Bde. 56th Div. Belgium; Harveng, south of Mons.

1/2nd (City of London) Battalion. (Royal Fusiliers). 4.8.14 9 Tufton Street, Westminster, S.W.; 1st London Bde. 1st London Div. 4 Aug. to war station guarding railway from Southampton Docks to Amesbury. 4.9.14 sailed from Southampton with 1st London Bde. for Malta arriving on 14 Sept. 2.1.15 sailed from Malta for France arriving Marseilles 6 Jan. 21.2.15 to 17th Bde. 6th Div. at Armentieres. 14.10.15 17th Bde. to 24th Div. 9.2.16 to 169th Bde. 56th Div., forming in Hallencourt area. 11.11.18 169th Bde. 56th Div. Belgium; Athis, north of Bavai.

1/3rd (City of London) Battalion. (Royal Fusiliers). 4.8.14 21 Edward Street, Hampstead Road, N.W.; 1st London Bde. 1st London Div. 4 Aug. to war station guarding railway Basingstoke to Eastleigh. 4.9.14 to Malta and record same as 1/2nd Bn. to Jan. 1915. 10.2.15 to Garwhal Bde. Meerut Div. 17.2.15 to Dehra Dun Bde. Meerut Div. 4.11.15 to 139th Bde. 46th Div. 16.11.15 to 142nd Bde. 47th Div. 9.2.16 to 167th Bde. 56th Div., forming in Hallencourt area. 31.1.18 to 173rd Bde. 58th Div. and absorbed 2/3rd Bn. becoming 3RD BN. 11.11.18 173rd Bde. 58th Div. Belgium; near Peruwelz, S.E. of Tournai.

1/4th (City of London) Battalion. (Royal Fusiliers). 4.8.14 112 Shaftesbury Street, City Road, N.: 1st London Bde. 1st London Div. 4 Aug. to war station guarding railway from Waterloo to Basingstoke. 4.9.14 to Malta and record same as 1/2nd Bn. to Jan. 1915. 20.2.15 to Ferozepore Bde. Lahore Div. 11.11.15 to 137th Bde. 46th Div. 15.11.15 to 140th Bde. 47th Div. 9.2.16 to 168th Bde. 56th Div., forming in Hallencourt area. 11.11.18 168th Bde. 56th Div. Belgium; Sars-la-Bruyere, north of Mons.

1/5th (City of London) Battalion. (London Rifle Bridgade). 4.8.14 130 Bunhill Row, E.C.: 2nd London Bde. 1st London Div. End Aug. Bisley. Sept. Crowborough. Nov. left division and landed at Havre 5.11.14. 17.11.14 to 11th Bde. 4th Div. at Bailleul. 19.5.15 to G.H.Q. and formed a composite bn. with 1/12th and 1/13 Bns. until 11 Aug. 25.10.15 to 8th Bde. 3rd Div. 10.2.16 to 169th Bde. 56th Div., forming in Hallencourt area. 11.11.18 169th Bde. 56th Div. Belgium; Erquennes, N.E. of Bavai.

1/6th (City of London) Battalion. (Rifles). 4.8.14 57a Farringdon Road, E.C.: 2nd London Bde. 1st London Div. Mid Aug. Bisley. Sept. Crowborough. 5.11.14 to 4th London Bde. 2nd London Div. at Watford. 18.3.15 landed at Havre. 11.5.15 formation became 140th Bde. 47th Div. 31.1.18 to 174th 58th Div. absorbing 2/6th Bn. and becoming 6TH BN. 11.11.18 174th Bde. 58th Div. Belgium; Beloeil, south of Ath.

1/7th (City of London) Battalion. 4.8.14 24 Sun Street, Finsbury Square, E.C.: 2nd London Bde. 1st London Div. Mid Aug. Bisley. Sept. Crowborough. 5.11.14 to 4th London Bde. 2nd London Div. at Watford. 18.3.15 landed at Havre. 11.5.15 formation became 140th Bde. 47th Div. 2.2.18 to 174th 58th Div. absorbing 2/7th Bn. and becoming 7TH BN. 11.11.18 174th Bde. 58th Div. Belgium; Grosage, south of Ath.

1/8th (City of London) Battalion. (Post Office Rifles). 4.8.14 130 Bunhill Row, E.C.: 2nd London Bde. 1st London Div. Mid Aug. Bisley. Sept. Crowborough. 6.11.14 to 4th London Bde. 2nd London Div. at Abbot's Langley, near Watford. 18.3.15 landed at Havre. 11.5.15 formation became 140th Bde. 47th Div. 2.2.18 to 174th Bde. 58th Div. absorbing 2/8th Bn. and becoming 8TH BN. 11.11.18 174th Bde. 58th Div. Belgium; Waudignies, south of Ath.

1/9th (County of London) Battalion. (Queen Victoria's Rifles).
4.8.14 56 Davies Street, Berkeley Square, W.: 3rd London Bde. 1st London Div. Mid Aug. Bullswater, near Pirbright. Sept. Crowborough. Nov. 1914 left 2nd London Div. and landed at Havre 5.11.14. 27.11.14 to 13th Bde. 5th Div. 10.2.16 to 169th Bde. 56th Div., forming in Hallencourt area. 1.2.18 to 175th Bde. 58th Div. absorbing 2/9th Bn. and becoming 9TH BN. 11.11.18 175th Bde. 58th Div. Belgium; Peruwelz, S.E. of Tournai.

1/10th (County of London) Battalion. (Hackney). 4.8.14 49 The Grove, Hackney, N.E.: 3rd London Bde. 1st London Div. Mid Aug. to Bullswater, near Pirbright. Sept. to Crowborough. April 1915 to East Midland Bde. East Anglian Div. at Norwich. 7.5.15 formation became 162nd Bde. 54th Div. and in May to St. Albans. End July 1915 sailed from Plymouth for Mudros. 11.8.15 landed at Suvla Bay. Dec. 1915 left Gallipoli and went to Egypt. 31.10.18 162nd Bde. 54th Div. Palestine; Beirut.

1/11th (County of London) Battalion. (Finsbury Rifles). 4.8.14 17 Penton Street, Pentonville, N.: 3rd London Bde. 1st London Div. Record same as 1/10th Bn.

1/12th (County of London) Battalion. (The Rangers). 4.8.14 Chenies Street, Bedford Square, W.C.: 3rd London Bde. 1st London Div. Mid Aug. Bullswater, near Pirbright. Sept. Crowborough. Oct. guarding railway from Waterloo to North Camp. Dec. Roehampton. Dec. 1914 left 1st London Div. and landed at Havre 25 Dec. to L. of C. 8.2.15 to 84th Bde. 28th Div. 20.5.15 to G.H.Q. Troops and formed a composite bn. with 1/5th and 1/13th Bns. until 11.8.15. 12.2.16 to 168th Bde. 56th Div. forming in Hallencourt area. 31.1.18 to 175th Bde. 58th Div. absorbing 2/12th Bn. and becoming 12TH BN. 11.11.18 175th Bde. 58th Div. Belgium; Peruwelz area, S.E. of Tournai.

1/13th (County of London) Battalion. (Kensington). (Army Order 408 of October 1914 changed the title to "13th (County of London) Princess Louise's Kensington Battalion").
4.8.14 Iverna Gardens, Kensington, W.: 4th London Bde. 2nd London Div. Aug. Abbots Langley, Herts. Nov. 1914 left 2nd London Div. and went to France landing at Havre on 4.11.14. 13.11.14 to 25th Bde. 8th Div. 20.5.15 to G.H.Q. Troops and until 11.8.15 formed a composite bn. with 1/5th and 1/12th Bns. for work on the L. of C. 11.2.16 to 168th Bde. 56th Div. forming in Hallencourt

area. 11.11.18 168th Bde. 56th Div. Belgium; Blaregnies, north of Maubeuge.

1/14th (County of London) Battalion. (London Scottish).
4.8.14 59 Buckingham Gate, Westminster, S.W.: 4th London Bde. 2nd London Div. Aug. Abbots Langley, Herts. Sept. 1914 left 2nd London Div. and went to France landing at Havre 16.9.14. To G.H.Q. Troops. 31.10.14 and early Nov. engaged at Messines and Ypres under Cavalry Corps. 7.11.14 to 1st Bde. 1st Div. 8.2.16 to 168th Bde. 56th Div. forming in Hallencourt area. 11.11.18 168th Bde. 56th Div. Belgium: La Dessous, near Blaregnies, north of Maubeuge.

1/15th (County of London) Battalion. (Prince of Wales's Own Civil Service Rifles).
4.8.14 Somerset House, Strand, W.C.: 4th London Bde. 2nd London Div. Aug. Bedmond, near Hemel Hempstead. Nov. 1914 billeted in Watford. 18.3.15 landed at Havre. 11.5.15 formation became 140th Bde. 47th Div. 11.11.18 140th Bde. 47th Div. Belgium; Tournai.

1/16th (County of London) Battalion. (Queen's Westminster Rifles).
4.8.14 Queen's Hall, 58 Buckingham Gate, Westminster, S.W.: 4th London Bde. 2nd London Div. Aug. Hemel Hempstead area. Nov. 1914 left 2nd London Div. and went to France landing at Havre 3 Nov. 12.11.14 to 18th Bde. 6th Div. 10.2.16 to 169th Bde. 56th Div. forming in Hallencourt area. 11.11.18 169th Bde. 56th Div. Belgium; Athis, north of Bavai.

1/17th (County of London) Battalion. (Poplar and Stepney Rifles).
4.8.14 66 Tredegar Road, Bow, E.: 5th London Bde. 2nd London Div. Aug. to St. Albans area. 16.3.15 landed at Havre. 11.5.15 formation became 141st Bde. 47th Div. 1.2.18 to 140th Bde. 47th Div. 11.11.18 140th Bde. 47th Div. Belgium; Tournai.

1/18th (County of London) Battalion. (London Irish Rifles).
4.8.14 Duke of York's Headquarters, Chelsea, S.W.: 5th London Bde. 2nd London Div. Aug. to St. Albans area. Mar. 1915 landed at Havre. 11.5.15 formation became 141st Bde. 47th Div. 11.11.18 141st Bde. 47th Div. Belgium; Tournai.

1/19th (County of London) Battalion. (St. Pancras).
4.8.14 76 High Street, Camden Town, N.W.: 5th London Bde. 2nd London Div. Record same as 1/18th Battalion.

1/20th (County of London) Battalion. (Blackheath and Woolwich).
4.8.14 Holly Hedge House, Blackheath, S.E.: 5th London Bde. 2nd London Div. Record same as 1/18th Battalion.

1/21st (County of London) Battalion. (First Surrey Rifles).
4.8.14 4, Flodden Road, Camberwell, S.E.: 6th London Bde. 2nd London Div. Aug. St. Albans area. 16.3.15 landed at Havre. 11.5.15 formation became 142nd Bde. 47th Div. 1.2.18 to 140th Bde. 47th Div. 11.11.18 140th Bde. 47th Div. Belgium; Tournai.

1/22nd (County of London) Battalion. (The Queen's).
4.8.12 2, Jamaica Road, Bermondsey, S.E.: 6th London Bde. 2nd London Div. Aug. St. Albans area. 16.3.15 landed at Havre. 11.5.15 formation became 142nd Bde. 47th Div. 11.11.18 142nd Bde. 47th Div. Belgium; Bizancourt, north of Tournai.

1/23rd (County of London) Battalion.
4.8.14 27, St. John's Hill, Clapham Junction, S.W.: 6th London Bde. 2nd London Div. Record similar to 1/22nd Bn. but on 11.11.18 at Kain, north of Tournai.

1/24th (County of London) Battalion. (The Queen's).
4.8.14 71, New Street, Kennington Park Road, S.E.: 6th London Bde. 2nd London Div. Record similar to 1/22nd Bn. but on 11.11.18 near Kain, north of Tournai.

1/25th (County of London) Cyclist Battalion.
4.8.14 Fulham House, Putney Bridge, S.W.: London District. 5 Aug. to war station on Kent and Sussex coast. 10 Aug. to Suffolk coast with H.Q. at Oulton Broad and in Jan. 1915 at Lowestoft. 2.12.15 to Chiseldon and re-organized as an infantry bn. 3.2.16 sailed from Devonport for India, arriving Bombay 25 Feb. Remained in India. (see 1/9th Hants. page 79).

1/28th (County of London) Battalion. (Artists Rifles).
4.8.14 Duke's Road, Euston Road, W.C. Army Troops attached 2nd London Div. Aug. to St. Albans area. Oct. 1914 left 2nd London Div. and landed in France 28.10.14. Became an Officers Training Corps at Bailleul and in April 1915 at St. Omer. 28.6.17 to 190th Bde. 63rd Div. 11.11.18 190th Bde. 63rd Div. Belgium; near Harmignies, S.E. of Mons.

2/1st (City of London) Battalion. (Royal Fusiliers).
Formed in London about Sept. 1914. By Dec. 1914 in Kent in 2/1st London Bde. 2/1st London Div. Feb. 1915 went to Malta landing 11 Feb. and relieved 1/1st Bn. 27.8.15 left for Alexandria. 25.9.15 landed at Suvla and attached to 88th Bde. 29th Div. Jan. 1916 to Egypt and attached to 53rd Div. April 1916 to France landing Marseilles on 24 April. To Rouen and disbanded by June (3/1st Bn. now became the 2/1st Bn.).

2/2nd (City of London) Battalion. (Royal Fusiliers).
Formed in London about Sept. 1914. Epsom Downs and Dec. 1914 to Tonbridge in 2/1st London Bde. 2/1st London Div. 23.12.14 sailed for Malta, arriving 31 Dec. and relieved 1/2nd Bn. 27.8.15 left for Alexandria. 13.10.15 landed at Helles and attached to 2nd Bde. Royal Naval Div. Jan. 1916 left Gallipoli and arrived Egypt 21 Jan. and attached to 53rd Div. April 1916 to France, arriving Marseilles on 24 April. To Rouen and Disbanded by June 1916 (3/2nd Bn. now became the 2/2nd Bn.).

2/3rd (City of London) Battalion. (Royal Fusiliers).
Formed in London about Sept. 1914. By Dec. 1914 in Kent 2/1st London Bde. 2/1st London Div. 23.12.14 sailed for Malta, arriving 31 Dec. and relieved 1/3rd Bn. Subsequent record similar to 2/1st Bn. but attached to 86th Bde. 29th Div. at Gallipoli. Disbanded by June 1916 3/3rd Bn. now became 2/3rd).

2/4th (City of London) Batatlion. (Royal Fusiliers).
Formed in London Sept. 1914. To New Barnet. Dec. 1914 Maidstone in 2/1st London Bde. 2/1st London Div. 23.12.14 left Southampton for Malta, arriving 31 Dec. relieving 1/4th Bn. 20–25 Aug. 1915 to Alexandria. 12.10.15 Mudros. 15.10.15 landed at Helles and attached to 1st Bde. Royal Naval Div. Jan. 1916 to Egypt and attached to 53rd Div. 16 to 24 April 1916 Alexandria to Marseilles, then to Rouen and disbanded by June 1916. (3/4th Bn. now became 2/4th).

2/5th (City of London) Battalion. (London Rifle Brigade).
Formed in London Sept. 1914 Nov. Haywards Heath in 174th Bde. 58th Div. May 1915 Norwich. June 1915 Ipswich. April 1916 Foxhall Heath, near Ipswich. July 1916 Sutton Veny. 25.1.17 landed at Havre. 6.2.18 disbanded at Moreuil.

2/6th (City of London) Battalion (Rifles).
Formed Aug. 1914 at Farringdon Road E.C. Oct. Walton-on-Thames. Nov. 1914 Burgess Hill in 174th Bde. 58th Div. May 1915 Norwich. June 1915 Ipswich. Oct. 1915 Stowmarket. Jan. 1916 Sudbury. April 1916 Foxhall Heath. July 1916 Sutton Veny. 25.1.17 landed at Havre. 31.1.18 absorbed by 1/6th Bn. which became 6th Bn.

2/7th (City of London) Battalion.
Formed in London Sept. 1914. Nov. 1914 Burgess Hill in 174th Bde. 58th Div. Subsequent record similar to 2/6th

Bn. and absorbed by 2/7th Bn. at Domart on 6.2.18 which became 7th Bn.

2/8th (City of London) Battalion. (Post Office Rifles).
Formed in London Sept. 1914. Nov. 1914 Cuckfield in 174th Bde. 58th Div. Subsequent record similar to 2/6th Bn. and absorbed by 1/8th Bn. on 6.2.18 which became 8th Bn.

2/9th (County of London) Battalion. (Queen Victoria's Rifles).
Formed in London Aug. 1914. Nov. 1914 Crowborough in 175th Bde. 58th Div. June 1915 Ipswich. May 1916 Bromeswell Heath, near Woodbridge. July 1916 Longbridge Deverell. 4.2.17 landed at Havre. 6.2.18 absorbed by 1/9th Bn. which became 9th Bn.

2/10th (County of London) Battalion. (Hackney).
Formed in London Sept. 1914. Record same as 2/9th Bn. until Feb. 1918. It was not disbanded and on 11.11.18 175th Bde. 58th Div. Belgium; Peruwelz area.

2/11th (County of London) Battalion. (Finsbury Rifles).
Formed in London Sept. 1914. Record similar to 2/9th Bn. until 6.2.18 when it was disbanded.

2/12th (County of London) Battalion. (The Rangers).
Formed in London Sept. 1914. Record similar to 2/9th Bn. until 6.2.18 when it was absorbed by 1/12th Bn., which became 12th Bn.

2/13th (County of London) Battalion. (Kensington).
Formed in London in Sept. 1914. Nov. at White City. Jan. 1915 Maidstone in 179th Bde. 60th Div. then to billets in London and Leatherhead. April 1915 Watford. June 1915 Saffron Walden. Jan. 1916 Sutton Veny. 28.4.16 crossed from Pembroke to Cork in H.M.S. Snowdon for security duty in Ireland after the rebellion. At Ballincollig and Macroom. 14.5.16 Rosslare to Fishguard and back to Sutton Veny. 22.6.16 landed at Havre. Nov. 1916 to Salonika, arriving 30 Nov. 2/5.7.17 Salonika to Alexandria. 31.10.18 179th Bde. 60th Div. Palestine; Jaffa. (For change in designation in Oct. 1914 see note under 1/13th Bn.).

2/14th (County of London) Battalion. (London Scottish).
Formed in London Sept. 1914. In London. Jan. 1915 Dorking in 179th Bde. 60th Div. Feb. 1915 billets in London. Mar. 1915 Watford. May 1915 Saffron Walden. Oct. 1915 Bishops Stortford. Jan. 1916 Sutton Veny. 28.4.16 to Ireland with 179th Bde. for security duty after the rebellion. 12.5.16 Rosslare to Fishguard and returned to Sutton Veny. 22.6.16 landed at Havre. 23.11.16 left Marseilles for Salonika, arriving 29 Nov. 30.6.17 Salonika to Alexandria on 3 July. 30.5.18 left 60th Div. and went to France via Taranto. 22.6.18 Audruicq. 2.7.18 to 90th Bde. 30th Div. 11.11.18 90th Bde. 30th Div. Belgium; Avelghem, S.E. of Courtrai.

2/15th (County of London) Battalion. (Prince of Wales's Own Civil Service Rifles).
Formed at Somerset House Sept. 1914. In London. Jan. 1915 Dorking in 179th Bde. 60th Div. Mar. 1915 Watford. June 1915 Saffron Walden. Jan. 1916 Longbridge Deverill. 30.4.16 to Ireland with 179th Bde. for security duty after the rebellion. To Ballincollig and Macroom. 12.5.16 Rosslare to Fishguard and back to Longbridge Deverill. 23.6.16 landed at Havre. 19 to 30.11.16 Marseilles to Salonika. June 1917 to Egypt. 30.5.18 left 60th Div. and went to France via Taranto (22 June) and arrived Audruicq 1.7.18. To 90th Bde. 30th Div. 11.11.18 90th Bde. 30th Div. Belgium; Heestert, S.E. of Courtrai.

2/16th (County of London) Battalion. (Queen's Westminster Rifles).
Formed in London Sept. 1914. Jan. 1915 Maidstone in 179th Bde. 60th Div. Subsequent record similar to 2/14th Bn.

2/17th (County of London) Battalion. (Poplar and Stepney Rifles).
Formed in London Aug. 1914. Jan. 1915 Reigate in 180th Bde. 60th Div. Mar. 1915 St. Albans area. May 1915 Bishops Stortford. Jan. 1916 Sutton Veny. 23.6.16 landed at Havre. Nov. 1916 to Salonika. June 1917 to Egypt. 27.5.18 left 60th Div. and went to France via Taranto (22 June). 30.6.18 Audruicq and to 89th Bde. 30th Div. at Ouest Mont, near Eperlecques. 11.11.18 89th Bde. 30th Div. Belgium; Flobecq, east of Renaix.

2/18th (County of London) Battalion. (London Irish Rifles).
Formed in London Aug. 1914. Record similar to 2/17th Bn. until May 1918 when it remained in 60th Div. 7.7.18 disbanded in Palestine, personnel to 1st Royal Irish Regt., 2nd Royal Irish Fusiliers and 1st Leinsters in 10th Div.

2/19th (County of London) Battalion (St. Pancras).
Formed in London Sept. 1914. Oct. White City. Jan. 1915 Reigate in 180th Bde. 60th Div. Mar. 1915 St. Albans. May 1915 Coggeshall. July 1915 Hatfield Broad Oak. Oct. 1915 Saffron Walden. Dec. Hertford. Jan. 1916 Sutton Veny. 24.6.16 landed at Havre. 25.11.16 left Marseilles for Salonika, arriving 1 Dec. 10-12 June 1917 Salonika to Alexandria. 31.10.18 180th Bde. 60th Div. Palestine; Sheik Muwannis, north of Jaffa.

2/20th (County of London) Battalion. (Blackheath and Woolwich).
Formed in London 3 Sept. 1914 Record similar to 2/19th Bn. until May 1918. Then left 60th Div. for France via Taranto (30 June). 17.7.18 attached 198th Bde. 66th Div. at Abancourt. 9.8.18 to 185th Bde. 62nd Div. at Thievres. 11.11.18 185th Bde. 62nd Div. France; Montplaisir, S.W. of Maubeuge.

2/21st (County of London) Battalion. (First Surrey Rifles).
Formed in Camberwell Aug. 1914. Jan. 1915 Redhill in 181st Bde. 60th Div. Mar. 1915 St. Albans area. May 1915 Braintree. Jan. 1916 Sutton Veny. June 1916 landed at Havre. Nov. 1916 to Salonika. June 1917 to Egypt. 3.6.18 disbanded in Palestine; personnel to 2/13th, 2/19th and 2/22nd Bns.

2/22nd (County of London) Battalion. (The Queen's).
Formed in Bermondsey Aug. 1914. Record same as 2/21st Bn. until May 1918 and then remained in 60th Div. 31.10.18 181st Bde. 50th Div. Palestine, near Jaffa.

2/23rd (County of London) Battalion.
Formed in Clapham Junction Aug. 1914. White City. Jan. 1915 Horley in 181st Bde. 60th Div. Oct. 1915 Braintree. Jan. 1916 Sutton Veny. 26.6.16 landed at Havre. Nov. 1916 to Salonika. June 1917 to Egypt. 26.5.18 left 60th Div. and went to France. Alexandria 24 June to Taranto 30 June. 8.7.18 Arques. To 21st Bde. 30th Div. 11.11.18 21st Bde. 30th Div. Belgium; Ellezelles area, east of Renaix.

2/24th (County of London) Battalion. (The Queen's).
Formed in Lambeth Aug. 1914. Oct. White City. Jan. 1915 Horley or Redhill in 181st Bde. 60th Div. Mar. 1915 St. Albans area. May 1915 Braintree. Jan. 1916 Sutton Veny. 26.6.16 landed at Havre. Nov. 1916 to Salonika. Jan. 1917 to Egypt. 26.5.18 left 60th Div. and went to France. Alexandria to Taranto 3-8 July. At Serqueux 15.7.18 and to 198th Bde. 66th Div. at Abancourt. 11.9.18 to 173rd Bde. 58th Div. at Guyencourt. 11.11.18 173rd Bde. 58th Div. Belgium; near Peruwelz, S.E. of Tournai.

2/25th (County of London) Cyclist Battalion.
Formed at Fulham 31.8.14. Nov. 1914 to coast defence in Sussex, attached 1st London Div. Bn. H.Q. at Lewes. April 1915 to coast defence in Norfolk with H.Q. at Holt; attached to 1st Mounted Div. April 1916 Bungay. Oct. 1916 Halesworth. Summer 1917 Saxmundham, attached

68th Div. To Peasenhall for the winter. Mar. 1918 Saxmundham attached 227th Bde. Aug. 1918 Wickham Market and by Nov. 1918 at Rendlesham still attached to 227th Bde.

2/28th (County of London). Battalion (Artists Rifles).
Formed in London Aug. 1914. Later to Richmond Park. July 1915 to High Beech in Epping Forest. In Nov. 1915 the 1/28th Bn. in France was recognised as an Officers Training Corps (Army Order 429 of 1915) and absorbed the 2/28th Bn. The 3rd line now became the 2/28th Bn. and by Mar. 1916 was at Hare Hall, Romford: it now became No. 15 Officer Cadet Bn. and remained at Romford. During the war 10,256 officers were commissioned after training with the Artists Rifles. They went to the Foot Guards, every Infantry Regiment and most of the other arms. The Royal Artillery alone had 953 officers and the London Regiment 783 officers from the Artists Rifles. (In June 1917 the 1/28th Bn. in France left G.H.Q. and joined 190th Bde. 63rd Div. on 28 June).

3/1st Battalion.
Formed Jan. 1915. April 1915 Tadworth in 3/1st London Bde. End May 1915 Bury St. Edmunds in 173rd Bde. 58th Div. June 1915 Ipswich. June 1916 became 2/1ST BN., after disbandment of original 2/1st Bn. in France. July 1916 Sutton Veny. Jan. 1917 landed at Havre. 6.2.18 disbanded in France, personnel to 2/2nd, 2/3rd, 2/4th and 1/4th Bns.

3/2nd Battalion.
Formed at Tottenham Corner, Epsom, Dec. 1914. April 1915 Tadworth in 3/1st London Bde. May 1915 Bury St. Edmunds in 173rd Bde. 58th Div. June 1915 Ipswich. June 1916 became 2/2ND BN., after disbandment of original 2/2nd Bn. in France. July 1916 Sutton Veny. 22.1.17 landed at Havre. 11.11.18 173rd Bde. 58th Div. Belgium, near Peruwelz, S.E. of Tournai.

3/3rd Battalion.
Formed Jan. 1915. Record similar to 3/2nd Bn. until 6.2.18 when it was disbanded and absorbed by 1/3rd from 56th Div. and then became 3RD BN. June 1916 became 2/3rd Bn.

3/4th Battalion.
Formed in Hoxton. Jan. 1915 Barnet. April 1915 Tadworth in 3/1st London Bde. Subsequent record similar to 3/2nd Bn. June 1916 became 2/4TH BN., after disbandment of original 2/4th Bn. in France. 24.1.17 landed at Havre. 12.9.18 disbanded in France, personnel to 2/2nd Bn.

3/5th Battalion.
Formed at Bunhill Row 26.11.14. April 1915 Tadworth. Oct. 1915 Sutton in billets. Jan. 1916 Fovant. 8.4.16 became 5th (Reserve) Bn. 1.9.16 in 1st London Reserve Bde. T.F. Nov. 1916 Exeter. Dec. 1916 Dawlish. April 1917 to Blackdown, Aldershot where it remained.

3/6th, 3/7th and 3/8th Battalions.
Formed early in 1915. April 1915 Tadworth. Oct. 1915 to Surbiton, Orpington and Blackheath in billets. Jan. 1916 to Fovant. 8.4.16 became Reserve Bns. 1.9.16 in 1st London Reserve Bde. T.F. Autumn 1916 to Newton Abbot, Dartmouth and Paignton. April 1917 to Blackdown, near Aldershot where it remained.

3/9th, 3/11th and 3/12th Battalions.
Formed early in 1915. April 1915 Tadworth. Oct. 1915 to Richmond, Sutton and East Sheen in billets. Jan. 1916 Fovant. 8.4.16 became Reserve Bns. 1.9.16 9th Reserve Bn. absorbed 11th and 12th Bns. in 1st London Reserve Bde. T.F. Autumn 1916 Exeter. About April 1917 to Deepcut, Aldershot where it remained.

3/10th Battalion.
Formed April 1915. Tadworth. Autumn 1915 Sutton. Jan. 1916 Fovant. 8.4.16 became 10th Reserve Bn. 1.9.16 absorbed 25th Reserve Cyclist Bn. in 1st London Reserve Bde. T.F. Autumn 1916 to Teignmouth. April 1917 Frith Hill, Aldershot where it remained.

3/13th Battalion.
Formed Dec. 1914. Richmond Park. Autumn 1915 Reigate. Jan. 1916 Winchester. 8.4.16 became 13th Reserve Bn. 1.9.16 in 2nd London Reserve Bde. T.F. (?) Reigate. July 1917 Richmond Park. About Jan. 1918 to 3rd London Reserve Bde. T.F. and was at Wimbledon or Orpington until Nov. 1918.

3/14th Battalion.
Formed Nov. 1914. Richmond Park. Autumn (?) East Sheen. Jan. 1916 Winchester. 8.4.16 became 14th Reserve Bn. 1.9.16 in 2nd London Reserve Bde. T.F. About Jan. 1918 to Chiseldon. By Aug. 1918 at Flixton, near Bungay and by Nov. 1918 at Wisbech.

3/15th, 3/16th and 3/17th Battalions.
Formed early in 1915. Richmond Park. Billets for the winter, 3/15th at Barnes. Jan. 1916 all bns. to Winchester. 8.4.16 became Reserve Bns. 1.9.16 in 2nd London Reserve Bde. Dec. 1917 to Wimbledon and newly formed 3rd London Reserve Bde. T.F. 15th and 16th Bns. remained at Wimbledon but 17th Bn. was at Orpington by Nov. 1918.

3/18th Battalion.
Formed May 1915. Richmond Park. Probably billets for the winter. Jan. 1916 Winchester. 8.4.16 became 18th Reserve Bn. 1.9.16 in 2nd London Reserve Bde. T.F. Nov. 1917 Chiseldon. Aug. 1918 at Flixton, near Bungay and by Nov. 1918 at Heacham, Norfolk.

3/19th and 3/20th Battalions.
Formed Mar. 1915. Richmond Park. Probably billets for the winter. Jan. 1916 Winchester. 8.4.16 became Reserve Bns. 1.9.16 in 2nd London Reserve Bde. T.F. Nov. 1917 Chiseldon. Mar. 1918 19th Bn. to 1st London Reserve Bde. at Blackdown where it remained. 20th Bn. went from Chiseldon to Flixton, near Bungay by Aug. 1918 and by Nov. 1918 was at March.

3/21st and 3/23rd Battalions.
Formed Mar. 1915. Tadworth. Billets for the winter. Jan. 1916 Winchester. 8.4.16 became Reserve Bns. 1.9.16 21st Bn. absorbed 23rd Bn. in 2nd London Reserve Bde. T.F. Nov. 1917 Chiseldon. July 1918 Benacre Park. Oct. 1918 Hunstanton.

3/22nd and 3/24th Battalions.
Formed Mar. 1915. Tadworth. Billets for the winter. Jan. 1916 to Winchester. 8.4.16 became Reserve Bns. 1.9.16 22nd Bn. absorbed 24th Bn. in 2nd London Reserve Bde. T.F. Nov. 1917 Chiseldon. July 1918 Saxmundham. Oct. 1918 Wells.

3/25th Cyclist Battalion.
Formed at Fulham Mar. 1915. Aug. 1915 to Hanworth. Nov. 1915 Feltham. 8.4.16 became 25th Reserve Cyclist Bn. May 1916 Richmond Park. 1.9.16 absorbed by 10th Reserve Bn.

3/28th Battalion.
Formed Sec. 1914. Richmond Park. Nov. 1915 became 2/28th Bn. (see above).

4/1st, 4/2nd, 4/3rd and 4/4th Battalions.
These fourth line battalions were formed in May 1915 when the third line units became operational and joined the 2/1st London Div. (173rd Bde. 58th Div.) in East Anglia. They were responsible for supplying drafts to the first and second line battalions overseas and the third line in the 58th Div. They were at first at Tadworth. Jan. 1916 to Hurdcott, west of Salisbury. 8.4.16 became reserve bns. 1.9.16 1st Bn. absorbed 2nd Bn. and 3rd Bn. absorbed the

4th in 1st London Reserve Bde. T.F. at Hurdcott. Nov. 1916 to Torquay. April 1917 to Blackdown, Aldershot where they remained.

The formation of a 26th Battalion was approved in A.C.I. 340 of 11 Feb. 1916 to be composed of men from the Dominions and Colonies. It would have two lines, 1/26th and 2/26th. However, on 1 March it was decided that as sufficient recruits had not been obtained the formation of the unit would not be proceeded with (A.C.I. 468 of 1 Mar. 1916).

29th (City of London) Battalion.
On 1.1.17 the 100th Provisional Bn. at Guildford in 212th Bde. 71st Div. became the 29th Bn. It had been formed in June 1915 from Home Service personnel. Mar. 1917 Colchester. Summer 1917 to St. Osyth in 226th Bde. By Jan. 1918 at Clacton where it remained in 226th Bde.

30th (City of London) Battalion.
On 1.1.17 the 101st Provisional Bn. at Guildford in 212th Bde. 71st Div. became the 30th Bn. It had been formed in June 1915 from Home Service personnel. Mar. 1917 Colchester. 5.2.18 to 226th Bde. at Walton-on-the-Naze where it remained.

31st (County of London) Battalion.
On 1.1.17 the 107th Provisional Bn. at Frinton in 226th Bde. became the 31st Bn. It had been formed in June 1915 from Home Service personnel. May 1917 St. Osyth. 7.9.17 disbanded.

32nd (County of London) Battalion.
On 1.1.17 the 108th Provisional Bn. at Frinton in 226th Bde. became the 32nd Bn. It had been formed in June 1915 from Home Service personnel. July 1917 Walton-on-the-Naze. 13.4.18 disbanded.

33rd (City of London) Battalion.
Formed at Clacton early in June 1918. 18.6.18 to Pirbright and absorbed cadre of 7th Bn. Rifle Brigade in 41st Bde. 14th Div. 3.7.18 landed at Boulogne. 11.11.18 41st Bde. 14th Div. France; Le Petit Tournay, N.E. edge of Roubaix.

34th (County of London) Battalion.
Formed at Clacton early in June 1918. 27.6.18 at Aldershot and absorbed cadre of 7th Bn. K.R.R.C. in 49th Bde. 16th Div. 1.8.18 landed at Boulogne. 11.11.18 49th Bde. 16th Div. Belgium; south of Tournai.

NOTES

1. The missing 26th and 27th Battalions:
When the Territorial Force was formed in 1908 the battalion numbers 26th and 27th were allotted to the H.A.C. and Inns of Court. These two historic regiments, both going back over 300 years, were not pleased with their high numbers and were allowed to retain their old titles: so the 26th and 27th Battalions did not exist.

2. The London Reserve Brigades:
1st London Reserve Brigade.
Formed at Fovant on 1.9.16 with 1st, 3rd, 5th, 6th, 7th, 8th, 9th and 10th Reserve Bns. and Reserve Bn. H.A.C. Nov. 1916 to South Devon with H.Q. at Torquay, but H.A.C. went to the Tower of London where they remained. April 1917 to Blackdown, Aldershot. Mar. 1918 19th Reserve Bn. joined the Bde. No further change.

2nd London Reserve Brigade.
Formed at Winchester 1.9.16 with 13th to 22nd Reserve Bns. Jan. 1918 to Chiseldon and 13th, 15th, 16th and 17th Reserve Bns. to new 3rd London Reserve Bde. 19th Reserve Bn. to 1st London Reserve Bde. July 1918 to Bungay area. Oct. 1918 to North Norfolk with H.Q. at Hunstanton.

3rd London Reserve Brigade.
Formed at Wimbledon Jan. 1918 with 13th, 15th, 16th and 17th Reserve Bns. No change.

INNS OF COURT OFFICERS TRAINING CORPS

4.8.14 10 Stone Buildings, Lincoln's Inn, W.C. The unit had an establishment of one squadron of cavalry and three companies of infantry. For the first weeks of the war the unit remained in London and trained at Lincoln's Inn and Temple Gardens with day visits to Regents Park, Wimbledon and Richmond Park. The squadron had no horses. In Sept. the establishment was increased to eight companies—four double companies. On 28 Sept. the unit moved to Berkhamsted. Here it spent the war training officers; there was no lack of recruits who had to be approved by the Corps Selection Committee. The cavalry squadron received their horses in Oct. 1914. In August 1915 the establishment was increased to six double companies.

By early 1916 the strength was well over 3000 and in Feb. four cadet companies were formed and on 5.9.16 these companies were formed into No. 14 Officer Cadet Battalion. In Dec. 1916 the squadron left to join the 13th Reserve Cavalry Regiment at Maresfield.

On 22 Jan. 1918 the 14th Officer Cadet Bn. moved to Catterick and a school for officer instructors in Cadet Bns. was formed at Berkhamsted. During the war between 11,000 and 12,000 men who had served in the Inns of Court O.T.C. received commissions.

THE HERTFORDSHIRE REGIMENT

1/1st Battalion.
4.8.14 Hertford: East Midland Bde. East Anglian Div. Aug. Bury St. Edmunds. Nov. 1914 left East Anglian Div. and landed in France on 6 Nov. 20.11.14 to 4th (Guards) Bde. 2nd Div. 19.8.15 to 6th Bde. 2nd Div. 29.2.16 to 118th Bde. 39th Div. at Renescure. 8.2.18 to 116th Bde. 39th Div. 11.5.18 to 112th Bde. 37th Div. 22.5.18 absorbed 30 officers and 650 men from 6th Bedfordshire Regt. which had been reduced to cadre. 11.11.18 112th Bde. 37th Div. France; Ghissignies, south of Le Quesnoy.

2/1st Battalion.
Formed at Hertford Sept. 1914. Jan. 1915 in Newmarket area in 207th Bde. 69th Div. 17.11.15 formed 4/1st Bn. June 1916 Harrogate. Oct. 1916 Darlington. April 1917 Carburton Camp Notts. 20.9.17 disbanded.

3/1st Battalion.
Formed at Hertford Dec. 1914. By Oct. 1915 at Halton Camp, Tring. 8.4.16 became 1st Reserve Bn. 1.9.16 in East Anglian Reserve Bde. at Halton Park. 11.7.17 combined with 5th Reserve Bn. Bedfordshire Regt. at Halton Park.

4/1st Battalion.
Formed by 2/1st Bn. on 17.11.15 at (?) Thetford in 206th Bde. 69th Div. July 1916 to Harrogate. April 1917 Welbeck. Aug. 1917 disbanded.

THE HEREFORDSHIRE REGIMENT

1/1st Battalion.
4.8.14 The Barracks, Hereford: Welsh Border Bde. Welsh Div. Aug. to war station at Pembroke Dock. 10 Aug. Oswestry. End Aug. Wellingborough area—Irchester and Rushden. Dec. 1914 Bury St. Edmunds. 24.4.15 to North Wales Bde. Welsh Div. May 1915 Bedford. 13.5.15 formation became 158th Bde. 53rd Div. 16.7.15 embarked at Devonport for Gallipoli. 9.8.15 landed at Suvla Bay. 12.12.15 left Gallipoli for Egypt arriving Alexandria 22 Dec. 1.6.18 left 53rd Div. for France. From Alexandria 17 June; Taranto 22 June. At Proven 30.6.18 and to

102nd Bde. 34th Div. 11.11.18 102nd Bde. 34th Div. Belgium; west of Courtrai.

2/1st Battalion.
Formed at Hereford Sept. 1914. Dec. 1914 Aberystwyth. April 1915 Northampton in 205th Bde. 68th Div. 30 May to 17 June at Billericay working on north London defences. July 1915 Bedford. Nov. 1916 Lowestoft. May 1917 Herringfleet. 10.9.17 disbanded.

3/1st Battalion.
Formed Feb. 1915 at Hereford. 1915 Abergavenny. Sept. 1915 Oswestry. 8.4.16 became 1st Reserve Bn. 1.9.16 in Welsh Reserve Bde. T.F. at Oswestry. 24.7.17 combined with 4th Reserve Bn. K.S.L.I. at Swansea.

THE NORTHERN CYCLIST BATTALION

1/1st Battalion.
4.8.14 Drill Hall, Hutton Terrace, Sandyford Road, Newcastle-on-Tyne: Northern Command. Aug. 1914 to war station Morpeth. By 1916 at Alnwick where it remained until the end of the war. (Tyne Garrison).

2/1st Battalion.
Formed in 1914. July 1915 formed 10th Provisional Cyclist Coy. 1916 Skegness. June 1918 Burton Constable where it remained. (Humber Garrison).

3/1st Battalion.
Formed at Newcastle in 1915. Mar. 1916 abolished and personnel posted to 1/1st and 2/1st Bns. and Machine Gun Corps.

THE HIGHLAND CYCLIST BATTALION

1/1st Battalion.
4.8.14 Kirkcaldy: Scottish Command. Aug. 1914 to war station East Linton, East Lothian. July 1916 St. Andrews. About May 1918 to Ireland and at Enniskillen and Randalstown.

2/1st Battalion.
Formed Nov. 1914. July 1915 personnel for 1st Provisional Cyclist Coy. 1916 Montrose. 1917 Arbroath. About May 1918 to Ireland at Athlone and Aug. 1918 the Curragh.

3/1st Battalion.
Formed in 1915. Mar. 1916 abolished and personnel posted to 1/1st and 1/2nd Battalions and Machine Gun Corps.

THE KENT CYCLIST BATTALION

1/1st Battalion.
4.8.14 Drill Hall, Tonbridge: Eastern Command. Aug. 1914 to war station Canterbury. 1915 on coast defence of Kent and Sussex attached to 57th Div. 2.12.15 to Chisledon and reorganised as an infantry bn. 8.2.16 sailed for India where it remained. (see 1/9th Hants. page 79).

2/1st Battalion.
Formed in 1914 or 1915. July 1915 personnel for 9th Provisional Cyclist Coy. 1916 Canterbury. Mar. 1917 at Ramsgate attached 5th Cyclist Bde. Mar. 1918 to the end of the war attached to The Cyclist Div. and in Aug. at Lydd.

3/1st Battalion.
Formed in 1915. May have been disbanded in 1916.

THE HUNTINGDONSHIRE CYCLIST BATTALION

1/1st Battalion.
4.8.14 St. Mary's Street, Huntingdon: Eastern Command. Aug. 1914 to war station at Grimsby. 1916 at Scarborough. By June 1918 at Whitby where it remained.

2/1st Battalion.
Formed in October 1914. 1916 at Sutton-le-Marsh, near Mablethorpe. Mar. 1917 Alford. July 1917 Chapel St. Leonards. May 1918 Skegness where it remained.

3/1st Battalion.
Formed in 1915. Mar. 1916 disbanded: personnel posted to 1/1st and 2/1st Battalions and Machine Gun Corps.

CHANNEL ISLANDS MILITIA

THE ROYAL MILITIA OF THE ISLAND OF JERSEY

In August 1914 the Jersey Militia included three battalions of infantry. Early in Mar. 1915 a company of 6 officers and 224 men joined the 7th (S) Bn. Royal Irish Rifles in Ireland at Ballyvonare, near Buttevant.

In 1916 the Royal Jersey Garrison Bn. was formed from the Militia. It was taken over by the War Office in December 1916 and remained in Jersey (Jersey Garrison).

ROYAL GUERNSEY

In Aug. 1914 the Guernsey Militia included two battalions of Infantry. Early in Mar. 1915 a company of 7 officers and 238 men joined the 6th (S) Bn. Royal Irish Regiment in Ireland at Fermoy.

In 1916 the Militia formed two battalions—1st (Service) and 2nd (Reserve) Battalions, Royal Guernsey Light Infantry. They were taken over by the War Office in Dec. 1916.

The 1st (Service) Battalion moved to England in May 1917 and was at Bourne Park, near Canterbury, in 202nd Bde. 67th Div. It left the 67th Div. in Sept. 1917 and went to France, landing at Havre on 27 Sept. On 2.10.17 it went to 86th Bde. 29th Div. On 27.4.18, after heavy casualties in the Battles of the Lys, it went to G.H.Q. Troops where it remained.

The 2nd (Reserve) Battalion remained in Guernsey (Guernsey Garrison).

Officer Cadet Battalions

The great expansion of the army in 1914 created the problem of finding officers for the hundreds of new units which were formed. Retired officers returned to their regiments and many young men were granted temporary commissions. A typical New Army battalion with an establishment of 29 officers—but often over strength—might have three Regulars, several from the Reserve of Officers and the Retired List and others with previous military experience. Apart from a few warrant officers and N.C.O.s promoted to commissioned rank, the subalterns would be newly gazetted 2nd Lieutenants who had been trained in the Officers Training Corps at their universities and schools.

The Officers Training Corps was formed in 1908 as one of the far-sighted measures of the Haldane reforms. It consisted of the Senior Division at Universities, the Junior Division at Public Schools and the Inns of Court. In 1914 there were 23 contingents in the Senior Division and 166 in the Junior. Between August 1914 and March 1915 20,577 temporary commissions were granted to former members of the O.T.C.

After a few months these sources were almost exhausted and as, by now, there were a number of potential officers serving in the ranks with a basic military training, it was decided in January 1915 that N.C.O.s and men, who were recommended by their commanding officers, would be given a short course of four weeks. This training was to be in such units as the Artists Rifles, Inns of Court and Senior Contingents of the O.T.C. and the candidates were commissioned if suitable. They then went to Young Officer Companies, which were attached to the Reserve Brigades, for further training while waiting to be posted to their units.

Sandhurst and Woolwich continued to train candidates for Regular commissions with shortened courses of four and six months: later extended to eight months and a year.

In February 1916 a new system of training officers was introduced with the formation of Officer Cadet units (A.C.I. 357 of 14 February 1916). In future, temporary commissions were granted only to those who had passed through the ranks of a cadet unit; unless they had previous service as an officer. Candidates for admission to a cadet unit had to have served in the ranks or in an O.T.C. contingent and reached the age of 18½ years and approved by a senior officer. The course lasted for four months and at the end of it, commissions were granted to those who qualified. A cadet battalion had an establishment of 400 cadets which was increased to 600 in the following May if accommodation was available. Cadet units were also formed for other arms.

By June 1916 there were about a dozen cadet battalions and more were formed so that by July 1917 there were 22 battalions. These are shown on the following page with their locations.

OFFICER CADET BATTALIONS

July 1917

Household Brigade Officer Cadet Battalion. Bushey, Herts.
No. 1 Officer Cadet Battalion. Newton Ferrers, Devon.
" 2 " " " Pembroke College, Cambridge.
No. 3 Officer Cadet Battalion. Bristol.
" 4 " " " Oxford.
" 5 " " " Trinity College, Cambridge.
" 6 " " " Balliol College, Oxford.
" 7 " " " Moore Park, Co. Cork.
" 8 " " " Lichfield.
" 9 " " " Gailes, Ayrshire.
" 10 " " " Gailes, Ayrshire.
" 11 " " " Pirbright.
" 12 " " " Newmarket.
" 13 " " " Newmarket.
" 14 " " " Berkhamsted, Herts.
" 15 " " " Romford.
" 16 " " " Kinmel, Rhyl.
" 17 " " " Kinmel, Rhyl.
" 18 " " " Bath.
" 19 " " " Pirbright.
" 20 " " " Crookham, Aldershot.
" 21 " " " Crookham, Aldershot.
Garrison Officer Cadet Battalion.
Jesus College, Cambridge.

The only changes before the end of the war were:—

No. 3 Officer Cadet Battalion moved to Parkhurst, Isle of Wight in 1918.

No. 14 Officer Cadet Battalion moved to Catterick in January 1918.

The Garrison Battalion became No. 22 (Garrison) Officer Cadet Battalion in August 1918.

No. 23 Officer Cadet Battalion was at Catterick having been converted from a Machine Gun Corps Officer Cadet Bn.

During the war over 73,000 officers in the Infantry were commissioned after training in the Officer Cadet Battalions.

THE HOUSEHOLD BATTALION

Formed at Knightsbridge Barracks, London on 1.9.16 as an infantry battalion with personnel from the Household Cavalry Reserve Regiments. 9.11.16 landed in France. 17.11.16 to 10th Bde. 4th Div. 10.2.18 disbanded in France sending drafts to the Household Cavalry and Foot Guards.

THE RESERVE HOUSEHOLD BATTALION

Formed about September 1916 to supply reinforcements to the Household Battalion in France. Stationed at Windsor until disbandment early in 1918.

(The history of the Household Battalion, formed from the three Household Cavalry Reserve Regts., is given on page 1 of Historical Records of British Cavalry and Yeomanry Regiments in the Great War 1914-18. It is repeated in this book so that it will also be with the other infantry battalions of the Army).

WARTIME CAMPS IN THE UNITED KINGDOM

Before the Great War the barracks in the United Kingdom provided quarters for 175,000 men and as over a million had enlisted by the end of December 1914 the existing accommodation was quite inadequate.

As a first step the families were moved out of the married quarters, increasing the barracks capacity to 262,000. Tented camps were erected (often on the camping grounds used by the Territorials for annual training) and institutions, schools and empty factories and warehouses were taken over. In addition, a large number of men were billeted in private houses during the first winter of the war.

Towards the end of October 1914 the weather broke. An exceptionally heavy rainfall and gale force winds turned the tended camps into quagmires and blew down the canvas. The troops had to move into unfinished huts and billets.

Immediately on the outbreak of war plans were made for hutted camps to be built and the first plans were ready by 14 August. By the summer of 1915 hutment camps were ready for 850,000 men but many of the occupied buildings were retained until the end of the war.

By 1917 all the New Army and Territorial divisions had gone overseas and the hutments were occupied by the British and Dominion reserve formations and units. In August 1917 there were 1,700,000 troops in the U.K.—1,505,000 British and 195,000 from the Dominions.

A complete list of the hutted and tented camps and all occupied buildings can be found in a War Office publication "List of Lands and Buildings in the occupation of the War Department" dated 1st June 1918.

The following paragraphs give the locations of some of the hutment camps mentioned in this book. Aldershot had over a dozen and there were about fifteen on Salisbury Plain.

England and Wales.
Aldershot. Cannock Chase, Staffs. Catterick. Clipstone, Notts. Crowborough, Sussex. Halton Park, Bucks. Hursley Park, Winchester. Kinmel, Rhyl. Park Hall, Oswestry. Pembroke Dock. Prees Heath, Shropshire, Ripon. Salisbury Plain. Wareham, Dorset.

Scotland.
Bridge of Allan, Stirling. Dunfermline, Fife. Glencorse, Edinburgh. Kinghorn, Fife. Wormit, Fife.

Ireland.
Aghada, Cork. Ballinvonear, Buttevant. Buncrana, Donegal. Clandeboye, Down. Curragh. Randalstown, Antrim.

Sources

OFFICIAL PUBLICATIONS AND RECORDS

Army Lists.
Army Orders and Army Council Instructions.
Monthly Distribution of the Army.
Official History of the Great War. Military Operations (32 volumes) 1922–1949.
Official History of the Canadian Forces in the Great War. General Series. Volume 1. 1938.
Battle Honours awarded for the Great War. 1925.
Battles Nomenclature Committee Report. 1921.
A Brief Record of the Advance of the Egyptian Expeditionary Force, 1917–1918. 1919.
List of Land and Buildings in the Occupation of the War Department. 1st June 1918.
Orders of Battle.
  Composition of the Headquarters of the Forces for Home Defence 1915–1917.
  Commanders Home Forces 1916 and 1917.
  Officers in Command, Home Forces 1918.
  Officers in Command Forces in Great Britain 1918.
  Composition of Headquarters and Officers in Command Forces in Ireland 1918.
  Distribution of Home Defence Troops and Reserve Units 1917 and 1918.
Peace Establishments, Regular Forces, 1914–1915.
Peace Establishments, Territorial Force, 1913–1914.
Statistics of the Military Effort of the British Empire during the Great War. 1922.
War Diaries.

OTHER SOURCES.

Regimental and Battalion Histories. (over 200 volumes).
Divisional and Brigade Histories. (44 volumes).
DUNLOP, Colonel John R., The Development of the British Army, 1899–1914. 1938.
EDWARDS, Major T. J., Regimetal Badges. 1957.
FREDERICK, J. B. M., Lineage Book of the British Army. 1969.
HAMPSHIRE TERRITORIAL FORCE ASSOCIATION, History of the Association and War Records of Units, 1914–1918. 1921.
HARRIS, Henry, The Irish Regiments in the First World War. 1968.
MACEACHERN, Dugald, The Sword of the North. 1923.
MAGNUS, Laurie, The West Riding Territorials in the Great War. 1920.
MILITARY HISTORICAL SOCIETY BULLETINS.
MONTGOMERY, Major-Gen. Sir Archibald, The Story of the Fourth Army, August 8th to November 11th 1918. 1920.
RICHARDS, Walter, His Majesty's Territorial Army (4 volumes). 1910–11.
WALLACE, Edgar, Kitchener's Army and the Territorial Forces. No date.
WHITE, Arthur S. A., Bibliography of Regimental Histories of the British Army. 1965.
WHITE, Charles, Our Regiments and their Glorious Records. 1915.
WILLIAMS, Captain Basil, Raising and Training the New Armies. 1918.

Mr. J. E. Lambert, West Kilbride (formerly of Nobel's Explosives Co. and I.C.I.) kindly supplied the history of the Ardeer Company T.F. of the Royal Scots Fusiliers.

Appendix 1 to Part 11

REGIMENTS AND THEIR BATTALIONS
TABLES SHOWING THE NUMBER AND TYPES OF BATTALIONS IN EACH REGIMENT
TABLE A. FOOT GUARDS

REGIMENTS	REGULAR BATTALIONS		RESERVE BATTALIONS	TOTAL
	Pre-war	*Formed during the war*		
GRENADIER GUARDS	3	1	1	5
COLDSTREAM GUARDS	3	1	1	5
SCOTS GUARDS	2	—	1	3
IRISH GUARDS	1	1	1	3
WELSH GUARDS	—	1	1	2
	9	4	5	18

1. The Welsh Guards were formed in February 1915.
2. The two Provisional Battalions (one Grenadier and one Coldstream) which were formed in August 1918 are not included above.

TABLE B. INFANTRY OF THE LINE
BATTALIONS

Regiments	Regular	Reserve and Extra Reserve	Territorial Force		New Army		Garrison, Service etc. (1918)	Labour, Transport Docks etc.	Graduated and Young Soldier	Total
			Field Units	Reserve Units	Service	Reserve				
	1	2	3	4	5	6	7	8	9	10
Royal Scots	2	1	14	6	6	2	2	1	—	34
Royal West Surrey Regiment	2	1	6	2	5	2	1	5	3	27
East Kent Regiment	2	1	5	2	3	1	1	—	—	15
Royal Lancaster Regiment	2	1	5	2	5	2	—	—	—	17
Northumberland Fusiliers	2	1	10	4	19	8	4	—	3	51
Royal Warwickshire Regiment	2	2	9	4	6	3	1	—	3	30
Royal Fusiliers	4	3	—	—	17	8	7	5	3	47
Liverpool Regiment	2	2	14	6	8	4	5	5	3	49
Norfolk Regiment	2	1	8	3	3	1	1	—	—	19
Lincolnshire Regiment	2	1	5	2	4	2	2	1	—	19
Devonshire Regiment	2	1	10	4	3	1	2	3	3	29
Suffolk Regiment	2	1	8	3	5	2	2	—	—	23
Somerset Light Infantry	2	1	6	2	3	1	3	—	—	18
West Yorkshire Regiment	2	2	8	4	9	4	2	1	3	35
East Yorkshire Regiment	2	1	3	1	7	3	2	—	—	19
Bedfordshire Regiment	2	2	3	1	3	2	3	2	3	21
Leicestershire Regiment	2	1	4	2	5	2	2	1	3	22
Royal Irish Regiment	2	2	—	—	2	—	4	—	—	10
Yorkshire Regiment	2	1	5	2	7	3	3	1	—	24
Lancashire Fusiliers	2	2	9	4	10	3	1	—	—	31
Royal Scots Fusiliers	2	1	6	2	3	1	2	1	—	18
Cheshire Regiment	2	1	9	4	8	2	4	5	3	38
Royal Welsh Fusiliers	2	1	11	4	10	5	7	—	—	40
South Wales Borderers	2	1	2	1	8	3	1	—	3	21
King's Own Scottish Borderers	2	1	4	2	3	1	1	—	—	14
Scottish Rifles	2	2	9	4	4	1	2	3	—	27
Royal Inniskilling Fusiliers	2	2	—	—	7	1	1	—	—	13
Gloucestershire Regiment	2	1	7	3	7	3	1	—	—	24
Worcestershire Regiment	4	2	4	2	4	2	2	2	—	22
East Lancashire Regiment	2	1	4	2	5	2	1	—	—	17
East Surrey Regiment	2	2	4	2	5	3	—	—	—	18
Duke of Cornwall's Light Infantry	2	1	3	2	4	2	—	1	—	15
West Riding Regiment	2	1	8	4	3	1	2	1	—	22
Border Regiment	2	1	4	2	5	2	—	—	—	16
Royal Sussex Regiment	2	1	8	3	6	2	1	—	3	26
Hampshire Regiment	2	1	11	6	5	2	2	—	3	32
South Staffordshire Regiment	2	2	4	2	3	2	1	1	—	17
Dorsetshire Regiment	2	1	2	1	2	1	2	—	—	11
South Lancashire Regiment	2	1	5	2	6	2	—	3	—	21
Welsh Regiment	2	1	9	4	12	4	—	—	3	35
Royal Highlanders	2	1	10	4	3	1	—	1	—	22
Oxfordshire and Buckinghamshire Light Infantry	2	1	5	2	4	1	3	—	—	18
Essex Regiment	2	1	13	5	4	2	3	—	—	30
Nottinghamshire and Derbyshire Regiment	2	2	9	4	8	3	1	1	3	33
Loyal North Lancashire Regiment	2	1	7	3	5	1	2	—	—	21
Carried Forward	94	59	290	124	264	104	87	44	45	1111

BATTALIONS

REGIMENTS	Regular	Reserve and Extra Reserve	TERRITORIAL FORCE		NEW ARMY		Garrison, Service etc. (1918)	Labour, Transport Docks etc.	Graduated and Young Soldier	TOTAL
			Field Units	Reserve Units	Service	Reserve				
	1	2	3	4	5	6	7	8	9	10
Brought Forward	94	59	290	124	264	104	87	44	45	1111
Northamptonshire Regiment	2	1	3	1	3	1	2	—	—	13
Royal Berkshire Regiment	2	1	2	1	4	1	1	4	—	16
Royal West Kent Regiment	2	1	5	2	5	2	1	—	—	18
Yorkshire Light Infantry	2	1	4	2	6	2	4	—	3	24
Shropshire Light Infantry	2	1	3	1	4	1	—	—	—	12
Middlesex Regiment	4	2	12	4	12	6	2	4	3	49
King's Royal Rifle Corps	4	2	—	—	12	6	1	—	3	28
Wiltshire Regiment	2	1	2	1	3	1	—	—	—	10
Manchester Regiment	2	2	13	6	12	4	2	—	3	44
North Staffordshire Regiment	2	2	4	2	3	2	4	—	—	19
York and Lancaster Regiment	2	1	4	2	8	2	1	2	—	22
Durham Light Infantry	2	2	12	5	10	4	3	1	3	42
Highland Light Infantry	2	2	10	4	8	3	1	—	3	33
Seaforth Highlanders	2	1	6	3	3	1	1	—	—	17
Gordon Highlanders	2	1	8	4	3	1	1	—	3	23
Cameron Highlanders	2	1	3	1	3	1	2	1	—	14
Royal Irish Rifles	2	3	—	—	11	4	1	—	—	21
Royal Irish Fusiliers	2	2	—	—	5	1	4	—	—	14
Connaught Rangers	2	2	—	—	2	—	—	—	—	6
Argyll and Sutherland Highlanders	2	2	11	5	4	2	—	—	—	26
Leinster Regiment	2	3	—	—	2	—	—	—	—	7
Royal Munster Fusiliers	2	3	—	—	4	—	*2	—	—	11
Royal Dublin Fusiliers	2	3	—	—	5	1	—	—	—	11
Rifle Brigade	4	2	7	1	8	3	—	—	3	28
	148	101	399	169	404	153	120	56	69	1619

TABLE C. INFANTRY—TERRITORIAL FORCE.

BATTALIONS

Regiments	Field Units	Reserve Units	Total
Honorable Artillery Company	2	1	3
Monmouthshire Regiment	7	3	10
Cambridge Regiment	3	1	4
London Regiment	62	26	88
Hertfordshire Regiment	3	1	4
Herefordshire Regiment	2	1	3
Northern Cyclist Battalion	2	1	3
Highland Cyclist Battalion	2	1	3
Kent Cyclist Battalion	2	1	3
Huntingdonshire Cyclist Battalion	2	1	3
	87	37	124

SUMMARY

BATTALIONS

	Regular	Reserve and Extra Reserve	Territorial Force		New Army		Garrison, Service etc. (1918)	Labour, Transport Docks etc.	Graduated and Young Soldier	Total
			Field Units	Reserve Units	Service	Reserve				
	1	2	3	4	5	6	7	8	9	10
Foot Guards	13	5	—	—	—	—	—	—	—	18
Infantry of the Line	148	101	399	169	404	153	120	56	69	1619
Infantry Territorial Force	—	—	87	37	—	—	—	—	—	124
	161	106	486	206	404	153	120	56	69	1761

1. The above does not include the Inns of Court O.T.C., the three Channel Islands battalions and the twenty-four Officer Cadets battalions, or the Household Battalion.
2. The titles of regiments in this Appendix are as directed to be used in official correspondence by the August 1914 Army List.
3. The total number of battalions in a regiment in these tables does not always agree with the figure given in the 1925 List of Battle Honours and in the Army List. The discrepancy is due to different methods of counting battalions.

Appendix 11 to Part 11

THE NEW ARMY BATTALIONS
1914-1918

When war broke out on 4th August 1914 the Prime Minister, Mr. Asquith, was also acting as Secretary of State for War. On 6th August Lord Kitchener, on leave from Egypt where he was British agent, was appointed to this post. Immediately on assuming office he said that we must be prepared for a three years war and that we would require an army of seventy divisions.

On 7th August a poster and notices in the newspapers called for an addition of 100,000 men, between 19 and 30, to the Army, serving for three years or the duration of the war. The response was overwhelming and within a few days the First Hundred Thousand had joined up and by the middle of September half a million men had enlisted. They included the best of their generation, eager to serve their country. Many gave their lives in the Somme battles of 1916 where the New Army battalions suffered grievous losses.

Kitchener decided that the massive expansion must be achieved by the creation of new armies separate from the Regulars and Territorials so he did not make use of the framework of the Territorial Force as envisaged in the Haldane plans.

The new army consisted of over 500 battalions (including the reserve units) and was popularly known at the time as Kitchener's Army. It was organised in thirty divisions formed in groups of six. The new battalions were raised as additional battalions of the regiments of Infantry of the Line sharing their traditions and regimental spirit. They were numbered consecutively after the existing battalions of their regiments and were distinguished by the word "Service" in brackets after the number (Note 1). Later Second Reserve and Local Reserve battalions were formed as explained below.

A large number of new units were also raised for the Royal Artillery, Royal Engineers and other arms for the thirty new divisions. They did not, however, have the word "Service" in their titles.

There are five categories of New Army battalions:—

A. The service battalions raised in August and September 1914 formed the eighteen divisions of the three new armies. First (9th to 14th Divisions), Second (15th to 20th Divisions) and Third (21st to 26th Divisions) (Note 2). The three new armies were sometimes abbreviated to K.1, K.2 and K.3. In addition to the twelve battalions for each division a number of Army Troops units were raised and attached to divisions for training. All these Army Troops battalions eventually went to regular or new army divisions. The 37th Division was formed in 1915 with thirteen Army Troops battalions.

B. Another series of service batatlions was formed in the autumn of 1914 with men from the reserve and extra reserve battalions, which were now well over establishment, to form the original Fourth Army (30th to 35th Divisions) known as K.4 (Note 3). Later in order to provide reinforcements for the first eighteen divisions it was decided in April, 1915 to break up the divisions of the Fourth New Army and reconstitute the infantry as reserve battalions to train recruits and send drafts to the first three new armies. (The battalions became second reserve battalions and were organized in eighteen reserve infantry brigades (Note 4). On 1st September 1916 all these second reserve battalions were absorbed in the Training Reserve (Note 5).

C. At the same time as the units of the first four armies were being formed a number of service battalions were being raised by committees from cities, towns, organizations and individuals. These battalions were clothed, housed and fed by these committees until the War Office took them over in 1915 and refunded the raisers' expenditure (Note 6).

These battalions supplied most of the infantry for the 30th to 41st Divisions. The new Fourth New Army divisions took over their numbers, 30th to 35th, from the original Fourth Army (see B above). The Fifth New Army (36th to 41st Divisions) included the 36th (Ulster) and 38th (Welsh) Divisions which were raised in Northern Ireland and Wales. The locally raised battalions had an additional title in brackets showing their connection with the district or organization which helped to form them (Note 9).

D. The locally raised service battalions formed depot companies (Note 7) and in 1915 these companies were grouped to form local reserve battalions, with numbers following the parent battalions, to supply reinforcements to their service battalions (Note 8). On 1st September 1916 these battalions were absorbed in the Training Reserve (Note 5).

E. A few more service and reserve battalions were formed in 1915 and 1916 in addition to those in the above four categories.

In the summer of 1918 about twenty garrison and other battalions were renamed service battalions. They were used to supply some of the infantry for the reconstitution of the 14th, 16th, 40th and 59th Divisions in France, which had been reduced to cadre after heavy casualties in the German offensives. These battalions had no connection with the service battalions of the New Army formed in the early years of the war.

REFERENCES

(A.O. Army Order. A.C.I. Army Council Instruction)

Note.
1. A.O. 324—1914
2. A.O.'s 382 and 388—1914
3. A.O. 389—1914 and A.C.I. 76—October 1914
4. A.C.I. 96—April 1915
5. A.O. 259—1916 and A.C.I. 1528—August 1916
6. A.C.I. 397—September 1914 and 172—January 1915
7. A.C.I. 13—December 1914
8. A.C.I. 109—July 1915
9. The locally raised battalions formed in the first months of the war were not, at first, numbered and were known by titles showing their local association. In November 1914 it was decided to number them following the battalions of the original Fourth New Army, keeping their local names as second titles. A.C.I. 28 of 3 December 1914 allotted numbers to the existing 66 battalions and after this they were numbered as they were raised.

SUMMARY

	Service Battalions	Reserve Battalions
K.1	80	—
K.2	80	—
K.3	90	—
K.4 (2nd Reserve)	—	76
Locally Raised	142	—
Local Reserve	—	68
Others	12	9
Total	404	153

GRAND TOTAL 557 BATTALIONS

NOMENCLATURE OF NEW ARMY BATTALIONS

Lieut. General Sir Arthur Codrington, Military Secretary to Lord Kitchener, said that he was in Lord Kitchener's room at the War Office when Kitchener was asked what he wanted to call the battalions of the New Army. The suggestion was made that they should be numbered from one upwards. But Sir Arthur Codrington intervened, saying that the men would have no regimental traditions to uphold and that the battalions should be parts of existing regiments. Kitchener said "I don't care as long as we get the men". Sir Arthur had his way and the new battalions were raised as additional battalions of the regiments of Infantry of the Line.

Appendix III to Part II

THE TRAINING RESERVE

In 1915 two kinds of reserve battalions were formed from New Army Service Battalions to supply their reinforcements. In April the 75 battalions of the original Fourth New Army, which were formed by the Reserve and Extra Reserve Battalions in October 1914, were converted to 2nd Reserve Battalions. In the summer of 1915 the depot companies of the Locally Raised Battalions formed 68 Local Reserve Battalions. These reserve battalions were organised in 24 Reserve Brigades.

In 1916 it was found that the regimental reserve battalions were unable to cope with the number of recruits coming in after the introduction of conscription and it was decided to form a new organization to receive and train the recruits and despatch drafts abroad to regiments which could not be supplied from regimental reserves. It was called the Training Reserve and came into being on 1st September, 1916.

The Training Reserve was formed from the 2nd Reserve and Local Reserve Battalions which discarded their designations and became numbered battalions of the Training Reserve from 1st to 112th. The 24 Reserve Brigades became Training Reserve Brigades and where the number of new battalions in a brigade was less than the existing ones the surplus units were absorbed in the new battalions.

The Reserve, Extra Reserve and T.F. Reserve Battalions were retained as regimental reserves and recruits were posted to them until they were up to strength and then to the Training Reserve. When drafts were required for regiments overseas they were first taken from the regimental reserves. If the number of trained men was insufficient they were taken from the Training Reserve.

The Irish regiments had no 2nd Reserve battalions and there were only six Local Reserve battalions, for the Ulster Division, in the 15th Reserve Brigade. These battalions did not form part of the Training Reserve.

In 1917 the Training Reserve was reorganized and the battalions became more specialized in their training. In May 14 were designated Young Soldier Battalions which took in recruits aged 18 years and one month and after basic training they were posted in companies to a Graduated Battalion. There were 28 of these, linked in pairs to each Young Soldier Battalion.

It was now decided that the Graduated Battalions would be used for Home Defence while completing their recruit training and they were posted to the eight Home Service divisions replacing 2nd Line and Home Service Territorial battalions which were disbanded. These battalions were now numbered from 201st onwards and increased to 46. Only six of the Reserve Brigades remained for the Young Soldier Battalions, now increased to 23.

On 27th October, 1917 the Graduated and Young Soldier Battalions were allotted to 23 Infantry Regiments and numbered 51st and 52nd for the Graduated and 53rd for the Young Soldier Battalions. Early in 1918 the Home Service divisions were reduced to four and, except for one brigade, all their battalions were now the Graduated ones. The remaining Training Reserve Battalions, after providing six Recruit Reception Battalions and four for training Machine Gun Corps recruits, were disbanded.

After the armistice some of the Graduated and Young Soldier Battalions went to the Rhine Army to replace Regular and disbanded battalions.

Appendix IV to Part 11

THIRD LINE AND PROVISIONAL TERRITORIAL BATTALIONS

A. Third Line Battalions

By June 1915 practically all Territorial battalions had formed a Third Line unit for the supply of reinforcements to the First and Second Line battalions. They had the designation 3/ followed by the number of the parent battalion.

In the autumn of 1915 the Third Line battalions were assembled in 14 Third Line Groups; one for each of the pre-war T.F. Divisions. In April 1916 these battalions dropped the fractional designation and became Reserve Battalions T.F. e.g. 4th Reserve Battalion, Lincolnshire Regt. T.F.

On 1st September, 1916 the Reserve Territorial battalions of each regiment were amalgamated into one unit or in a few large regiments into two units. At the same time the Third Line Groups became 14 Reserve Brigades T.F. There were no further changes.

B. Provisional Battalions

During the summer of 1915 a number of battalions known as Provisional Battalions were formed from the personnel of 2nd and 3rd Line Territorial battalions not available for posting overseas. They included men of low medical categories and Territorials who had not volunteered to serve abroad. Some of the battalions were disbanded but by 1916 there were 41 serving in the ten Provisional Brigades.

In November 1916 the 6th, 8th and 9th Provisional Brigades were used to make up the new Home Service divisions, 71st, 72nd and 73rd. Almost all these battalions were disbanded when the Graduated Battalions were posted to the Home Service divisions (see Appendix III, paragraph 7).

On 1st January, 1917 the Provisional battalions became numbered Home Service Territorial battalions in the Infantry Regiments. The remaining seven Provisional Brigades were numbered from 221st to 227th and later called mixed Brigades. They were stationed on the East Coast until the end of the war.

Appendix v to Part 11

LIST OF BRITISH DIVISIONS (INFANTRY) WHICH SERVED IN GREAT WAR, 1914–1918

KEY	DIVISIONS	NOTES
A	1st, 2nd, 3rd, 4th, 5th & 6th	Regular formations in existence prior to 4th August, 1914.
B	Guards 7th 8th, 27th, 28th & 29th	Regular formations formed after 4th August, 1914. Formed August, 1915 with 8 Bns. in France and 5 from England. Formed Sept. 1914 with 4 Bns. from U.K. and 8 from overseas. Formed in 1914 and (29th) 1915 with Bns. from overseas garrisons.
C	42nd (East Lancashire) 43rd (Wessex) 44th (Home Counties) 46th (North Midland) 47th (2nd London) 48th (South Midland) 49th (West Riding) 50th (Northumbrian) 51st (Highland) 52nd (Lowland) 53rd (Welsh) 54th (East Anglian) 55th (West Lancashire) 56th (1st London)	Territorial Force Divisions that were in existence before 4th August, 1914. They received numerical designations in May 1915 and were numbered in the order in which they went overseas. After the formation of 2nd Line Territorial formations they sometimes had the fractional 1/ or 1/1st before the territorial title.
D	9th (Scottish) 10th (Irish) 11th (Northern) 12th (Eastern) 13th (Western) 14th (Light) 15th (Scottish) 16th (Irish) 17th (Northern) 18th (Eastern) 19th (Western) 20th (Light) 21st, 22nd, 23rd, 24th, 25th and 26th	First, Second and Third New Armies formed in 1914. The 14th Division was the 8th Division until 11th September, 1914.
E	30th, 31st, 32nd, 33rd, 34th and 35th. 36th (Ulster) 37th 38th (Welsh) 39th, 40th and 41st	Fourth and Fifth New Armies formed in 1915.

KEY	DIVISIONS	NOTES
F	45th (2/Wessex) 57th (2/West Lancashire) 58th (2/1st London) 59th (2/North Midland) 60th (2/2nd London) 61st (2/South Midland) 62nd (2/West Riding) 63rd (2/Northumbrian) 64th (2/Highland) 65th (2/Lowland) 66th (2/East Lancashire) 67th (2/Home Counties) 68th (2/Welsh) 69th (2/East Anglian)	Second Line Territorial Force Divisions formed in 1915. They received numerical designations in Aug. 1915. The 63rd, 64th, 65th, 67th and 68th and 69th did not leave the United Kingdom. The 63rd Division was broken up in July 1916. The 65th Division was broken up in March 1918.
G	63rd (Royal Naval) 71st, 72nd and 73rd 74th (Yeomanry) 75th	Royal Naval Division was formed in Sept. 1914 and numbered 63rd in July 1916. These three divisions were formed for home service in Nov. 1916 and were broken up by Mar. 1918. Formed in Egypt in Mar. 1917 from dismounted yeomanry regiments. Formed in Egypt in June 1917.

SUMMARY

Key	Served overseas	Remained in United Kingdom	Total
A	6	—	6
B	6	—	6
C	14	—	14
D	18	—	18
E	12	—	12
F	8	6	14
G	3	3	6
	67	9	76

Appendix VI to Part II

TITLES OF INFANTRY REGIMENTS IN 1914 AND 1974

The list of Infantry Regiments in 1914 is arranged in order of seniority. Following each one, on the next line and slightly indented, is the title of the regiment in 1974 or, in the case of amalgamations, that of the successor regiment.

FOOT GUARDS

Grenadier Guards.
   No change.
Coldstream Guards.
   No change.
Scots Guards.
   No change.
Irish Guards.
   No change.
   Welsh Guards (formed in 1915).

INFANTRY OF THE LINE

The Royal Scots (Lothian Regiment).
   The Royal Scots (The Royal Regiment).
The Queen's (Royal West Surrey Regiment).
   The Queen's Regiment.
The Buffs (East Kent Regiment).
   The Queen's Regiment.
The King's Own (Royal Lancaster Regiment).
   The King's Own Royal Border Regiment.
The Northumberland Fusiliers.
   The Royal Regiment of Fusiliers
The Royal Warwickshire Regiment.
   The Royal Regiment of Fusiliers.
The Royal Fusiliers (City of London Regiment).
   The Royal Regiment of Fusiliers.
The King's (Liverpool Regiment).
   The King's Regiment.
The Norfolk Regiment.
   The Royal Anglian Regiment.
The Lincolnshire Regiment.
   The Royal Anglian Regiment.
The Devonshire Regiment.
   The Devonshire and Dorset Regiment.
The Suffolk Regiment.
   The Royal Anglian Regiment.
Prince Albert's (Somerset Light Infantry).
   The Light Infantry.
The Prince of Wales's Own (West Yorkshire Regiment).
   The Prince of Wales's Own Regiment of Yorkshire.
The East Yorkshire Regiment.
   The Prince of Wales's Own Regiment of Yorkshire.
The Bedfordshire Regiment.
   The Royal Anglian Regiment.
The Leicestershire Regiment.
   The Royal Anglian Regiment.
The Royal Irish Regiment.
   Disbanded 31 July 1922.
Alexandra, Princess of Wales's Own (Yorkshire Regiment).
   The Green Howards (Alexandra, Princess of Wales's Own Yorkshire Regiment).
The Lancashire Fusiliers.
   The Royal Regiment of Fusiliers.
The Royal Scots Fusiliers.
   The Royal Highland Fusiliers (Princess Margaret's Own Glasgow and Ayrshire Regiment).
The Cheshire Regiment.
   No change.
The Royal Welsh Fusiliers.
   The Royal Welch Fusiliers.
The South Wales Borderers.
   The Royal Regiment of Wales.
The King's Own Scottish Borderers.
   No change.
The Cameronians (Scottish Rifles).
   Disbanded 14 May 1968.
The Royal Inniskilling Fusiliers.
   The Royal Irish Rangers.
The Gloucestershire Regiment.
   No change.
The Worcestershire Regiment.
   The Worcestershire and Sherwood Foresters Regiment.
The East Lancashire Regiment.
   The Queen's Lancashire Regiment.
The East Surrey Regiment.
   The Queen's Regiment.
The Duke of Cornwall's Light Infantry.
   The Light Infantry.
The Duke of Wellington's (West Riding Regiment).
   The Duke of Wellington's Regiment (West Riding).
The Border Regiment.
   The King's Own Royal Border Regiment.
The Royal Sussex Regiment.
   The Queen's Regiment.
The Hampshire Regiment.
   The Royal Hampshire Regiment.
The South Staffordshire Regiment.
   The Staffordshire Regiment (The Prince of Wales's).
The Dorsetshire Regiment.
   The Devonshire and Dorset Regiment.
The Prince of Wales's Volunteers (South Lancashire Regiment).
   The Queen's Lancashire Regiment.
The Welsh Regiment.
   The Royal Regiment of Wales.
The Black Watch (Royal Highlanders).
   The Black Watch (Royal Highland Regiment).
The Oxfordshire and Buckinghamshire Light Infantry.
   The Royal Green Jackets.
The Essex Regiment.
   The Royal Anglian Regiment.
The Sherwood Foresters (Nottinghamshire and Derbyshire Regiment).
   The Worcestershire and Sherwood Foresters Regiment.
The Loyal North Lancashire Regiment.
   The Queen's Lancashire Regiment.
The Northamptonshire Regiment.
   The Royal Anglian Regiment.
Princess Charlotte of Wales's (Royal Berkshire Regiment).
   The Duke of Edinburgh's Royal Regiment (Berkshire and Wiltshire).
The Queen's Own (Royal West Kent Regiment).
   The Queen's Regiment.

134 Appendix VI to Part II

The King's Own (Yorkshire Light Infantry).
   The Light Infantry.
The King's (Shropshire Light Infantry).
   The Light Infantry.
The Duke of Cambridge's Own (Middlesex Regiment).
   The Queen's Regiment.
The King's Royal Rifle Corps.
   The Royal Green Jackets.
The Duke of Edinburgh's (Wiltshire Regiment).
   The Duke of Edinburgh's Royal Regiment (Berkshire and Wiltshire).
The Manchester Regiment.
   The King's Regiment.
The Prince of Wales's (North Staffordshire Regiment).
   The Staffordshire Regiment (The Prince of Wales's).
The York and Lancaster Regiment.
   Disbanded in 1968.
The Durham Light Infantry.
   The Light Infantry.
The Highland Light Infantry.
   The Royal Highland Fusiliers (Princess Margaret's Own. Glasgow and Ayrshire Regiment).
Seaforth Highlanders (Ross-shire Buffs, The Duke of Albany's).
   Queen's Own Highlanders (Seaforth and Camerons).
The Gordon Highlanders.
   No change.
The Queen's Own Cameron Highlanders.
   Queen's Own Highlanders (Seaforth and Camerons).
The Royal Irish Rifles.
   The Royal Irish Rangers.
Princess Victoria's (Royal Irish Fusiliers).
   The Royal Irish Rangers.
The Connaught Rangers.
   Disbanded 31 July 1922.
Princess's Louise's (Argyll and Sutherland Highlanders.
   The Argyll and Sutherland Highlanders (Princess Louise's).
The Prince of Wales's Leinster Regiment (Royal Canadians).
   Disbanded 31 July 1922.

The Royal Munster Fusiliers.
   Disbanded 31 July 1922.
The Royal Dublin Fusiliers.
   Disbanded 31 July 1922.
The Rifle Brigade (The Prince Consort's Own).
   The Royal Green Jackets.

INFANTRY TERRITORIAL FORCE

Honourable Artillery Company.
   The Honourable Artillery Company.
The Monmouthshire Regiment.
   The Royal Regiment of Wales.
The Cambridgeshire Regiment.
   The Royal Anglian Regiment.
The London Regiment.
   Royal Regiment of Artillery.
   Royal Corps of Signals.
   The Queen's Regiment.
   The Royal Regiment of Fusiliers.
   The Royal Irish Rangers.
   The Duke of Edinburgh's Royal Regiment (Berskshire and Wiltshire).
   The Gordon Highlanders.
   The Royal Green Jackets.
   Special Air Service Regiment.
The Hertfordshire Regiment.
   The Royal Anglian Regiment.
The Herefordshire Regiment.
   The Light Infantry.
The Northern Cyclist Battalion.
   Royal Regiment of Artillery.
The Highland Cyclist Battalion.
   Royal Corps of Signals.
The Kent Cyclist Battalion.
   Royal Regiment of Artillery.
The Huntingdonshire Cyclist Battalion.
   The Royal Anglian Regiment.

Appendix VII to Part II

BATTLE HONOURS

In August, 1919 the Army Council appointed the Battles Nomenclature Committee. Its task was to tabulate and classify the actions fought in the war and to define the geographical and chronological limits of each action. The report was completed by July, 1920 and published in the following year under the title THE OFFICIAL NAMES OF THE BATTLES AND OTHER ENGAGEMENTS FOUGHT BY THE MILITARY FORCES OF THE BRITISH EMPIRE DURING THE GREAT WAR, 1914-1919. It consists of sixty-three pages and cost nine pence.

Now, regimental committees had to work out the battle honours for their regiments. The first step was to decide on the entitlement of each battalion. In order to qualify for a battle honour a unit had to have its headquarters and 50% of its strength within the boundaries of a battle between the dates laid down in the report. Then the results were combined to form a list of battle honours for the regiment to be approved by the War Office.

A complete list of battle honours for the Great War was issued with Army Orders for February 1925. Ten of the honours were selected to be borne on the King's Colour. The battle honours for each regiment are shown in the Army List, following those of previous campaigns, and the ten King's Colour ones are printed in heavier type. 1958 saw the beginning of the amalgamation of some Infantry Regiments and the successor regiment's battle honours are a combination of those borne by the regiments they have absorbed.

Service in a theatre of war counted as a battle honour. The principal campaign honours are given below and the figures in brackets indicate the number of regiments bearing it, but not always with the dates shown, which are for the total period of the campaign.

"France and Flanders 1914-18"	(80)
"Italy 1917-18"	(33)
"Macedonia, 1915-18"	(50)
"Gallipoli, 1915-16"	(53)
"Palestine, 1917-18"	(41)
"Mesopotamia, 1914-18"	(51)

Some of the operations on the Western Front were on a very large scale and lasted for months. They consisted of a series of operations and the Nomenclature Committee decided to treat them as a Group of Battles under the title "Battles" and the various phases were each called 'Battle'. For example, The Battles of the Somme, 1916 (1st July to 18th November) consisted of twelve individual battles and the Battles of Ypres, 1917 (31st July to 10th November) had eight battles. Regiments received battle honours for the main Battles as well as the individual ones, so for example, those with any of the twelve fought on the Somme in 1916 also have "Somme, 1916".

When several battles were fought over the same ground they are distinguished by the year in which they took place, e.g. "Ypres, 1914" and "Ypres, 1915". Two or more dates are combined as "Arras, 1917, '18".

Army Order 136 of 1951 approved the grant of more battle honours to various regiments from the Seven Years War to the Great War. A few new ones were awarded for the Great War and some changes made in the King's Colour Honours.

VICTORIA CROSSES

Deciding on the number of V.C.s earned by each regiment is by no means as simple as might be expected. Sometimes the decoration was awarded to an officer or soldier while attached to another regiment, another arm or the Royal Flying Corps. In some cases both claim the award in their histories.

The figures in this supplement have been compiled from various sources and I wish to thank Miss R. E. B. Coombs of the Imperial War Museum for her help in the research.

The first figure in the Victoria Cross column of the tables is the total number awarded to all ranks of the regiment during the Great War. If there is a second figure, in brackets it shows the number of Victoria Crosses awarded to officers and soldiers while attached to other regiments.

CASUALTIES

The casualty figures are based on two official publications which give the names of every officer and other rank from the United Kingdom who lost his life in the Great War. There are four categories; Killed in action, Died of wounds, Killed, other than in action and Died from natural causes.

The first is OFFICERS DIED IN THE GREAT WAR, 1914-1919, published by H.M.S.O. in 1919, which contains the names of about 39,000 officers. It is divided into two parts: Part I Old and New Armies and Part II Territorial Force. They are listed by regiments and each entry gives the full name of the officer, his rank, decorations, usually the battalion with which he was serving and date of death.

The other publication is SOLDIERS DIED IN THE GREAT WAR, 1914-1919, published by H.M.S.O. in 1921. It is in eighty parts and contains about 667,000 names; the Infantry take seventy-two parts. Each entry usually shows the full names of the soldier, his place of birth, place of enlistment, rank, decorations, and dates of death and country in which it occurred.

Some of the regimental histories give the casualties for their regiments and these figures have been used when available after checking with the official lists.

The casualty figures in this Supplement are only approximate as it was not possible to count over half a million names and there were various complications such as the question of officers and other ranks who were killed while attached to another arm or regiment. However, the total of approximately 589,000 all ranks in the infantry regiments agrees closely with an official estimate of 591,000 killed and died in the Infantry during the Great War.

The British Army suffered its heaviest losses of the war in the Battles of the Somme, 1916 and in the Battles of Ypres, 1917. The total casualties for the Somme were 419,000 and at Ypres they were 240,000. In each of the Battles 54 divisions (including ten from the Dominions) took part and some were engaged six times.

NORTH RUSSIA 1919

The official Great War records of Battle Honours and Casualties cover the operations in North Russia so they are included in the Schedule below.

There are two battle honours for North Russia, "Archangel" and "Murman" which are shared by eleven regiments. Two non-commissioned officers of the Royal Fusiliers were awarded Victoria Crosses.

This appendix has been compiled with great care from many sources. Should there be any errors I hope that they will be excused.

January 1976.   E.A.J.

SCHEDULE

Regiments	Battle Honours	Victoria Crosses	Casualties (Estimated)
Foot Guards			
Grenadier Guards	34	7	4680
Coldstream Guards	36	7	3860
Scots Guards	30	5	2840
Irish Guards	30	4	2250
Welsh Guards	20	1	860
Infantry of the Line			
Royal Scots	71	6 (1)	11160
Royal West Surrey Regiment	74	4 (2)	8000
East Kent Regiment	48	1	6000
Royal Lancaster Regiment	59	8	5500
Northumberland Fusiliers	67	5	16000
Royal Warwickshire Regiment	70	5	11610
Royal Fusiliers	80	12	15600
Liverpool Regiment	58	6 (1)	14200
Norfolk Regiment	70	1 (1)	6000
Lincolnshire Regiment	58	3	8800
Devonshire Regiment	59	2	5790
Suffolk Regiment	73	2	6550
Somerset Light Infantry	60	1	4760
West Yorkshire Regiment	57	4	12700
East Yorkshire Regiment	56	4	7480
Bedfordshire Regiment	74	7 (1)	6500
Leicestershire Regiment	37	3	6870
Royal Irish Regiment	42	1	2780
Yorkshire Regiment	56	10	7500
Lancashire Fusiliers	63	17	13640
Royal Scots Fusiliers	58	4	5600
Cheshire Regiment	75	2	8420
Royal Welsh Fusiliers	77	8 (1)	9800
South Wales Borderers	64	6 (1)	5600
King's Own Scottish Borderers	66	4	7740
Scottish Rifles	56	3	7070
Royal Inniskilling Fusiliers	46	7	5890
Gloucestershire Regiment	72	4 (1)	8100
Worcestershire Regiment	72	8 (1)	9460
East Lancashire Regiment	61	4	7000
East Surrey Regiment	62	7	6750
Duke of Cornwall's Light Infantry	57	1	4510
West Riding Regiment	63	5	7870
Border Regiment	64	5	7450
Royal Sussex Regiment	69	3	6550
Hampshire Regiment	82	3	7580
South Staffordshire Regiment	56	3	6360
Dorsetshire Regiment	57	—	4060
South Lancashire Regiment	59	4	5450
Welsh Regiment	71	3	8360
Royal Highlanders	69	4 (1)	8390
Oxford and Buckinghamshire Light Infantry	59	2	5880
Essex Regiment	62	1	8860
Nottinghamshire and Derbyshire Regiment	57	9 (1)	11410
Loyal North Lancashire Regiment	68	3	7590
Northamptonshire Regiment	58	4	5950
Royal Berkshire Regiment	55	2	7140
Royal West Kent Regiment	69	3 (1)	6900
Yorkshire Light Infantry	59	8	9450
Shropshire Light Infantry	52	1	4710
Middlesex Regiment	81	5	12720
King's Royal Rifle Corps	60	7	12840
Wiltshire Regiment	60	1	5200
Manchester Regiment	72	11	13770
North Staffordshire Regiment	52	4 (1)	5430
York and Lancaster Regiment	59	4	8810
Durham Light Infantry	59	6	12530
Highland Light Infantry	65	7	10030
Seaforth Highlanders	60	7	8830
Gordon Highlanders	57	4 (1)	8870
Cameron Highlanders	57	3	5930
Royal Irish Rifles	40	3	7010
Royal Irish Fusiliers	40	2	3330
Connaught Rangers	42	1	2050
Argyll and Sutherland Highlanders	68	6 (3)	6900
Leinster Regiment	32	4	1980
Royal Munster Fusiliers	51	3	3070
Royal Dublin Fusiliers	49	3	4780
Rifle Brigade	52	10	11580

Regiments	Battle Honours	Victoria Crosses	Casualties (Estimated)
Territorial Force			
HONOURABLE ARTILLERY COMPANY INFANTRY	38	2	840
MONMOUTHSHIRE REGIMENT	22	—	2430
CAMBRIDGESHIRE REGIMENT	27	—	870
LONDON REGIMENT	64	9	29100
HERTFORDSHIRE REGIMENT	26	2	900
HEREFORDSHIRE REGIMENT	16	—	480
NORTHERN CYCLIST BATTALION*	—	—	10
HIGHLAND CYCLIST BATTALION*	—	—	11
KENT CYCLIST BATTALION	2	—	45
HUNTINGDONSHIRE CYCLIST BATTALION*	—	—	16
Channel Islands Militia			
ROYAL JERSEY LIGHT INFANTRY*	1	—	4
ROYAL GUERNSEY LIGHT INFANTRY	7	—	330
		351	588526

The titles of the regiments are as shown in the Army List for August 1914.

* Did not serve overseas.

Index to Part 11 for

REGIMENTS, BATTALIONS AND INDEPENDENT COMPANIES.

The Index is based on the Table of Contents in the Army Lists for 1914-1918. In some cases, for brevity or clarity, the official titles of regiments have not been used, but the names shown will be easily identified with the regiments concerned.

A number of Territorial battalions and all the locally raised New Army battalions had second titles showing the place in which they were raised or some other particular association. All these second titles are shown in the Index followed by the unit's battalion number and regiment.

	Page
Accrington Bn.—11th (S) East Lancs. Regt.	74
Alexandra, Princess of Wales's Own (Yorks. Regt.)	62
Anglesey, Carnarvonshire &, Bn.—6th R. W. Fus. TF	67
Angus & Dundee Bn.—5th Black Watch TF	84
Antrim, Central, Bn.—12th (S) R. Irish Rifles	106
— South, Bn.—11th (S) R. Irish Rifles	106
Ardeer Coy.—R. Scots Fus. TF	64
Ardwick Bn.—8th Manchester Regt. TF	97
Argyll & Sutherland Highrs.	107
Argyllshire Bn.—8th A. & S. Highrs. TF	108
Armagh, County, Bn.—9th (S) R. Irish Fus.	107
Artists' Rifles—28th London Regt. TF	114
Arts & Crafts Bn.—18th (S) K.R.B.C.	95
Ayr & Lanark Yeo. Bn.—12th R. Scots Fus. TF	65
Banff & Donside Bn.—6th Gordon Highrs. TF	104
Bankers' Bn.—26th (S) Royal Fus.	50
Barnsley Bns. 1st & 2nd—13th & 14th (S) York & Lancs. Regt.	100
Battersea Bn.—10th (S) R. West Surrey Regt.	44
Bedfordshire Regt.	59
Belfast, East, Bn.—8th (S) R. Irish Rifles	106
— North, Bn.—15th (S) R. Irish Rifles	106
— South, Bn.—10th (S) R. Irish Rifles	106
— West, Bn.—9th (S) R. Irish Rifles	106
Berkshire Regt., Royal	89
Bermondsey Bn.—12th (S) East Surrey Regt.	75
Bermuda Volunteer Rifle Corps—see 1st Lincs. Regt.	53
Birkenhead Bns. 1st & 2nd—15th & 16th (S) Cheshire Regt.	66
Birmingham Bns. 1st to 3rd—14th to 16th (S) R. Warwick Regt.	48
Black Watch (Royal Highlanders)	83
Blackheath & Woolwich Bn.—20th London Regt. TF	114
Blythswood Bn.—7th H.L.I. TF	102
Border Bn.—4th K.O.S.B. TF	69
Border Regt.	77
Borderers, King's Own Scottish	69
— South Wales	68

	Page
Bradford Bns. 1st & 2nd—16th & 18th (S) West Yorks Regt.	58
Brecknockshire Bn.—S. Wales Borderers TF	68
Bristol Bn.—12th (S) Gloucester Regt.	72
— City of, Bn.—4th Gloucester Regt. TF	72
British Empire League Bn.—17th (S) K.R.R.C.	95
— Pioneers Bn.—20th (S) K.R.R.C.	95
Buchan & Formartin Bn.—5th Gordon Highrs. TF	104
Buckinghamshire Bn.—Oxford & Bucks L.I. TF	85
— Oxford &, L.I.	85
Buffs (East Kent Regt.)	44
Cadet Battalions, Officer	119
Caithness, Sutherland &, Highland Bn.—5th Seaforth Highrs. TF	103
Cambridgeshire Regt.	112
— Bn.—11th (S) Suffolk Regt.	56
Cameron Highlanders	105
Cameronians (Scottish Rifles)	70
Canadians, Royal (Leinster Regt.)	109
Cardiff City Bn.—16th (S) Welsh Regt.	83
Carmarthenshire Bn.—15th (S) Welsh Regt.	83
Carnarvonshire & Anglesey Bn.—6th R. Welsh Fus. TF	67
Channel Islands Militia	118
Chatsworth Rifles Bn.—16th (S) Sherwood Foresters	87
Cheshire Regt.	65
— Shropshire and, Yeo. Bn.—10th K.S.L.I. TF	92
Church Lads Brigade Bn.—16th (S) K.R.R.C.	95
Cinque Ports Bn.—5th R. Sussex Regt. TF	77
Civil Service Rifles Bn.—15th London Regt. TF	114
Coldstream Guards	41
Connaught Rangers	107
Cornwall Pioneers Bn.—10th (S) D.C.L.I.	76
Cumberland & Westmorland Bn.—4th Border Regt. TF	77
— Bn.—5th Border Regt. TF	77
Cyclist Bns. Territorial Force	
10th Royal Scots	42
6th Norfolk Regt.	53
7th Devonshire Regt.	54
6th Suffolk Regt.	56
5th East Yorks Regt.	59
5th R. Sussex Regt.	77
9th Hampshire Regt.	79

	Page
7th Welsh Regt.	82
8th Essex Regt.	86
25th London Regt.	114
Northern Bn.	118
Highland Bn.	118
Kent Bn.	118
Huntingdonshire Bn.	118
Deeside Highland Bn.—7th Gordon Highrs. TF	104
Denbighshire Bn.—4th R. Welsh Fus. TF	67
— Yeo. Bn. 24th R. Welsh Fus. TF	68
Derbyshire, Notts &, Regt.	86
Derry Bn.—10th (S) R. Innis. Fus.	71
Devon Yeo. Bn.—16th Devonshire Regt. TF	55
Devonshire Regt.	54
Donegal & Fermanagh Bn.—11th (S) R. Innis. Fus.	71
Donside, Banff &, Bn.—6th Gordon Highrs. TF	104
Dorsetshire Regt.	81
Down, County, Bns. 1st & 2nd—13th & 16th (S) R. Irish Rifles	106
Dublin Fusiliers, Royal	110
Duke of Albany's (Seaforth Highrs.)	103
—Cambridge's Own (Middlesex Regt.)	92
—Connaught's Own Bn.—6th Hampshire Regt. TF	79
— Cornwall's Light Infantry	75
— Edinburgh's Wiltshire Regt.	96
— Wellington's (West Riding) Regt.	76
Dumbartonshire Bn.—9th A. & S. Highrs. TF	108
Dumfries & Galloway Bn.—5th K.O.S.B. TF	69
Dundee, Angus &, Bn.—5th Black Watch TF	84
— City of, Bn.—4th Black Watch TF	84
Durham County Bns. 1st, 2nd & 3rd—18th, 19th & 22nd (S) Durham L.I.	101
— Light Infantry	100
Earl of Chester's Bn.—5th Cheshire Regt. TF	65
East Anglian Bn.—12th (S) Suffolk Regt.	56
— Ham Bn.—32nd (S) Royal Fus.	50
— Kent Regt.	44
— Lancashire Regt.	73
— Surrey Regt.	74
— Yorkshire Regt.	59
Edinburgh Rifles, Queen's—5th Royal Scots TF	42

Index to Part II

Entry	Page
Edinburgh Rifles Queen's—Bns. 1st & 2nd—15th & 16th (S) R. Scots	43
Empire Bn.—17th (S) Royal Fus.	49
Essex Regt.	85
Fermanagh, Donegal &, Bn.—11th (S) R. Innis. Fus.	71
Fife Bn.—7th Black Watch TF	84
Fife & Forfar Yeo. Bn.—14th Black Watch TF	84
Finsbury Rifles—11th London Regt. TF	113
Flintshire Bn.—5th R. Welsh Fus. TF	67
Football Bns. 1st & 2nd—17th & 23rd (S) Middlesex Regt.	93
Forest of Dean Bn.—13th (S) Gloucester Regt.	72
Formartin, Buchan &, Bn.—5th Gordon Highrs. TF	104
Frontiersmen Bn.—25th (S) Royal Fus.	50
Fusiliers, Dublin, Royal	110
— Inniskilling, Royal	71
— Irish, Royal	106
— Lancashire	63
— Munster, Royal	109
— Northumberland	46
— Royal	49
— Scots, Royal	64
— Welsh, Royal	66
Galloway, Dumfries &, Bn.—5th K.O.S.B. TF	69
Glamorgan Bn.—6th Welsh Regt. TF	82
— Bns. 1st & 2nd—17th & 18th (S) Welsh	83
— Pembroke &, Yeo. Bn.—24th Welsh Regt. TF	83
— Pioneer Bn.—19th (S) Welsh Regt.	83
Glasgow Bns. 1st to 4th—15th to 18th (S) H.L.I.	103
— City of, Bn.—5th H.L.I. TF	102
— Highland Bn.—9th H.L.I. TF	102
Gloucestershire Regt.	72
Gordon Highlanders	104
Grenadier Guards	41
Grimsby Bn.—10th (S) Lincoln Regt.	54
Guards Machine Gun Regt.	41
Guernsey Militia, Royal	118
— see 6th (S) R. Irish Regt.	61
Gwent Bns. 1st to 3rd—10th to 12th (S) S.W.B.	69
Hackney Bn.—10th London Regt. TF	113
Hallamshire Bn.—4th York & Lancs. Regt. TF	99
Hampshire Regiment	78
Herefordshire Regiment	117
Hertfordshire Regiment	117
Highland Cyclist Bn.	118
— Deeside Bn.—7th Gordon Highrs. TF	104
— Glasgow Bn.—9th H.L.I. TF	102
— Light Infantry	102
— Ross, Bn.—4th Seaforth Highrs. TF	103
— Sutherland & Caithness, Bn.—5th Seaforth Highrs. TF	103
Highlanders, Argyll & Sutherland	107
— Bn.—9th Royal Scots TF	42
— Cameron	105
— Gordon	104
— Royal	83
— Seaforth	103
Home Counties Bn.—24th Rifle Bde. TF	111
Honourable Artillery Coy.	112
Household Bn.	119
Hull Bns. 1st to 4th—10th to 13th E. Yorks Regt.	59
Huntingdonshire Cyclist Bn.	118
Inniskilling Fusiliers, Royal	71
Inns of Court O.T.C.	117
Irish Bn.—8th King's (Liverpool Regt.) TF	51
— Fusiliers, Royal	106
— Guards	41
— Horse, North—9th R. Irish Fus.	107
— Horse, South—7th R. Irish Regt.	61
— London, Rifles—18th London Regt. TF	114
— Regiment, Royal	61
— Rifles, Royal	105
Isle of Man Volunteer Bn.—7th King's (Liverpool Regt.)	51
Isle of Man 1st Manx Coy.—see 2nd Cheshire Regt.	66
Isle of Wight Rifles—8th Hampshire Regt. TF	79
Islington Bn.—21st (S) Middlesex Regt.	94
Jersey Militia, Royal	118
— see 7th (S) R. Ir. Rif.	106
Jewish Bns.—38th to 40th (S) Royal Fusiliers	50
Kensington Bn.—22nd (S) Royal Fus.	50
— 13th London Regt. TF	113
Kent, County Bn.—10th (S) R. West Kent Regt.	90
— Cyclist Bn.	118
— East, Regt.	44
— East Yeo. Bn.—10th East Kent Regt. TF	45
— Weald of, Bn.—5th East Kent Regt. TF	44
— West, Regt., Royal	90
— West Yeo. Bn.—10th East Kent Regt. TF	45
King's (Liverpool Regt.)	51
— Own (Royal Lancaster Regt.)	45
— Own Scottish Borderers	69
— Own Yorkshire Light Infantry	91
— Royal Rifle Corps	94
— Shropshire Light Infantry	92
Lambeth Bn.—11th (S) R. West Surrey Regt.	44
Lanark Bn.—8th H.L.I. TF	102
Lanark Ayr &, Yeo. Bn.—12th R. Scots Fus. TF	65
Lancashire, East Regiment	73
— Fusiliers	63
— North, Regiment, Loyal	88
— South, Regiment	81
— South-East Bns. 1st & 2nd—17th & 18th Lancs. Fus.	64
Lancaster Regiment, Royal	45
— York and,	99
Leeds Bns. 1st & 2nd—15th & 17th (S) W. Yorks R.	58
— Rifles—7th & 8th West Yorks Regt. TF	57
Leicestershire Regiment	60
Leinster Regt. (Royal Canadians)	109
Lewisham Bn.—11th (S) R. West Kent Regt.	91
Light Infantry, Duke of Cornwall's	75
— Durham	100
— Highland	102
— King's Shropshire	92
— King's Own Yorkshire	91
— Oxford & Buckinghamshire	85
— Somerset	56
Lincolnshire Regiment	53
Liverpool Regiment, The King's	51
Liverpool City Bns. 1st to 4th—17th to 20th (S) Liverpool Regt.	52
London Bn.—18th Rifle Bde. TF	111
London City of, Bns.—London Regt. TF	113
— County of, Bns.—London Regt. TF	113
— Irish Rifles—18th London Regt. TF	114
— Rifle Bde.—5th London Regt. TF	113
— Scottish—14th London Regt. TF	114
— Welsh Bns. 1st & 2nd—15th & 18th R. Welsh Fus.	67
Lonsdale Bn.—11th (S) Border Regt.	77
Lothian Regiment (Royal Scots)	42
Lovat's Scouts Bn.—10th Cameron Highrs. TF	105
Machine Gun Guards	41
Manchester Regiment	96
Manchester City Bns. 1st to 8th—16th to 23rd (S) Manchester Regt.	97
Merioneth & Montgomery Bn.—7th R. Welsh Fus. TF	67
Middlesex Regiment	92
Midland Pioneers Bn.—11th (S) Leicester Regt.	61
Midland Bn.—21st Rifle Bde. TF	111
Miners Bn.—12th (S) K.O.Y.L.I.	91
Monmouthshire Regiment	112
Montgomery, Merioneth &, Bn.—7th R. W. Fus. TF	67
— & Welsh Horse Yeo. Bn.—25th R. W. F. TF	68
Morayshire Bn.—6th Seaforth Highrs. TF	103
Munster Fusiliers, Royal	109
N.E.R. Bn.—17th (S) Northumberland Fus.	46
Newcastle Bn.—16th (S) Northumberland Fus.	46
Norfolk Regiment	53
Norfolk Yeo. Bn.—12th Norfolk Regt. TF	53
North Irish Horse—9th R. Irish Fus.	107
— Lancashire Regt., Loyal	88
— Staffordshire Regiment	98
— Wales Bns. 1st & 2nd—13th & 17th (S) R. W. F.	67
— Western Bn.—23rd Rifle Bde. TF	111
Northamptonshire Regiment	89
Northern Bn.—20th Rifle Bde. TF	111
— Cyclist Bn. TF	118
Northumberland Fusiliers	46
Nottingham Bn.—15th (S) Sherwood Foresters	87
Notts & Derby Regiment (Sherwood Foresters)	86
Officer Cadet Bns.	119
Oldham Bn.—24th (S) Manchester Regt.	98
Oxfordshire & Bucks. Light Infantry	85
Pembroke & Glamorgan Yeo. Bn.—24th Welsh Regt. TF	83
Perthshire Bn.—6th Black Watch TF	84

140 Index to Part II

Entry	Page
Poplar & Stepney Rifles—17th London Regt. TF	114
Portsmouth Bns. 1st & 2nd—14th & 15th (S) Hampshire Regt.	80
Post Office Rifles—8th London Regt. TF	113
Prince Albert's (Somerset L.I.)	56
— Consort's Own (Rifle Bde.)	110
— of Wales's Bn.—5th Devonshire Regt. TF	54
— of Wales's Leinster Regt.	109
— of Wales's (North Staffordshire) Regt.	98
— of Wales's Own. Civil Service Rifles—15th London Regt. TF	114
— of Wales's Own (West Yorks) Regt.	57
— of Wales's Volunteers (South Lancs. Regt.)	81
Princess Beatrice's Isle of Wight Rifles—8th Hampshire Regt. TF	79
— Charlotte of Wales's (R. Berkshire Regt.)	89
— Louise's (A. & S. Highrs.)	107
— Louise's Kensington Bn.—13th London Regt. TF	113
— of Wales's Own, Alexandra (Yorkshire Regt.)	62
— Victoria's (Royal Irish Fusiliers)	106
Public Schools Bn.—16th (S) Middlesex Regt.	93
— Schools Bns. 1st to 4th—18th to 21st (S) Royal Fus.	50
Public Works Pioneers Bns. 1st, 2nd & 3rd—18th, 19th & 26th (S) Middlesex Regt.	94
Queen Victoria's Rifles—9th London Regt. TF	113
Queen's—22nd & 24th London Regt. TF	114
— Edinburgh Rifles—5th Royal Scots TF	42
— Own Cameron Highlanders	105
— Own Royal West Kent Regiment	90
— Royal West Surrey Regiment	43
— Westminster Rifles—16th London Regt. TF	114
Rangers—12th London Regt. TF	113
Renfrewshire Bn.—5th A. & S. Highrs. TF	108
Rhondda Bns. 1st & 2nd—10th & 13th (S) Welsh Regt.	83
Rifle Bn.—6th King's (Liverpool Regt.) TF	51
— Brigade	110
— Corps, King's Royal	94
Rifles Bn.—6th London Regt. TF	113
Robin Hood Bn.—7th Sherwood Foresters TF	87
Rosebery Bn.—17th (S) Royal Scots	43
Ross Highland Bn.—4th Seaforth Highrs. TF	103
Ross-shire Buffs. Seaforth Highrs.	103
St. Helens Bn.—11th (S) South Lancs. Regt.	82
— Pancras Bn.—16th (S) Rifle Bde	111
— Pancras Bn.—19th London Regt. TF	114
Salford Bns. 1st to 4th—15th, 16th, 17th & 20th (S) Lancs. Fus.	64
Scots Fusiliers, Royal	64
— Guards	41
— Royal (Lothian Regt.)	42
Scottish Bn.—10th King's (Liverpool Regt.) TF	51
— Borderers, King's Own	69
— Horse — 13th Black Watch TF	84
— Rifles (Cameronians)	70
Seaforth Highlanders	103
Severn Valley Bn.—14th (S) Worcester Regt.	73
Sheffield Bn.—12th (S) York & Lancs. Regt.	100
Sherwood Foresters (Notts & Derby Regt.)	86
Shetland Coys.—Gordon Highrs. TF	104
Shoreditch Bn.—20th (S) Middlesex Regt.	94
Shropshire & Cheshire Yeo. Bn.—10th K.S.L.I. TF	92
— Light Infantry	92
Somerset Light Infantry	56
— Yeo. Bn.—12th Somerset L.I. TF	57
South Down Bns. 1st to 3rd—11th to 13th (S) Royal Sussex Regt.	78
— Irish Horse—7th R. Irish Regt.	61
— Lancashire Regiment	81
— Staffordshire Regiment	80
— Wales Borderers	68
Sportsman's Bns. 1st & 2nd—23rd & 24th (S) Royal Fus.	50
Staffordshire, North, Regiment	98
— South, Regiment	80
Stepney, Poplar and, Rifles—17th London Regt. TF	114
Suffolk Regiment	55
— Yeo. Bn.—15th Suffolk Regt. TF	56
Surrey, East, Regiment	74
— Rifles, First—21st London Regt. TF	114
— West, Regiment, Royal	43
Sussex, Regiment, Royal	77
— Yeo. Bn.—16th R. Sussex Regt. TF	78
Sutherland & Caithness Highland Bn.—5th Seaforth Highrs. TF	103
— Argyll &, Highlanders	107
Swansea Bn.—14th (S) Welsh Regt.	83
Tees-side Pioneers Bn.—12th (S) Yorkshire Regt.	62
Tyneside Irish Bns. 1st to 4th—24th to 27th (S) Northd. Fus.	47
— Scottish Bns. 1st to 4th—20th to 23rd (S) Northd. Fus.	47
— Pioneer Bns. 1st & 2nd—18th & 19th (S) Northd. Fus.	47
Tyrone, County Bn.—9th (S) R. Innis. Fus.	71
Volunteer Bn. (Isle of Man)—7th King's (Liverpool Regt.)	51
Wales, South, Borderers	68
Wandsworth Bn.—13th (S) East Surrey Regt.	75
Warwickshire, Regiment, Royal	48
Weald of Kent Bn.—5th East Kent Regt. TF	44
Wearside Bn.—20th (S) Durham L.I.	101
Welbeck Rangers Bn.—17th (S) Sherwood Foresters	87
Wellington's, Duke of, (West Riding Regt.)	76
Welsh Fusiliers, Royal	66
— Guards	41
— Horse, & Montgomery, Yeo. Bn.—25th R. W. F. TF	68
— Pioneers Bn.—23rd (S) Welsh Regt.	83
— Regiment	82
Wessex & Welsh Bn.—22nd Rifle Bde. TF	111
Westminster Rifles, Queen's—16th London Regt. TF	114
West Ham Bn.—13th (S) Essex Regt.	86
— Kent Regt., Royal	90
— of England Bn.—14th (S) Gloucester Regt.	72
— Riding Regiment (Duke of Wellington's)	76
— Surrey Regiment, Royal	43
— Yorkshire Regiment	57
Western Bn.—19th Rifle Bde. TF	111
Westmorland, Cumberland &, Bn.—4th Border Regt. TF	77
Wiltshire Regiment	96
Wool Textile Pioneers Bn.—21st (S) West Yorks Regt.	58
Woolwich, Blackheath &, Bn.—20th London Regt. TF	114
Worcestershire Regiment	73
Yeoman Rifles—21st (S) K.R.R.C.	95
York & Lancaster Regiment	99
Yorkshire, East, Regiment	59
— Light Infantry	91
— Regiment	62
— West, Regiment	57
Young Citizens Bn.—14th (S) Royal Irish Rifles	106

www.ingramcontent.com/pod-product-compliance
Lightning Source LLC
Chambersburg PA
CBHW082013220426
43670CB00014B/2616